WHITE HULL, BUFF FUNNEL

Also by the author

Under A Big Blue Star: Exotic Voyages of a Deck Cadet

ISBNs: pbk 978-1-7397590-8-7; ebk 978-1-7397590-9-4

WHITE HULL, BUFF FUNNEL

A Personal Voyage from
Dartmouth to Deep Ocean

Phil Carroll

Copyright © 2025 Phil Carroll.

The right of Phil Carroll to be identified as the author of the work has been asserted by him in accordance with the Copyright, Designs and Patents Act 1988.

All rights reserved. No part of this book may be reproduced, stored in a retrieval system, or transmitted, in any form or by any means, electronic, mechanical, photocopying, recording or otherwise, without the prior written permission of the publisher, except as permitted by UK copyright law.

For permissions contact: philipjcarroll@btinternet.com

ISBN pbk 978-1-0685716-6-4
      ebk 978-1-0685716-7-1

Designed and typeset www.ShakspeareEditorial.org

Dedication

TO ALL MY OLD SHIPMATES WITH WHOM
I SERVED AT SEA OR ASHORE.

TO SHIPMATES WHO HAVE CROSSED THE BAR

Cdr Ian Bartholomew
Cdr Peter Hobson
Lt Cdr Mark Rowledge
Lt Cdr Don Ventura
Lt Cdr 'Scouse' Labone
Lt Andy Skinner
Lt Simon Wall
CPO(SR) Bob McGovern
CPO(Sea) Pete Edwards
CPO(SR) 'Ginge' Woodhouse
CPO(SR) 'Spike' Hughes
LS(SR) Brian Humphries
LS(SR) 'Kipper' Herring
AB(SR) 'Artie' Shaw

MAY THEY REST IN PEACE

Contents

Figures viii
Glossary xvii
Abbreviations xix
Acknowledgements xxiii
Foreword 1

1. Altering Course 3
2. We Joined the Navy 11
3. Mediterranean Cruise – Navy Style 63
4. A Bleak Midwinter in Rosyth 93
5. Armilla Patrol – Up the Gulf 123
6. Back to Pompey 167
7. Makie-Learnie Droggy 179
8. Back to School – Basic H Course 197
9. First Job Droggy – Wrecks and Bottom Texture 211
10. To Brazil and West Africa 247
11. Happy Days in the Country Club 281
12. A Season in the North Sea 311
13. A Bajan Interlude 323
14. Hydro School for Long Course 335
15. Happy *Hecla* Again! 347
16. A Dark, Miserable Period 387
17. A Happy Interlude 391
18. Postscript 397

Note on Sources 413
References 415
About the Author 419

Figures

1. ALTERING COURSE
1.1 Dad, David, James 8
1.2 Two trout in one day! 9

2. WE JOINED THE NAVY
2.1 BRNC crest 11
2.2 BRNC dominates Dartmouth from its hill-top location 11
2.3 College façade 12
2.4 View to mainmast, overlooking Dartmouth town and river
    and Kingswear on the opposite side 13
2.5 Hawke Division frontage 14
2.6 'Main drag' from Chapel to SGR 17
2.7 Me in the detested battledress uniform 18
2.8 BRNC, key features annotated 19
2.9 My seaman's knife and spike combo, well-used but now careworn ... 21
2.10 View from Upper Dorm balcony 22
2.11 Hawke A-Block 23
Table 2.1 Standard rigs 24
2.12 My class prepped for an acquaint flight in a Wasp helicopter
     from Norton Airfield 30
2.13 PB3 at sea 32
2.14 PBs manoeuvring in Start Bay 34
2.15 Hawke Division, viewed from the lawn 35
2.16 View from Cabin B15 37
2.17 In B15 38
2.18 Invitation to Combined Mess Dinner 40
Table 2.2 Daily toasts 40
2.19 SGR, its gallery at far end 41
2.20 Dressed in my swanky Gieves & Hawkes mess kit 42
2.21 Kev Seymour in river activity rig writing his WAR in Upper Dorm ... 44
2.22 Example of formal letter – acknowledgement of appointment 45
2.23 Our PLX campsite behind Ditsworthy Warren House 48
2.24 PLX points of interest in west half of Dartmoor National Park ... 50

2.25 Sandquay, with PBs berthed at pontoon 52
2.26 Cheverton2 alongside PB2 in the River Dart 53
2.27 BRNC tennis squad, summer term 1984 55
2.28 BRNC façade 58
2.29 Platoons formed up for Divisions 59

3. MEDITERRANEAN CRUISE – NAVY STYLE
3.1 *Fearless* crest 63
3.2 *Fearless* 63
3.3 DTS Mediterranean cruise 68
3.4 *Fearless* in Barcelona 71
3.5 In 'whites' at the Maritime Museum 72
3.6 Open to visitors 73
3.7 LCUs on Loutra beach 76
3.8 Setting up camp at dusk 77
3.9 At the Parthenon with 'Stumpy' Haldane and others 77
3.10 *Fearless* anchored in Bosphorus 80
3.11 Waiting for a liberty boat 81
3.12 CTP invitation 82
3.13 Me, Monty and the belly-dancer 84
3.14 'Hands to bathe' somewhere in the Med 85
3.15 Taking it easy on flight deck 85
3.16 Parade ground layout for POP 89
3.17 DGEs, schoolies and GLs passing out. 90
3.18 Typical ball programme 91
3.19 Ball venue plan 91

4. A BLEAK MIDWINTER IN ROSYTH
4.1 *Gavinton* crest; *Brinton* crest 93
4.2 *Gavinton* 93
4.3 Typical Ton foc's'le 96
4.4 Typical Ton bridge 97
4.5 Armed team sweep 99
4.6 Oropesa sweep 100
4.7 Team sweep 100
4.8 Ship's Log, Tuesday 22 January 1985 103
4.9 *Brinton* under Forth Rail Bridge 104
4.10 Simon Wall on *Brinton's* port bridge wing 105
4.11 *Abdiel* 108

4.12 *Brinton's* voyages 109
4.13 Ship's Log sea state and visibility codes.................................... 112
4.14 A typical day's minehunting in Scapa Flow 113
4.15 Scapa Flow... 114
4.16 'Banana boat' 117
4.17 Top Gun ready for his flight... 121

5. ARMILLA PATROL – UP THE GULF

5.1 *Exeter* crest 123
5.2 *Exeter* 123
5.3 *Exeter's* main features.. 124
5.4 *Exeter's* Armilla Patrol 128
5.5 Suez Canal 131
5.6 View from *Exeter's* bridge... 132
5.7 View aft.. 133
5.8 Great Bitter Lake anchorage 133
5.9 Stuarts distance meter 135
5.10 Formation Foxtrot starboard 136
Table 5.1 OOW routine for three OOWs 137
5.11 Costumed elephants at the Perahera, surrounded by festive crowds 146
5.12 Neil and Kieran playing tennis … 147
5.13 … and leaping into the pool.. 147
5.14 Ready to rumble!.. 150
5.15 Ossie and me on the dusty red road to nowhere................... 152
5.16 Overnight lodge, Tsavo National Park................................... 152
5.17 Mike and elephants 152
5.18 Muscat's Corniche backed by mountains in afternoon sun. Mutrah Fort in centre.. 154
5.19 Banjo, Max and me in the GOO... 154
5.20 Neil, Omani fast attack craft, *Charybdis* in background....... 155
5.21 Kieran on bridge-wing of *al-Sharqiyah*................................... 155
5.22 RAS with *Kitty Hawk* 156
5.23 *Kitty* and me.. 157
5.24 Banjo, Ray and Neil loafing on the beach............................... 158
5.25 *Exeter's* Ship's Log, Wed 6 Nov 85. My handwriting for Daily Summary and Last Dog initialled 160
5.26 *Newcastle* slides passed … 161
5.27 … followed by *Jupiter* 161

Figures xi

5.28 Both Armilla Patrol groups, seen from *Exeter* 162
5.29 Kieran and me witnessing a gunnery shoot 163
5.30 *Exeter*, home for six glorious months 165

6. BACK TO POMPEY
6.1 Newly striped-up Lieutenant RN 167
6.2 OOW 55, drawn by Bob Edwards 169
6.3 *Northella* entering Pompey harbour, Isle of Wight ferry astern 171
6.4 D-Day Map Room, Southwick House 173

7. MAKIE-LEARNIE DROGGY
7.1 *Gleaner* crest 179
7.2 *Gleaner* 179
7.3 'Cap'n Bob', me and some of his motley crew 188
7.4 HI243, Ramsey Bay to King William Banks 189
7.5 Trisponder network 190
7.6 Trisponders at: Balladoole; Maughold Head; Point of Ayre lighthouse . 191
7.7 Extract from sounding collector 191
7.8 Sidescan sonar and multibeam echo sounder images of *Resurgam* 193
7.9 My travels in *Gleaner* 194
7.10 HI266, Needles Channel 195
7.11 Present from *Fawn's* wardroom 196

8. BACK TO SCHOOL – BASIC H COURSE
8.1 Hydrographic Office crest 197
8.2 Tellurometer 201
8.3 Station-pointer 203
8.4 Station-pointer fix 203
8.5 SMB, off Newport, South Wales 206
8.6 Example (not on an SMB) of Kitchener gear 'buckets' 207
8.7 Basic H Course certificate 210

9. FIRST JOB DROGGY – WRECKS AND BOTTOM TEXTURE
9.1 *Fox* crest 211
9.2 *Fox* 211
9.3 *Fox* voyages 1987 213
9.4 CSV survey capabilities 214
9.5 Sidescan sonar recorder; towfish 216
9.6 *Fox* surveying 217
9.7 Williamson turn 218
9.8 Main parts of a Shipek grab 219

9.9 Wreck on a sonograph; interpretation of sonograph 222
9.10 Wreck investigation 224
9.11 Calculating wreck's height above seabed 225
9.12 Flag Officer Plymouth presented his Commendation to Aussie Austin 226
9.13 *Fox* conducting a lead-through 227
9.14 HI 389 Loch Ryan 229
9.15 Pilotage view of Cairn Ryan Jetty 230
9.16 H525 for an obstruction found during HI389B 231
9.17 Capt Hope presents Hope Operational Efficiency Trophy to Steve Shipman. In background, 'Abes' Abrams 234
9.18 Recovered mines on fo'c'sle; one of the mines 236
9.19 BBC Shipping Forecast areas, adopted 1949 238
9.20 *Fox* voyages 1988 240
9.21 *Fox*, St Malo 1–5 July 241
9.22 HI439 Padstow Bay 242
9.23 Progress of HI429 Celtic Deep as at 30 September 88 244
9.24 Tawny owl hitching a ride 245

10. TO BRAZIL AND WEST AFRICA
10.1 *Hecla* crest 247
10.2 *Hecla* 247
10.3 Survey Department 248
10.4 Features of an H-boat 250
10.5 *Hecla* voyages 1989 251
10.6 Feigning interest at Hydrographic Institute 253
10.7 King Neptune's thugs; 'policemen' carry a victim to Neptune's Court; the punishment 255
10.8 Recife, post-beach debacle 256
Table 10.1 1-in 4 watch routine 257
10.9 LStwd 'George' Nicholson and Stwd Warren Strickland 258
10.10 Graham, Martin, me and Mick at Mercado Modelo 259
10.11 Off Trindade and Martim Vaz islands 261
10.12 Me and Graham on bridge wing at Ascension; loading stores/parts from Mexeflote 262
10.13 PO (Cook) McCann and Gary the Pusser chat with Capt H in the galley 265
10.14 In the throng at Lome market: Martin, Russell and Graham; me 267
10.15 Circuit training, Buffer in charge; gym – tanned, buffed-up 'muscle-bosuns'. Buffer and AB 'Tiny' Little on weights 268

10.16 Flight deck sports 269
10.17 *Hecla's* rugby team 271
10.18 Gary Lewis sets off on Ringbolt Relay; Ringbolt Relay team 272
10.19 Horse race meeting on flight deck 273
10.20 Scenes from the SODS Opera 273
10.21 AB (Cook) Ted Hobbs' chicken divine recipe 274
10.22 21-gun salute off Tenerife 275
10.23 Martin, Higgy and me, Mount Teide in background 275
10.24 Ship's company 277
10.25 Survey department T-shirt 278

11. HAPPY DAYS IN THE COUNTRY CLUB
11.1 BRNC crest 281
11.2 *Britannia* and *Hindostan* at Sandquay 282
11.3 BRNC façade, wardroom, Captain's House 283
11.4 Access to wardroom 285
11.5 BRNC's magnificent Chapel 288
11.6 Peterel and Sandpiper 292
11.7 Getting things done; check list of leadership actions 293
11.8 PLT at the mainmast 295
11.9 Ditsworthy Warren House 297
11.10 Royal Oak, Meavy 298
11.11 Leopard crawl across a chasm; crossing a chasm on parallel
    ropes; ascent or descent of a tor 299
11.12 Clay pits near Cadover Bridge, scene of many sinking rafts! 299
11.13 Main doors, through which passers out marched 306
11.14 'Dining-Out': front and back covers; menu and wines 310

12. A SEASON IN THE NORTH SEA
12.1 NP1008 crest 311
12.2 *Marine Explorer* *311*
12.3 *Marine Explorer* alongside Grimsby 313
12.4 Stern and A-frame; looking aft, sidescan sonar winch and
    cable's block on A-frame 314
12.5 HI554 (Whitby Fine Ground to Inner Bank) 315
12.6 *Marine Explorer* *317*
12.7 Grimsby Dock Tower on starboard quarter, *Marine Explorer* exiting ... 318
12.8 HI555 (Southern North Sea Deep Water Route) 319
12.9 HI581 (Celtic Sea) 321

13. A BAJAN INTERLUDE
13.1 Home for the duration 324
13.2 A choice of boats, excluding the big one astern!................................. 325
13.3 Climbing St Ann's Tower; Daz conducting GPS observations; me conducting observations, *Alacrity* in background; conducting trisponder calibration; Geraint at Signal Station 326
13.4 Control stations... 328
13.5 HI 568 Bridgetown Deep Water Harbour 329
13.6 Daz in Coastguard dory 329
13.7 Our cox'n driving the Port Authority's boat, Trisponder receiver to his right... 330
13.8 Daz in the boat, me holding the distance line to maintain distance-off for lines parallel to wharf 331
13.9 Extract from HI568 fair sheet, drawn by Daz, checked by me, approved by Geraint 332
13.10 Panoramic view of berths 333

14. HYDRO SCHOOL FOR LONG COURSE
14.1 Class photo, for the SMS Newbury module 335
14.2 Long H Course certificate... 345

15. HAPPY *HECLA* AGAIN!
15.1 *Hecla* crest.. 347
15.2 *Hecla*... *347*
15.3 Atlantic Ocean deployment... 348
15.4 Rattler in the gym 356
15.5 Christmas drinks in Senior rates Mess... 357
15.6 Dickie, Martin, me in Maceio 357
15.7 Saturday night in The Zoo 359
15.8 Jimmy Chan in his laundry 362
15.9 Indian Ocean deployment.. 365
15.10 Exiting Suez Canal... 366
15.11 Entrance to Massawa Port 367
15.12 War-damaged Eritrean Navy vessels 368
15.13 HI636 Massawa Harbour... 368
15.14 Footie at dawn.. 369
15.15 Destroyed tanks and armoured vehicles in Massawa's streets 370
15.16 Battlefield remnants; standing beside a destroyed tank 371
15.17 Diego Garcia.. 374

15.18 Board showing plan of copra plantation in front of the manager's office 375
15.19 Flying-boat wreck and explanatory noticeboard 376
15.20 Muscat, one of the world's most beautiful natural harbours; road winding its way from Mina Qaboos to old Muscat city 377
15.21 Part of unspoilt Bandar Khayran 378
15.22 Extract of HI21b fair sheet; detail extract 379
15.23 Camels grazing outside Job's tomb 380
15.24 Sod's Opera starring: 1 Mess; our own Supremes (4/5 Mess) and Village People (2 Mess Stokers) 381
15.25 Stan and Katrina, still together today 382
15.26 1 Mess deployment T-shirt 383
15.27 Entering 3 Basin 383
15.28 Bicentenary fireworks at Canary Wharf 384
15.29 Departing London, *Roebuck*, *Bulldog*, *Hecla* pass through the Thames Barrier 385
15.30 Bicentenary certificate 386

16. A DARK, MISERABLE PERIOD
16.1 *Beagle* crest 387
16.2 *Beagle* 387

17. A HAPPY INTERLUDE
17.1 *Scott* crest 391
17.2 *Scott* *391*
17.3 Capt H's offices and glass porch; overlooked by Capt H's residence 392
17.4 *Scott's* silverware table-piece 394

18. POSTSCRIPT
18.1 Reunited with Monty in his boatshed; we haven't changed a bit since summer 1984 397
18.2 With Paddy Watson; with Bob and Wendy, BRNC in background 398
18.3 Exeter's OUTs reunited – Kieran, me, Max, Neil, Feb 2024 400
18.4 With Graham, Oct 2021 401
18.5 Surrounded by Steve, Daz and Mick, Oct 2019 402
18.6 With Dusty, Sep 2021 403
18.7 *Exeter* at ship-breakers, between *Invincible's* remains and a ferry 405
18.8 HV *Fox*, as MY *Toy Heaven* 407
18.9 *MY Aqua Blu* *408*
18.10 *SV Bligh* looking shabby in 2002 408
18.11 *Herald's* sad end as *SV Somerville* at Alang 409

18.12 SAS *Protea*, Simonstown, March 2006...410
18.13 3 Basin with two H-boats and a CSV, two CSVs berthed outside on 3 Wharf..411

Glossary

Also see Abbreviations

Adrift	late for work or duty
Bosun's call	high-pitched, two-note metal whistle used for making 'pipes'
Bubblehead	mine-clearance diver
Buffer	Bosun's right hand man; Leading Seaman, PO or CPO, depending on ship size
Chief Petty Officer	RN senior non-commissioned officer
Clanky	slang for an engine room rating
Div Chief	Divisional Chief Petty Officer, one per Division at BRNC, a Division's backbone
Div Sub	Divisional Sub Lieutenant; an OUT selected as leader of a Division's OUTs at BRNC
Divisions	Naval parade
Dodgy deacon	Chaplain/padre, also sin bosun, god botherer, sky pilot
Droggy	hydrographic survey officer
Duty Mid	Duty Midshipman, at BRNC
Executive Officer	second-in-command of a warship or establishment
Goffers	Huge green waves breaking over the fo'c'sle; also a soft drink (Coke, etc)
Greeny	slang for a heavy-duty electrics maintainer
Guzz	slang for Devonport, Plymouth
H-boat	*Hecla*-class Ocean Survey Ship
Heads	toilets
Helo	helicopter
Int	Officer-Under-Training from overseas
Junior Rate	any sailor up to and including Leading Seaman
Killick	slang for Leading Seaman, Leading Hand, Leading Rate
Leading Hand of the Mess	Killick in charge of his mess responsible for its cleanliness and good order, also Killick of the Mess
Leading Seaman	RN junior non-commissioned officer
Makie-learnie	Probationary Hydrographic Survey Officer (Prob H)

Marine Engineering Officer	officer responsible for all ship's engineering systems in the engine room
Mid/Middy	Midshipman
Officer-of-the-Day	Duty officer responsible for the safety of a ship's company, warship or shore establishment
Officer-of-the-Watch	Seaman Officer on watch on the bridge; responsible for the safety of the ship's company and safe navigation
Oily-Qs	Officer-like qualities
Oppo	mate, friend, pal
Petty Officer	Navy senior non-commissioned officer
Pinky	slang for an electrical rating maintaining delicate electronic systems
Pompey	slang for Portsmouth
Pusser	Supply Officer, responsible for stores, victuals, administration, correspondence
Rig	uniform; Daily Orders include stating the Rig of the Day
Schoolie	Instructor Officer, responsible for training and teaching
Scuttle	porthole
Serial	an exercise/event scheduled in a ship's programme
Senior Rates	sailors from Petty Officer up to Warrant Officer
Senior Sub	Senior Sub Lieutenant; selected as leader of all OUTs at BRNC
Stand easy	tea/coffee break
Stoker	marine engineering sailor
Stone frigate	naval shore establishment
Weapon Engineering Officer	officer responsible for all ship's weapon and electrical systems

Abbreviations

AB	Able Seaman
ADO	Assistant Divisional Officer
AIB	Admiralty Interview Board
AMP	Assisted maintenance period
ARs	active rudders, fitted as part of conversion of *Ton*-class minesweepers into minehunters
A/SLt	Acting Sub Lieutenant
BM	Bosun's Mate, assistant to the QM at sea and in harbour
BNA	British Naval Attaché
BRNC	Britannia Royal Naval College
BUFFS	buck up, for f***'s sake
C&L	Character and leadership, qualities assessed at BRNC
CCF	Combined Cadet Force
Cdr	Commander
CJH	Casper John Hall, large auditorium at BRNC (400-man sleeping-bag)
CO	Commanding Officer
CPO	Chief Petty Officer
CSV	Coastal survey vessel, *Bulldog*-class
DGPS	Differential GPS)
DO	Divisional Officer
DTS	Dartmouth training squadron/ship, *Fearless* in my case
EMA	Early morning activity
EODM	electronic optical distance measuring
E-O-L	End of line, a survey line is completed and survey ship turns onto next line
EPF	electronic position fixing
EXAS	Exercise areas, usually adjacent to a naval base (Pompey, Portland, Guzz, Rosyth)
FAA	Fleet Air Arm, the Navy's flyers
GI	Gunnery instructor, a senior rate drill instructor at BRNC
GL	General list, a full career commission
GOO	Gulf of Oman

HGR	Hawke Gun Room, 'space' for the Divisional briefings, presentations, meetings
HOD	Head of department
HQ	headquarters
JGR	Junior Gun Room, dining room for BRNC Juniors
JRDH	Junior Rates' Dining Hall
LHOM	Leading Hand of the Mess, also Killick of the Mess
LS	Leading Seaman
Lt	Lieutenant
Lt Cdr	Lieutenant Commander
LWEM(R)	Leading Weapons Electrical Mechanic (Radio)
MBDD	Machinery breakdown drills
MCDO	Mine Clearance Diving Officer
MCM3	3rd Mine Countermeasures Squadron, based at Rosyth
MCMV	mine countermeasures vessel (minehunter or minesweeper)
MDW	mine disposal weapon
ME	Marine engineering
MEO	Marine Engineering Officer
METOC	Meteorology and oceanography
MLO	mine-like object
MN	Merchant Navy
MOBEX	Man overboard exercise
MOD	Ministry of Defence
NAAFI	Navy, Army and Air Force Institutes, supports bases, deployments and warships worldwide
NBCD	nuclear, biological, chemical and damage control
NBCDX	fire-fighting and damage control exercise
NCE	Naval College Entry
NCO	Non-Commissioned Officer, a Navy senior rate (Petty Officer, Chief Petty Officer, Warrant Officer)
NEX	New Entry Exercise
NGT	Naval General Training
NO	Navigating Officer
OIC	Officer-in-Charge
OOD	Officer-of-the-Day
OOW	Officer-of-the-Watch
OSS	Ocean survey ship, *Hecla*-class or H-boat
OST	Operational Sea Training

OUT	Officer Under Training
PB	picket boat, BRNC had eight
PDR	precision depth recorder
PLT	Practical leadership task
PLX	Practical Leadership Exercise
PO	Petty Officer
POP	Passing out parade
PSO	Personnel selection officer
PTI	Physical Training Officer
PWO	Principal Warfare Officer
QM	Quartermaster
RAS	Replenishment at sea, a method of transferring fuel, munitions and stores from one ship to another while under way
RFA	Royal Fleet Auxiliary, civilian-manned supply ships supporting RN warships
RM	Royal Marines (bootnecks)
RN	Royal Navy
RNOV	Royal Navy of Oman Vessel
ROR	Rule of the Road
RoS	Report of Survey
S&S	Supply and Secretariat
SAM	supply, administration and management
SGR	Senior Gun Room, dining room for BRNC Seniors
SINS	Ship's Inertial Navigation System
SIPS	Ships Information Processing System
S/Lt	Sub Lieutenant
SL	Supplementary list, a short career commission
SMB	Survey motor boat
SMP	Self-maintenance period
S-O-L	Start of line, a new survey line is commenced
SO	Supply Officer, responsible for stores, victuals, administration, correspondence
SR	Survey Recorder
UKHO	UK Hydrographic Office
USN	US Navy
USS	United States ship (USN warship)
VERTREP	vertical replenishment
WE	Weapon Engineering

WEO	Weapon Engineering Officer
WFT	Withdrawn From Training
WO	Warrant Officer
XO	Executive Officer, a warship's second-in-command; also First Lieutenant or The Jimmy

Acknowledgements

My wife, Lynne, encouraged me to pen these memoirs. Frequently, our general chit-chat leads into a 'salty' dit from my seafaring days in the Merchant Navy and Royal Navy. She suggested I write them down as, surely, old shipmates, oppos and fellow mariners would find my tales and anecdotes of interest and trigger nostalgia for their own past maritime career. As I completed each draft chapter, Lynne avidly read and critiqued it. Given she's a landlubber, it was gratifying she grasped the gist of my life at sea.

I'm greatly indebted to Bob Mark. I had great pleasure in serving with Bob over several years in different ships. Bob kindly agreed to write the Foreword and acted as my second beta-reader. He pops up frequently throughout, from my first days at Dartmouth until when I moved on from his newly commissioned survey ship *Scott* to my first overseas appointment some 13 years later.

I was delighted that David Smiley (ex-Blue Star Line, ex-Master Mariner, marine consultant) was my other beta-reader. With his wealth of Merchant Navy experience, David reviewed every chapter from a Merchant Navy perspective as I hope this volume will appeal to all seafarers and anyone of a maritime bent.

I was thrilled that a large number of old oppos kindly spared their time to read, review, comment and correct chapters in which they appear. In rough chronological/chapter order, Nick 'Monty' Birch, Mark Allibon, Neil Hunter, Kieran Nash, Max Rance, Mike 'Banjo' West, Mick Slater, Steve Hawes, Martin Clegg, Graham Turnbull, Bob Eadie, Darren Wake, Geraint West, Rob Lawson, Gary 'Barney' Barnard, Dave 'Rattler' Morgan, Paul 'Dusty' Miller and David 'Stan' Baxter and Pat Mowatt.

I must give especial mention and thanks to Mick Slater. He's swiftly provided answers to my numerous out-of-the-blue WhatsApp messages with 'noddy' questions on minute details at any time. Thanks, Mick, for your patient, tolerant assistance.

I thank Dickie Bird, our 'man in Oman', for emailing me the Bandar Khayran *Report of Survey*

I'm grateful to other folks who allowed me to use their photos: BJ Newton, John Woodward, Rob Hoole, Max Rance, Bob Mark, Martin Jones, Mick Slater, Graham Turnbull, 'George' Nicholson, Geraint West, Dusty Miller, Stan Baxter, Willy Wilcock, Dave Olner, Gerry Quinn, Chris Coulter and Tony Jenks.

Other photographs were sourced from a variety of agencies to whom I am equally indebted: UK Hydrographic Office Archive, BRNC Archive, Historic England, *Ton* Class Association, Britannia Association. I possessed photos of some of my ships but fortunately Fotoflite, Maritime Quest, Graham Stevens, Photoship, Ships Nostalgia, Super Yacht Times and ShipSpotting allowed use of theirs.

Similarly, my survey ships' crests are on the wall of my study. Nick Barwis kindly allowed me to use his magnificent paintings of missing crests of 'proper' warships in which I served. Incidentally, Nick has a vast library of ships' badges and warships. Visit his website (www.jackstaxi.net) to view his excellent products.

I don't have any photos of Dartmoor so I'm very grateful to Steve Foster for his excellent photos of Ditsworthy Warren House, The Royal Oak at Meavy and other significant places. Check out his excellent website if you're seeking information on Dartmoor walks.

Other oppos and ex-surveyors have answered questions I posted to a couple of Facebook sites (HMS *Hecla* Old Timers, Survey Ships RN, Survey Squadron Reunion, *Ton* class MCMVs) and, particularly, Mick Slater's immensely popular WhatsApp group. Primarily established to organise and manage Mick's highly successful annual Survey Ships Reunions on a Saturday afternoon in June in Guzz, attendance increases year on year. They are a great opportunity to meet up with folks not seen for so many years. I'd certainly encourage anyone who's served in 'the white navy' to join Mick's WhatsApp group. It is a great forum for spinning dits and recalling collective memories of our time in the branch over the decades.

Whilst I'm blessed with an excellent memory for faces, people, places, dates and events, this book would be neither complete nor accurate without access to official records and documents.

I'm deeply grateful to Dr Richard Porter and Dr Jane Harrold, who allowed me the freedom to roam through BRNC's Archive. Richard was one of the College's academic staff during my time as a Divisional Officer in 1990–1992. Jane 'hosted' my visit to Dartmouth and escorted me up to the archive, a large walk-in cupboard at the rear of Richard's study/office. Richard's absence meant I occupied his desk uninterrupted for the entire day. It was a pity I didn't meet Richard that day, some 30 years after I left BRNC.

Ian Killick and his colleagues at UKHO Archive, Taunton, were equally helpful and sympathetic to my research requests. The Archive sits in a shiny new building adjacent to the old charting building that I recollect from day-trip visits during basic and long hydrographic survey courses. Ian had prepared all the material I sought, laid out on one of the Archive's vast chart tables, and left me to my own devices to rummage through files pertaining to *Gleaner, Fox, Hecla, Beagle* and NP1008, which brought back so many memories of my time as a droggy. Commanding Officers' monthly *Reports of Proceedings* were invaluable, as were *Reports of Survey*, describing surveys we'd undertaken. *Annual Returns of Survey* added a little more flesh, as did various articles in *Hambone*, the now-defunct annual journal that collated Survey Squadron activities. Ian was readily available to answer my queries and attempted to find other material for me. I'm truly indebted to him for all his help.

I spent a whole day at The National Archives, Kew, reading through and photographing a multitude of Ship's Logs, the official monthly record of RN warships' activities, packaged in large cardboard cartons that filled a desk. I eagerly accessed Ship's Logs from *Fearless, Gavinton, Brinton* and *Exeter*, plus a few from my survey ships. It was a right old trip down memory lane about what we did in those long-dead warships, decades ago. I was transported back to the Junior Rates mess-deck in *Fearless* during our second term of general naval training, to the cramped conditions in *Ton*-class minehunters and the Mids' Grot in *Exeter*. It was poignant to recognise the initials for each watch in those Ship's Logs. I noted my own neat manuscript detailing exercises and incidents and my 'PJC' initials at the end of my watch. The staff at Kew were equally supportive and sought additional Ship's Logs for me. It was an invaluable day's research.

Throughout those research days, my internet research and correspondence with oppos not seen for so many years, I was perpetually swamped in nostalgia. So many happy memories of a bygone era. I hope my scribblings evoke the same emotional reminiscences in you, dear reader.

Foreword

Rear Admiral Bob Mark, FRIN

This second volume of Phil Carroll's autobiography captures his transition from mature, experienced merchant marine 2nd Mate to aspiring naval officer through the lens of new entry training at Britannia Royal Naval College, a somewhat less than inspirational voyage in the Dartmouth Training Squadron, and then a refreshing pick-me-up in the finishing school of 'fleet time' in minesweepers operating from Rosyth, and in HMS *Exeter*, a destroyer on patrol in the Gulf. Despite the inevitable ups-and-downs of service life, good fellowship, humour, resilience, coupled with a quiet determination to succeed, shine through. All a good grounding for when, a few short years later, Phil was to find himself as a Divisional Officer on the BRNC staff, with his own experience fresh enough to help shape and inculcate a new cohort of midshipmen into the ways of the Service. Both thoughtful and descriptive, these chapters capture very well the twin aims of testing and honing the character and leadership qualities of young officers embarking on not only a new career but also a new, absorbing way of life.

Phil's choice of Seaman Officer sub-specialisation, hydrography, enabled him to live through, and chronicle, a now vanished time at the end of the Cold War, when a sizeable Royal Navy Hydrographic Flotilla spanned the globe. It surveyed the data which enabled the RN to carry out successful surface and submarine operations, and contributed to Admiralty charts and publications, which were and still are, available to all mariners. The span of naval surveying activity Phil describes encompass the Celtic and North Seas, Atlantic, Caribbean and Indian Oceans with innumerable exotic, and sometimes not so exotic, port visits. All part of life in 'a blue suit'. He admirably captures the comradeship and atmosphere of those times. The book goes beyond an entertaining log of events as the period described is on the cusp of the introduction of two new, now ubiquitous, then transformative, technologies, the global positioning system (GPS) and the digital computer. Phil's first early hydrographic training – his 'Basic H Course' pre-dates both, imparting the distilled wisdom of two centuries of hard-won analogue surveying know-how which formed the foundation for all surveyors of Phil's and earlier generations. In less than a decade, these two new technologies had transformed the science and practice of hydrography. Phil's 'Long H Course' chapter details how these innovations were swiftly adopted, together with the best of the hydrographic branch heritage and fixed determination to deliver accurate, reliable results – no matter the level of effort required which, as Phil describes could be considerable, particularly in winter north Atlantic conditions! Phil's description of his sea-time on the survey ground in *Gleaner, Fox, Hecla* and *Marine Explorer* both detail and celebrate the dedication of the teams involved and his own satisfaction in playing his part.

All in all, a splendid read, charting Phil's personal journey and shining a perceptive light on the Royal Navy Hydrographic branch at a time when its activities spanned over half the globe.

1.

Altering Course

I served my Deck Cadetship in the Merchant Navy (MN) from September 1980 to April 1984. I had a fantastic time at sea with Blue Star Ship Management. I was incredibly fortunate as I circumnavigated the world on my first trip to sea, including transits of the Suez and Panama Canals. I had trips in every type of ship in Blue Star's fleet (containers, general and refrigerated cargo, heavy-lift) and went to myriad ports in Europe, North and South America, Middle East and Australasia.

I earned my 2nd Mate's Certificate of Competency via 24 months sea-time and college phases at Liverpool Polytechnic. This culminated in written exams and a fearsome oral exam, an interrogation by the fearsome Principal Examiner of Masters and Mates in Liverpool.

At the end of my previous book, *Under a Big Blue Star*, I decided to 'alter course'. I was born and brought up in Gosport, surrounded by the Royal Navy (RN). My father was a Civilian Instructional Officer at HMS Sultan (RN School of Marine Engineering) and my mother was a civil servant at Royal Naval Armament Depot Elson. Influenced by this naval environment, I was also captivated by television series such as *Warship* (a 1973–1977 action drama set in *Hero*, a *Leander*-class frigate) and *Sailor* (a fantastic documentary about life on board *Ark Royal* in 1976 and her deployment to the US, with plenty of footage of Buccaneer and Phantom jets catapulted from and landing on her flight deck). Real boy's-own stuff.

By the mid-1980s, the MN was in a sad, sorry, deep malaise. British ships were increasingly registered to flags of convenience, British crews were being made redundant and the UK shipbuilding industry was unable to compete with foreign yards. I was 25 and the upper age limit for graduate entry as a Seaman Officer was 26. So, it was now or never.

My application to join the RN yielded an invitation to attend the Admiralty Interview Board (AIB). It must have been February/March 1984 as I didn't pay-off from *New Zealand Star* in Colombo until 23 January. I avidly read the joining instructions and buffed up on news topics and the Navy (ships, bases, deployments, commitments). I felt I was as ready as possible by the time I arrived on the afternoon of the first day. Luckily, the AIB was a lodger unit at HMS Sultan so I had only a short taxi ride from my folks' house in Alverstoke, on the beach at Gosport.

The AIB selection procedure lasted three days, during which we candidates were assessed via a variety of psychometric tests, leadership and syndicate exercises, and interviews. We were briefed on the programme and completed a biographical questionnaire to update the Board on our qualifications and achievements, if any. It also asked about our view of positive and negative aspects of service life and participation in sports, clubs and hobbies.

After that, we were free to settle in, unpack in our cabins, take tea/coffee in the candidates' restroom. Everyone was a bit nervous, unsure of how these life-defining three days would pan out: deemed to have potential to be naval officers, or not; be sent away with the Board President's advice ringing in our ears and have another go next year; or, worst of all, be advised to simply forget any thought of a naval career.

Age and experience varied from wet-behind-the-ears, A-level schoolboys, to graduates, to mature blokes like me. After dinner, several were tempted to cross the road for a pint or two in The Cocked Hat. I chose a quiet night in, read a couple of newspapers (quality broadsheets, naturally) and editions of *Navy News*, the RN's monthly newspaper. I braced myself for tomorrow.

A rather restless sleep overnight, unusual for me, and into breakfast in suit, tie and polished shoes. The Board President (Captain, RN) welcomed and briefed us about the AIB and what was expected of us. He explained the Board composition: himself, a Commander, a Personnel Selection Officer (PSO, usually a Lieutenant), and a visiting headteacher or university lecturer. For the remainder of the morning we sat general knowledge tests, then psychometric tests: verbal, non-verbal, numeracy and 'clerical accuracy', followed by a diagnostic written communication skills test to identify grammatical and spelling errors. The climax to the morning was an essay and a precis. Crikey, we needed lunch after that lot.

We changed into overalls and were transported to the venue used for gym tasks. It was a section of one of Sultan's old hangers, partitioned off for AIB use. We walked through and practised the leadership tasks we'd do tomorrow. Divided into teams of six (I think), 'staff' explained the various tasks. We had a go at a couple, learned to swing on ropes and use cantilevers. We'd each lead a dry or a wet (cross a large tank of water) task. Every task required the leader to brief his team, devise a plan and execute it whilst maintaining control throughout. Specific items of kit were provided on site and the entire team had to cross the 'chasm' or 'river'.

On returning to the AIB, staff explained the discussion planning exercise. I was mentally exhausted by the end of the day. It was pleasant to relax in the restroom before retiring (watch television, have dinner, watch more television). Another restless night. Nerves? Adrenalin? Not sure if anyone went for a pint in The Cocked Hat that evening.

Fortified by another hearty breakfast, we were delivered to the gym tests. We each took turns at being 'leader', given the exercise briefing from the staff and a short time to think of a plan. The leader briefed the task, his plan and allocated jobs to team members. Then it was crash, bang, wallop as we worked hard to build a bridge/raft/whatever and cross the chasm/river/whatever, using ropes, barrels, staves, planks.

Although it was pleasing to complete a task as leader, that wasn't the sole criterion noted by the staff observing and assessing each task. It was only much later that I realised the important things were to take charge, show leadership, power of command, determination, grit, courage in the face of adversity – or the team's numpty (because there's always one!) doing something stupid to reduce the task to a shambles. Inevitably, one or more candidates fell into the raging river and remained sodden until all tasks were finished. I don't recall whether I completed my task or not.

We returned to the AIB for the next phase. The discussion planning exercise was in syndicates and leaderless. The syndicate was given a disaster scenario. A map and calculations of speed/time/distance were provided. After a short time to study the scenario and develop a plan, we then collectively discussed, developed and agreed a group plan. We were quizzed individually and as a group by the PSO. Finally, we each gave a 60-second summary of the plan to the Board. Throughout, the assessors observed proceedings, made copious notes. Do many notes equal a good thing? Who knows? And about who? It was difficult to ignore their presence, hanging on our every word and gesture.

On the afternoon of the third day, we were subjected to individual interviews by the Board and the PSO. The Board interview comprehensively covered news topics, the Navy, NATO, the military and almost any other subject that came to mind. I know I had to stand up and point to a particular country on a giant wall-map of the world. It was a standard question. The PSO's interview was more concerned with personal and family stuff.

Mentally exhausted after another intense day, we waited nervously in the restroom whilst the Board discussed and considered each candidate's overall performance, measured against inflexible criteria and scores. This process decided our future.

In late afternoon, each candidate was summoned to the Board. I don't recall any particular order, possibly alphabetical. When my turn came, I strode purposefully along the corridor, knocked on the door, was bidden entry and told to sit. I felt four pairs of eyes focus on me, the President at the centre, flanked by the Commander and PSO to his left, the visiting headmaster to his right. I remained calm and erect in what seemed the most uncomfortable chair in Christendom, braced for the outcome of three days of concentrated mental effort. At last, the Captain spoke. I don't remember anything except that I'd passed and would receive a letter from the RN in due course. I was chuffed to bits. All that hard work before and throughout this selection process, plus my performance within it, had paid off. The Board wished me well. I said thank you and marched out the door with a distinct skip in my step.

I packed my bag, left my cabin neat and tidy, went downstairs and said cheerio to the Chief Petty Officer (CPO) who'd met us on arrival. I phoned home and my father picked me up from The Cocked Hat car park. We got home and enjoyed a celebratory cup of tea.

Sometime later, a letter arrived from the Ministry of Defence (MOD). I was to join Britannia Royal Naval College (BRNC) at Dartmouth on 25 April 1984 as an Acting Sub Lieutenant Direct Graduate Entry Supplementary List Seaman Officer sub-specialising in Hydrography. I learned this verbose description was abbreviated to A/SLt DGE SL X(H). I expected to acquire a new lexicon and a myriad abbreviations and acronyms at BRNC. Joining instructions from Dartmouth followed later. My parents were delighted. I was thrilled and relaxed for a couple of months.

My father suggested a lads' fishing week in Snowdonia before Easter for himself, his brother David, my brother James and me. He arranged accommodation in the village of Trawsfynydd. We drove up in convoy: Dad and David in one car; me and James in his Opel Manta. I'm not into cars at all, but James' Manta was a beauty: sleek, black, coupé-style, with lots of grunt under its bonnet as she purred her way to Snowdonia.

Our family had history in Trawsfynydd. When my father bought his first car, we had a family holiday on the Isle of Wight, via car ferry instead of our usual foot-passenger ferry. Dad's driving experience increased and he suggested a holiday in North Wales. Despite the slow, torturous car journey

1. Altering Course

from Gosport, we annually holidayed in Trawsfynydd in Snowdonia, staying at the Cross Foxes Hotel in the village.

During the war, my paternal grandfather was a Royal Artillery RSM stationed at the nearby training camp. The family lived in a cottage in Trawsfynydd. My father was the eldest of four children and attended school in nearby Blaneau Ffestiniog but spent most of his time truanting in the countryside, fishing and hunting rabbits. Not a great scholar, he didn't like school.

Trawsfynydd is in a beautiful part of Snowdonia, beside a man-made lake created to serve the ugly nuclear power station at the far end. This contrasted, strangely, with the engineering beauty of the hydroelectric dam at Ffestiniog. We visited many castles, sites of interest and natural beauty during those holidays.

The long, winding, blacktop, gently rising and falling across the mountain, with Lake Bala on one side, is a particular memory. We stopped in a lay-by on one occasion and my father, James and I walked up the hillside and perched ourselves on an exposed rocky outcrop to enjoy panoramic views. My mother took a photo showing her 'boys' halfway up the steep hillside, neatly dressed in jeans and cable-knit sweaters she'd knitted.

I enjoyed the castles: Harlech, Conwy, Caernarfon. Barmouth had a decent expanse of sandy beach. Undoubtedly the best trip was the train ride to the top of Snowdon. Such spectacular scenery and it was nice being atop a real mountain. Gosport's only 'hill' was the bridge over the redundant railway line where hill-starts were practised for driving-tests. Yes, simple, but truly great family holidays from a bygone era.

This time, the journey was much faster. Our accommodation was a recently built, self-catering house adjacent to the Cross Foxes Hotel. Dad got the key from the hotel, owned and run by the same family. The matriarch, Sally, who I dimly remembered was old when we first stayed there in the early-1970s, had died a few years before. Her daughter Mary was in charge. We settled in. Dad and I had single bedrooms, David and James shared the twin. Excellent!

We walked through Trawsfynydd, and stopped outside the cottage in which Dad and David had lived during the war. Not only that, but we bumped into umpteen villagers who recognised the brothers, despite the intervening decades. David was the youngest of the siblings, my Dad the eldest (mid-teens then). These villagers, of a similar age to Dad and David, called out 'Teddy Carroll' – and most of them were 'girls'. I got the impression my Dad liked, and was popular with, the village girls in those far-off days. He was like Tom Sawyer or Huckleberry Finn on Snowdonia's foothills. Perhaps I've over-romanticised. Who cares?

After the long day's travel and excitement of being in Trawsfynydd again, we had dinner in the Cross Foxes and returned to our house to turn in. Each morning, Dad cooked a great breakfast. We packed our fishing-rods and sundry kit. Dad chose our several different fishing venues, but the best was lakeside at Trawsfynydd.

I had my own foul-weather gear but I'd never fished before, so Dad lent me one of his rods. We focused mainly on fly-fishing for trout (brown or rainbow). I gradually got used to casting. We mainly used Dad's flies. He made many varieties of lure in his workshop at the back of the garage at home. The days passed slowly, relaxation was paramount. We occasionally 'lifted and-shifted' along the bank and resumed fishing.

We'd each caught a few beautiful little trout by the end of the week. Dad and David shared the filleting and gutting duties, followed by grilling the tasty trout. I've never been a fish-eater but enjoyed the novelty of eating fish we'd caught that very day. On other evenings, we ate out in the Cross Foxes or at nearby restaurants. One of these was a short drive up into the hills at the refurbished remains of my grandfather's wartime training camp.

1.1 Dad (in distance), David (foreground), James (under umbrella)

1. Altering Course

1.2 Two trout in one day!

We had a brilliant week, with good weather throughout. We got on well together, much cheerful bonhomie and laughter. I enjoyed my first experience of fly-fishing and relaxing lakeside. I felt a thrill when I got a 'bite', patiently reeled in a trout (size didn't matter, it was a 'catch'), and tried not to lose it whilst doing so. I was pleased to have done it, with limited success, but fly-fishing failed to 'grip' me.

We drove home at the week's end as 20–23 April was Easter. I prepared as best I could for Dartmouth. I packed my civvies, adhering to the kit list included in the joining instructions. I felt I was 'ready in all respects' to begin my new adventure.

2.

We Joined the Navy

2.1 BRNC crest

2.2 BRNC dominates Dartmouth from its hill-top location

On the bright sunny morning of Wednesday 25 April 1984, I crammed my grips and bags into the boot of my gold-coloured Morris Marina 1.3 Coupe. I said cheerio to my folks and set off for Dartmouth dressed in shirt, cufflinks, tie, chinos and polished shoes, with my blazer carefully laid across the back seat. It was a long flog westwards. When I got off the A38 I thought I was nearly there. Not so. The winding country road via Totnes, hippy capital of Devon, meant another half-hour to Dartmouth. At the final crest, with Norton Airfield and its petite control tower on my right, I glimpsed the town and river below.

Down the hill, idyllic scenery hove into view. Townstal Gate, uppermost access to the College, was to my left, as the frighteningly steep road with its shingled escape lanes took me down to the entrance. I turned left through the main gate, under the wrought-iron arch with 'Britannia Royal Naval College' in gold lettering. BRNC dominated Dartmouth, perched atop an incredibly steep grass-sloped hillside. It was an impressive building in an enviable location.

2.3 College façade
Main door surmounted by clock tower, parade ground in front, ramp at left foreground

A few cars, each driven by a smart besuited young man, waited at the gate. A MOD Plod (Ministry of Defence Policeman) checked my papers. An impeccable, uniformed Midshipman (Middy) checked my name and directed me to Hawke Division. I drove up a steep winding road, which dissected the nine-hole golf course, and turned left. I cut across BRNC's extensive red-brick and Portland stone façade, the parade ground at its front to my right. On my left, the mainmast and a spectacular panorama overlooked town and river.

2.4 View to mainmast, overlooking Dartmouth town and river and Kingswear on the opposite side

As I drove slowly past the parade ground, several coaches disgorged smartly attired young men scrambling about to retrieve their kit from the luggage compartments. New entrants travelling by train alighted at Totnes, where uniformed Middies shepherded them to coaches for the last leg of the journey to BRNC.

These new entrants milled about whilst Middies barked orders at them to form lines three-deep. Names were called out, answered, then they were marched off, clutching their kit, to their respective Divisions (similar to a boarding school's house) in the main building. New Hawkes were eventually marched up the hill, away from the main College buildings, to the Division. The opening 15 minutes of *We Joined the Navy* depicted this scene well. Adapted from John Winton's 1959 novel, the frenetic arrival at BRNC had changed little in the interim.

The road rose again past an accommodation block (The Hostel, where unaccompanied or single staff officers were billeted) and a couple of houses (married quarters for BRNC's Supply Officer and Training Commander).

At the end of the road, I arrived at Hawke Division. We quickly learned that the building immediately adjoining Hawke was the Commander's house, BRNC's second-in-command. We were told to minimise noise levels when outside Hawke's front door so as not to disturb the Commander and his family.

2.5 Hawke Division frontage
Div Chief's office (left), DO's office (right) on ground floor, HGR across width of first floor

Several cars were outside Hawke's front door. Like me, their owners retrieved suitcases and grips from the boot. Another impeccable Middy told me to put my stuff in the hall inside Hawke, take my car to the designated car park somewhere on the other side of the sports field, and return ASAP. Swiftly following his orders, I returned to Hawke. Yet another Middy checked my name and directed me to Upper Dorm. I picked up my bags and dashed up the staircase.

There was a wide hallway at the top of the stairs. I walked along a passageway, with cabins and heads (toilets) and bathrooms either side, through the double-doors into the Upper Dorm. Ranged along each side were metal double-bunks, heads to the outside wall, feet towards the centre. Shabby, scratched wooden wardrobes/drawers surmounted with shoe-racks were between each set of bunks. Along the centreline were several long tables plus a few more wardrobe/drawer/shoe-rack combos.

I was allocated a bunk and wardrobe, my home for the next 14 weeks. Sharing a bedroom was alien to me. I'd never done so with anyone, at home, university or as a MN deck cadet. However, my experience in Upper Dorm did me no harm.

I had a bottom bunk. This avoided clambering up-and-down, especially for a wee during the night. I unpacked, stowed my stuff and moved my empty bags to the nearest baggage room, down the passageway. Others did likewise. There were brief introductions. It was about 1700, the bustling dorm seemed full.

The uniformed Middies were Seniors. Their role was to guide/lead us Juniors through New Entry Phase, our first four weeks at BRNC. Seniors had completed two terms, first at BRNC, the second in the Dartmouth Training Squadron (DTS). Now they were 3rd termers, others were 4th termers. They were all Naval College Entry (NCE) as they'd joined straight from school. Supplementary List (SL) officers completed three terms at Dartmouth, General List (GL) stayed beyond for a fourth term. The former were on eight-year short career commissions (SL shags), the latter held full career commissions (lifers).

Seniors rounded up the Juniors from Upper and Lower Dorms. We mustered (quietly!) outside Hawke, formed three ranks, marched down the road, bore left at a junction and arrived at Caspar John Hall (CJH).

We got to know CJH well. Many presentations, briefings and lectures took place there. It was a large auditorium with a stage at the front. Nicknamed 'The 400-man Sleeping-Bag', its cosy temperature, comfy seats and dim lighting were perfect for exhausted Juniors to catnap or go comatose during even the most interesting lectures. With luck your oppo (mate) elbowed you if you started nodding in slumber. A heinous crime, punished by enforced standing at attention for the remainder of the lecture.

Time pressed. We were seated by 1715, ready for the Captain's introduction at 1720. I knew punctuality was a cornerstone of the military, but BRNC took it to a new level. Hawke Juniors were joined by Juniors from the other three Divisions (Blake, Cunningham and St Vincent). Seniors surrounded us, monitored our noise level and silenced us just before the Captain entered CJH. We were ordered to 'sit at attention'.

Mounting the stage, Captain Bevan was a huge man with a booming Churchillian voice. His physical presence gave him natural authority and, on walkabout, he filled BRNC's corridors. His distinguished career included command of frigates and destroyers, plus service in Royal Yacht *Britannia*. He exuded the countenance, bearing and power of command required of a military officer. What a great man!

After another couple of briefings, Seniors ushered Juniors back to their respective Divisions. When 'dismissed', we rushed into Hawke, upstairs to Hawke Gun Room (HGR) for the next serial, as programmed events were called in the RN. All seated, a Senior stationed at the door ordered us to 'sit at attention' as our Divisional Staff Officers entered. Time for introductions.

Our leader (Divisional Officer, DO) was Lieutenant Commander (Lt Cdr) Woolston. Dark-haired, bearded and softly spoken, he seemed a dull, uninspiring chap. A contrast to the massive impression that Captain Bevan had made on me. His staff were Assistant Divisional Officers (ADOs), each responsible for a group of Juniors and Seniors.

My ADO was Lt Cdr Paddy Watson, the most pukka officer I ever met in my entire naval career, well-spoken with clipped tones and invariably impeccably dressed (Gieves & Hawkes, naturally). He even wore a stiff white collar when in 'woolly-pully' uniform. Accompanied everywhere by his black labrador, Lt Cdr Watson was a fearsome officer of enviable ramrod, erect bearing, uncompromising in demanding extraordinarily high standards if officer-like qualities (Oily-Qs). I greatly respected him and felt fortunate he was my ADO.

A Division's lynchpin was its Divisional Chief (Div Chief). Hawke's was CPO Ross. Like his colleagues in the other Divisions, he'd completed a long, unblemished naval career. Div Chiefs provided continuity to College and Division routine and administration, while Staff Officers were appointed for two years and moved on.

Finally, the Divisional Sub Lieutenant (Div Sub) introduced himself. Midshipman John Dryden was a pleasant, easy-going bloke. This impression concealed a steely young man who ceaselessly strove to maintain high standards from Hawke's Officers-Under-Training (OUTs). His role was Hawke's chief OUT.

Each Division had a Div Sub but top dog was the Senior Sub Lieutenant (Senior Sub). He had his own cabin in the College, separate from the Divisions. He was king of the OUTs, selected by cross-division staff officer recommendation and discussion. The role attracted great kudos and was potentially a launch pad to a great naval career.

After Hawke Staff Officers had introduced themselves, it was our turn to stand and spout a quick couple of minutes of biography when called. It was important to speak clearly and articulately to avoid a monotonous drone and to camouflage any nerves. Our performances provided Divisional Staff with their first impression of us. The assessment of our qualities and potential as a naval officer began.

We mustered outside Hawke and marched down that hill again (we never 'walked' or 'ambled' anywhere at BRNC!), all the way to the chapel at the far end of the College's 'main drag'. This parquet-floored, highly polished passageway ran the entire length of the College's façade. At 201m, it was one of the longest corridors in the world, every footstep echoed. On both sides, stretches of wall between doorways and windows were lined with framed photos of previous passing out groups, stretching back decades. I eagerly looked forward to my own passing out photo joining the others. I would then proudly become an integral part of Dartmouth's illustrious history.

2.6 'Main drag' from Chapel to SGR

In the magnificent chapel, a short new entry prayers service was led by the three College chaplains (sin bosuns or dodgy deacons): Church of England, Roman Catholic, Church of Scotland. Then we were marched out to eat dinner in the Junior Gun Room (JGR) on the ground floor of D Block, the College's rearmost main building, in which Cunningham and St Vincent Divisions were housed. Blake Division occupied the upper floors of A Block and the front west façade overlooked the parade ground.

As Juniors, we took all our meals in the JGR. After dinner, we mustered again – this mustering malarkey was never-ending! We marched back up to CJH for a presentation on uniforms at 2000 and then returned to Hawke.

We felt bewildered at the whirlwind of activity since passing through the gates that afternoon – and this was only day one. The frenetic pace never slackened, so the sooner we got used to the routine, the better.

Call the hands was at 0630 and by 0700 we were at breakfast in plain clothes (civvies). A long day ensued. We were divided into small groups and escorted by a Senior to follow a matrix of locations and offices: dentist/sickbay; barber (everyone had a haircut, regardless); stationery store; clothing store; photographer; pay office; Owens Tailors (for contract uniform measurement); chaplain; and a tour of the College. Sometime lunch occurred. Luckily, tea in the JGR was at 1615.

2.7 Me in the detested battledress uniform

We also went to Wrangaton, a naval supply depot between Ivybridge and South Brent, to be issued with a mountain of uniform. We stuffed everything into our newly-issued, tan canvas, kit-bags.

2. We Joined the Navy

We were in CJH at 1730 for the College task presentation then back to Hawke for respite until dinner at 1900. This was our first outing in uniform. We dressed in white shirts, black tie, black trousers, new black leather shoes and name tally and cap. On top, despised by all Juniors, was a black battledress jacket of serge, ill-fitting regardless of body-shape (short, tall, fat, thin, muscular … it made no difference) and uncomfortable, barely long enough to reach the waist. Everyone looked like a sack of spuds with exposed white shirt between trouser-waist and jacket hem.

Friday was our first day in uniform. After breakfast, we mustered in HGR. The DO and ADOs listened to the remainder of our short biographies. There was a wide range of folks. As well as Brits, there were Internationals (Ints), mainly from the Caribbean and Persian Gulf states, with a sprinkling from Kenya, Singapore and Brunei. The rest of the morning comprised more briefings in CJH.

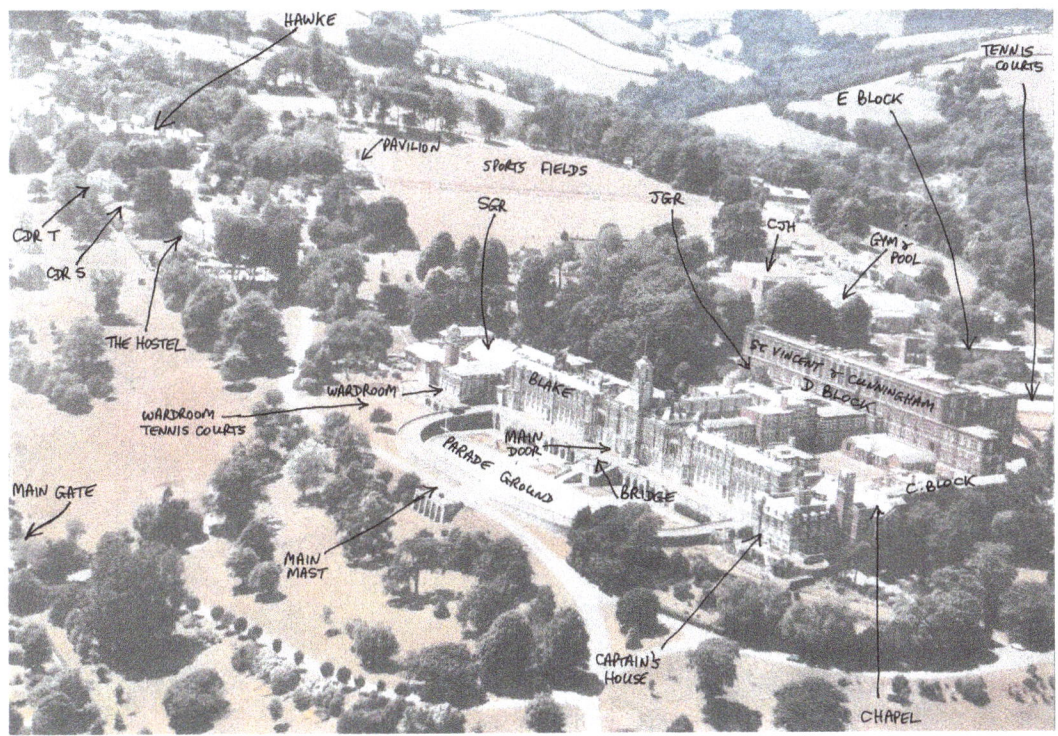

2.8 BRNC, key features annotated
(BRNC Archive)

On top of our busy Wednesday and Thursday, over two hours on Friday in a warm, comfy CJH, listening to a succession of important but dull briefings proved too much for a few Juniors. I noted some nodding heads and occasionally saw someone elbow his neighbour in the ribs and the startled face of the awakened miscreant. And we were only on Day 3, Week 0.

We were 'acquainted' with the river in the afternoon. It was a long trek down hundreds of steps to Sandquay, where BRNC's fleet of boats was berthed: whalers, Cheverton motor boats, picket boats (PBs), bosun dinghies, sail training craft (STC or yacht), dories and Geminis (a boat with a rubber buoyancy tube, flat fabric floor and a wooden transom on which an outboard motor was mounted). The river was a big focus and we'd be required to practise and pass a 'ticket' for each type of craft.

On Saturday, we experienced our first en masse parade training session. The fearsome, loud, barking parade training staff (gunnery instructors, GIs) ordered us about. They introduced the basics of drill: march, turn, about-turn, wheel, halt, stand at attention, stand at ease. Rigorous, inflexible standards were explained: clean-shaven, no wristwatches, highly-bulled parade boots, sparkling-clean white cap covers, perfect creases in trousers and shirts. If a wristwatch was spotted, the offender was ordered to double around the ramps at either end of the parade ground, arms vertical, shouting 'I MUST NOT WEAR MY WATCH ON THE PARADE GROUND, STAFF'. No one repeated the offence after being caught out once!

The morning rounded off in Hawke where Lt Cdr Woolston briefed us on and discussed 'What is an Officer?' Indeed!

The rest of the day was quieter and devoted to sorting out, ironing and folding our kit to fit into drawers. We also started bulling (polishing) our boots and shoes in earnest, a long process. An oft-repeated cry from Seniors and Sea Dads was 'Don't forget the welts', the leather rim sewn round the edge of a shoe's upper to which the sole was attached. Inspections by GIs and Divisional Staff always noted the state of your welts.

Every Junior was allocated a Sea Dad. Mine was Nick Richardson, a tall, confident, good-humoured Northerner. He was Flight, so he'd joined the Navy directly to be Fleet Air Arm (FAA) aircrew (pilot or observer), pilot in Nick's case. Flight OUTs completed two terms at BRNC. As Seniors, their second term was academic and included flight grading in Navy Chipmunk aircraft at Roborough Airport, Plymouth. Those who failed grading could either leave the Service or become a Seaman Officer.

Years later, I learned that Nick had completed his flying training and was selected to fly Sea Harriers. He embarked in *Ark Royal* in 1994, was shot down over Gorazde in Bosnia, survived and then escaped when the Serbs stormed the city. His book, *No Escape Zone*, is a cracking tale.

A Sea Dad initiated his protégé into the ways of life in the Division and the wider College. Nick's primary focus was guiding me through the intricacies of uniform, particularly how it must be laid out in our drawers and wardrobe for standing rounds (inspection).

The various tricks included:
- buy another pair or two of Pusser's daps (Navy-issue plimsolls) purely for show on my shoe-rack – as not only the plimsolls but their white laces had to be immaculate
- likewise, the white lanyards for our newly issued knife and spike

2.9 My seaman's knife and spike combo, well-used but now careworn

- be careful when ironing black and bow ties; both were nylon so, after ironing, they'd be shiny – unacceptable – therefore, put a folded handkerchief on top and then iron them
- soak my beret in lukewarm water, place it on my head and mould it to the right shape; carefully remove it to maintain the shape and leave it to dry – perfect!

Summer 1984 entrants were the first to be issued with combat high boots and we spent an awful lot of time in them. We soaked them for a few hours, got them out and put them on before letting them dry overnight on the Upper Dorm balcony. The boots had moulded slightly to your feet, which reduced the chance of blisters. Throughout our first term, there were always Juniors hobbling round in Pusser's daps because of painful blisters from their combat high boots. Ouch!

In Upper Dorm, we got to know each other better. Nick Birch was the other graduate Seaman Officer and the same age as me. Post-university, he'd worked as a skilled builder and repairer of wooden vintage boats in Stratford-Upon-Avon. Monty, as he was affectionately nicknamed, arrived in his red MG convertible, roof folded away as it was a lovely sunny day. He'd also brought his own ironing board, stowed upright in the passenger seat. He was a well-spoken, smart, smooth, cool guy, blessed with blond hair and blue eyes. Like me, he was well-travelled and worldly wise – and as organised. No wonder we got on famously.

Among the non-graduate entrants were a couple each of Engineers and Supply Officers (Pussers), several Seaman Officers and some potential aircrew. I found the list of entrants for my first term in the BRNC Archive and was instantly transported back to April 1984 in Hawke when I read those names: Richie Blackwell, Kev Seymour, Nigel Rhind, Andy Skinner, Johnny Park, Matt Thorsby, Dougie 'Dinger' Bell (all Bells were nicknamed Dinger). Ah, such heady, happy days.

2.10 View from Upper Dorm balcony

Of the Ints, Al-Ameri from the UAE was an excellent chap. Orlando Forbes and Thomas Clearie were relaxed but well-disciplined Bahamians. Thomas was gregarious, perpetually cheerful, with a permanent broad smile. He was also an expert buller and offered to do it for others who weren't quite so competent, me included. He sat at the centreline tables, happily bulling away most evenings. Sometimes, he continued bulling despite falling asleep. Orlando, an equally good guy, was quietly serious and calm. He let slip he'd exchanged fire with a Cuban patrol boat somewhere in the Caribbean and was instantly nicknamed Orlando the Cuban Killer.

I was no stranger to Caribbean blokes. My first two trips with Blue Star (*ACT 5* and *Benedict*) were Barbadian-crewed with UK officers. Their laconic approach to work on deck and West Indian patois were different to anything I'd previously experienced. They were great fun to work with on deck.

2.11 Hawke A-Block
Upper Dorm (first floor), Lower Dorm (ground floor)

The Saudi Arabians were in Lower Dorm, as were a pair of Instructor Officers (Schoolies), several NCEs across the specialisations and some Flight. Hawke Juniors totalled 28 in a total intake of 110. Summer term entry was always the smallest. Autumn's (September) was always the largest, as those who'd completed school or graduated from university chose to join up straightaway. The winter (January) entry was between these two.

A quiet start to Sunday, with a new entry church service at 1000. The three denominations had their own chapel: the Church of England had BRNC's Chapel; Catholics and Church of Scotland each had a small chapel elsewhere in the College; there was also a Muslim prayer room. Afterwards, everyone gathered for tea and biscuits on the quarterdeck. Staff, lecturers

(BRNC's civilian academic staff), Seniors and Juniors rubbed along together in social conversation. Very civilised.

New entry mini-sports occupied the afternoon. Competition was intense between the Divisions. Pride was at stake across a range of games on the parade ground, such as sprints and relays, culminating with tug-of-war. It was morale-boosting and fertilised camaraderie in a tribal, raucous atmosphere. The parade ground was filled with Seniors screaming encouragement, Juniors in Divisional T-shirts (Hawke red, Blake navy blue, Cunningham yellow, St Vincent purple), shorts and daps.

The day ended with dinner. On Monday, naval general training (NGT) and our new entry phase began in earnest. Confined to BRNC for four weeks of intense activity at a relentless pace under perpetual time pressure. Our daily routine began at 0610 through to post-2100. Seniors focused on their academic studies and left Juniors to fend for themselves.

The other Divisions had two- or four-man cabins. In Hawke a tighter bond developed in Lower and Upper Dorms. Hawke Staff and Seniors impressed on us that we were fortunate and privileged to be in Hawke, the Country Club. We were up the hill and far from the madness and chaos of the main College. Yep, we felt fortunate in Hawke.

We swiftly learned that personal organisation was key. With the number of different 'rigs' (uniforms) across the syllabus (see Table 2.1), it was a long way to climb that hill and get back in time for class if we forgot to pack the right rigs in a Pusser's grip for the day's classes and activities. Divisions in the main building had the luxury of sufficient time to return to their cabins to change or collect items they'd forgotten. That simply wasn't possible for us in the Country Club, as it was just too far away. So we in Hawke packed a full day's kit in our grips – little wonder we developed Popeye-like forearms.

Table 2.1 Standard rigs

Rig	When worn
No.5 Reefer jacket and trousers, white shirt, stiff detached collar, black shoes, black tie, name tally	Ceremonial occasions, Sundays
No.5J White collar-attached shirt, woolly pully, No.5 trousers, black tie, black shoes, cap, name tally	Daily working rig (academics)

Rig	When worn
No.5JP Blue AWD (action working dress) shirt (open neck), woolly pully, battledress trousers, black shoes or parade boots, cap, name tally	Daily working rig (naval general training)
Mess undress Soft dress shirt, black bow tie, mess jacket, trousers, cummerbund, black shoes, cap	Evening rig
Battledress Serge blouse and trousers, white shirt, stiff collar, black shoes, black tie, cap, name tally	Evening rig, ceremonial occasions, Sundays
River duty rig No.12 shirt, tie, woolly pully, battledress trousers, plimsolls, knife, lanyard, beret, name tally	River duty
River instructional rig Appropriate day dress modified: beret, AWD trousers, plimsolls, knife, lanyard	River instruction and sea training in *Peterel* or *Sandpiper*
River activity rig White sports shirt, AWD trousers, plimsolls, knife, lanyard, name tally	Activity or recreation on river

We gleaned two basic rules at BRNC: never be adrift (late); always be in the correct rig. If you got them right, life at BRNC was a breeze! Or so you thought.

The morning of Monday 30 April began with a rude awakening. The Duty Mid (Duty Midshipman) bellowing as he crashed through the Upper Dorm's double-doors. The sun streamed through the windows. I'd woken a bit earlier, got a head-start with my ablutions, knowing it would be chaos given the limited number of washbasins and showers. Freshly shaved, we mustered outside Hawke's front door. A Senior marched us down to the gym for our first early morning activity (EMA).

EMAs were an embuggerance to lengthen our days. They occurred daily, except Sunday, and comprised gym, parade training, squad run, pulling. The last entailed doubling down hundreds of steps to Sandquay to clamber into the College whalers and pull (row) up-river for about ten minutes. It was exhausting. We were all novices with only a vague idea of technique. To make any headway, our Senior bellowed out the stroke. A vain attempt to coordinate his numpty crew. We turned around, rowed back, disembarked, secured the whalers and raced back up to Hawke. Futile? Character-building?

All non-Divisional College staff were affiliated to a designated Division. Hawke's EMA parade training was conducted by Colour Sergeant Spiewack, a fine Royal Marine with a great sense of humour. Like all his colleagues on the parade training staff, he was extremely professional and rigorously upheld standards of drill. He brooked no clumsiness or inability to march properly.

The other EMAs were organised and run by the Duty Divisional Officer (DDO), a Senior nominated by rota. Depending on this bloke's personality, the EMA was fun, chaos or farce.

I enjoyed the squad run most of all. We formed up, three deep, in front of Hawke, were turned left and doubled (jogged) in step at a reasonable pace. Dartmouth's early morning birdsong was interrupted by the steady rhythmic pounding of umpteen pairs of combat high boots chuffing along like a train on its tracks. There was something soothing and reassuring about a body of military blokes moving perfectly in concert around the College's grounds for about 30 minutes.

Somewhere during Week 0, we passed the naval swimming test. We changed into bathers, donned black overalls and mustered poolside. In we jumped, swam 50m within four minutes, trod water for two minutes in the deep end and surface dived to collect a rubber brick from the pool's bottom and climbed out unaided. Most passed. The poor sods who failed did remedial swimming for EMA until they passed. If they hadn't succeeded by the end of New Entry, they were placed under Captain's Warning and, ultimately, withdrawn from training (WFT), ending a very short naval career.

It was after our first pulling EMA that we fully appreciated just how isolated Hawke was from the rest of the College. The flog up Sandquay steps and then up the hill to Hawke severely reduced time for ablutions. Dressed in the correct rig, we raced down to the JGR for breakfast, filling our faces with food, then hurtled to the correct venue to be punctual for after breakfast activity (ABA) at 0800.

Monday was Divisional Officer's period, when the Division assembled in HGR for a particular purpose, otherwise, an opportunity for ADOs to conduct progress interviews with their OUTs. Wednesday and Friday were used for lessons. Divisions (parade) was held on Tuesday, Thursday and Saturday. The first two were Training Divisions. Saturday was the more formal Ceremonial Divisions and usually included BRNC's Royal Marines Band. Its stirring martial music made for a great parade.

Sundays were largely free, but hardly a rest day as there was always something to do: sorting kit, dhobying (laundry), ironing, afternoon activities. Wearing a suit was required for attending compulsory church services at 1000, compensated for afterwards by multi-denominational tea/coffee and biscuits on the quarterdeck.

From 0900 to 1305 on Monday to Saturday we attended classes. Afternoon lessons ended at 1615 on weekday afternoons (except Monday and Wednesday). Monday afternoons were for sports clubs. Wednesday and Saturday afternoons were for organised sports fixtures against external opponents.

We took tea in the JGR until 1700, akin to feeding the chimps at London Zoo. I thoroughly enjoyed stuffing myself with two, three or even four rounds of buttered toast and jam, washed down with a mug of tea. Our days were so action-packed and full of movement and activity around the College that my appetite sky-rocketed, yet I remained lean, slender and wiry.

As it was light well into the evening, BRNC ran its summer routine, which meant activities from 1700 to 1855. It was an opportunity for Juniors to get onto the river and gain expertise in handling a variety of boats and get our boat tickets as soon as practicable.

We rushed back up to Hawke to get changed for dinner in the JGR. Time pressure increased because we were obliged to clean Hawke's heads and bathrooms and our own accommodation space by 1955. 'Standing Rounds' occurred at 2000. For this, we were immaculately turned out in battledress, caps on (with pristine white cap cover), shiny shoes and name tallies. We stood at ease by our bunks to await the Inspecting Officer.

For our first standing rounds, Sea Dads were at our side, ready to note and action any deficiencies raised by the Inspecting Officer. Sea Dads did their utmost to ensure our appearance, kit, bunks and footwear were of an acceptable standard and presented correctly. There was no room for civvies, save for a suit, blazer and chinos, a couple of quality shirts and ties, and shoes (polished, of course). We repacked the remainder of our civvies in grips and bags to stow in Hawke's baggage rooms. We didn't need them due to our confinement in the College throughout our new entry phase.

That first evening of standing rounds left an impression on us all. Time severely pressed. No one went to dinner as we focused entirely on preparing for rounds. We were each allocated a specific space and guided through the standard to be achieved.

Heads were scrubbed thoroughly, with a new roll of bog-paper (plus a spare) in each cubicle. Showers and washbasins cleaned and wiped dry. Nylon shower curtains were a nightmare to dry. If a washbasin's tap had a drip, the shiny white basin would never be bone dry. Washbasin plugs were 'cheesed down': plug placed on the basin between the taps and then slowly rotated so its chain gradually and perfectly spiralled around the plug until there was no slack in the chain. The red, tiled decks were swept and mopped out. A pungent odour of bleach and detergent lingered, matched by furniture and shoe polish in Upper Dorm.

When allocated either a bathroom or set of heads, the time remaining to get personal space sorted significantly reduced. It required extremely efficient organisation to achieve the standard in both places. Little wonder we skipped dinner.

At 1955 we got into position. Those involved in heads and bathrooms stood ready to salute and report the space ready for inspection to the Inspecting Officer. Everyone else stood 'at ease' beside their bunk, shoulder-to-shoulder with Sea Dad. The tension was tangible in Upper Dorm. We didn't know what to expect.

That first inspection was interminable. Ground floor was inspected first, so we had a long wait. Hawke was totally silent. Seniors remained in their cabins or escaped elsewhere. The Rounds Party was led by Duty Mid, followed by Inspecting Officer and DDO (notebook and pen in hand). Duty Mid piped 'The Still' on his bosun's call (traditional naval whistle) to signal their approach. At each space, the Junior reporting it stood at attention and made his report.

Time wore on. The piping grew louder, the rounds party got closer. Upper Dorm's double-doors were already open. You could hear a pin drop. The Inspecting Officer slowly proceeded around Upper Dorm, inspecting each kit layout, boots, shoes and the Junior standing rigidly at attention, eyes focused unswervingly ahead.

He passed comment here and there, mainly that boots and shoes required more shine. Frequently, he took an item from a drawer and inspected it. He'd either drop it or chuck it somewhere. Not much shouting or abuse occurred, unlike in films, merely a rise in volume of his authoritative voice, showing disdain and displeasure.

The Inspecting Officer rummaged through my kit. All was in order. Eventually, he exited Upper Dorm and turned to face our reporting bloke who requested if rounds were complete. Apparently, we'd barely achieved the standard and had much more work to do. With that, he about-turned and headed off to the next space.

Occasionally, re-scrubs were decreed, particularly heads and bathrooms deemed unacceptable in some minute way. A re-scrub meant the unlucky

Junior responsible for that space had to re-clean it by 2130, re-report to the DDO and hope it now met the standard.

By now it was about 2100. We closed the doors and reflected on our non-stop, first day's new entry training. Crikey, if every day was like that, the next four weeks would be an eternity. Yep, every day we were constantly on the move from 0530 to completion of standing rounds at about 2100, depending on the Inspecting Officer.

With only five Hawke ADOs, responsibility for conducting standing rounds included Hawke's Affiliated Officers. The College's uniformed staff, although not directly involved, were affiliated to a Division, instilling a sense of inclusivity and belonging. College Non-Commissioned Officers (NCOs) were also affiliated to a Division. Each Division had a GI, PTI, river instructor and several other senior rates from BRNC ship's company. There was even an Attached Band Sergeant from BRNC's Royal Marines Band. Most of these folks were never seen, but it was a worthwhile part of inclusivity.

Monday evenings from 2000, Juniors were available for interviews and discussions on progress with their nominated tutor, a member of the civilian academic staff. They acted more as a sounding board for Juniors if any were unhappy, unsettled or struggling, rather than for academic problems.

Many tutors had been at BRNC for decades. Mine had joined in 1964. Michael Scott-Scott ('Scott squared' as he was affectionately known) was a science lecturer, a long-standing member of the Wardroom Mess Committee (especially the laying-down of port and wine), and the Armed Services Arts Society. We had tennis in common as he was Assistant Tennis Officer. Scott-Scott was a pukka old boy, with thinning white hair, tall but stooped. His appearance made him look older than my father, who was the same age. Due to his seniority, his office/study overlooked the parade ground, Dartmouth town, the river and beyond to Kingswear.

We were divided into classes containing blokes from all four Divisions. This blend of Juniors ensured we had substantial contact with our peers in Blake, Cunningham and St Vincent. Each class had a mix across all types of entry and specialisation. Thus, everyone made new friends and a collective camaraderie among Juniors evolved. The Ints were in separate classes.

Each week, a class leader was designated, responsible for ensuring the class was in the right place, at the right time, in the right rig. It was a test of character and leadership (C&L) and management skills.

In BRNC the 'five minute rule' was golden. Classes must be at the venue five minutes before start time. Class Leaders went over the top, demanding we muster five minutes before that, so, ten minutes before start time. Everyone knew this was daft and impossible to achieve for every lesson or activity. Nevertheless, as Class Leader, that logic evaporated. If the class was adrift, it was the Class Leader's fault and he'd failed, regardless of circumstances. A bad week as Class Leader was noted, and a snotty-gram sent to the Division, attracting an ADO's interview and a bollocking.

Early on, Juniors picked up choice phrases from Seniors and Staff Officers. 'SORT YOUR LIFE OUT!', 'GET YOUR S**T IN ONE SOCK!', 'SWITCH ON!' 'BUFFS!' ('Buck up for f***'s sake!') were bellowed or shrilled interminably all over College. Class Leaders frustrated by dismal timekeeping and/or incorrect rig of the class muppet (there's always one) used these phrases. Lack of a name tally attracted particular condemnation.

If instructors felt a Class Leader had performed well, good feedback was sent to his ADO. For impressive showing in lessons, a positive chit could be added. These titbits from numerous sources developed a picture of the Junior, greatly assisting his ADO in assessing progress and the content of termly personnel reports.

2.12 My class prepped for an acquaint flight in a Wasp helicopter from Norton Airfield.
Front (left to right): BJ Newton, Kev Seymour, me, Chris Davies, Charlie Coull, Mark Ledger. Rear (left to right): Nigel Rhind, Steve Williams, Jon Pentreath, Steve Kenny, Sam Toothill, Towner, Neil Hicking, Neil Boughton (BJ Newton)

2. We Joined the Navy

The timetable, unlike school, varied week to week. The programme was published on Fridays for the following week, especially pertinent for the incoming Class Leader.

The curriculum was wide-ranging: navigation; operations and weapons ('ops and wops'); seamanship; supply, administration and management (SAM); marine engineering (ME); weapon engineering (WE); parade training; gym; and leadership. Most subjects were interesting.

I was already a competent and knowledgeable navigator after my deck cadetship. I knew of types of warships and gun/missile systems as I'd enjoyed touring warships at Portsmouth Navy Days for years and reading *Navy News* monthly. Now, I learned their exact role: anti-ship; anti-missile; anti-aircraft; anti-submarine. Seamanship lessons reinforced knowledge gained with Blue Star, but introduced RN methodology for anchoring, berthing and manoeuvring, which differed slightly from MN practices.

ME opened my eyes to powerplants fitted in warships: jet engines 'marinised' into gas turbines; steam; diesel; nuclear power in submarines. It also introduced the principles of nuclear biological chemical and damage control (NBCD), a vast but very important topic. WE was an entirely new subject, covering the wiggly-amp bits that actually powered and moved the weapon systems and electronics.

By far the dullest classes were SAM. Utter tedium! I thanked God I'd chosen to be a Seaman Officer, the Executive Branch, the Master Race, to command warships, charge round the oceans on missions critical to our nation's security. And thanked God again that there were people who volunteered to be bean-counters and blanket-stackers.

Our instructors were professional, competent and knowledgeable. They largely succeeded in putting the information across to us.

New entry phase weekends were occupied with a series of new entry exercises (NEX). My class was one of those designated for the first weekend. Instructions were issued early in Wcek 1. At the end of that frenetic week, we heaved a sigh of relief but braced ourselves for whatever NEX hurled our way. I packed the specified kit into my bergen rucksack.

On Saturday afternoon, class leaders marched us down to Sandquay to embark in eight PBs. For each PB, a Senior was Coxswain and ordered us to collect this, fetch that, stow the other. 'SORT YOUR LIFE OUT!' 'GET YOUR S**T IN ONE SOCK!' echoed around Sandquay from irate Seniors. The Coxswain was assisted by another Senior (Mate of the Upper Deck) to control us on deck for seamanship. A Staff Officer was nominated for each PB. He boarded shortly before we slipped from the pontoon and satisfied himself that the PB was ready in all respects to proceed. The Coxswain ordered a Junior to take the Staff Officer's bergen down to the for'ard cabin. RHIP (rank has its privileges).

2.13 PB3 at sea
(BRNC Archive)

The PBs slipped in an impressive, organised fashion and loitered clear of Sandquay. Coxswain and Staff Officer demonstrated a PB's handling characteristics and evolutions (berthing, coming to a buoy, recovering a man overboard). At the specified time, the 'Guide' PB ordered the others to form up in line astern and collectively headed upriver towards Dittisham.

On a very pleasant, warm evening in May, late afternoon sunshine bathed the Dart and its forested banks. The picturesque towns of Kingswear and Dartmouth were downstream, astern of our PB convoy. It was a short passage to Dittisham.

The Senior on deck ordered us to 'stand by to come to a buoy', explained the procedure and ensured we rigged the mooring line correctly. The PB approached the buoy, Coxswain loudly issued orders. All went smoothly, our PB secured to the buoy by mooring line passed through the PB's bull-ring, out to the buoy's ring, back inboard and secured to the cleat on the bow.

It seemed to go well to our uninitiated eyes, but I glimpsed our Staff Officer scribbling notes. I realised that it was not only Juniors being assessed, but also Seniors, still under the spotlight until they passed out.

We tidied up and secured the fo'c'sle. A brief lull ensued. We went below and settled into the PB's aft cabin, where we'd sleep overnight. But the space doubled as galley, dining-room and saloon. It was cramped as half a dozen Juniors tried to organise themselves whilst bent almost double due to the low headroom.

The for'ard cabin was also cramped but could accommodate the Staff Officer, Coxswain and Senior. These two spaces were separated by the wheelhouse and a well deck. The former's kit included the helm, throttles for the twin engines, echo sounder, a few dials showing engine revs, basic radar and a VHF radio.

Our next task was to cook dinner, our introduction to 'pot-mess', a unique dining experience found across all three services. A Junior was designated chef and, guided by the Seniors, tipped the contents of a 24-hour ration pack (except desserts, biscuits and chocolate) into a large saucepan on the galley's gas ring. It was heated and stirred frequently. The kettle was boiled on the other ring for a brew, because British soldiers, sailors and airmen brewed a cuppa at any opportunity.

Our chef announced dinner was ready. Strict etiquette was followed: Staff Officer first, Seniors next, lastly Juniors. We squeezed around the table in the aft cabin and tucked in. Pot-mess was delicious and slices of a large white loaf mopped up the dregs on our plates. Tea was most welcome. For dessert, tins of fruit were opened and we tucked in again. Conversation continued throughout.

Sated, we sat back as best we could. Not for long! Coxswain ordered us to clear away the table, wash up the pan, plates and cutlery, dry them off, put them back in their correct stowage. We remained in the aft cabin for our Staff Officer's briefing on the next stage: a march around the countryside.

Several Geminis, driven by more Seniors, ferried Juniors ashore where each PB team navigated a slightly different route to avoid a huge mass of OUTs tramping all over this rural idyll. We were given a target time to complete the trek and it was up to us to navigate.

Bergens on our backs, we set off. I remember nothing of the march, but a delightful trudge through the glorious South Hams. The sun dipped below the hills around 2030, replaced by a moonlit night. We finished in good time at Dittisham's Red Lion Inn, at the top of the village. Our leader reported to the Exercise Director. He ordered us to continue down to the landing-stage, then disappeared back into the pub to resume his pint.

At the landing-stage, Dittisham's other pub, The Ferry Boat Inn, looked inviting but those pesky Seniors ferried us back to our PB. We clambered aboard and sorted ourselves out for as comfortable a night as practicable in the tight confines of the aft cabin.

Call the hands was early on Sunday morning. We did our best to ablute, given a PB's limited facilities. Another chef cooked a hearty breakfast. Following the Senior Ship's lead, we conducted colours at 0800, the Jack hoisted for'ard, White Ensign aft. A Junior was designated padre and each PB held a very short service before shattering Sunday's peace and quiet with lusty singing (mangling?) of the naval hymn.

We slipped from the buoys, formed up in line astern of the guide and steamed downstream on a bright, warm, sunny morning. We passed Higher Ferry, Dart Marina Hotel and The Floating Bridge pub to starboard. A little further, Dartmouth quayside and Kingswear were to starboard and port respectively. BRNC dominated the skyline from its lofty perch. Onwards we steamed, between the castles at the Dart's mouth and into Start Bay.

Officer-of-the-Watch manoeuvres took place on an empty, open sea. A commonplace serial in which two or more warships manoeuvred in close formation, changed course, speed and formation shape, using a series of pre-determined tactical signals by flag hoists or VHF. The guide PB ordered each manoeuvre. The other PBs used course and speed alterations to get into and maintain station relative to the guide. It was impressive to witness eight PBs in one formation. Then, using VHF radio, the order 'Stand By … Execute' triggered all PBs to whizz into the new formation.

2.14 PBs manoeuvring in Start Bay
(BRNC Archive)

At last, we returned to Sandquay, where we off-loaded our bergens, stowed all PB kit in the correct place, scrubbed out the cabins, wheelhouse and well deck. Staff Officers didn't loiter for long. At 1700, we made our weary way back up the endless Sandquay steps to our Divisions. In Upper Dorm, I unpacked and stowed my kit, checked the time and planned for a shower and preparations for standing rounds.

Here, Week 1 ended. Crikey, this set the pace and tone for the remaining 13 weeks of our first term.

2.15 Hawke Division, viewed from the lawn

Hawke Juniors' diligence at cleaning for standing rounds paid off as we were reprieved early in Week 4. This provided respite from the slog of our daily routine and freed the evenings a little. Evening rounds occurred instead, but were less severe, provided we maintained the standard.

The evening's cleaning didn't require all Juniors. Like everyone else in BRNC, we were divided into four duty parts – 1st and 2nd Port Watch, 1st and 2nd Starboard Watch – so duty one day in every four. This mirrored routine life (and daily drudgery for our sailors) in warships and shore establishments.

Occasionally, Hawke conducted a skirmish of and around the Division. With Seniors in charge, Juniors spent a half-hour in Hawke's immediate environs picking up scraps of litter. A waste of time? No, a warship was a fighting machine to be kept spick-and-span at all times. Litter and debris weren't tolerated. As aspiring officers, cleaning for rounds and skirmishing helped instil this ethos for when we served in the Fleet.

New entry phase ended after Ceremonial Divisions at lunchtime Saturday 25 May. At last, we were permitted to go ashore. College Orders stated that OUTs proceeded ashore on leave in 'plain clothes'. Time to break out blazer, shirt, tie, chinos and polished shoes.

During new entry, Divisional Staff Officers explained in great detail about 'plain clothes'. Lt Cdr Watson stood rigidly at the lectern in CJH to describe various rigs while his colleagues modelled them. Four decades later, I clearly hear his clipped tones: 'Leather is worn on the foot, not the back.' 'Officers do not wear white socks or grey shoes.' 'Use wooden coat hangers, never plastic ones.' 'A suit is worn, with polished shoes, on Sundays, even when cleaning one's car.' And he was serious. Jeans were, and still are, absolutely forbidden in BRNC.

We wore 'dog robbers' (blazer, chinos, shirt, tie) in the evenings when not on duty. On hot summer days, the blazer was relaxed to 'planters' (collar-and-tie, chinos). Dress in the Mess was inflexible. Tracksuits or football/rugby/hockey boots or any other studded footwear were not permitted. Sports and river rigs were also forbidden, although, if clean, they were acceptable when worn with a cravat and blazer for tea. Blimey, who wore a cravat in 1984?

Before going ashore, we reported to the Hall Porter's office by the main door for 'liberty boat inspection' by Officer-of-the-Watch 1 (rostered Senior on duty), who checked our dress was acceptable. We deposited our Leave Cards with the Hall Porter and exited the building from either the West or East Door. OUTs weren't allowed to use the main door. We headed down the steep path, through the main gate and into Dartmouth. That first pint in the Royal Castle was the very taste of freedom.

Although confined to BRNC during new entry, Monty Birch and Andy Skinner had circumvented this restriction. As experienced riders (Andy was a jackaroo on an Australian cattle station for several months), they were allowed out to exercise the College's horses in the countryside. Sneaky!

Post-new entry phase there was improved status for graduates/schoolies. We moved from the Dorms in Hawke A-Block into two-man cabins in B-Block. Monty and I lifted-and-shifted to Cabin B15. B Block, first floor, first cabin on the left. It was well-appointed, with a bay window looking between the trees towards Kingswear. Our desks faced each other in the bay window. With Monty's ironing board, our own steam irons, plus my kettle, teapot, mugs and Earl Grey tea, we were largely self-contained and self-sufficient. With our mature, professional attitude to training and general enthusiasm, we were popular with Hawke Seniors. We got to know them far better than if we'd remained in Upper Dorm. The lucky ones were invited for tea in B15. Yep, a real privilege for our favoured Seniors!

2.16 View from Cabin B15

Nevertheless, we continued to slum it in the café-style JGR. For a beer on-site, we went across to the NAAFI bar in the old, wooden pavilion beside the sports field. It was a short walk for Hawkes, while those in other Divisions had to come up the hill. Even in 1984, it was a rickety, shabby, neglected relic with rusty, spindly steel rafters, a vaulted wooden ceiling, creaking and chipped floorboards, and bright neon lighting. A rustic, basic alternative to Dartmouth's pubs.

2.17 In B15
Bay window (left); my own space in B15 (right)

Some blokes frequented Torquay on Saturday nights. It was a long return journey. The 'duty driver' couldn't drink and had to wait around until nightclub chucking-out time to drive back to BRNC via Higher Ferry. No thanks! Besides, Dartmouth had some lovely pubs for warm summer evenings.

The majority got used to BRNC's daily routine, improved without the twin burdens of EMAs and standing rounds at each end of the day. Some struggled. We could see they may not survive. A few resigned, others were WFT'ed. We were saddened when someone in Hawke was WFT'ed. But comforted that it was likely the correct decision by Divisional Staff, Commander (Training) and Captain Bevan, and in the best interests of the Navy and the poor bloke himself.

The programme varied every week and wasn't too onerous, but diligent preparation in the evening for the following day's classes and activities was essential. Allied to the ever-changing programme were the variety of rigs needed for a day in the main college, particularly if it included lessons at Sandquay. Hawke Juniors flitted about the College all day carrying a grip full of rigs, so 'personal admin' was key.

The RN was deeply steeped in social etiquette customs. We were taught about invitations to social events and the need to respond promptly and correctly, whether accepting or declining. We learned the behaviour expected at such events, making polite and interesting conversation with fellow guests of whatever rank.

Captain Bevan hosted occasional dinner parties 'at home' for a blend of staff officers, academics and their wives, plus a sprinkling of Seniors and Juniors. I don't know how the latter were selected but, in Week 3, I felt fortunate and privileged to be invited.

The formal invitation arrived on quality printed card. As etiquette required, I RSVP'd swiftly using the format in the SAM handout: 'Sub Lieutenant P Carroll, Royal Navy, has much pleasure in accepting the kind invitation of Captain and Mrs T Bevan to dinner on Wednesday 16 May at 7.30 pm.'

In battledress uniform, I checked for fluff and odd threads, slipped on my freshly polished shoes and marched from Hawke, down the hill, across the College façade and knocked on the Captain's front door. A steward let me in, indicated where to leave my cap and ushered me into a large reception room. There, I met and mingled with fellow guests. Blimey, what a lucky bloke I was. The room was beautifully furnished, heavy quality curtains at the windows. I was made welcome and felt comfortable, not overawed.

The gong sounded, dinner was announced and we crossed the wide hallway into the equally beautiful dining room. The seating plan alternated boy-girl-boy-girl. I found my seat and away we went. Dinner was delicious, with excellent silver service from Captain Bevan's immaculate stewards. Before dessert, male guests moved around the table a couple of places to the right, affording everyone the opportunity to converse with other guests. The evening culminated in coffee and port.

Afterwards, I marched back to Hawke, reflecting on a brilliant, interesting and thoroughly enjoyable evening. I was impressed by the smooth choreography. I certainly appreciated my good fortune in being chosen to attend. No idea how it happened, but who cares?

Naturally, I hand wrote my 'thank you' letter to Mrs Bevan, using my fountain pen on plain vellum paper, slipped into a matching envelope, according to the rules of etiquette.

Wardrooms dined formally together for special occasions, including Trafalgar Night (21 October), Taranto Night (11 November, when FAA celebrated their destruction of the Italian Navy in 1940), dining-in a new Commanding Officer (CO), or dining-out officers leaving the ship. Ladies' Nights were great evenings when our wives/girlfriends joined us for a mess dinner on board. We wore mess undress, the ladies 'frocked up' in evening dress. Great nights that boosted camaraderie and esprit de corps.

At BRNC, mess dinners were considered 'training serials'. We were briefed on etiquette and the evening's format and were expected to host a member of staff. Every term, each Division held a Divisional Dinner in the SGR. For Juniors, it was our first such experience and the only occasion when the whole Division sat down to a formal dinner together.

Sometimes a Divisional Dinner spawned pranks beyond post-dinner drinks in the SGR Bar. Blake's Dinner led to a raid on Hawke. About 2300, Blake yobs strode up the hill, crashed through the front door and attempted to create mayhem. Hawke Seniors were aware of this planned invasion and were ready to repel the unwelcome boarders. Some pathetic fisticuffs occurred and the Blake boys retreated. Their ringleader, Mid. Randolph Churchill, was captured, stripped naked and forced to return to Blake in his birthday suit.

Once per term a Combined Mess Dinner was held. I was fortunate to be invited, possibly because the Guest of Honour was Rear Admiral Haslam, Hydrographer of the Navy, and I was a going to be a hydrographic survey officer.

2.18 Invitation to Combined Mess Dinner

Mess dinners culminated in passing the port and at least two toasts, first to our sovereign, followed by that day's daily toast.

Table 2.2 Daily toasts

Monday	Our ships at sea
Tuesday	Our men
Wednesday	Ourselves
Thursday	A bloody war or a sickly season
Friday	A willing foe and sea room
Saturday	Wives and sweethearts, may they never meet
Sunday	Absent friends
21 October (Trafalgar Night)	The immortal memory of Admiral Lord Nelson (drunk in silence)

Mess dinners were fantastic evenings of delicious food, classy wine, smooth port and great conversation. The SGR's sumptuous surroundings of wood panelling, polished parquet floor, portraits of famous admirals, vaulted ceiling with light fittings decorated with wooden models of ships and intricate colourful bosses, added to the occasion's elegance. Glorious. I felt incredibly privileged and honoured to be a member of this exclusive and prestigious club, an armed force so rich in culture and with a long, proud and distinguished history.

2.19 SGR, its gallery at far end

We Juniors struggled along in battledress for Hawke Divisional Dinner. Shortly after, our swanky No.5 uniform and mess kit were delivered from the tailors. At last, we threw off the loathed battledress. During induction, we were measured for 'contract' No.5, part of our kit issue supplied by Owens

Tailors. But there was a choice of other quality tailors for a 'best' No.5 and mess kit, mostly covered by a kit upkeep allowance and I chose Gieves & Hawkes. The kit was made of an expensive English cloth, a thick, heavy, quality barathea that was closely woven, with a slight diagonal weave that gave a broken rib effect but was smooth to the touch. My Gieves & Hawkes uniforms lasted until I retired, by which time the jackets had been taken out to their full extent. The high-waisted mess trousers fitted perfectly and were of a far superior quality to those issued to me when I transferred to the Royal Australian Navy. I increasingly felt more like a 'proper' naval officer.

2.20 Dressed in my swanky Gieves & Hawkes mess kit

We had to get to grips with the peculiarities and precision of service writing. Everything we needed to know was captured in *Joint Service Publication 101 Defence Writing Guide* (*JSP 101*), although I never read it during my naval career. I picked up what I needed as I went along, recalled stuff we did at Dartmouth and sought guidance from colleagues (usually supply officers).

JSP 101 included examples of how to write English in the Services, with formats for papers, letters and studies. It simplified written communication so anyone following its principles could pass on information in a concise, understandable form. It demanded accuracy, brevity, clarity, relevance and logic. Conventions for document formats covered the use of spacing and capital letters, types of headings, spelling and rules for numerals. Temporary memoranda and loose minutes were for ship's internal correspondence. At BRNC we quickly became familiar with various types of memorandum, particularly training office temporary memoranda (TOTEMs) which described every serial, exercise and event to inform the College population.

Incredibly, there were various types of letter. Like any normal person, I thought a letter was a letter. But, no! There were laborious lessons on, and practice in, formal letters, routine letters, business letters, demi-official letters and social correspondence (invitation, reply, thank you). Amazing. Each type had a specific use and format. Clearly, service writing differed from normal writing and used the 'keep it short and simple' principle. It was not to entertain, provoke or amuse but to inform the reader.

Every week we submitted a weekly activity report (WAR). It was utter torture to get the content on a single side of A4 paper absolutely correct. The WAR tabulated the activities attended during the previous week and any amplifying remarks (passed a boat test, played tennis for BRNC). Sunday evenings in the Upper Dorm were silent hives of activity as we sat along tables each side of the centreline, heads bowed, focused on writing another perfect WAR.

Essential items were a fountain pen and black ink refills. Luckily, the NAAFI shop near the JGR maintained a good stock. We gleaned that ADOs easily discerned if a fountain pen had been used ... or not. Paddy Watson had doubtless mastered this skill. The blank forms were on standard A4 printer paper, but we placed a sheet of lined paper beneath to ensure that every entry we laboriously and painstakingly wrote was perfectly straight and equally spaced. Frequently, the silence was shattered by loud expletives as someone made a tiny mistake, scrunched the A4 sheet into a ball and cast it into the wastepaper basket. Whoever it was had to start again. When I'd finished, I scrutinised my handiwork. If happy, I hole-punched the top left corner and slipped this latest edition into my manila WAR file, using the india-tag looped through the holes either side of the spine. On the left-hand side, I wrote a short entry on the minute sheet stating the WAR was attached.

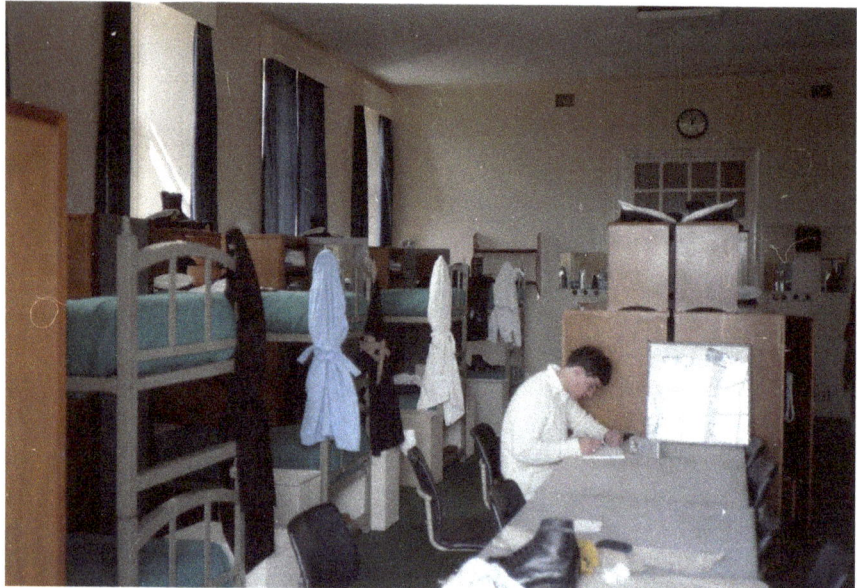

2.21 Kev Seymour in river activity rig writing his WAR in Upper Dorm

Returning to Hawke at the end of Monday's instruction, we collected our WARs. ADOs checked them as soon as possible on Mondays. I dreaded opening mine. What had Paddy Watson spotted? How much red ink littered my work? What snotty comment in his neat hand might I find? The biggest fear was getting a rescrub, meaning I must rewrite and resubmit it by 0800 Tuesday, consuming time I didn't really have to spare.

I realised it was all part of the game, an important lesson on naval paperwork and setting standards as an officer. No good whining and whingeing, just get on with it. But – apart from responding to social invitations, followed by brief thank you letters – my only piece of official writing was the formal letter of acknowledgement all officers were required to submit to the CO when appointed to a warship. The first one we all did was to *Fearless* before embarking in her for our second term.

It was stressed that this letter was extremely important as it represented the first impression that the CO got of an officer joining his warship. First impressions counted, so it was vital that I wrote it as perfectly as possible,

2. We Joined the Navy 45

even though *Fearless'* Captain had a hundred-odd letters to read through, all exactly the same, except for names and addresses. Nevertheless, I got the message and punctiliously wrote and checked my subsequent 'acknowledgements of appointment' before posting them. If it was only me joining, the CO would surely make time to properly examine my letter?

> DISASTER Division
> Britannia Royal Naval College
> Dartmouth
> Devon
> TQ6 0HJ
>
> The Commanding Officer   31 February 1984
> HMS NONESUCH
>
> Sir
>
> 1. I have the honour to acknowledge the receipt of my appointment to Her Majesty's Ship NONESUCH, under your command, to date 1 April 1984.
>
> 2. I am directed to request joining instructions.
>
> 3. My address will be as above until 12 February 1984. Thereafter, until joining, I will be on leave at:
>
>   Heathfield
>   12 Oildrean Lane
>   Glasshields
>   Dorset   (Telephone Glasshields 140)
>
>   I have the honour to be,
>   Sir,
>   Your obedient Servant
>   J. Carstammers-Waghorn
>   J. CARSTAMMERS-WAGHORN
>   Midshipman Royal Navy

2.22 Example of formal letter – acknowledgement of appointment
(BRNC Archive)

I retained and used my home-made lined template, with extra lines to demarcate the 2cm clear margin all round and a line dividing the A4 sheet vertically down the centre. I always used a fountain pen, just in case my new CO was as pernickety as Paddy Watson.

BRNC's training focused on character and leadership (C&L). Without us realising, it began immediately we arrived and stood up in HGR to spout our short biography. Woolston and his ADOs noted every performance and quickly formed an impression of each of us.

Leadership was defined as the 'function of communicating with subordinates in order to get them to do things willingly and in concert with others to achieve a common aim'. BRNC espoused functional leadership (task, team, individual).

The C&L package had four phases and we'd already completed the first, NEX. We then moved on to formal classroom instruction on the basic principles of leadership. This included lively playlets on the CJH stage, performed by divisional staff: *Social Behaviour*, *Plain Clothes*, *Divisional System*, *Loyalty*, and *Discontent*. We watched our, hitherto stuffed-shirt, divisional staff role-play on stage. The scripts had an element of comedy but conveyed important messages for us to hoist in.

We prepared and presented talks of 3-, 10- and 30-minute duration. The first two on our own topics. The subject of the last was foisted upon us. It required much time and effort to research, write, prepare overhead projector slides, and rehearse to get content and timing spot on. No PowerPoint in those far-off days. These performances required an organised, well-rehearsed presentation using home-made slides, delivered with a power of command and questions confidently answered at the end.

The third phase was practical leadership tasks (PLTs) within the College grounds. Classes were divided into teams of six under the direction of a staff officer. In AWD, combat boots, beret and name tally, we were equipped with four wooden staves, a 120-foot rope, and a couple of heaving lines. We marched around the estate from stance to stance, adhering to a strict timetable for each leadership task.

In turn, each of us was designated leader to get us from one task to the next, doubling if necessary. At the site, the Staff Officer briefed the task to the leader and allowed a short time to assess the situation and concoct a plan. When ready, the leader briefed his plan using NATO's sequence of orders: ground (area of operations); situation (background to the task); mission (the task); execution (the plan); service support (rig, equipment, rations, water, medical); command and signal (who's the leader?); questions; time check – and designated a timekeeper. This last was crucial because we had no idea how quickly task-time evaporated. Time was precious. Don't waste a minute, particularly when under the microscope as leader.

After every PLT, our Staff Officer comprehensively debriefed us on the leader, his plan, the team, the overall task execution and its success or failure.

It was a very full, non-stop forenoon. We were exhausted when we finished at lunchtime.

The culmination of leadership training was the practical leadership exercise (PLX), a three-day exercise on Dartmoor. PLX loomed large for ages. Finally, about halfway through term, it was upon us. In teams of six, we carried all our kit plus four staves, a 120-foot rope, a couple of heaving lines and, as it was a hot summer, a five-gallon jerrycan of water. Overall, we covered some 40km of Dartmoor during the three-day exercise, camping out overnight.

We mustered in our teams on C-Block car park, behind the main building. The Exercise Director inspected each of us and rummaged through our bergens to ensure no one had packed illicit nutty bars. He scrupulously checked our polished combat high boots. We climbed into Bedford three-ton trucks with our kit and relaxed as best we could on the rock-hard plank benches for the journey to Dartmoor. Knowing we'd be starved of sleep during PLX, the wise Junior grabbed some kip. I certainly did as I can sleep anywhere, any time.

At Princetown, the Bedfords stopped. Tailgates lowered and out we jumped. We fell in at the roadside in teams under our respective leader. Each team was accompanied by a Staff Officer. Ours was Lt Niner, a US Navy exchange officer. Unlike many of his countrymen, he seemed fairly relaxed and certainly not your typical loud, brash, gung-ho American. Staff Officers took team leaders aside and briefed them on the route for the march-on (different for each team) and ETA at Ditsworthy Warren House, PLX HQ.

We set off at a decent pace in warm late-afternoon sunshine. Dartmoor looked its best. Bracken, heather, gorse and thin, scrubby grass added green shades to the tors' harsh grey. Lt Niner stayed astern of us to check our navigation and monitored our pace. We divided the extra kit between us: one with three staves, a pair with the heavy rope, another with the heaving lines and another pair with the fourth stave through the jerrycan's handle as it was incredibly heavy. Too much for one man, unless he was Arnie Schwarzennenger!

All teams arrived at Ditsworthy Warren at roughly the same time. It was first come, first served to make camp on the hillside behind the house. Ponchos were used to construct bivouacs. We flashed up the hexamine stove. This standard bit of army kit folded in on itself to retain the solid fuel cake, making it compact and lightweight. We had a brew and cooked rations for dinner.

Team leaders were briefed about overnight arrangements. Sleep deprivation was integral to PLX so every team had a sentry to keep watch overnight. We split the pain between us. We were to be left alone overnight until call the hands at 0530 the next morning. Of course, a fitful sleep in a green 'slug' on a bed of thin grass and rock was shattered at an ungodly hour by the loud bang and intense brightness of several thunderflashes, pyrotechnic sticks used to simulate battlefield conditions. Staff bawled at everyone to get up, break camp and scuttle away to a rendezvous position as we were under attack. Yeah, right!

2.23 Our PLX campsite behind Ditsworthy Warren House
(Steve Foster, www.treksandtors.co)

About a quarter of an hour later, we returned to our original camp sites and settled down again. All too soon, we were rudely awakened by Staff as the sun rose above the tors on the horizon. A beautiful dawn on Dartmoor. Priorities were shaving and boot polishing. Breakfast swiftly followed. Our bergens got lighter as we consumed our ration packs.

Our leader hurried us along to the muster point for the morning inspection. Don't be adrift! Exercise Director inspected everyone, particularly our clean-shaven faces and polished boots, then any other sloppiness in dress. Not shaving was a heinous crime, a black mark against the offender. Don't bother whining, there'd been no time to polish boots either. No excuses were acceptable.

Team leadership changed before we set off for a day's hike around Dartmoor. In turn, we were selected to lead the march to the next stance and conduct the task there. It was tiring but the weather was warm, fine and sunny, almost a pleasure to be here, but for the heavy bergen digging into my back and sharing jerrycan-carrying duty with BJ. It was warm enough to relax to shirt sleeves. We circumnavigated Burrator reservoir, through copses, over rolling grassland and up and down treacherous rocky tors. I remember many of the tasks. We ascended Sheeps Tor, descended another tor, leopard crawled across the river at Meavy (near the Royal Oak pub and ford), and crossed the clay pits at Cadover on a home-made raft.

After a day's slog, our team camped on the beach at Cadover clay pits. Lt Niner distanced himself from us and set up his own pup tent and camp for the night. We maintained an alert watch overnight but otherwise enjoyed undisturbed sleep. In the morning, we roused ourselves to shave, polish boots and breakfast with a brew. Lt Niner did his own thing until we mustered for his inspection, which was less intimidating than the Exercise Director's.

We resumed our march from stance to stance for an interminable morning. We were tired and grubby. But at least the weather remained excellent. And the jerrycan emptied enough to be one-man portable.

After the final task, we set course for PLX HQ. The end was in sight as we crowned the crest of a hill and saw Ditsworthy Warren in the valley below. We crossed the small leat and marched up to the dry-stone wall enclosure. We were told to find a spot and cooked lunch. Eventually all the teams arrived back and relaxed.

We still had to exit the moor on foot. This wasn't possible for a few poor sods as they'd developed painful, red-raw blisters and were unable to get their boots on. How would this affect their Staff Officer's assessment of performance and C&L. Might they be rescrubbed?

At last, team leaders were briefed on the march-off, the reverse of the march-on but our destination was Cornwood, at the south end of Dartmoor. Each team set off, radiating from Ditsworthy Warren on a slightly different track. The first half was predominantly uphill but, on reaching Shell Top's crest, it was nearly all downhill. Lt Niner, like his colleagues, encouraged his team to set and maintain a stiff pace. It was only during the descent from the moor that we saw other teams converging on the same gate at the bottom of the hill. 'March-off' was the wrong description, 'race-off' was more accurate! No Staff Officer wanted to be last into Cornwood. Our pace quickened as adrenalin coursed through our exhausted bodies, elbows sharpened to fend off other teams and gain the advantage.

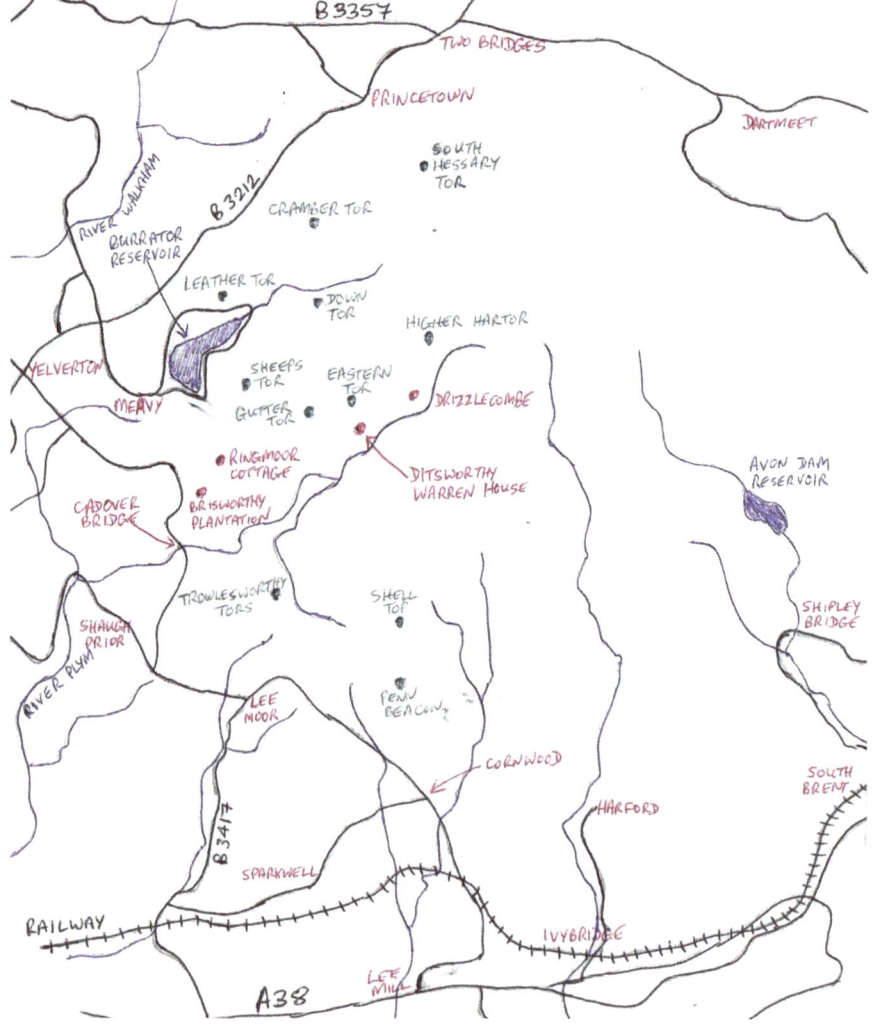

2.24 PLX points of interest in west half of Dartmoor National Park

We galloped along, through the gate, onto the tarmac lane, amazingly still in step, a rhythmic pounding of rubber soles on metalled road. The final 50-60m became a sprint as we pulled clear of a chasing team. At the finish line, Lt Niner told us to move off the track and, in an officer-like manner, collapse in the glade. We thirstily swigged from our water bottles, sweat ran from brow to face and dripped onto our sweaty, smelly clothes.

When ordered to by the Exercise Director, we climbed into the three-tonners and flopped onto the benches. Too exhausted to chatter, and relieved PLX was over, I fell into deep slumber, lulled by the Bedford's rhythmic engine and clunky gear-changing. Eventually, the trucks stopped. Like a scene from a World War II prisoner-of-war movie, staff shouted at us to disembark.

We were shocked. Our PLX ordeal wasn't over. We were on a narrow lane in a wood with a steep slope down to the river. What's going on now? We grabbed our kit, fell in and were directed in teams to make our way down to the shore. There, Seniors told each team to embark in beached dories and Geminis. They ferried us to a whaler, into which my team clambered with our kit, joined by another team. We sat and waited until Lt Bradshaw, a short, squat, blond, bespectacled, aggressive Hawke ADO, embarked from the Staff Gemini.

The climax to PLX was to pull down-river to Sandquay. Lt Bradshaw told us we were at Blackness Point, up-river from Dittisham. Crikey, after our exhausting Dartmoor experience, we now had a lengthy distance to pull home. We sorted out positions in the boat, designated a coxswain, slipped from the buoy, and off we went. Slowly, we rounded Higher Gurrow Point and then Lower Gurrow Point. Dittisham and the pink Ferry Boat Inn hove into view. We knew where we were and how far to go, but we'd never pulled such a distance.

We rotated through as coxswain. When I took the tiller, my crew was pulling at a reasonable rate. Lt Bradshaw seemed happy enough. We were desperate not to run aground on a falling tide, marooned with an exceedingly unhappy and grumpy Staff Officer until the rising tide lifted the whaler off the mud hours later.

My abiding memory was the rhythmic strokes of the oars. As their paddles pulled the whaler through the water, so the crew lent backwards. Neil Hicking was right in front of me. Each time he pulled, his meat-and-two-veg appeared as his trousers were split at the crotch and he was 'commando' (wearing no skiddies). Not a pretty sight. Even today, BJ recalls the same appalling image when he cox'ed.

At last, we came alongside at Sandquay, dumped our kit on the pontoon and cleaned the boat. Lt Bradshaw inspected it and us, formed up in a line beside the whaler. He released us and we made our way up Sandquay steps to our respective Divisions. I enjoyed a long, hot soak in the bath, relieved PLX was over and that Lt Niner's debrief of my performance was flattering. No PLX rescrub for me.

BRNC's leadership package had been honed over many years. It seemed to hit the spot as we gradually learned of and then practised leadership, culminating in PLX. Of course, only a muppet believed that success in PLX was the end to learning about leadership. Everything we did at BRNC was critically appraised by staff, with an emphasis on our C&L. Leadership was a never-ending process, even when we went to sea as trained naval officers.

2.25 Sandquay, with PBs berthed at pontoon

The river was a priority. Instruction by Seniors covered the evolutions required to pass boat tests: slipping from and berthing at the pontoon; coming to and slipping from a buoy; turning round in a confined space (equivalent to a car's three point turn); recovering a man-overboard (which could occur at any time); anchoring (whalers, single screw Chevertons and twin screw PBs). Not much of a list, but with four or more Juniors per boat and less than two hours on the water per session, time was precious. When not being coxswain, the other Juniors were occupied putting out and pulling in fenders when ordered to by the coxswain; and conducting the correct drill as bowman on a Cheverton or PB.

On the river, we obeyed the International Regulations for Preventing Collisions at Sea 1972 (Rule of the Road or ROR), every mariner's highway code of the sea. Having learned it by rote and used it for real throughout my four-year deck cadetship, I wasn't worried. Navigation lessons gradually introduced ROR so, initially, many Juniors weren't familiar with the basic rules. If a Junior, as coxswain, failed to obey ROR, Seniors gave you rocks and Staff Officers' bollockings echoed across the water.

2.26 Cheverton2 (foreground) alongside PB2 in the River Dart
(BRNC Archive)

It was an art form to decide when to put fenders out prior to berthing. Too early earned a bollocking. Too late and berthing became rushed and easy to screw up. It was triggered by the coxswain's 'STAND BY TO COME ALONGSIDE, PORT/STARBOARD SIDE TO. OUT PORT/STARBOARD FENDERS'. In reflex, the bowman performed his boathook drill and the crew flipped the bright blue fenders outboard. On slipping from a berth, 'IN PORT/STARBOARD FENDERS' was ordered as soon as possible. It was a heinous crime to trail fenders through the water, attracting more bellowing from Seniors and Staff Officers.

I was never attracted to sailing, despite a childhood by the sea in a naval town. BRNC had laser and bosun dinghies and each Division had a Contessa 38 yacht. I delayed contact with sailing as long as possible. Luckily, BRNC sailing required only an 'acquaint'. I detested the 'bosun dinghy acquaint'. Despite a warm summer, the water was cold if I got wet. In river rig and a lifejacket, perched on the dinghy's gunwale, water sloshed around in the bilge, soaking my Pusser's daps or my bum. A truly miserable experience. I was just relieved to complete two afternoons and get my ticket. I've never been anywhere near such horrible little boats since.

The STC acquaint in Hawke's Contessa 38 was more civilised. On a beautiful sunny afternoon, Phil Warwick, one of Hawke's keen sailors, was skipper and I was part of his crew. We set off down-river under power, passed between the castles and out into a flat calm Start Bay. Phil hoped there'd be some wind outside, but alas there wasn't. We puttered around and loitered off Blackpool Sands, a delightful cliff-backed cove. We shared the binoculars to spy on topless young women sunbathing on the beach. This concluded my only experience of sailing a yacht ... and we didn't hoist a sail!

Every class completed a practical life raft drill. As programmed, several classes mustered at Sandquay for a briefing one evening, dressed in a once-only suit. This orange rubber overall was worn when abandoning ship, zipped up to prevent one getting wet when immersed in the sea. It had elasticated neck and wrist seals and a hood. Having contorted into it, it was critical to squat down to squeeze out trapped air via one of the cuffs and then knot the ankle-ties.

We donned lifejackets and clambered onto the wharf. Lifejacket inflated, we were told how to enter the water. One forearm across the chest, the other arm raised to pinch the nose. The former prevented a smack in the face when the solid inflated lifejacket hit the water, the latter stopped a surge of water shooting up the nostrils.

When ordered, we stepped off the wharf and entered the water. Luckily it was summer. BRNC's once-only suits were used umpteen times. The rubber neck and wrist seals had small or large splits. We all got waterlogged. If there was any air in the suit, buoyant feet floated on the surface, head and body were submerged, and we struggled not to drown.

Floundering in the water, we swam on our backs to the inflated life raft, tethered from Sandquay's old boatshed. In turn, we hauled ourselves in. Those first on board helped pull others inboard. We'd been briefed on procedures and organisation in a life raft. The class leader took charge and we sat around the raft circumference as comfortably as practicable.

Staff Officers demanded to know what we were up to. What organisation was in place? Were lookouts designated and in position? The summer evening drew on, light faded, the river was mirror-like. To simulate rough weather, Seniors drove a Gemini at speed around our orange craft in a pathetic attempt to create waves to rock the life raft and induce seasickness. A forlorn, unsuccessful hope. We were released from this water torture about 2100 and trudged up Sandquay steps to our respective Divisions to get dry.

As I was on top of my boatwork and tickets, I could focus increasingly on tennis as my activity. Tennis Officer was Lt Cdr Richard Clapp, a calm, relaxed Navy pilot. As University Training Officer, his great job entailed plenty of visits to naval undergraduates attending universities throughout the UK. His office was in prime position next to the main door, with views across the parade ground to the river and castles beyond.

2.27 BRNC tennis squad, summer term 1984
(BRNC Archive)

I attended the club trial at start of term. As a pretty handy player, I was selected to join BRNC's squad. We had decent strength in depth and fielded three good pairs for fixtures against local tennis clubs, despite personnel absences due to curriculum commitments like PLX. Martin Jones and I were the only Juniors in the squad. Martin was in Blake and, by now, we had many mutual friends across the Divisions: Jamie McMichael-Phillips, BJ, 'Traps' Doolan, 'Woody' Coussens, Steve Kenny and my cabin-mate Monty.

My usual doubles partner was Mark Allibon, a red-headed Hawke Senior. We had some sort of on-court telepathy and played well together, usually as BRNC's second pair. The designated club captain, although he wasn't one of our best players, was Randolph Churchill, a fresh-faced, jolly, teenage Middy, a bit naïve and immature but full of smiles and bonhomie.

Home matches were played on the hard courts behind D Block, in the shadow of the Navigation Block. It was tranquil back there. The only sound on those Wednesday and Saturday afternoons was the thwack of gut against ball during rallies and frequent calls of 'Mine', 'Leave it', 'Out', 'Shot' and the score. Afterwards, tea was laid on.

It was pleasant to escape BRNC for an afternoon of away matches at a nice little local club. It reminded me of my boyhood tennis at Brune Park Comprehensive School, partnered with Andy Atkins, a brilliant all-round sportsman, with Jimmy Clarke and little Arthur Lloyd. My brother and some of our friends were members of Alverstoke Lawn Tennis Club. We'd had coaching and spent long summer afternoons playing on the club's beautifully manicured grass courts. After adult club matches, a huge tea was provided and we loitered to mine-sweep leftover cakes and sandwiches.

BRNC tennis team enjoyed a successful season in 1984. We played 14, won 11, drew 1 and lost only 2. I was awarded colours for tennis, not quite as notable as an Oxford/Cambridge blue. Nevertheless, an achievement. I still have the tie in my wardrobe.

Every term, sports weekends were held against Sandhurst and Cranwell. The precursor to these were the DartMan Games, held midweek beforehand. After passing out from BRNC, RN engineers studied and gained an engineering degree at Royal Naval Engineering College, Manadon, Plymouth. As BRNC was small in numbers compared to Sandhurst and Cranwell, Combined Naval Colleges teams were selected after DartMan Games. Summer term sports were cricket, golf, tennis, riding, swimming, water polo, clay pigeon and .22 shooting, windsurfing, sailing, rowing.

Our tennis team fared well against the engineers. I was selected, surprisingly, to captain the Combined team. The first and second pairs were from Manadon and BRNC respectively. I formed the third pair with Andy Mills from Manadon. We'd never met before, never mind played together, but we seemed to click on court, as I'd done with Mark.

The following Friday, the Combined teams travelled by coach to RAF Cranwell, home of RAF officer training. With comfort breaks, the protracted 470km journey took all day. We settled in and went ashore to nearby Sleaford. There were some rather shabby-looking naval sportsmen at breakfast on Saturday morning.

On Saturday afternoon, after all sports had finished, an enormous piss-up started, interrupted by the announcement of all the results and prize-giving. Overall, we were victorious. Most importantly, we beat Cranwell 6–3 in tennis, after each of the three pairs had played each other. Our pairs each won two of their three matches. A few hardy souls went into Sleaford that evening. Most of us had dinner in the Mess and a few more beers with our hosts, then bed. It was a long, slow, quiet coach trip to Dartmouth on Sunday.

The following weekend, BRNC hosted Royal Military Academy Sandhurst. As tennis captain, I met our opponents when they alighted from their coach and escorted them to their accommodation in the College. On Saturday, games commenced. For reasons unknown, instead of using our hard courts, we played on the two lovely grass courts in front of the wardroom, adjacent to the West Ramp and parade ground. I'd marched past them every day but never seen them used. It was brilliant to play tennis sandwiched between BRNC's magnificent façade and the glorious panorama of Dartmouth, Kingswear and the river.

Andy and I played our final match together against Sandhurst's third pair. This was truly a privilege. The Army's top and second pairs occupied the wardroom courts, but their third pair played on the grass court hidden behind the high hedges of the Captain's House. It was definitely somewhere that Staff Officers, never mind OUTs, ever saw, much less played on. A close match but we triumphed, witnessed by Captain and Mrs Bevan. What an afternoon.

A drinks and smally-eats party in the marquee on the sports field followed the day's exertions. Andy and I were nearly adrift. We were the last to finish as it was such a tight match. Overall, the Combined team won and we earned a 7–2 victory in tennis. Those two weekends certainly represented a most satisfying pinnacle to my tennis career. Years later, I learned Andy was a long-standing member of the RN bobsleigh team, frequently bombing down the Cresta Run.

Part of the curriculum included PT in BRNC's antiquated gym. It and the pool were eventually Grade 2 listed, as was the dilapidated sports pavilion. Lessons were conducted by a PTI, immaculate in pristine white vest (crossed clubs branch badge emblazoned on his chest), perfectly ironed white shorts, dazzling white daps, muscles bulged everywhere. PTI's instruction was unique, as they explained every exercise in detail, then ordered, with a little jump, 'THIS POSITION … READY'. Then 'EXERCISE … COMMENCE', and off we went.

Fitness tests occurred in Weeks 10 and 11: a 2.4km run in less than 11½ minutes; 6-length swim of the pool; rope climb, sit ups, squat thrusts and a 6-length sprint in the gym. Nothing too onerous, although some blokes really struggled, despite PTIs teaching us correct rope climbing techniques and the physically active life we now led. Failure meant a black mark and remedial PT.

For parade training, we packed highly bulled parade boots in our grips, slipping a sock over each toecap to protect that precious shine. The West Door's hallway was always full of neatly aligned Pusser's grips as we marched down the West Ramp onto the parade ground for a drill lesson. PO Jones was our class GI. A short, stocky Welshman with a great sense of humour, spotless white blancoed gaiters, toecaps like mirrors, pace stick tucked under his arm. His lessons always had an element of fun but required concentration throughout as he fell like a ton of bricks if anyone screwed up. However, PO Jones always castigated with wit.

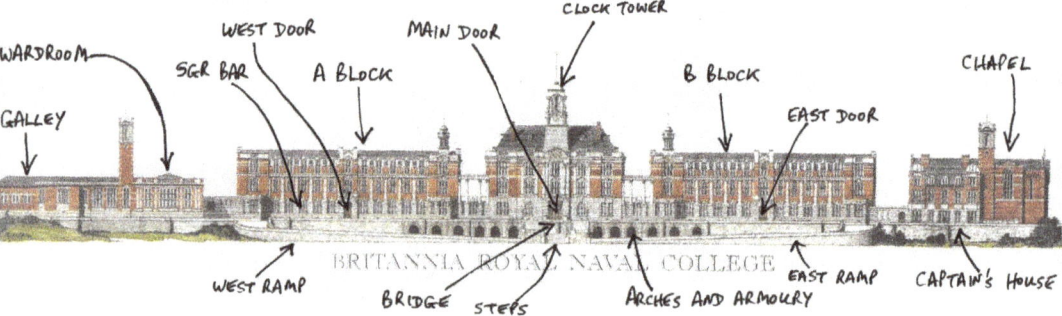

2.28 BRNC façade
(Britannia Association)

I enjoyed parade training despite the intense focus required. Keeping in step was easy. For manoeuvres (turns, wheels, about-turns), it was vital to remain 'switched on' at all times. I found coming to a halt the most difficult to grasp. PO Jones, like all GIs, demonstrated every move in minute detail and explained each element and the relative positions of arms and legs at that moment.

Divisions (parade) was held three times per week. Tuesdays and Thursdays were Training Divisions, Saturday was Ceremonial. The latter was more formal and we were in immaculate No.5 uniform; the former were excellent practice and required Juniors to be perfectly turned out in No.5JP uniform. We paired up with an oppo to check each other, using loops of Sellotape to pat down and collect tiny threads and fluf – more effective than a clothes brush.

We mustered at 0750 in platoons, which snaked back along the narrow road behind the wardroom, SGR and Galley. There was a strict order for marching-on: Hawke led Cunningham, Blake and St Vincent, then Talbot (trainee WRNS officers) and St George (Senior Rates who'd worked their way up from sailor to officer trainee). Our four Divisions had Juniors and Seniors platoons, each commanded by a Senior.

The platoons marched onto the parade ground and halted at their designated position. This was potentially traumatic for the Senior commanding us. If he got the timing of his orders wrong, Hawke Juniors undershot or overshot the spot. The GIs' wrath was wrought upon the poor sod. Overseeing everything was Parade Training Officer WO Kent, whose voice boomed across the parade ground. His keen eye never missed the slightest error.

On most Tuesdays and Thursdays, BRNC's Royal Marine Band was present. Wow, were they brilliant? At colours, they struck up one verse of 'God Save the Queen'. If the band was away on tour, a lone Royal Marine bugler sounded the 'Alert' and the 'Carry on'. Equally brilliant.

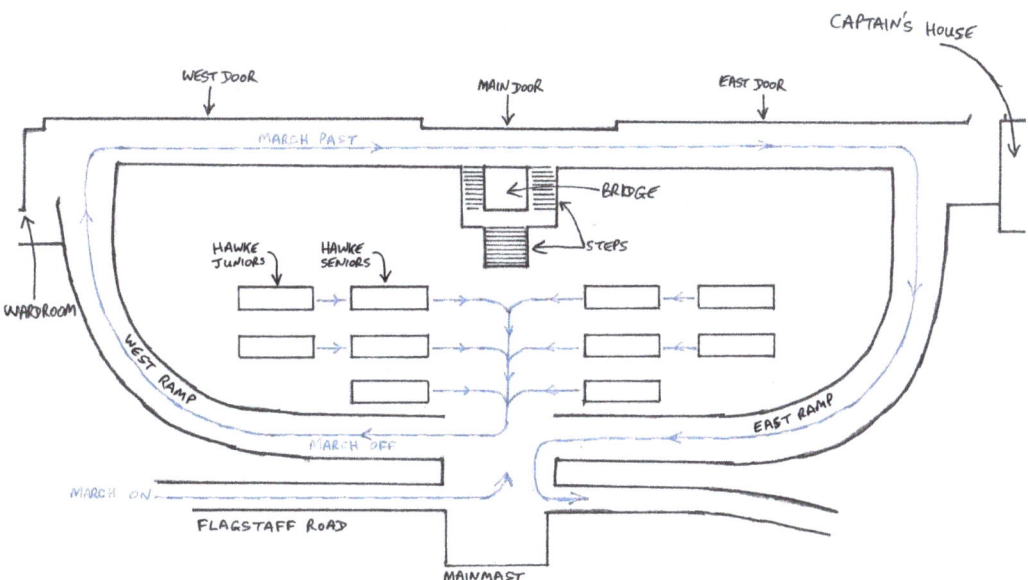

2.29 Platoons formed up for Divisions

The march past was the finale. Platoons turned inwards 90° to face the parade ground centre and then marched off in strict order. Wheeling right, Hawke Juniors followed Hawke Seniors toward the mainmast. The other Divisions followed on. Another right wheel and we marched up the West Ramp, rounded the corner by the wardroom and headed along the College frontage, the Captain's House dead ahead at the far end.

Approaching the main door (left) and the Bridge (right), we braced to salute the Captain as we passed. Our platoon commander tensed as he judged when to order 'HAWKE JUNIORS…… … EYES…… … RIGHT.' We swivelled our heads to the right. Then he ordered 'HAWKE JUNIORS…… … EYES…… … FRONT.' Phew! Now all we had to do was keep in step until we'd marched down the East Ramp, passed the mainmast and back to the side road by the Galley. If our march past and 'Eyes right!' were deemed substandard, the Captain ordered 'Round again!' This was to be avoided at all costs as Hawke Divisional Staff would be very unhappy that we'd let Hawke down – and ourselves.

Saturday's Ceremonial Divisions was similar. We marched on as usual. Next, the Guard (Guard Commander and 24 OUTs) and Colour Party (Escort Officer, plus one OUT each side of the OUT Ensign Bearer) marched on. Impressive, especially when the Band was playing rousing martial music. I always felt incredibly proud, standing rigidly at attention, in immaculate No.5 uniform, shiny parade boots and dazzling white cap cover as the Band's music blared and echoed round the parade ground.

Before the march past, each platoon was inspected by a critical Staff Officer. He eyed each of us from cap badge and glossy peak to shiny toecaps, spotting any minute fault, loose thread or tiny piece of fluff missed despite our last-minute dabbing down with Sellotape.

Standing at attention for long periods was difficult. Feet were gradually crimped by parade boots, creating a strange tingling sensation in the toes. Caps tightened around the skull, akin to a tourniquet. Concentration was key, focus purely on standing rigidly at attention. Wiggling toes helped a little. It was a relief to get orders to turn and march off.

Occasionally, in peripheral vision, I saw the odd OUT sway backwards and forwards. Oh dear, if unchecked, fainting and a face-plant on the parade ground in front of the entire College population followed. Immediately, the First Aid Party (a pair of OUTs) dashed to the fallen, hooked an arm under each armpit and hauled them off the parade ground to the Armoury.

The Divisions programme dictated occasional wet weather Divisions. These followed the same routine but took place on the Quarterdeck. This magnificent, high-vaulted, rectangular space was considerably smaller than the parade ground. Divisions were on a tighter scale but with the same personnel as the outdoor version, made even more awkward by the row of stone columns along each side of the Quarterdeck. Also, the highly buffed parquet floor was a potential slipping hazard.

Term ended with various events for those passing out of BRNC, protracted rehearsals culminated in the Passing Out Parade with a Divisional Cocktail Party that evening and then a Summer Ball on Friday night. Monty had a hotel room with his girlfriend and drove into BRNC for the ball. He got plastered so his girlfriend drove Monty's red MG down the hill, missed a tight corner, slid down the steep grassy slope, but regained the road before the main gate. Amazingly, there were no witnesses and nothing was mentioned on Saturday morning about the skid marks on the golf course. A lucky escape.

Saturday morning on 28 July was post-ball torture as everyone just wanted to go home. But leave wasn't piped until we'd cleared up the mountains of ball debris, the Divisions and our cabins to a satisfactory standard. Our first term in the RN was complete. We'd learned so much, became leaders of some sort, moulded by the Staff into naval officers. Our 'Oily Qs' (officer-like qualities) honed via the entire spectrum of life in BRNC.

We'd earned summer leave before our second term in *Fearless* on a Mediterranean cruise. How lucky were we?

3.

Mediterranean Cruise – Navy Style

3.1 *Fearless* crest
(Nick Barwis, www.jackstaxi.net)

3.2 *Fearless*

(Michael W Pocock, www.MaritimeQuest.com)

During summer leave we were obliged to do an activity. There was a large selection on offer. Some glamorous (US Naval Academy, Annapolis), others not (PB cruise). I wasn't bothered so chose the BRNC-based Combined Cadet Force (CCF) Camp (29 July to 6 August). Superficially, it sounded horrendous – having charge of 180 teenage CCF cadets – but the score or so of us OUTs were ably supported by some 'old-and-bold' Royal Naval Reserve and CCF officers.

We had important roles as Divisional staff. The cadets were divided into six Divisions named after Type 22 frigates (*Broadsword, Battleaxe, Brilliant, Brazen, Boxer, Beaver*). I was in charge of *Broadsword* and had a quartet of OUTs as assistants, a CCF officer and, importantly, a terrific retired submariner Lt Cdr with a fantastic sense of humour. Collectively, we ensured my Division had a great time.

The cadets ate in JGR. We were victualled in SGR, a delightful treat. The week was jam-packed with activities: parade training, boatwork, seamanship, gym, swim, run, a river night exercise in PBs, and a mini-sports competition. The cadets were on the move all day. Specialist instruction was from BRNC's river staff, GIs, PTIs and others. This left us with a quasi-monitoring role for most of the time.

Parade training climaxed with Ceremonial Divisions on Saturday morning and a swimming gala and sports competitions in the afternoon. The cadets relaxed watching a film in CJH that evening. The final day had a church service, cross-country run and regatta, ending with a sod's opera in CJH. After rounds on Monday morning, the cadets were transported to Totnes station for the train home. We packed up and bomb-burst for leave after a week everyone greatly enjoyed.

Our leave ended on the evening of Sunday 16 September when we joined HMS Excellent, a stone frigate (shore establishment). It occupied Whale Island, at the north end of Pompey Harbour, beyond the Naval Base. It was home to the Gunnery School and several lodger units. We were allocated messes and settled in, rekindling friendships from BRNC.

It was a busy week of internal security training. Gunnery School instructors described and explained the RN's personal weapons: 7.62mm SLRs (self-loading rifle); Browning 9mm pistols; Sterling sub-machine guns (SMG); and light machine guns (LMG). Instruction included naming the parts of each weapon and the drills associated with loading, firing, unloading, plus methods of clearing a stoppage and making the weapon safe on returning it to the armoury. We spent time at nearby Tipner Range, firing live rounds with each weapon at the standard NATO 'figure 11' target, an unkempt male combatant charging towards the viewer, eyes in shadow, bayonet fixed, just as we novices imagined our dehumanised, savage enemy. My shooting would never make me a sniper!

Daily at Excellent someone was bollocked by the resident GIs for failing to march correctly across the parade ground, a large, shingled rectangle. We took a somewhat laissez faire attitude at Excellent. Our daily routine was easy compared to BRNC. No duties, no night leave restrictions and our plain clothes' standard 'relaxed'.

After weekend leave, we endured a long coach journey from Pompey to join *Fearless* in Guzz at noon on Tuesday 25 September. *Fearless* (L10) and her sister-ship *Intrepid* (L11) were amphibious assault ships (landing platform dock, LPD, in NATO parlance). The former was built by Belfast's famous Harland & Wolff shipyard in 1963 and commissioned in 1965. Her long, distinguished career included action in the Falklands War, after which *Fearless* was re-tasked as Dartmouth Training Ship (DTS).

Post-World War II, the RN had a dedicated Dartmouth Training Squadron, administratively named 17th Frigate Squadron, comprising Type 15 and *Whitby*-class frigates. It was disbanded in 1972 and replaced by either *Fearless* or *Intrepid*.

Fearless was 160m long, 24m beam, 6.4m draught and displaced 12120 tons fully loaded and with a complement of 580. Similar physical dimensions to my last ship in Blue Star, *New Zealand Star*, a fully refrigerated cellular container ship which was crewed by only 32. *Fearless'* propulsion system was two English Electric, shaft-geared, steam turbines, yielding a top speed of 21kts. The for'ard two-thirds comprised the fo'c'sle and accommodation block, while the aft-most third was a large flight deck and adjoining hangar with a capacity for five Sea King helicopters.

A feature typical of assault ships was the dock beneath the flight deck. This could be flooded and the stern-gate opened to allow her four LCUs (landing craft utility) to exit loaded with tracked or wheeled vehicles and troops for amphibious assault. There were also four LCVPs (landing craft vehicle personnel) on davits, a pair on each side of the accommodation. These assets were the responsibility of 4th Assault Squadron Royal Marines. A further 400 marines (bootnecks) were embarked for operations and exercises.

For'ard of the dock and below the accommodation was the Tank Deck with capacity for 15 tanks and 27 vehicles.

Our accommodation was in Junior Rates' messes, small compartments of 12 to 24 bunks stacked 3-high, without a scuttle (porthole), so neon tubes provided light. Each bunk space had a small shaded reading-light and curtains for privacy. A maze of pipework, some encased in thick (asbestos?) lagging, criss-crossed the deckhead. Storage space for personal possessions was limited to a small locker containing a short pole to hang jacket and uniform and a set of drawers for clothing. A small table fixed to the deck was in the centre of each mess (mess square). Everything was battleship grey, save for the white pipework and the brightly coloured tapes indicating a pipe's use and our towels of all hues and patterns.

Located in the port or starboard wall either side of the dock, these messes were occupied by the Royal Marines when embarked. We were allocated five messes in the starboard wall: 2N1, 3N1, 3M1, 4K1 and 4M1. About 100 marine engineering artificer apprentices occupied the port wall messes.

Every compartment in a warship was identified by a three-character serial number. The first number was the deck, numbered from 1 Deck for the upper deck downwards. Superstructure decks above 1 Deck were numbered 01, 02 and so on. A letter indicated in which compartment it was, where A was right up for'ard. The second number showed on which side of the ship the compartment lay, where 1 meant starboard, 2 was port side, 0 meant the compartment straddled the warship's centreline.

I was allocated 2N1: starboard side, quite a way aft, on 2 Deck (one deck below the upper deck). There were 12 in our mess. Nigel Rhind was an oppo from Upper Dorm, Charlie Coull (an engineer) was, like Nigel, in my BRNC class. I knew Martin Jones as we'd played tennis for BRNC. Steve Kenny was also an ex-merchant seaman and was selected to be our Senior Mid, equivalent of a BRNC Div Sub. We universally saw Steve as the right man for this job. He proved excellent. I didn't really know either 'Granny' Grantham or Richie Rayner, both engineers in Cunningham. 'Granny' was a graduate entry engineer. Richie was an Upper Yardman. He'd joined the Navy as a sailor and had been identified as a potential officer. The Upper Yardman scheme required a sailor not only to show his mettle as a specialist, but more importantly as a leader amongst his peers. It was a slow process and required stamina and determination to succeed. Kenny McCulloch was a Cunningham seaman officer, a gentle giant with an extremely broad, almost incomprehensible Scottish accent. There were four Ints: a couple of Bahamians; a Malay I didn't know; and a Hawke Saudi Arabian. Richie was our Leading Hand of the Mess (LHOM), responsible for all aspects of life in our mess.

Heads and bathrooms were along the passageway. The whole accommodation thing made us fully aware of the conditions in which 'Jack' lived – limited (if any) privacy, cramped space, minimal stowage for personal belongings and shared facilities. We were victualled in the Junior Rates Dining Hall (JRDH).

The remainder of our first day on board was used to draw bedding and loan clothing, become acquainted with the ship and have an interview with our respective DO. The Officer Training Department (OTD) Staff embarked for each term's deployment, under the command of the Officers' Training Officer (OTO). There were eight DOs, eight Divisional Senior Rates (DSR) and a Leading Writer to manage correspondence and general admin. The 70 OUTs were divided into classes of nine or eight, blended from across BRNC's Divisions and specialisations and at least one Int. My DO was Lt Cdr Thornton, a tall, skinny, pleasant, easy-going Schoolie and my DSR was Chief Yeoman Hill, a tactical communicator by trade. My interview with Lt Cdr Thornton went well. So ended the first day of DTS. Night leave was granted to non-dutymen.

Wednesday was the first proper day's routine. We mustered on the Tank Deck at 0745 and were briefed successively by OTO, Training Planning Officer, CO (Captain Roger Trussell), Executive Officer (XO, *Fearless'* second-in command), First Lieutenant (responsible for the efficient running of the ship's routine), and Fleet Master-at-Arms (*Fearless'* police chief). It was bewildering, mind-numbing, tedious but important. At some point we had stand easy (tea/coffee break) and eventually lunch. In the afternoon, we cleaned the OTD areas of the ship and the DOs completed their interviews. At last, night leave was piped.

The next day, the OTD routine was established. An early start, as every day we had EMA. If the weather was suitable, we were on the flight deck. If not, we got filthy doing press-ups and sit-ups on the oily, grubby, smelly tank deck, which we grew to detest. Daily, there followed a melee in the bathrooms, jostling to shave at a washbasin or take a shower. Dressed, we queued for breakfast in the JRDH. There was always plenty of decent, basic fare available. Our daily routine quickly resembled Groundhog Day.

We had to complete a ship knowledge questionnaire by 0900 Friday. We wandered around *Fearless*, in our own time, filling in answers about the locations of certain compartments, fire-fighting kit, hoses, fire hydrants, life rafts. She was a big ship with a maze of passageways, hatches and ladders. Initially, it was easy to get disorientated or temporarily lost. The questionnaire was therefore a worthwhile exercise. In everyday life on board and certainly in an emergency, it became instinctive to know the quickest route to our designated emergency station. Everyone gashed a shin climbing over a hatch coaming or banged his head going up a ladder.

Our time in Guzz ended with a last run ashore, supping a few beers in Plymouth's Barbican, ending with fish and chips from Cap'n Jasper's van on the Barbican quayside. On Friday, 'hands to harbour stations' was piped at 0715 and by 0725 we'd fallen in on deck for Procedure Alpha, where ship's company lined the upper deck for port arrival or departure. Captain Tullis, Captain Bevan's successor at BRNC, was piped on board and sailed with us down harbour.

Following the buoyed channel, *Fearless* rounded Devil's Point to port and left Drake's Island to starboard. The red and white bands of Smeaton Tower dominated Plymouth Hoe and the waterfront lido as we turned to starboard and left them astern. *Fearless* briefly secured to a buoy in Plymouth Sound and ballasted to her deep condition. The stern gate opened to allow the LCUs to drive into the dock and then closed, dock pumped out so the flat-bottomed LCUs settled on the dock floor. At noon, *Fearless* slipped from the buoy and steamed past the breakwater and out to sea.

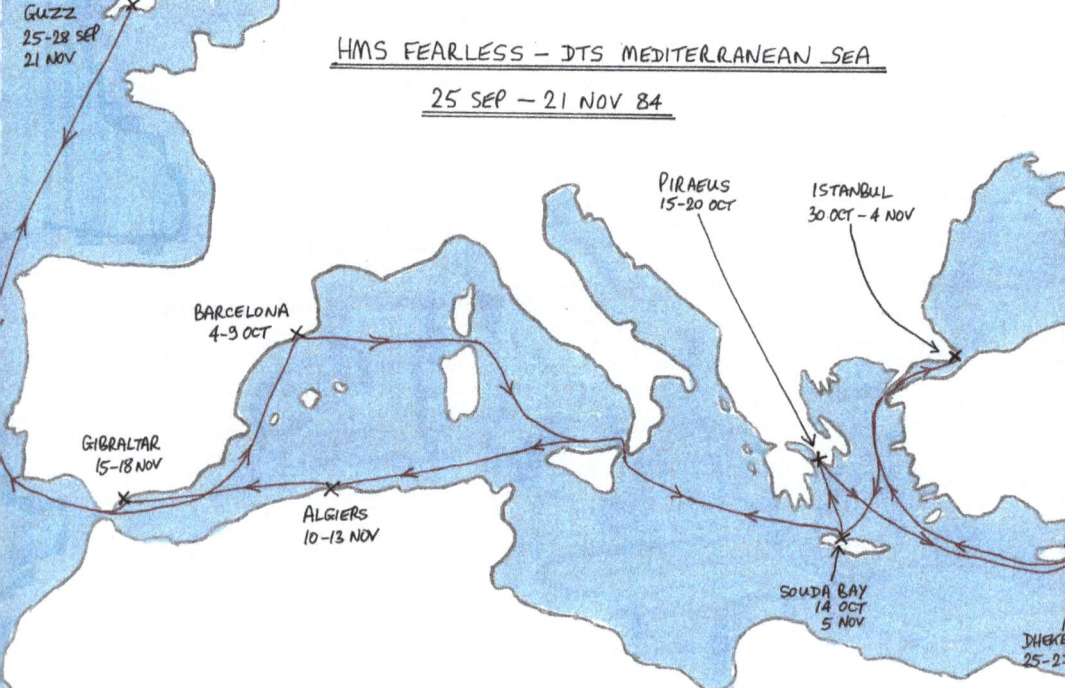

3.3 DTS Mediterranean cruise

Flying stations was piped for a helicopter (helo) to land and carry Captain Tullis back to BRNC. After all that novel excitement, we headed south across the Channel. Ship's company settled into the evening routine: dinner; cleaning for rounds; pipe down at 2230. The silent hours followed as passage to Barcelona continued.

Although it was Saturday, *Fearless* was put through her paces with a set of machinery breakdown drills (MBDD) in the forenoon. Late afternoon witnessed a fire exercise during which the OTD went to emergency stations. The seaboat, used at sea primarily for man overboard (MOB) recovery, was launched and recovered. On Sunday, another set of MBDD took place. Was there no respite? Going to sea in a warship was quite different from being on a merchantman. In Blue Star, we steamed as fast as possible between ports on a tight schedule. Time was money. No messing about. In the Navy, the ship's programme was arranged months in advance and, during passages, exercises of all sorts were planned by the ship's hierarchy. Training obligations and targets had to be met and recorded.

I learned nuances of Jackspeak (naval slang): a porthole was now a scuttle; smoko was stand easy; instead of being *on* a ship, I served *in Fearless* but served *on Active*, not *in Active*; warships were ships, submarines were boats; brightwork (any brass accessory or finishing on bits of kit like the centreline pelorus on the bridge) was polished with bluebell; I no longer went 'up the road' but for a 'run ashore'.

Overlaid on the ship's programme was our own training schedule. We were divided up by classes into each of the departments on board. We had classes in Portakabins on the tank deck and, for navigation training, on the bridge deck, and worked with sailors in each department or sub-department on board. Living and working with Junior Rates was great experience and certainly gave us an insight into their lives, attitudes, mannerisms and habits. I'm sure it was difficult for them, but I never detected animosity towards us. Naturally, we were fair game for pranks and jokes. After BRNC's hectic first term, life in *Fearless* was more relaxed and without responsibility.

Every day during daylight, *Fearless* undertook training serials: at least one set of MBDD, flying stations, fire exercises, MOB and seaboat drills. It was relentless for the ship's company. We remained uninvolved unless a 'whole ship' fire and damage control exercise occurred. At emergency stations, we formed a pool of spare hands to be used when fire teams and damage control parties were short of bods.

We steamed through the Strait of Gibraltar, passed the Rock itself and its southernmost tip, Europa Point. We continued east, paralleling the Spanish Costas frequented by millions of British holidaymakers and rounded Cap Marti. Ibiza was over the horizon to the east. Our north-east course through the Balearic Sea led us to Barcelona, our first port, arriving on 4 October. It was a pleasant passage, consistently light westerly winds and sea state 2.

Barcelona wasn't a natural harbour as it was built on a gently shelving coastline. Lengthy, substantial breakwaters built parallel to the coast shielded the wharves and provided a safe haven for ships. It was one of the top ten busiest ports in Europe and Spain's third largest.

Fearless fired a gun salute and embarked the pilot. We passed between the outer mole and the main breakwater to enter the port, turned at rest in Darcena Nacional and nestled starboard side to Muelle de Bosch y Alsina. Our berth was in easy walking distance of La Rambla and the old areas of El Raval and the Gothic quarter, with their maze of narrow cobbled streets.

I found it very odd not being on the bridge, observing everything on entering Barcelona. As an MN Deck Cadet, I was always on the bridge for port arrivals and departures, annotating the Bridge Movement Book, writing up the Deck Log, operating the telegraphs, wetting the tea/coffee for the master and pilot. On *Benedict*, a small general cargo ship, in the Amazon delta I was on the helm too because the mates and every Barbadian able seaman (AB) were on the fo'c'sle or poop deck. I was a one-armed wallpaper hanger. When Captain 'Flash' Harris disappeared into the bridge heads for a pee, it was just me and the pilot on the bridge.

As *Fearless* was the first RN warship to visit Barcelona in the post-Franco era, Flag Officer 3rd Flotilla (FOF3), Vice Admiral Fitch, had embarked in Guzz. His Flotilla comprised our aircraft carriers, assault ships, and a few odd destroyers. 1st Flotilla comprised 1st , 6th and 7th Frigate Squadrons (22 *Leander*-class frigates) and 3rd Destroyer Squadron (five Type 42 destroyers). 2nd Flotilla had 2nd , 4th and 8th Frigate Squadrons (respectively six Type 22, six Type 21 and nine *Leander*-class frigates) and 5th Destroyer Squadron (five Type 42s). Those were the days when Britain had a Navy and an impressive fleet of sleek grey warriors of death.

Admiral Fitch was in post until 1985, when he was promoted and became Second Sea Lord, before retiring in 1988. He was a Lloyds Name but alas, faced with large underwriting debts, he committed suicide by carbon monoxide poisoning in his car in 1994. A tragic end to a distinguished naval career. He and Captain Trussell went ashore to call on local military and civic dignitaries, returning a couple of hours later. This archaic standard courtesy was observed by all warships visiting a home or foreign port.

3.4 *Fearless* in Barcelona

Alongside, there was no training programme for us, but we were kept busy with *Fearless*' duty routine, acting as 2nd or even 3rd Officer-of-the-Day (OOD) learning the ropes of this vital role. If we were duty part of the watch, we cleaned our mess decks, heads and bathrooms for evening rounds. We stood gangway watches with the QM (Quartermaster) and his BM (Bosun's Mate), maintaining ship security and ensuring returning sailors pegged back in on the pegboard.

Alas, EMAs continued daily, usually a squad run around the port area. The OTD PTI was a horrible specimen. We nicknamed him POPT Gutbucket as he was the only PTI with a beer belly that I ever came across in my 25 years' service. He shouted at us at any opportunity. His wingman was another PO. Between them, they took charge of squad runs.

One morning in Barcelona, we formed up on the wharf at 0625 and set off at 0630. Gutbucket set the pace and led the way into the old quarter, our boots rhythmically clattering on the ancient cobbles. After 15 minutes, we ought to be heading back to the ship. We assumed Gutbucket had a pre-determined route and we'd circle back to *Fearless*. It was obvious at 0655 that Gutbucket had no idea where we were relative to the wharf. He was lost. Grumbling rumbled through our ranks. Gutbucket and his mate bellowed at us. We got back on board about 0715. Ablutions and breakfast were compressed. Some of us never made it to the JRDH as the morning muster was still at 0800 regardless. Gutbucket was the most detested man on the Staff. He never conceded he was at fault for this debacle. Arsehole.

If not duty, we went ashore in BRNC-style plain clothes. Barcelona's old quarters, just up the road from our berth, were narrow cobbled streets with plenty of small lively bars. We were warned not to go ashore alone, but in groups to ensure collective safety. In Blue Star, I usually went ashore solo, making my way back unscathed in dodgy ports like Rio, Santos and Belém. We heard on the ship's grapevine that a sailor had been beaten up and mugged by some local yobs. The bootnecks decided to prevent a recurrence. They lay in wait as one of their number acted drunk wobbling along the street. The yobs jumped on him but his mates appeared from the shadows and exacted violent retribution. Naturally, there were no more muggings of *Fearless'* sailors in Barcelona.

3.5 In 'whites' at the Maritime Museum

3. Mediterranean Cruise – Navy Style

Any port visit included organised visits to cultural sites. We traipsed across the main road in tropical rig (short-sleeved white shirt, white shorts or 'Empire-builders', long white socks, white canvas deck shoes, caps) to the Maritime Museum. We wandered around exhibits of boats through the ages and an array of seamanship items. It was interesting but we'd almost have preferred to be duty.

A typical event in a warship's visit was 'Ship open to visitors'. This was viewed as an excellent public relations opportunity to fly the flag and build good relations with the local populace. These events attracted large numbers of visitors. They snaked around the upper deck route, ogled the anchor cable, windlass, weapon systems and our helos on the flight deck. It was a success and worth the ship's company's effort.

3.6 Open to visitors

There was also a defence sales aspect to the deployment. Stowed on the tank deck was a variety of military hardware. Defence sales reps eagerly pushed their pitch to invited local military hierarchy in each port visit.

Admiral Fitch disembarked at 0900 before we sailed at 1000 on Tuesday 9 October. It was nice to settle back into our training routine at sea. *Fearless'* rigorous daily schedule of exercises and drills resumed. I gathered this was the norm for a warship on passage between ports.

For the first couple of nights at sea, we practised co-nav (coastal navigation) around Sardinia and the north coast of Sicily as *Fearless* progressed east towards Italy. Throughout the cruise, the navigation plan took every overnight opportunity for OUTs to hone their co-nav skills. We took visual bearings and radar ranges, plotted them on the chart to determine position, course and speed made good. Our expertise improved, save for the occasional cocked hat where position lines didn't intersect at a point, but formed a triangle instead. Bad bearing? Poor plotting? Range from a misidentified prominent cape or headland? Tough luck. Take another fix immediately. BUFFS!

On the morning of 12 October, *Fearless* transited the Strait of Messina. Between the eastern tip of Sicily (Punta del Faro) and the western tip of Calabria (Punta Pezzo) on mainland Italy, this narrow strait connects the northern Tyrrhenian Sea with the Ionian Sea to the south. Its width varies between 3.1km and 5.1km and a maximum depth of 250m. Our transit was made trickier by the almost constant ferry traffic criss-crossing the Strait and the ubiquitous fishing boats.

Heading east-south-east, we transited the Ionian Sea, the rocky coast of Greece's Peloponnese region over our northern horizon. It was Saturday afternoon and, after yet more exercises, *Fearless* stopped in the water somewhere west of Crete. The sterngate was lowered. 'Hands to bathe' was imminent. This seafaring tradition dated back to before the foundation of the RN. Personal hygiene was a luxury and a ship's limited fresh water was reserved for drinking, not washing. Hands to bathe gave sailors an opportunity to freshen up with a swim in the ocean.

Before 'hands to bathe' was piped, safety measures needed to be put in place. Machinery was tagged out to ensure the propellors didn't turn. Sonar switched off. Eductors, discharges, and other ballast fluid systems were off. The seaboat was lowered into the water to patrol the immediate vicinity, ready to rescue anyone in difficulty. In tropical seas, one of the seaboat crew was on shark watch, armed with a rifle. A scrambling net was rigged on the lee side so that if any wind took the ship towards the bathers they could climb back on board. When all was ready, the pipe was made. All those not on watch were free to participate.

I wasn't enthused. I couldn't see the point of jumping off a perfectly safe ship into a bottomless sea for no good reason. Much like parachuting. Still, my shipmates enjoyed the experience, especially stepping off the sterngate into the sea rather than leaping from the upper deck. An hour later, everyone was safely back on board, seaboat recovered, engines flashed up, and *Fearless* resumed passage to Crete.

On 14 October, *Fearless* passed Rodopos Peninsula, crossed the entrance to Chania Bay, rounded Akrotiri Peninsula to enter Souda Bay. A major base for the Hellenic Navy, it was also NATO's largest, most prominent naval base in the eastern Mediterranean. Its deepwater port was the only one in the Mediterranean capable of accommodating America's largest aircraft carriers. We berthed at the NATO fuelling jetty at 0945 and sailed at 1400 with full fuel tanks. A short visit, no run ashore – it reminded me of being on a container ship.

We steamed north and arrived off Piraeus the next morning, alongside at lunchtime. Soon after the gangway was set, dignitaries came aboard. Senior Naval Officer, Aegean arrived first. What a cracking job that must have been, sadly long since gone as the RN gradually shrank in numbers of warships and personnel. Later, the British Ambassador boarded. They both left a couple of hours later, which allowed Captain Trussell to do his own calls ashore. He returned in time for the official reception (cocktail party, CTP). As taught at Dartmouth, we acted as hookers to collect guests at the gangway, make some polite chit-chat as we trundled them along the upper deck to the flight deck and deposited them at a circle of waiting officers.

We didn't see much of Piraeus or Athens because we had an exped to nearby Kithnos. We stored ship, handing down cases of ration packs and chilled steaks and joints into the LCUs outboard of *Fearless*. The bootneck crews stowed the victuals wherever they could. We clambered aboard, with pup tents and our personal kit.

We departed Piraeus under a grey overcast sky, on a light green sea. An LCU's accommodation was non-existent. Its superstructure aft comprised only bridge and engine room, as far as we knew. We slumped and sprawled on the open deck usually occupied by a tank or jeeps en route to an amphibious landing. The weather was cool as the sun just couldn't break through the cloud cover. The LCUs approached Kithnos and ran into the sandy beach in a small cove. Loutra village perched on the surrounding low hills.

The weather cooled at the onset of dusk. We unloaded the LCUs and walked to a sandy square just outside Loutra. Camp was set up. Tents pitched under the direction of Gutbucket and his mate. These two herberts were the only accompanying OTD staff on the exped. How unlucky were we?

Time for dinner. We couldn't find our chilled steaks and joints and realised the bootnecks had purloined the lot. We complained to Gutbucket but he just laughed and said we should have looked out for our victuals. How typical of him, but fair comment. 'Look after your kit, and your kit will look after you' was a popular maxim. We'd have to be content with ration packs. However, the trio of Blake's Saudi Arabians, nicknamed 'the good (Assery), the bad (al Shenji) and the Ageeli', turned up in a pick-up with a farmer from whom they'd purchased a lamb, which they butchered, halal-style, on the beach. We dug a pit under their instruction and built a fire with lots of stones underneath. The lamb was put in after the fire had died down and covered with a tarpaulin. When cooked, it was most welcome, if slightly rare in places and lacking in flavour. After dinner, we visited Loutra's taverna for liquid sustenance.

3.7 LCUs on Loutra beach

I don't recall what we did on Kithnos. We strolled around a bit after Gutbucket and his mate had got us up for EMAs, followed by breakfast. The weather remained overcast and cool. We mostly wore sports shorts, trainers and T-shirts, covered permanently by our nylon foulie (foul-weather) jackets, barely waterproof or windproof and good at retaining damp sweat. Although Gore-Tex was invented in 1969, it hadn't yet been acquired by the RN for foulies.

Carrying our memories of a couple of days and nights camping on Kithnos, the LCUs used astern power to get off the beach. The voyage to Piraeus was in more inclement conditions. The flat-bottomed, shallow draft LCUs pitched and rolled in sea state 3 or 4. Goffers (big waves) broke over the for'ard ramp. Sea water sloshed around the exposed deck, forcing us to stand and grimly hold on. Our kit was soaked. After an eternity, we got alongside *Fearless* and disembarked, relieved the thoroughly unpleasant, miserable exped was over.

3.8 Setting up camp at dusk

Some of us went to Athens, a contrast in bright, warm sunshine. We visited the Parthenon. Its white stone reflected and radiated the sun's heat. Hordes of tourists clambered over this famous monument, feet kicking up swirling dust clouds. I was impressed by the Parthenon and all its decorative sculptures, standing proudly atop the Acropolis. I was pleased I'd seen something of Athens but, like my fellow OUTs, disappointed that I'd missed out on so much more because of the futile exped.

3.9 At the Parthenon with 'Stumpy' Haldane (right) and others

Fearless sailed from Piraeus at 1000 on Saturday 20 October. After lowering the stern gate and flooding the dock to allow the LCUs to drive in, we steamed through the Dodecanese Islands. In the afternoon, *Fearless* anchored off the north coast of Mykonos for another 'hands to bathe'. We remained at anchor overnight for the wardroom to enjoy Trafalgar Night dinner. Many of us were jobbed as extra stewards for the evening. For each course, we speedily flitted from galley to wardroom, providing silver service to the officers, loitered in and around the pantry, waiting for the call to whizz round clearing the tables. The CPO (Steward) ran us ragged.

Our rotations through the ship's departments included supply and secretariat (S&S). In the galley, we were used and abused in the scullery on 'pot-wash', endlessly washing up pots, pans, plates, bowls and cutlery every mealtime. I don't think *Fearless* was fitted with a dishwasher. We sweated in the ambient heat, hands constantly immersed in hot soapy water that got increasingly greasy, cool and grey. We'd empty the large sink, refill with hot water, squirt in washing-up liquid and continue. On and on it went. Endless. We dried up with dishcloths, which quickly became damp and were frequently replaced with fresh ones.

We weren't involved in food preparation or assisting the chefs in cooking. They were always hard-pressed, with no time to instruct or monitor an OUT buggering up some dish. Caterers were another S&S sect, responsible for ensuring the right quantities of ingredients were delivered from stores, fridges and freezers deep down in *Fearless*. Stores Accountants (SAs or Jack Dusties) held anything and everything a ship needed when at sea. I'm afraid these sub-specialisations were tedious and dull. Again, I thanked God I was a Seaman Officer, the Executive Branch, the master race.

The passage to Cyprus was under pleasant conditions. Each night classes continued co-nav off Crete's north coast followed by Cyprus' south coast. On Wednesday, a splash target was streamed astern, its framework designed to create visual white sea froth to enable either another ship to fire its gun at it or an aircraft to bomb or strafe it. Naturally, the role of 'splash target coxswain' was a practical joke on innocent sailors or, better still, naïve OUTs. The word went out, calling for volunteers to apply for this prestigious job. A few did, most of us smelt a rat but naturally encouraged others to apply. Cruelly, we had a good laugh at their expense. All part of Jack's famous sense of humour.

The splash target (without a coxswain) was streamed, ready for the attacking aircraft, a detachment of Lightnings based at RAF Akrotiri, Cyprus. As a pair strafed, I recalled going to Air Day at HMS Daedalus,

Lee-on-Solent, as a boy. We lived in Gosport, so I got a bus to Daedalus and enjoyed watching aircraft whizzing around in the sky. One year, a RAF Lightning appeared, certainly off the scale for beauty, power and machismo. I stared in awe and wonder as this glistening silver beast took off and went vertical at max power. Its jet engines roared at full throttle, afterburner flames issued from twin exhausts. It disappeared high into the wild blue yonder. Chapter 9 of James Hamilton-Paterson's *Empire of the Clouds* describes the Lightning's development and brilliantly evokes the thrill of seeing it perform at air shows. The Lightnings made *Fearless'* pair of Wessex helos look very tame and pedestrian. Alas, the upper deck was out of bounds so we didn't see them.

The next morning, we anchored off Dhekelia, Cyprus. Ship's company had 50% leave. We were taken ashore by LCU and had an informative trip inland to visit the Green Line. This UN Buffer Zone was a demilitarized zone, patrolled by the UN Peacekeeping Force in Cyprus (UNFICYP), established in 1964. After the Turkish invasion the ceasefire of 16 August 1974 extended it and it became the de facto partitioning of Cyprus. The Republic of Cyprus (excluding British Sovereign Base Areas) controlled the southern half and the largely unrecognised Turkish Republic of Northern Cyprus the northern. This Green Line stretched for 180km from Paralimni in the east to Kato Pyrgos in the west. We were briefed on the situation by the local British Army unit's commander and saw their barracks and views towards the Turkish side. Apparently, it was usually very quiet with occasional outbursts of random gunfire.

Fearless remained at anchor for a couple of days and departed on 27 October. We were on our way to Istanbul, a city I'd often dreamed of visiting … now was my opportunity. Northwards we steamed, through the Aegean Sea, littered with Greek islands.

On Monday 29 October, *Fearless* transited the Dardanelles. This narrow strait connects the Aegean to the Sea of Marmara and onwards to the Bosphorus and the Black Sea. It is 61km long and 1.2–6km wide, with an average depth of 55m, deepening to 103m at its narrowest point at Çanakkale. To starboard was the ancient city of Troy but further along to port lay Gallipoli, scene of a long campaign in 1915.

In an attempt to force Turkey out of World War I, the Allies dispatched a naval force to steam through the Dardanelles and Sea of Marmara and seize Constantinople (Istanbul). French and British warships were shelled from both shores and struck mines laid by the Turks. The losses and damage to several battleships forced the Allies to retreat. To negate Turkish defences, large-scale amphibious landings on both sides of the Dardanelles were conducted. British, Australian and New Zealand forces landed at several beaches on Gallipoli, the French on the Asian shore. This (in)famous Gallipoli campaign began in April 1915 and ended with the Allied withdrawal by 9 January 1916 – 56707 Allied soldiers and 56643 Turks were killed. The Turkish defence of Gallipoli was masterminded by Colonel Mustafa Kemal, later known as Ataturk, the founder of modern Turkey.

Viewed from *Fearless*' flight deck, the Dardanelles was a constricted channel. I imagined the Allied dreadnoughts, battleships and battlecruisers attempting to penetrate, despite close range artillery shelling from both sides, plus the mined channel. Further north, *Fearless* passed through the pinch point at Çannakale and Eceabat, between which frequent ferries operate. We steamed through the Sea of Marmara to anchor the next morning, 30 October, in the Bosphorus, off Dolmabahçe Palace, with its impressive waterfront façade.

3.10 *Fearless* anchored in Bosphorus

This palace, was built between 1843 and 1856 by the Ottoman Empire's Sultan, Abdülmecid I. The Sultan and his family lived in the medieval Topkapı Palace, but it lacked contemporary style, luxury and comfort compared to the palaces of European monarchs. So he built the modern Dolmabahçe Palace near the site of the old demolished Beşiktaş Sahil Palace. Dolmabahçe is the largest palace in Turkey, filling 44,500m², with 285 rooms, 46 halls, 6 baths (hamam) and 68 toilets. It contains eclectic elements from the Baroque, Rococo and Neoclassical styles, blended with traditional Ottoman architecture. It was home to six Sultans until the abolition of the Caliphate in 1924, when ownership was transferred to the new Turkish Republic. Atatürk, founder and first President of the Republic, used it as a summer presidential residence. He spent his final days there as his health deteriorated, dying on 10 November 1938.

We had great views to the Palace on one side, Istanbul's suburbs on the Asian shore opposite, 15 July Martyrs Bridge to the north-east (which links Europe and Asia) and, south-west, a skyline of Hagia Sofia, Topkapi Palace and Blue Mosque. The problem with being at anchor was the necessity for liberty boats. Luckily, this was well-organised by the British Naval Attaché (BNA). A regular ferry service was established so no one waited too long to get ashore or to return on board.

3.11 Waiting for a liberty boat.
Kim Godfrey, me, Steve Williams, Woody Coussens, BJ, Steve Kenny and John Pentreath

Our plain clothes weren't inspected as in BRNC, but we were required to wear the correct rig of chinos, shirt, tie and, as it was a bit nippy, a sweater. We went ashore in groups and made our way by taxi across the Golden Horn, the natural estuary and waterway that formed the northern boundary of the peninsula of old Istanbul. We visited Hagia Sophia, Topkapi Palace, Blue Mosque and Grand Bazaar, collocated in the old quarter of Fatih. All were absolutely magnificent in their own way. I was chuffed to see and tour these historical monuments, symbols of where East met West, Asia met Europe, blending Christian and Muslim cultures.

Hagia Sofia was a vast edifice, with its rather ugly, substantial but necessary buttresses. Its chequered history dates from AD360, including periods as Byzantine and Catholic cathedrals, a mosque and a museum until 2020, when it became a mosque again. Inside was astounding. We walked around and admired the magnificent dome some 55m above us. At a lower level, there were galleries to stroll around and look down on the expanse of the ground floor. Dim lighting added to the building's ancient atmosphere.

The Grand Bazaar is one of the world's largest and oldest covered markets. Construction began in 1455 and grew to cover 30,000m² a in a vast grid of 61 criss-crossing streets with over 4000 shops under vaulted and arched ceilings. Some streets were dedicated to particular products: jewellery; gold; furniture; carpets; leather goods; casualwear; vibrant herb and spice stalls; and, naturally, plenty of stalls flogging fake designer clothes, football shirts and crappy souvenirs for the daily tourist hordes.

I don't think we had sufficient time to get into Topkapi Palace or the Blue Mosque. Nevertheless, my romantic soul was just thrilled to be in old Istanbul.

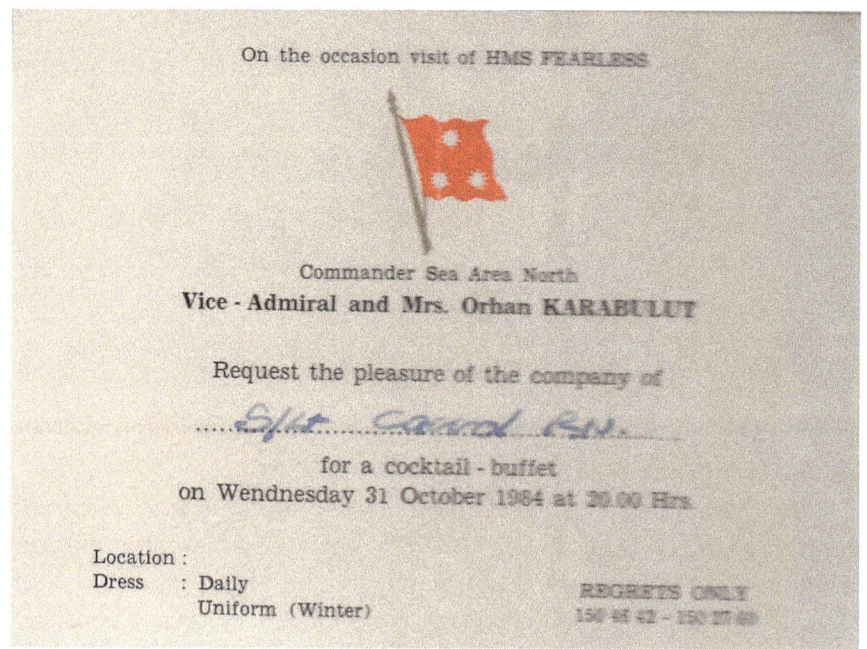

3.12 CTP invitation

On our second evening, a number of OUTs were invited, among *Fearless'* officers, to attend a reception held by Vice Admiral Karabulut, Commander Sea Area North. I have no idea where this was held but it was an enjoyable evening, chatting to Turkish Navy officers, drinking G&T and sampling the buffet. Curious, I recently 'googled' Karabulut and discovered his distinguished naval career culminated as Commander of the Turkish Navy from August 1988 to August 1990.

Many of us were jobbed for a day trip to Turkey's Naval High School on Heybeliada Island. I'm not sure how we got there, either by boat from *Fearless* or coach and then a boat to the island, but it was a flog as Heybeliada was some 20km by sea from Dolmabahçe Palace. It was back down the Bosphorus, into the Sea of Marmara and along the Asian coast to Princes' Islands archipelago, of which Heybaliada was the second largest.

Founded in 1773, the Naval High School was one of Turkey's oldest high schools. From 1784, the Imperial Naval Engineering School provided a three-year course, divided into two parts. The first focused on navigation and plotting, the second trained the cadets in naval architecture. The curriculum evolved and, in the early 20th century, adopted a similar training syllabus to BRNC's. When Turkey became a Republic in 1923, it was renamed Naval High School and the training comprised a year's English prep and four years high school. Graduates were automatically admitted to the Turkish Naval Academy in Tuzla, Istanbul.

There was a guided tour of classrooms and facilities – yawn! We got the impression the cadets lived a monastic lifestyle and weren't afforded too many opportunities to get ashore to the mainland. We'd raised a basketball team to play against them and finished the visit scoffing the buffet before the long trip back to *Fearless*. Another example of fostering friendly and valuable relationships with a NATO partner.

Undoubtedly my best memory of Istanbul was realising Monty's ambition to see a belly dancer. He'd found a venue and off we trotted about a mile from Dolmabahçe Palace. Kervansaray Restaurant-Night-Club was on Cumhuriyet Cadessi, close to the famous Taksim Square. Inside, there was dim lighting and an array of small tables with tablecloths and a candle gave a further modicum of light. I don't think the drink prices were exorbitant but the belly dancer's performance was fantastic. We had a great evening. Our trip to Istanbul was complete.

I recently found Kervansaray on the internet, offering a similar experience but in plusher surroundings. It had moved a few doors further away from Taksim Square. Its original building was now 'Cavalli in Istanbul Club' with terrible reviews on Trip Advisor, a tourist scam. How sad our days of 'innocents abroad' no longer occur.

3.13 Me, Monty and the belly-dancer

After a busy port visit, *Fearless* weighed anchor on Sunday 4 November and steamed south-west into the Sea of Marmara. We transited the Dardanelles in late afternoon and we were in the Aegean Sea again for the short overnight passage to Souda Bay. We went alongside for a couple of hours for bunkers (refuelling) before setting off to Algiers.

The next day focused on an NBCDX (fire and damage control exercise) beginning with, and remaining at, 'action stations' until the exercise ended at 1409. Our collective reward was 'hands to bathe'.

Fearless transited the Strait of Messina the following afternoon, continued west along the north coast of Sicily, our course tweaked slightly to west-south-west. The now-familiar round of exercises, seaboat drills and flying serials continued during this passage, as well as small arms firing. We cut across the Bay of Algiers and entered Algiers port on the morning of Saturday 10 November.

3. Mediterranean Cruise – Navy Style

3.14 'Hands to bathe' somewhere in the Med
Stern-gate lowered, two LCUs in foreground

3.15 Taking it easy on flight deck
Woody Coussens (foreground), Wessex helos (background)

The usual flurry of activity occurred. Captain Trussell went ashore for his calls, returning in time to receive local VIPs. These formalities and courtesies took up a lot of the Captain's time on arrival in any port. Perks of the job.

I don't recall much about Algiers. We attended *Fearless'* CTP on the flight deck on the first evening. My only other clear memory was as one of a group of OUTs invited to the British Embassy for drinks and canapes, followed, weirdly, by watching *The Right Stuff* (a brilliant 1983 film about the selection of Mercury astronauts and the rivalry with Chuck Yeager's test pilots at Edwards Air Force Base in the high desert) on a reel-to-reel projector.

Our nondescript visit to Algiers ended when we sailed on Tuesday 13 November. *Fearless* rounded Raïs Hamidou and headed west towards Gibraltar (Gib), our final port visit. We rounded Europa Point and anchored at 1800 on 14 November, 6½ cables (1300yds) west-north-west of 'A' Head on the north end of South Mole, one of the breakwaters built to shelter warships berthed in the Naval Base.

Gib was so near and yet so far. We weighed anchor at 0530 to spend the day in the adjacent exercise areas. Weapon training included gunnery serials and air defence exercises with RAF Jaguars from Gib. Sadly, the upper deck was out of bounds to spectators. A long day ended when we finally went alongside at 41 Berth.

The massive Jurassic limestone crag of the Rock of Gibraltar (426m high) dominated the base, town and the narrow strip of land stretching back to the Spanish border. I almost strained my neck looking upwards to espy its peak. Gib's history goes back hundreds of years. An excellent book with a particular focus on its defence in World War II is Nicholas Rankin's *Defending the Rock*.

To make Gib torpedo-proof, the South and North Moles were extended and the Detached Mole built in the 19th century. Later, three large dry docks were constructed to enhance Gib's facilities and importance as a British naval base and dockyard. The senior naval officer was Flag Officer Gibraltar (FO Gib), a post that existed in various guises under a Rear or Vice Admiral from 1902 to 1992, when it was rationalised to Commander British Forces Gibraltar under a Commodore. The incumbent FO Gib, called on Captain Trussell.

Our routine was more relaxed in Gib. We thought the OTD staff were winding down at the end of the cruise, looking forward to getting home and off-loading these pesky OUTs. Even Gutbucket didn't demand his

3. Mediterranean Cruise – Navy Style

EMA squad runs. In the evenings, we enjoyed runs ashore, along Rosia Street to Main Street to numerous pubs. The Gib Arms and The Horseshoe (Donkey's Flip-Flop in Jackspeak) in particular.

Before departure on Sunday 18 November, we were ordered to do the Rock Race. It was traditional for visiting ship's companies to run up the Rock. It was an ungodly hour but there was daylight at least, as sunrise was 0730. Only OUTs participated. Our cripples and sickies acted as guides, stationed at various points on the 4.3km route, rising 400m to the summit. I was knackered soon after jogging only a short distance uphill, many OUTs soon slowed to a walk. The road curved and contoured its way, a blessing although still steep. I was relieved to reach the top and then walked down many flights of steps to the Dockyard and *Fearless*. I don't know what my time was, but certainly nowhere near the record of 17 minutes 29 seconds set in 1986.

After a shower and swift breakfast, we went to our allotted stations for departure at 0900. My class was in the Marine Engineering Department, so I went down the engine room. Luckily, the on-watch stokers took pity on us. And we were left to loaf as we were exhausted, exacerbated by the engine room's heat. That forenoon watch melted away. I don't remember anything.

The last leg to Guzz was very quiet. We didn't do anything noteworthy. The pace and relentless ship's exercises also eased. Back through the Strait of Gibraltar, northbound up the Portuguese coast, Lisbon and Porto unseen over the distant eastern horizon. *Fearless* rounded the north-west tip of Spain and headed north-north-east across the Bay of Biscay, a little rougher and windier than in late September. Past Ushant, we steamed across the Channel and entered Plymouth Sound via the western entrance. *Fearless* moored to 'C' Buoy at 1315 on 21 November.

We'd had a little bit of a Channel Night, scuppering our daily beer allowance of three cans. We packed our kit. Customs boarded to clear ship's company and us. We loaded ourselves and our kit into the LCUs and disembarked from *Fearless*. The LCUs off-loaded us at Mill Bay Docks. Abandoned by the OTD Staff, we made our way home. Most got taxis to Plymouth station to catch a train, others shared hire cars to drive home. It was Wednesday and we were rejoining BRNC on Sunday.

Our DTS experience was over. Although I'd had a good time living together in our cramped messes, it was certainly an unenviable way of life. Living and working with Jack gave me an invaluable insight to their working conditions and routines. Each department had given us stupid, nonsensical, futile jobs to do. We considered the OTD Staff weren't of a quality comparable to BRNC Staff Officers.

When we returned to BRNC on Sunday, the NCEs and Ints returned to their respective Divisions to start their academic classes. As September was the largest term entry, the Divisions were full. So, we DGEs, schoolies and NCE engineers were banished to 'C' Block as we were passing out at the end of term. 'C' Block was nicely tucked away, behind the Chapel and off the main drag. Our cabins were on the first floor with plentiful heads and bathrooms compared to *Fearless*. We were very much out of the way and realised that provided we behaved sensibly, we'd be left alone. Divisional Staff were fully engaged with our fellow DTS returnees joining their divisional groups and writing OUTs' reports.

Like everyone else, I had an interview with my ADO. Lt Cdr Watson had moved upwards from Hawke to become Cunningham's DO. His relief, Lt Cdr Andy Willmett, was now my ADO. He was a personable, approachable, cheerful bloke, in contrast to Watson's curt manner. Nevertheless, he expected the same high standards befitting BRNC. We had a good old chat. He'd gleaned details from my file and DTS report and was genuinely interested in my pre-BRNC life as a deck cadet. He informed me that my year's fleet time would commence in Rosyth with *Gavinton*, a wooden, 32-year-old, *Ton*-class minehunter. Winter in Scotland over January to April, then to *Exeter*, a Pompey-based Type 42 destroyer on her deployment to the Gulf for the remainder of 1985.

Our timetable was pretty empty. We kept our heads down, cleaned our cabins and heads/bathrooms nightly. As Seniors, we enjoyed meals in the magnificent SGR and beers in the civilised, relaxed SGR Bar. We attended whatever noddy classes were timetabled. These included presentations on RN sub-specialisations (submarines, FAA, hydrography), RM, RNR, career patterns, behaviour in a wardroom and drug awareness.

Our penultimate week at BRNC was filled with passing out parade (POP) rehearsals. We were constantly on the parade ground (fine weather) or on the quarterdeck (wet weather practice). We had refresher lessons on marching and sword drill. Importantly, we learned steps drill for POP's climax when we slow marched up the steps and through the main door.

Steps drill required absolute focus. If one of us fell out of step or stumbled slightly as we climbed the steps, the whole thing could go to an embarrassing ball of chalk in front of family and friends. It was critical that as we passed through the main door, we maintained our marching rhythm along the main drag until everyone had entered the building. Then, the doors were slammed shut behind us and we could whoop, cheer and throw our caps in the air.

The rehearsals were relentless, daily from 0830 to 1200 or even to 1600. Sometimes with the RM Band, or just a bass drummer to provide the beat. Sometimes the Guard participated. The GIs pushed us hard. At the end of our last rehearsal at Wednesday lunchtime, we stood on the parade ground. WO Kent addressed us from the bridge. He warned of the dangers of over-imbibing this evening, and claimed the weather would be good for our big day. PO Jones echoed his words and, as he roared, his clip-on black tie pinged from his shirt collar. We dissolved into laughter at his embarrassment.

My parents and my girlfriend, Sue, arrived late afternoon. It was nice to see them. We dined in Dartmouth and bumped into a few of my friends with their parents and girlfriends. Thursday 13 December dawned. I got back on board, ate a hearty breakfast and dressed in No.5. Boots were given a final clean, cap cover a brilliant white, peak shined, sword and scabbard brasso'ed, No.5 patted down with Sellotape for fluff. Muster at the West End was at 1000, where Staff Officers inspected the POP platoons. Another final whizz round with Sellotape. At 1033 the platoons were on Flagstaff Road, nerves in check, and marched on at 1045.

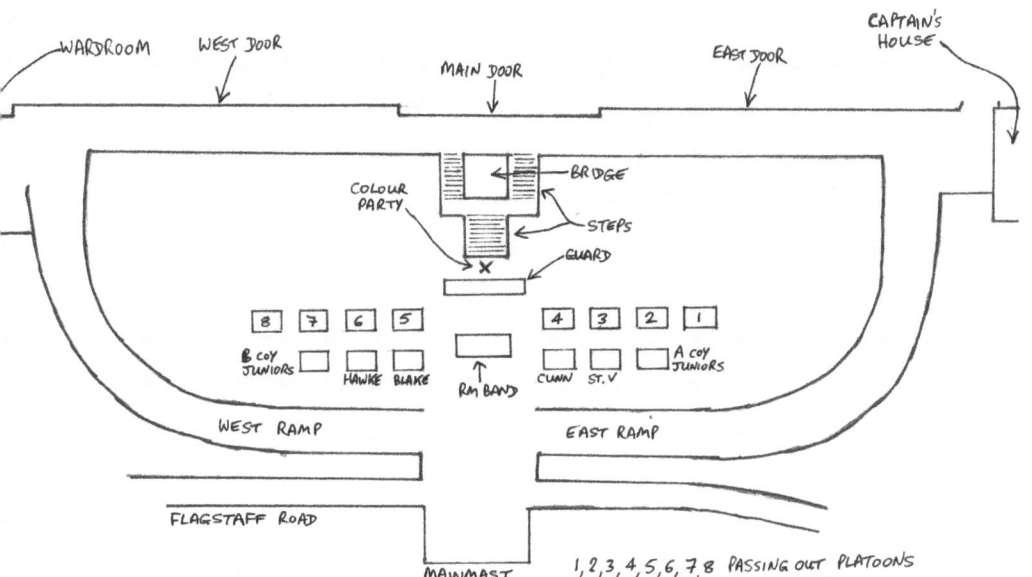

3.16 Parade ground layout for POP

At 1055, the Commander reported the Parade to the Guest of Honour, Vice-Admiral Sir Peter Stanford (Vice-Chief of the naval staff). Captain

Tullis escorted him down the steps to inspect the Guard and POP platoons. The march past followed and, while the Divisional platoons dispersed along Flagstaff Road, we were supposed to march back onto the parade ground to form up, advance in review order and do the steps drill.

Unfortunately, this didn't happen. The threatening sky opened up and rain fell. Our moments of glory were cancelled. The POP platoons were directed to continue up Flagstaff Road and disperse with the other platoons. We were appalled and disgusted, and couldn't fathom why this final bit of ceremonial, the end of our time at BRNC, had been cancelled. There was much disgruntlement. I think we're the only POP that didn't do the steps drill and pass through the main doors. It still rankles today.

3.17 DGEs, schoolies and GLs passing out.
Front row Monty (2nd left), BJ (3rd left). 2nd row me (2nd left). 4th row Jamie (3rd left). 6th row Traps (3rd left), Martin Jones (4th left)
(BRNC Archive)

Well, that's 'life in a blue suit'. We met up with family and friends inside the building. Lunch was laid on, after which visitors departed and we settled into helping with preps for the ball in respective Divisions. Later, dressed again in No.5, we reunited with our guests and went to the Chapel for the Leavers' Service, short, atmospheric and moving. BRNC's three Sin Bosuns shared duties and rousing hymns were sung, not least the Naval Hymn.

Afterwards, we made our way up the hill to Hawke as each Division held a CTP. In HGR, I introduced Sue and my parents to many of my peers and Staff Officers. G&T flowed freely, with trays of nibbles. Conversation volume reached fever pitch. I changed into plain clothes and walked down into Dartmouth with my guests.

Back at Hawke early next morning, we returned our swords to the Armoury, under the arches on the parade ground. The rest of the day was spent in the tumult of rigging ball decorations. It was very well organised by the Ball Officer and his Committee, formed a few weeks before. When completed, we were released and I escaped to the hotel to get into Mess Undress.

My parents, Sue and I had a great time. The ball started at 1930 and concluded at 0230. There was plenty of music and dancing, plus a delicious supper at 2130. The highlight was the RM Band's 'Beat Retreat' at 2030 on the quarterdeck. 'Carriages' at 0300.

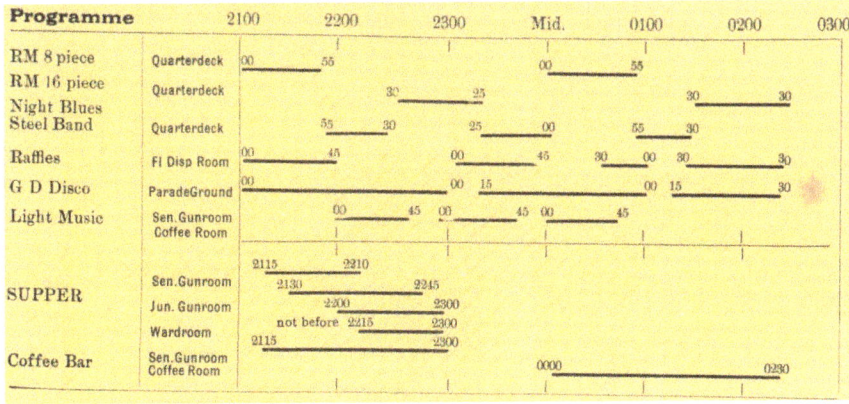

3.18 Typical ball programme

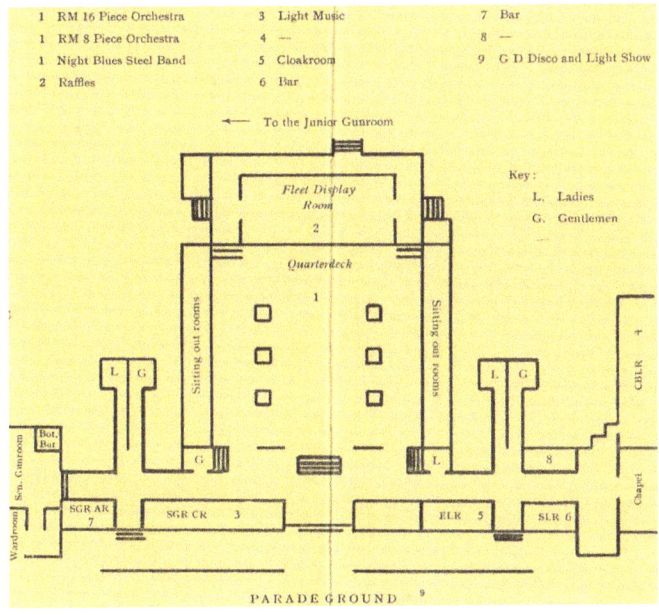

3.19 Ball venue plan

Christmas leave was spent at home. A welcome change after four consecutive festive seasons at sea on Blue Star ships: Panama Canal transits (1980 and 1982), mid-Atlantic (1981) and Fremantle (1983). I braced for joining *Gavinton* in Rosyth on 7 January 1985.

4.

A Bleak Midwinter in Rosyth

4.1 *Gavinton* crest (left); *Brinton* crest (right)
(Nick Barwis, www.jackstaxi.net)

4.2 *Gavinton*
(Ton Class Association)

After Christmas leave, I travelled north from my home town via Gosport ferry, train from Pompey Harbour to Waterloo, tube across to King's Cross for the train to Edinburgh. It was endless, but even then I needed a local train across the Forth to Inverkeithing and a taxi to Rosyth Naval Base. It was dark when I bowled up *Gavinton's* gangway on the evening of Sunday 6 January.

The QM met me and guided me and my kit to the wardroom. I don't recall if anyone was there, possibly Officer-of-the-Day (OOD). But I was tired and, after a mug of tea, climbed into the top bunk in XO's cabin for a deep sleep.

Breakfast was an opportunity to meet my brother officers: XO (Lt Robin Swaine), NO (Lt Alistair Halliday) and Guns/Corro (Gunnery and Correspondence Officer, Lt Richard Farrington). Robin was an old-and-bold special duties (SD) communicator, quiet, calm and unruffled. Throughout my time in *Gavinton*, nothing fazed him. Alistair and Richard were gregarious, outgoing young blokes, competent and professional in their respective duties. This trio got on well together and formed an efficient and effective team, fully supportive of their CO.

Robin asked if I knew who *Gavinton's* CO was. I hadn't a clue. He said Bernie Bruen. Nope, never heard of him. Robin was aghast at my total ignorance of Bernie, his legendary status in the mine clearance diving (MCD) world and Falklands War heroics. The then-Lt Bruen had been in charge of one of three clearance diving teams dispatched to the Falklands to defuse unexploded bombs. A 1000lb bomb struck *RFA Sir Galahad* and lodged itself in the hold with metal debris wrapped tightly around it. It took Bernie and his team 8½ hours to remove the bomb, mostly achieved while it rested on Bernie's legs as he sat in battery acid. Immediately after disposing of the defused bomb over the side, Bernie hastened to another warship to assist in defusing another bomb. He was awarded the Distinguished Service Cross.

Bernie was well-known as an eccentric. Apparently, as *Bulwark's* NBCD Officer, he walked around the ship with a blue flashing light on his hard hat and a red surcoat with yellow rank strips sewn on so 'people will know who I am and what I do'. After leaving the RN in 1988, he served in the Royal Navy of Oman until 1996. To relax, he played the fiddle and wrote poetry.

After Colours at 0900, Robin took me to meet the CO. I was face-to-face with Lt Cdr Bernie Bruen. He certainly was a tough-looking, rufty-tufty bloke, short but powerful stature and full black beard. Despite his rather scary appearance, we had a cheerful introductory conversation.

4. A Bleak Midwinter in Rosyth

He was, I think, pleased that his OUT was a mature graduate and had completed a four-year MN deck cadetship before joining the RN.

I'd seen much of the world on a variety of merchantmen. Now I found myself within the cramped confines of a vintage wooden minehunter. Gone was the open expanse of a container ship's weather deck and fo'c'sle. *Gavinton* was just 50% longer than the beam of my first ship (*ACT 5*), which was 4½ times longer (217m) and weighed in at 24212 gross tons compared to my little *Ton's* 440. Yet both ships had a similar sized crew. I was sharing Robin's cabin, half the size of my deck cadet's en suite accommodation in Blue Star Line.

Ton-class minesweepers were 1950s vintage. Thornycroft was lead constructor but also built at 15 other yards. Named after English towns suffixed '-ton', 119 were built and served in nine navies. Constructed from aluminium and other non-ferromagnetic materials, their hulls were double-layered mahogany planking. They were 46m long, 8.5m beam and 2.4m draught. As mine countermeasures vessels (MCMVs), their minesweeping equipment countered the threat of mines (seabed, moored or magnetic) laid in shallow coastal waters, rivers, ports and harbours. Later, 16 *Tons* (including *Gavinton* and *Brinton* in 1966–1968) were converted to minehunters, with the fitting of active rudders (ARs) and Type 193 minehunting sonar.

They also served as patrol vessels and in fishery protection. But *Tons* 'got around a bit'. When we had a Navy, 9th Minesweeping Squadron was based in Bahrain, 6th MCM Squadron formed 6th Patrol Craft Squadron in Hong Kong. A handful of *Tons* participated in mine clearance of the Suez Canal in 1974 and served in the Mediterranean and Red Sea. *Kirkliston* and *Maxton* even deployed to Mackay and Cairns in Queensland. Prince Charles commanded *Bronington* in 1976. For a full history of *Tons*, read *Last of the Wooden Walls*, an excellent publication by the Ton Class Association. *Jack of All Trades*, another Ton Class Association book, lists every *Ton's* service history.

By January 1985, 3rd MCM Squadron comprised ten *Tons* (*Gavinton, Brinton, Brereton, Hubberston, Iveston, Keddleston, Kellington, Nurton, Sheraton, Wilton*). Originally 1st MCM Squadron at Port Edgar, almost opposite Rosyth and beneath the Forth Road Bridge, a reorganisation of the MCM Flotilla moved these *Tons* to Rosyth to form 3rd MCM Squadron in January 1984. Also based at Rosyth were 1st MCM Squadron's *Hunt*-class MCMVs and the Fishery Protection Squadron. The latter 'fish boats' included a handful of *Tons* and several *Island*-class offshore patrol vessels (OPVs).

Warships were occasionally refitted at Rosyth Dockyard. From 1984, Rosyth was the sole location to refit our nuclear submarine fleet and eventually where several were berthed to await disposal after decommissioning. Add occasional visits from destroyers/frigates and regular RN/NATO maritime exercises to multiple daily movements of MCMVs and 'fish boats', Rosyth Naval Base was a very busy place with lots of warships.

Rosyth Dockyard had a synchrolift. This powered trolley lifted an MCMV from the water and transported it into a covered workshop. Maintenance and repairs were carried out around the clock, oblivious to external weather conditions.

4.3 Typical Ton foc's'le
(John Woodward)

After Robin's brief ship tour, I familiarised myself more deeply with *Gavinton*. It was nice to see wooden decks again. The fo'c'sle with its windlass, anchor cables, spurling pipes and hawse pipes were scaled down versions of a merchantman's. In front of the for'ard screen was the Bofors 40/60 gun. Aft, the sweep deck had a small capstan and the same small diameter mooring ropes. Scuttles were rare. I think there was one in the aft bulkhead of the wardroom, the others were in the wheelhouse and on the bridge. I'd been on *Fearless*' bridge and thought it small compared to a merchantman's. *Gavinton's* was petite.

4.4 Typical Ton bridge
(John Woodward)

The decks had a scattering of hatches, their lids clipped open against a bulkhead, allowing access to sections and compartments below. A large chest freezer was secured to the bulkhead outside the CO's and NO/Guns' cabins on the main drag, a common practice in *Tons*. Adjacent was the officers' heads and bathroom. Across the alleyway was the wardroom, pantry and XO's cabin.

The day ended. Sunset had been and gone, almost simultaneous with night leave being piped. RAs (rationed ashore, personnel who lived ashore rather than onboard in home port) disappeared. I remained on board as I was 2nd OOD. My fleet training as a seaman officer began in earnest. It was a good way to learn the ropes of being OOD in harbour. I familiarised myself with relevant BRs (Books of Reference) and FLAGOS (Fleet Administrative and General Orders). I accompanied OOD (Richard) as he conducted his duties: duty watch fire exercise (firex); evening rounds; muster OOD's safe; middle watch rounds. A new world was opening up.

Richard and I did Colours the next morning. We stood together on the sweep deck, faced aft towards the ensign staff. An AB stood by, another AB alongside Richard, another sailor on the bridge manned the 'prep', and yet another sailor manned the jack-staff on the fo'c'sle. It was almost a whole duty watch ceremony. With several MCMVs in port, it was important to coordinate Colours and Sunset. The 'senior ship' led, the others followed.

The Bridge Card (updated monthly to the Fleet) listed RN warships by squadron and role, named each CO, his rank and date of seniority. MCMV COs were Lieutenants or Lieutenant Commanders. Senior ship was that with the CO of highest rank and earliest date of seniority in that rank in port at that moment.

We followed the senior ship's waggling of the prep (one minute to colours) and hauling down at 0900. The shrill bosun's call piped 'The Still' from every ship, echoing around Rosyth, immediately followed by the ensign (aft) and jack (for'ard) simultaneously hoisted. The ceremony ended when we all followed senior ship's piping 'Carry on'. Bosun's calls reverberated again around the base, piercing Rosyth's eerie silence, especially at weekends.

It was certainly more low-key and far less stressful than the ceremony at BRNC. I found it an equally proud and moving twice-daily event, almost the bedrock of naval custom and tradition.

The fuel barge came alongside. At 1115, Special Sea Dutymen (Specials or SSDs, personnel required to berth/unberth a warship – bridge, fo'c'sle, sweep-deck, engine-room and tiller flat – the steering gear compartment) closed up. At 1130, *Gavinton* slipped from Romeo (North) in company with *Brinton* and *Bildeston*. I was on the fo'c'sle for slipping. A loud voice roared from the bridge wing, 'Sub Lt Carroll, where's your seaman's knife?' Oops, Bernie had caught me out. Shamefaced, I scuttled below to fetch it. Lesson learned! Thereafter, I never ventured on deck without my trusty knife/spike combo on its lanyard round my waist.

Post-Christmas leave, it was a busy week at sea. SQUADEX (squadron exercise) with *Bildeston* and *Brinton* in Rosyth's EXAs. The non-stop programme of the first day (OOW manoeuvres, MOBEX, light-line transfer with *Bildeston*, formation anchorage off Kirkcaldy, diving exercise) set the tone for the week.

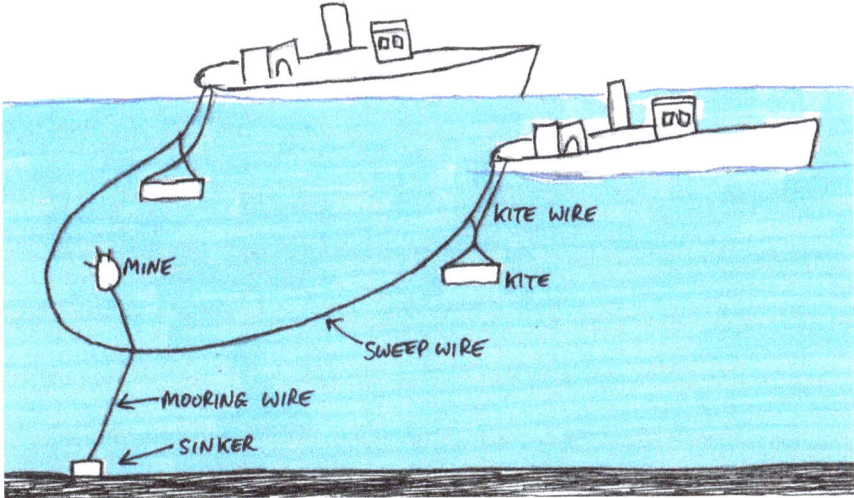

4.5 Armed team sweep

Wednesday focused on armed team sweeps with the other two ships, anchoring overnight in Kirkcaldy Bay. Gunnery shoots for GPMG and Bofors 40/60 on Thursday. The day rounded off with a double Oropesa sweep. It was novel, intriguing and exciting to observe the minesweeping kit laid out on the sweep deck and then streamed by our sailors. There were obviously lots of opportunities for things to go wrong very quickly. I appreciated the dangers of these procedures. We got alongside at Romeo (North) with *Brinton* berthed outboard on Thursday evening.

For an armed team sweep, a pair of minesweepers veered their sweep wires, joined in the middle and armed with explosive cutters. Kites pulled the sweep down to the required depth, adjusted by paying out equal lengths of kite wire (held down by the kite) from each ship. This method was used against deep moored mines. As the wire 'snagged' a moored mine, the mooring would gradually slide along the wire sweep as the ships continued ahead, until the mine's mooring wire was cut by one of the explosive cutters. When cut, the mine floated to the surface to be destroyed by the minesweepers later.

An armed team sweep was a dangerous serial. Minesweepers had a DOGGO drill, called if/when the ships got too far apart and the sweep wire pulled taut. This caused the ships to be pulled towards each other and could quickly end in a collision. 'Doggo, doggo, doggo! Close all red openings!' was piped on the main broadcast.

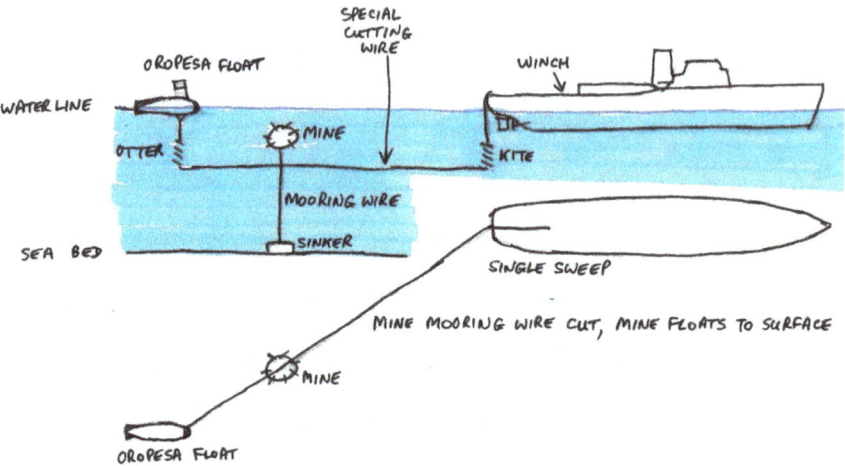

4.6 Oropesa sweep

An Oropesa sweep used the same sweep wire but pulled out to either side of the ship by the port or starboard otter, increasing the sweep's width. Otters were supported by the torpedo-shaped Oropesa floats above them. The sweep's depth was determined at the otter's end of the wire by the length of wire connecting the otter to the Oropesa float. The kite pulled the ship's end of the wire down to the required sweep depth. Kites and otters were the same bits of kit, but rigged and calibrated such that otters pulled the sweep wire to port or starboard and kites pulled it straight down. Calibrating them was hazardous as they'd occasionally leap spectacularly out of the water if they weren't 'tuned' correctly.

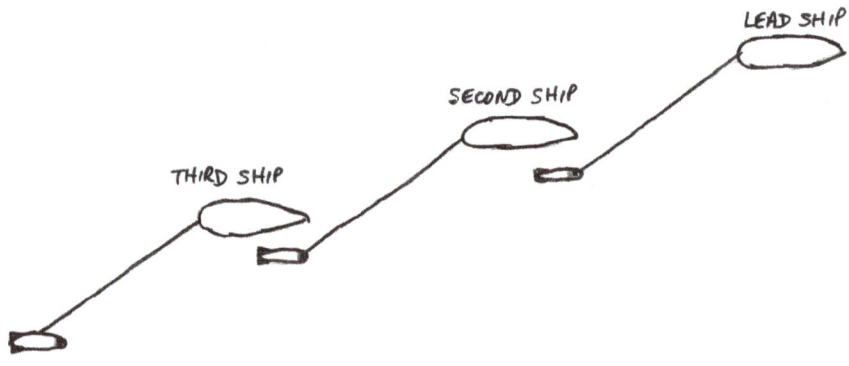

4.7 Team sweep

This form of minesweeping was developed in 1919 in the minesweeper *Oropesa* during the clearance of the northern mine barrage laid across the North Sea from the Orkneys to Norway's coast.

A team sweep involved two or more minesweepers in echelon, accurately following the lead minesweeper's orders to ensure that a maximum swathe of water was swept without gaps in coverage. It was crucial for each ship to maintain the correct distance and bearing from its neighbour.

So ended my first week in a *Ton*-class MCMV, an enjoyable and very busy period. I'd learned, albeit in simplistic terms, about minesweeping and witnessed a variety of exercises in which I'd gradually participate more fully as I accrued experience. It was great to be on watch on the bridge again, getting used to its compact size and the kit squeezed into it. I became comfortable in its confines with OOW (Alistair) and QM plus assorted occasional visitors: CO, XO, Guns, RO. Even more folks crowded into the space for SSDs. A complete contrast to my MN experience. My last trip was four months as 3rd Mate driving *New Zealand Star* (17000 tons, 171m long refrigerated cellular container ship) solo on the vast bridge for two round trips between the Gulf and Australia/New Zealand via the Indian sub-continent and Singapore. Transiting Hormuz at night, alone on the bridge.

Gavinton was also quite a change from the formality of a big ship like *Fearless*. I hadn't taken to the big ship environment. Already, I much preferred the intimacy and cosiness of little *Gavinton*, which appeared to enjoy more freedom and independence.

I grew accustomed to sharing XO's cabin with Robin, an absolute gentleman. I'd detected a close bond among the crews and wardrooms of *Tons* in MCM3. I knew I'd made the right decision to become a droggy after completing fleet time and passing Fleetboard.

Gavinton was alongside for the next 10 days. Life passed quietly in Rosyth. It was much too far to flog down to Eastbourne to see my fiancée at weekends. Instead, I went ashore a bit, mostly strolling around Edinburgh. Sundays were devoted to doing my dhobying in the laundry at HMS Cochrane. It was a leisurely time, reading the papers in the TV room while my dhobying washed and tumble-dried. I watched *The Big Match* and ironed my kit before trogging back to *Gavinton* for dinner. A simple life.

HMS Cochrane was the shore establishment within Rosyth Naval Base. First commissioned in 1938, it suffered a series of closures and reopenings until being recommissioned in 1968. It was the administrative and accommodation base for Rosyth-based warships, primarily MCMVs and fish boats. The wardroom was cheap and nasty, a shoddy construction.

A typical 1960s build of plasterboard walls and flat asphalted roofs. Winter was cold, with plenty of rain, so most corridors and rooms contained plastic buckets to collect the incessant drips through leaky ceilings. Luckily, the central heating worked properly. Most popular was Scruffs Bar, where we OUTs gathered in varying numbers for beer and to spin our growing collection of salty dits.

At 1145 Monday 21 January, *Gavinton* slipped from Romeo (North) and steamed under the Forth Road Bridge and the glorious red spans of the Forth Railway Bridge. Between Inchcolm, Inchmickery and Cramond Islands, we left Inchkeith to starboard and continued through the Rosyth EXAs. Heading north-east, with Isle of May a few miles off our starboard side, we rounded Craighead. Altering course north, we were in the unforgiving North Sea on passage to Clyde EXAs and Operation Pike, a regular operation to 'mine hunt' for Soviet-laid sonar buoys and listening devices along our nuclear submarine routes from/into Faslane.

The weather worsened. The easterly wind's speed increased dramatically from 40kts to 60kts (46–69mph), concomitant with sea state 5, then a steady 6. Wind and sea state on the beam caused *Gavinton* to roll heavily, even scarily! We continued passage overnight as conditions deteriorated further, from Force 9 to Force 10.

I was on middle watch with Alistair. At 0154, we had a steering gear failure. This was rectified by 0230, after a rather worrying period. A minor casualty in the mess deck was reported at 0222. We hove-to shortly afterwards. A busy middle watch climaxed when the port engine packed up due to lubricating oil pump failure. As Alistair wrote in the log, 'Substantial damage sustained to port garden wall and Gemini stowage in mountainous seas and Force 10'.

Bernie Bruen's article in *Ton Talk* (the Ton Class Association's magazine) described the actual damage sustained:

> A large rogue wave struck *Gavinton*, removed 10ft of the port garden-wall (bulwark) from the mine recovery fairlead to the Gemini petrol stowage and buckled the port garden gate. There were numerous deck leaks, power failures and a switch-fire in CO's cabin. Main lighting was reduced to 50% power. The fresh-water pump broke. The port name-board, miscellaneous bits-and-pieces on deck and the explosive-cutter locker were lost overboard. The provision

room fridge came off its mountings and the port engine lubricating oil pump failed.

The damage was far more extensive than I was aware of at the time.

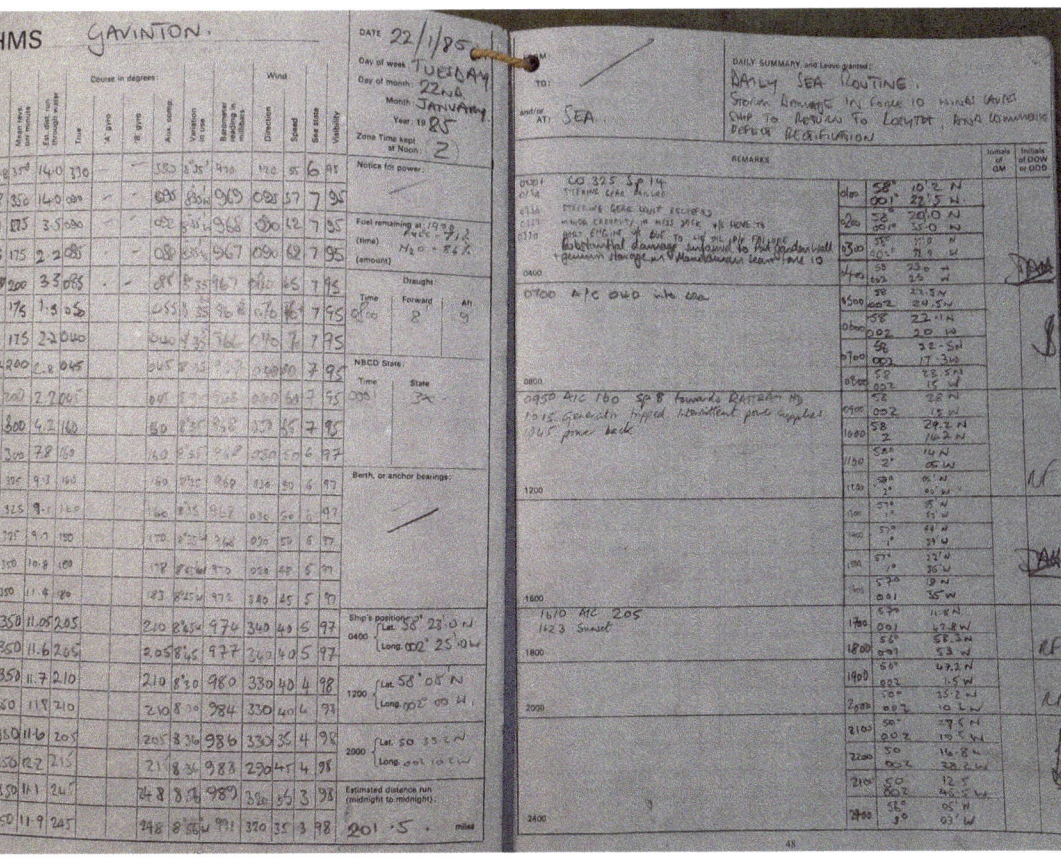

4.8 Ship's Log, Tuesday 22 January 1985
(National Archives)

The maximum recorded roll was 65°. Robin reported to Bernie that he'd observed the wardroom doorway curtain swing up to touch the deckhead, indicative of excessive rolling. We pressed slowly northwards until about 0700, when XO altered course to 040°, into the sea to reduce our rolling. Speed was about 2kts as we remained hove-to. Eventually, in daylight and after a thorough assessment of the damage and our parlous engineering state, CO decided at 0950 to return to Rosyth. We'd reached Rattray Head, a few miles north of Peterhead. Our troubles weren't quite over. A generator tripped at 1015, resulting in limited power until it was fixed 30 minutes later.

I'd experienced a Force 11 crossing the Great Australian Bight on *Mandama* (8220 gross tons, 160m long, a beautiful reefer) in ballast en route to Timaru to load 4500 tons of frozen lamb carcasses. But she was a bigger ship and the storm pushed us along. In tiny *Gavinton*, it was a more frightening experience, with similar ambient noise as wind whistled through wires and masts, visibility reduced by wind-blown spray, gigantic green walls of water streaked white.

Back on watch with Alistair for the afternoon, conditions had eased a little to Force 8 or 9 and the wind backed to north-west, pushing us along a bit. We made about 11kts, hugging the Scottish coast until turning into the Firth of Forth. There, *Gavinton* was in the lee, wind speed dropped perceptibly but was still some 30kts. Sea state had decreased to 2 as, much relieved, we approached the Forth Bridges. It was 0045 when SSDs closed up, tug *Cairn* assisted our manoeuvring to secure starboard side to on *Bildeston*, bows north on Romeo (North) on Wednesday 23 January.

4.9 *Brinton* under Forth Rail Bridge
(Ton Class Association)

Gavinton wasn't in a fit state to return to sea until the physical damage, engineering assessment and repairs had been effected.

On Friday, long weekend leave was piped. I took the opportunity to head south to see my fiancée. It was a long plod by train. I arrived in

Eastbourne late that night. All too soon, I headed back up to Rosyth, my first experience of a sleeper train, arriving about 0600 in Edinburgh. After the short local train ride to Inverkeithing, I walked down to Rosyth's main gate and got on board before leave expired.

By the end of Monday, Bernie had arranged my transfer to *Brinton*. Rightly, he considered that I wouldn't gain any training value by remaining in *Gavinton* for her prolonged defect rectification. The necessary paperwork and approvals were obtained. *Brinton's* CO was happy to take me on. All I had to do was pack my kit and make my way to Faslane to join her for the passage back to Rosyth.

I headed across Scotland to join *Brinton* in Faslane on Tuesday 29 January 1985. Lt Simon Wall, *Brinton's* CO, made me most welcome. A smart, trim, blue-eyed chap with a crown of neat blond hair and boyish good looks, he was every inch a naval officer. He was probably one of the most junior COs in the Fleet, not much older than me. We chatted about my previous life and *Gavinton* experience. During my research for this book, I was very saddened to learn that, due to deteriorating eyesight, he had to leave the RN shortly after commanding *Brinton* and died in April 2009, aged only 51 or 52. Tragic. RIP, Simon.

4.10 Simon Wall on *Brinton's* port bridge wing
(Rob Hoole)

My new wardroom was Jonathan Cody (XO), Steve Hopper (NO) and Pete Fiddy (Guns). I shared XO's cabin, neat and tidy but bloody cold as he steadfastly refused to use the Pusser's black heater affixed to the bulkhead. XO showed me around. The 'Banana Boat' was basically identical to *Gavinton*. I was left to roam at will to familiarise myself with her in more detail, meeting many of her crew. Wednesday saw preps for departure, storeship and bunkers.

Brinton replaced her ship's badge on the for'ard screen with a large plastic Fyffe's banana. Being MCMVs, several *Tons* displayed a diver's helmet and/or a mine: *Bossington*, *Laleston* (as divers' training ship), *Maxton* originally had a standard mine and keys but changed to a mine clearance diver's (MCD's or bubblehead's) helmet and a decompression chamber when converted from a sweeper to a hunter. *Upton* had Hagar the Horrible with one foot on a mine.

Others had alcohol symbols: *Soberton's* Belhaven Bill, emblem of Belhaven Brewery; *Sheraton's* was the Sandeman Port Don, later changed to the Sheraton hotel 'S' and Sandeman was affixed to an internal bulkhead door; *Hubberston* had a Martini bottle (motto: 'Any mine, any place, anywhere').

Several more had seemingly unrelated symbols: *Lewiston's* greyhound; Polly the Parrot took pride of place in *Pollington*; *Iveston's* ivy leaf; *Bronington* had a shield with a cockerel; *Bildeston's* boot; *Crichton* displayed Robertson's Golly; *Gavinton* had a pair of boxing gloves (which I don't recall seeing), as she had several Scotland and Northern Ireland boxing champions among the ship's company. Finally, *Wilton*, the newest (built in 1972) and only fibreglass *Ton*, had a great motto: 'Tupperware blows yer mines'.

It was 0035 when SSDs was piped and *Brinton* slipped from No.3 berth at 0050. Five minutes later a faulty throttle control on the port engine forced a return to No.3 berth at 0120. Oh dear, a short-lived voyage. We remained alongside overnight while repairs were effected and finally slipped at 1215. *Brinton* transited from Gare Loch, into the Firth of Clyde, rounded the Mull of Kintyre and turned northwards, making a healthy 14kts. A 15kt south-west wind and sea state 4 pushed us along.

It was an uneventful passage to Rosyth, around the top of Scotland, through the Pentland Firth. This strait separates the Orkneys from the north coast of Scotland and is infamous for the strength of its tidal stream, reportedly up to 16kts. Its highly complex flow is difficult to predict due to its sensitivity to meteorological influences and strong tidal forces, resulting in overfalls and tidal races. Add gale-force winds and the result is extremely violent sea conditions. Hence its reputation as a graveyard for ships. Fortunately, our Pentland transit was benign.

I doubled up on dogs/morning watches with XO and got to know him better. A tall, skinny bloke, well-spoken, pleasant and with, most noticeable, Mr Spock-like ears. We berthed outboard of *Maxton* on P2 at Rosyth at 0720 on Saturday 2 February. *Brinton* remained alongside until Monday 11 February when we spent a week day-running in company with a couple of *Hunts* and other *Tons* conducting minehunting exercises and OOW manoeuvres, returning alongside nightly.

Ton-class were phased out by their replacement *Hunt*-class MCMVs from 1980 onwards. *Wilton*, the last *Ton*, was decommissioned in 1994. Interestingly, she was the first major warship in the world to be built of glass reinforced plastic (GRP or fibreglass), of which the *Hunts* were constructed. *Tons* gave distinguished service for over four decades and provided outstanding platforms to nurture OUTs like me and gave junior seaman officers great experience as GOs, NOs and especially COs.

I spent all day every day on the bridge, doubled up on watch or being useful wherever I could. I gained invaluable experience of minehunting, manoeuvring using the active rudders (ARs). These were a small propeller fitted to each of *Brinton's* twin rudders, powered by separate Foden Steering Engines. Controlled from the bridge, they enabled a minehunter to hover close to an MLO (mine-like object), stemming the tidal stream or going around it in small circles, to obtain a better sonar picture to aid classification of the contact.

Today's minehunters use bow thrusters and innovative propulsion systems for hovering capability and remotely operated vehicles (ROV) to take visual imagery to identify MLOs. If deemed a hazard, the ROV can return with a warhead to neutralise the contact. Nevertheless, there's still a role for bubbleheads when the water is excessively murky and touchy-feely is the best/only solution.

I also learnt much about OOW manoeuvres, with signals sent by flag hoists. It was thrilling to be in a quartet of MCMVs suddenly whizzing about the Firth of Forth, cutting through the sea, diesel engines at full throttle, as they manoeuvred into the signalled formation.

The following week was in Rosyth, various defects (OPDEFs) repaired and maintenance conducted. XO's cabin was bitterly cold overnight. Jonathan got up daily about 0600 for a run. As soon as he closed the door behind him, I leapt from the top bunk, switched on the black heater and climbed into my bunk under the duvet. The heater took the chill off the cabin. Jonathan switched it off immediately on his return. He was definitely a cold-weather beast. After a few days of this rigmarole, I detected he was a bit irritated about the heater. So, I got out of bed a bit earlier to switch the heater off before he got back. He seemed happy with this compromise. I was conscious of being a 'house guest'.

The following week began with CCF Day, at sea with groups of CCF cadets in *Brinton, Cottesmore, Dulverton* and *Bildeston*, plus *Abdiel*. Minesweeping drills showed the cadets how we conducted our business, including a live mine disposal weapon (MDW) firing. MDW was a demolition charge attached by a bubblehead to an MLO or live mine and detonated to destroy it. We did a search and rescue (SAR) exercise with an RAF Wessex 4 helicopter. Another very busy day on the bridge ended alongside *Maxton* at P1.

4.11 *Abdiel*
(Ton Class Association)

Although designated an exercise minelayer, *Abdiel's* prime role was training RN personnel in minelaying operations and acting as a support/headquarters ship for MCM operations. She was capable of laying offensive mines during wartime, although British government policy since the mid-1960s opposed UK use of sea and land mines. Built by Thornycroft, *Abdiel* was launched and commissioned in 1967. At 1460 tons fully laden, she was 81m long, 11.73m beam and 3m draught, powered by a pair of Paxman Ventura diesel engines driving twin shafts to a maximum speed of 16kts. Her complement was 98 and she was armed with a Bofors 40/60 gun and 44 naval mines. She was decommissioned in 1988.

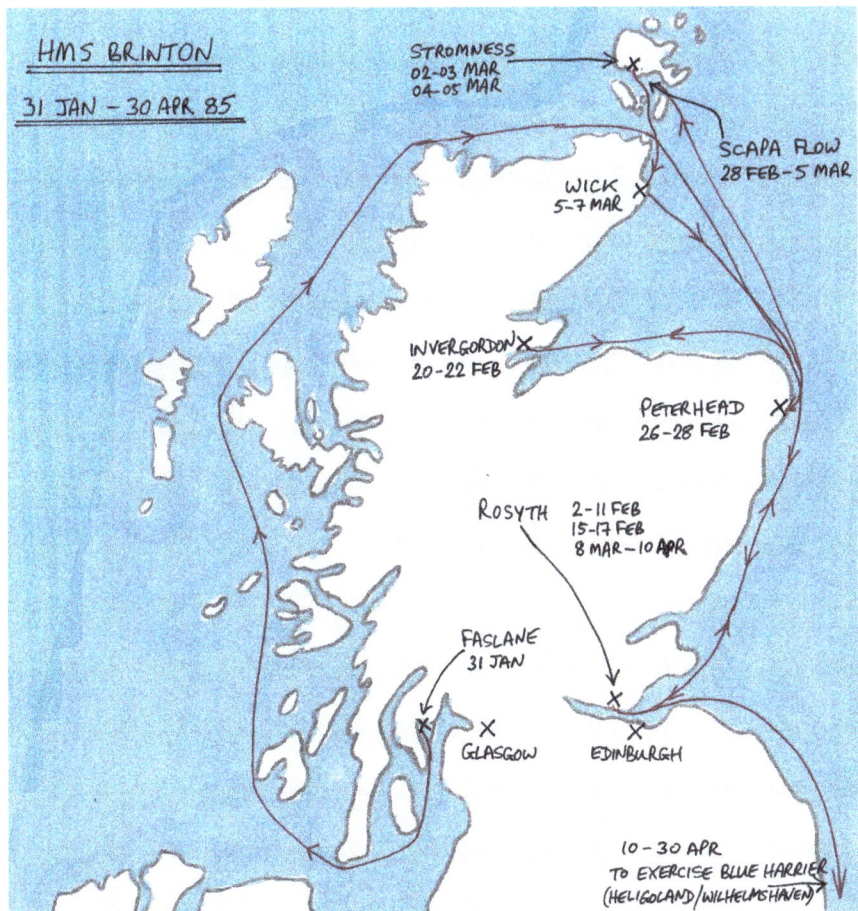

4.12 *Brinton's* voyages

Brinton and *Abdiel* sailed the next day, 19 February. Another busy day with a light-line transfer in the forenoon and fire exercises in the afternoon, including a funnel fire, perhaps the most catastrophic of potential fires in a *Ton*. I was now on forenoon/first. That night was my first solo watch, keeping station on *Abdiel* as we headed north towards Invergordon.

Wednesday forenoon began and ended with MBDD. Sandwiched between, the splash target was streamed for RAF Buccaneers to bomb while our 40/60 engaged them with break-up ammo. Post-lunch was action stations and a full NBCDX, after which *Brinton* headed into Invergordon and secured alongside *Abdiel* overnight. I'd experienced countless serials during my DTS cruise in *Fearless* but we OUTs were very much uninvolved. Here, I had an integral role in the ship's company.

The Invergordon Mutiny took place on 15 September 1931. Ten warships of the Atlantic Fleet, including the flagship *Hood*, arrived in Invergordon on 11 September. Officers and crew read newspapers containing reports of pay cuts as part of the government's sweeping austerity drive. Word spread among the sailors. That fateful morning, ships' companies refused orders. By midday, mobs of sailors gathered on fo'c'sles for boisterous speeches and sang songs, including the communist anthem *The Red Flag*. Several crews refused to put to sea for routine exercises.

The Mutiny had no casualties and lasted less than two days. But the British public were shocked at a mutiny in the RN. News reached London, the Stock Exchange went into meltdown, markets plummeted, there was a run on the pound and, days later, the government decided to leave the gold standard. The Invergordon Mutiny was viewed as a 'near miss' and a reminder of the real possibility of a communist uprising in Britain, a genuine fear from the inter-war years.

In summarising the mutiny, Rear Admiral Tomkinson (temporary commander of the Atlantic Fleet) reported that sailors remained respectful to their officers throughout, who had done their best to explain the government's reasons for the pay cut and complaints were taken seriously. He concluded that the mutiny was caused primarily by the 25% pay cut for junior ratings who had joined the service before 1925. There were no other grievances. Tomkinson believed their complaint was well founded and considered that use of force would have exacerbated the situation. The Cabinet accepted his conclusions but emphasised that further acts of mutiny would be severely punished.

We remained alongside the next day, a hot move to the other side of Admiralty Jetty and *Bildeston* secured outboard of us late forenoon. Later, we were soundly thrashed 9–2 by *Abdiel* at football. Doubled-up as OOD, I led evening rounds, mustered the OOD's safe and recorded in the Ship's Log that I'd 'sighted two pistols' (Very flare pistols and white, green and red flare cartridges in a locked cabinet on the bridge), repeated during middle watch rounds at 0100.

On Friday, we departed Invergordon with *Bildeston*. Both ships did MOBEXs for a half-hour. CO let MEO, Cox'n, Navigator's Yeoman (Nav's

Yeo) and me each do a MOBEX. I enjoyed 'driving' a small ship around to rescue the MOB dummy. Not a bad first effort, but definitely room for improvement.

In mid-afternoon, *Brinton* laid a danbuoy, used as the reference point for our minehunting. At 1600, we went to minehunting stations. The crew split into port and starboard watches, closed up for six hours on, six hours off. I was starboard watch as OOW with XO in the ops room, 1800 to 0001 and 0600 to 1200. Steve (bridge) and Pete (ops room) were port watch. All hands camped on 1 Deck to minimise noise and maximise crew safety in case we inadvertently detonated a mine. With ARs engaged, main engines at five minutes notice, we conducted a route survey off the north shore of Moray and Aberdeenshire over the next 36 hours. Alongside *Abdiel* on Peterhead's north wall by 1300 on Sunday 24 February, *Bildeston* berthed outboard soon after. She sailed six hours later to resume her route survey.

Peterhead is at the easternmost point of mainland Scotland and is the UK's biggest fishing port for total landings by UK vessels. Much of the port was constructed between 1818 and 1822 by famous Scottish builders John Rennie and Thomas Telford, notably the North Harbour and dry dock.

Three of Peterhead's four lighthouses were built by Stevensons. Buchan Ness (1827) and South Breakwater (1833) by Robert. His son Thomas built Harbour South in 1849 and was Robert Louis Stevenson's father. The fourth lighthouse, Harbour North was built in 1908.

Our brief respite in Peterhead ended when we sailed at 0830 on Monday morning. We continued our route survey for the day and overnight, berthing outboard of *Bildeston* at Peterhead again late afternoon, Tuesday 26 February.

Wednesday was spent leisurely in Peterhead. We lost 8–4 to *Abdiel* at rugby. After sailing on Thursday morning, *Brinton* embarked some RAF personnel and set off for the open sea where a helo transfer of the RAF folks took place. It was interesting to observe this from the bridge. The winching was from the sweep deck but the distance from there to the bridge meant the helo was almost directly atop the entire ship. The helo was incredibly loud and we felt the wash from its rotors. XO was Flight Deck Officer (FDO), clad in white boilersuit, yellow surcoat, earmuffs and red and green bats in hand to do his signalling stuff.

From there, *Brinton* continued north and anchored off Hoy Sound lighthouse, adjacent to Scapa Flow, at 2210 that night. During the middle, we weighed anchor, switched to 'ops control', flashed up the ARs and commenced minehunting for the day. Despite occasional defects on the

ARs (loss of oil pressure), minehunting in Scapa Flow continued overnight and into Saturday. At 1710, we berthed outboard of *Bildeston* in Stromness.

I enjoyed the responsibility as OOW during minehunting. Under 'ops control', XO directed *Brinton's* course and speed, but I retained charge of the ship, keeping her safe navigationally and monitoring other shipping movements in Scapa Flow. I found it easy to slip into the 6-on, 6-off routine. Weather conditions were kind: sea state 2, light easterly winds.

The RN required all its warships to maintain a daily record of events and incidents in the Ship's Log, similar to a merchantman's Deck Log. Our Ship's Log inevitably contained more detail because we did exercises continually and frequently anchored for brief periods, whereas a cargo ship steamed uninterrupted between ports and sped across oceans.

A Ship's Log front pages had detailed instructions on content to be included, plus useful tables and codes for Beaufort wind scale, sea state and visibility. The OOW noted hourly in each column on the left-hand page: log reading; speed; course (true, 'A' gyro, 'B' gyro, magnetic); variation; wind speed and direction; sea state; and visibility.

SEA STATE CODE				VISIBILITY CODE		
Code Figure	Descriptive terms	Height* Metres	Feet (approx.)	Code Figure	Yards/ Nautical Miles	Kilome
0	Calm (glassy)	0	0	90	<55 yd	<0·
1	Calm (rippled)	0–0·1	0–¼	91	55 yd	0·
2	Smooth (wavelets)	0·1–0·5	¼–2	92	220 yd	0·
3	Slight	0·5–1·25	2–4	93	550 yd	0·
4	Moderate	1·25–2·5	4–8	94	1100 yd	1
5	Rough	2·5–4	8–13	95	1·1 n m	2
6	Very rough	4–6	13–20	96	2·2 n m	4
7	High	6–9	20–30	97	5·5 n m	10
8	Very high	9–14	30–45	98	11 n m	20
9	Phenomenal	Over 14	Over 45	99	>27 n m	>50

* The average wave height as obtained from the larger well-formed waves of the wave system being observed.

NOTE.—If the visibility lies between two of the distances in the table, the code figure for the lower distance is rec

NOTE.—An exact upper height is to be assigned to the lower figure; e.g. a height of 4 metres is coded as 5.

4.13 Ship's Log sea state and visibility codes
(National Archive, Kew)

On the opposite page, events per watch were written (with a four-figure time): course/speed changes; exercises (start and end); boats lowered and hoisted; anchoring/weighing; SSDs; tugs secured/let go; change of machinery state; plus myriad details too numerous to mention. The final column was for OOW's initials. I was struck by emotional nostalgia at seeing my own initials as OOW in my ships' logs during my day's research at National Archive, Kew.

I felt like I was living in *The Cruel Sea*, a white coastal forces roll-neck jumper replaced the standard woolly-pully. This feeling was emphasised when contacting the CO. To call him, I pulled the stopper from my end of the brass voice-pipe and bellowed 'Captain, Sir, Officer-of-the-Watch'. My ear to the voice-pipe, I waited for his response, then made my report. Usually, he'd 'Roger' and tell me to carry on. Stirring stuff!

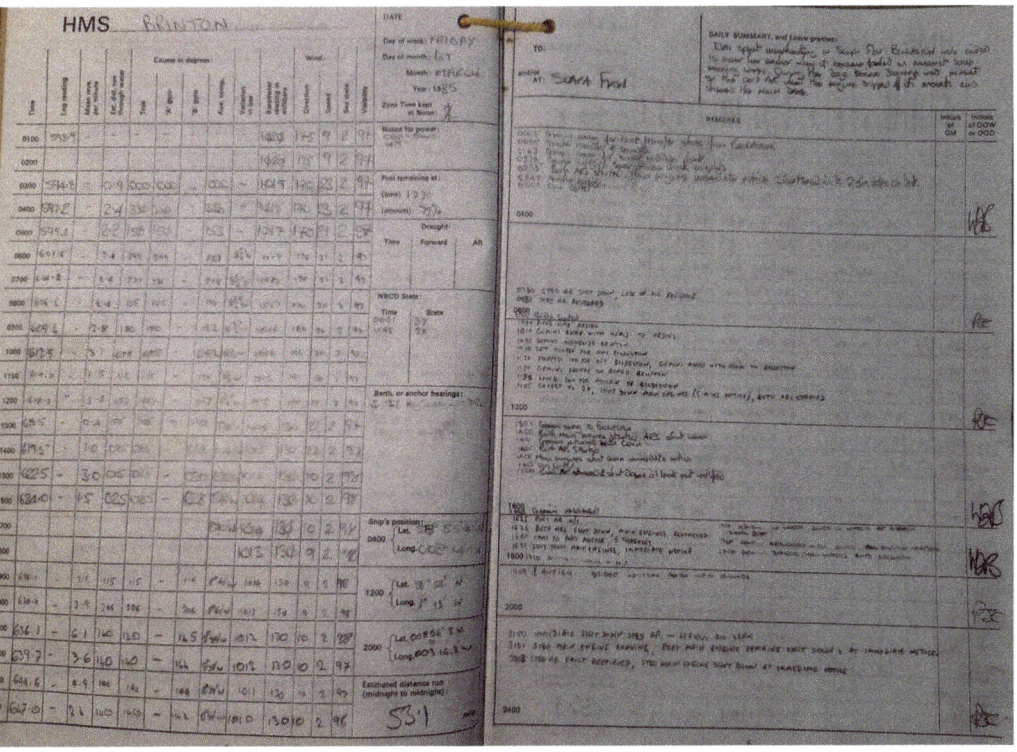

4.14 A typical day's minehunting in Scapa Flow
(National Archive, Kew)

The following day, route surveys continued until we berthed outboard of *Abdiel* in Stromness at 2317. After a few hours respite, another long day's route survey followed, returning to Stromness. We set off again later that night to complete the route survey before leaving Scapa Flow to arrive at Wick with *Bildeston* early forenoon on Tuesday 5 March. Both ships remained alongside on Wednesday and played a rough game of rugby, which *Brinton* won 14–10. There were some sore bodies after that, anaesthetised by post-match beer.

Wick straddled the River Wick, derived from Norse 'vík' meaning bay, and belonged to Norway until the mid-13th century. Not much else occurred in Wick until the 19th century when herring fishing took off, leading to the building of the harbour in 1803–1811. Wick became a bustling harbour with ships from Orkney, Scotland, Wales, Shetland and the Isle of Man. With the rise in fisheries, the town's size increased and eclipsed Thurso as the centre of shipping and trade in Caithness.

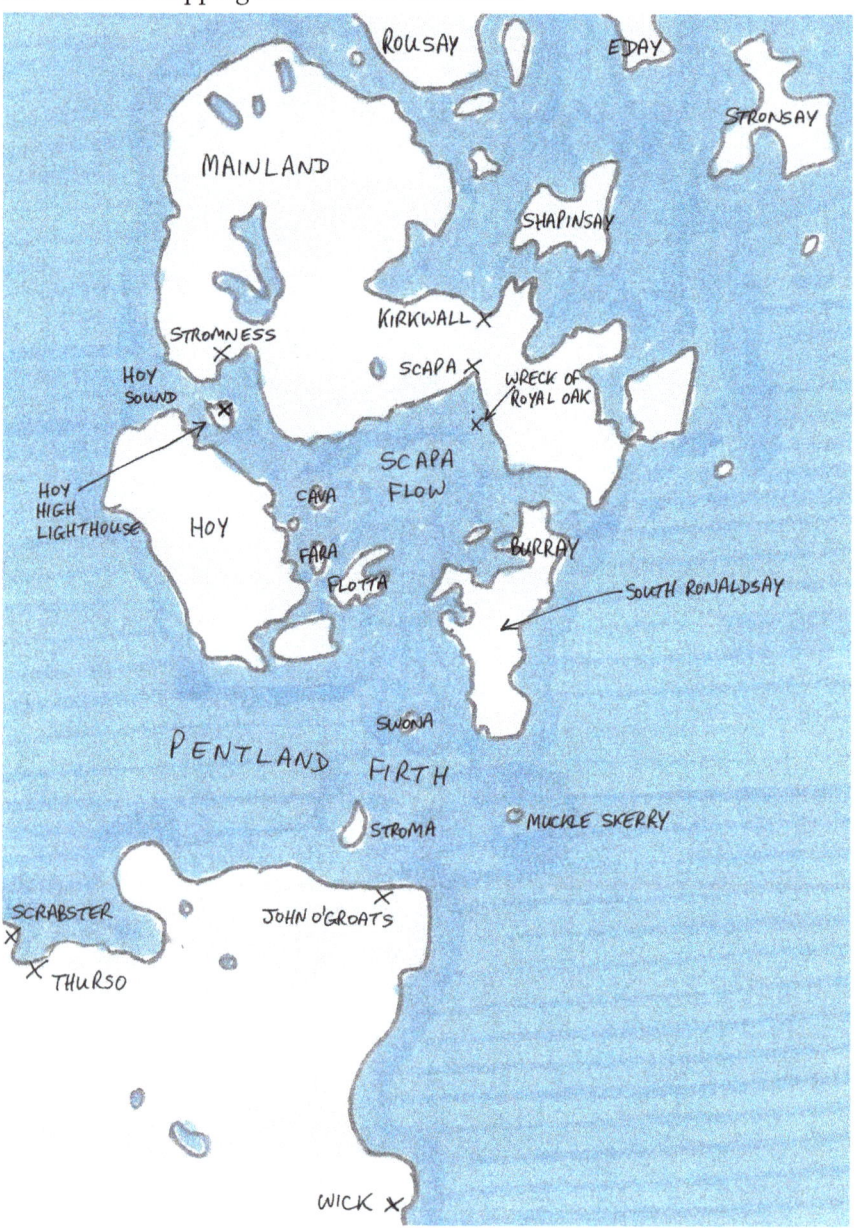

4.15 Scapa Flow

In 1939, Wick's airfield became an RAF base. It was improved with hard runways and hangars to become one of 14 airfields from Iceland to North Yorkshire administered by No. 18 Group, RAF Coastal Command, headquartered at Pitreavie. Sorties engaged in reconnaissance, anti-submarine patrols, convoy escort, defence of Scapa Flow and strikes against the Germans in Norway and Norwegian waters. The German occupation of Norway left Wick more vulnerable. It was bombed six times and the first daytime bombing of the UK caused 15 dead and several shops and houses destroyed or damaged.

On Thursday, *Brinton* returned briefly to Scapa Flow for diving ops before heading to Rosyth, where we berthed outboard of *Walkerton* on P4, mid-afternoon Friday 8 March. *Brinton* remained alongside at Rosyth for a maintenance period and Easter leave, which ended on 9 April.

We sailed with *Abdiel*, *Sheraton* and *Kellington* the next day. After several exercises together and NBCDX in the Forth EXAs, we headed south-east across the North Sea to participate in Exercise Blue Harrier, an annual NATO MCM exercise, mostly focused on minehunting. The multinational MCMVs were tasked to hunt pre-laid exercise mines.

OOW manoeuvres and TOWEX took place on Thursday morning but the afternoon's serials were cancelled as sea state had gradually increased from 3 to 5 with a south-easterly 30kt wind. I enjoyed spending all the daylight hours on the bridge, gaining more experience in routine exercises carried out by warships at sea. My trusted presence allowed the OOW to focus on the unfolding serial, while I monitored navigation, kept lookout and filled in the log.

Overnight, clocks were advanced an hour to European time. On Friday we arrived off Heligoland. This small archipelago in the German Bight is part of Schleswig-Holstein on mainland Germany and lies about 70km from Cuxhaven, at the Elbe's mouth. That afternoon, we laid a danbuoy 10km north of the islands, then laid and detonated a live MDW. There was quite a spectacular shaking of the sea surface and eruption of a large plume of water and spray as we stood off at the designated safe distance.

Sheraton and *Brinton* did OOW manoeuvres before entering Heligoland's small harbour. We berthed outboard of *Sheraton*. Heligoland was British until the late-19th century, when Queen Victoria exchanged it for Zanzibar with Kaiser Wilhelm II. It was hardly Jack's run ashore, but it was duty-free so at least booze was available.

Saturday was a full day, kicked off with OOW manoeuvres. Danbuoy laid, then double Oropesa minesweeping exercises with *Sheraton* and

Kellington. We were alongside in Heligoland at 1822, starboard side to on *Kellington* with *Sheraton* outboard of *Brinton*. Sunday formed a similar pattern, OOW manoeuvres followed by an armed team sweep with our accompanying *Tons*. MCM3 embarked in *Brinton*, leaving his 'flagship' *Abdiel* for the day.

On 15 April, the *Tons* followed *Abdiel* out of Heligoland in thick fog. According to the log, visibility was only 50m and persisted for the short passage across the German Bight's busy shipping routes. We managed a safe speed of about 7kts but it was a proper 'pea-souper'. Lookouts for'ard and aft listened acutely for merchantmen's fog horns, traversing to/from Hamburg. It was a relief to get alongside the German naval base, Wilhelmshaven at 1550, outboard of *Sheraton*.

The naval base brimmed with warships. It was home to the then Bundesmarine's destroyer squadrons and auxiliary ships, now joined by MCMVs from Germany, Belgium and the UK for Exercise Blue Harrier. Uniquely, the Bundesmarine's five Type 352 *Ensdorf*-class minesweepers used the Troika Plus MCM system. One part of this was a single Type 352, controlling up to four remote-controlled Seehund (in English, Seal) drone boats. The Seehunds simulated acoustic and magnetic signatures of large warships to trigger mines. The drones' small size and special construction helped them survive the effects of exploding mines. At 25m long and displacing 99 tons, they were too large to be carried on board an *Ensdorf* minesweeper so they were manned when manoeuvring in harbour.

During the couple of days alongside at Wilhelmshaven there were exercise briefings for COs and XOs, while the ship's company were employed on deck and had night leave each day. I don't recall anything about Wilhelmshaven or what I did in the evenings. I know the gin pennant was hoisted that first evening and the wardroom was full of officers from our *Tons* and *Abdiel*.

I was OOD on 17 April, ready for departure at lunchtime the next day. The MCMVs sailed in formation. The weather was cold, with light airs and a thick fog reduced visibility to about 400m. Blind pilotage was used for the exit and we cleared the channel at 1730. Slipping into ops control, *Kellington* led *Brinton* to the start of the route survey and flashed up the ARs.

Minehunting continued overnight, throughout Friday and into Saturday. Fog persisted and thickened in the afternoon, reducing visibility to 50m before it slowly improved to a few kilometres. The bridge was quite eerie at times, in silence, fog swirling around, listening for other ships' fog signals, keeping a sharp visual lookout and monitoring the radar. Our minehunting yielded a couple of MLOs. One was identified as a World War II sinker. Alas, a strong tidal stream prevented accurate classification of the second contact.

4.16 'Banana boat'
(Ton Class Association)

The fog cleared on Saturday, replaced by a westerly wind which increased to a Force 8 gale and sea state 6. *Brinton* waited in a patrol box until wind and sea state abated, whereupon we headed into Heligoland and berthed outboard of *Abdiel* around 0100 on Sunday. Ships dressed overall for the Queen's birthday and we lost 4–2 at football against *Abdiel*. We sailed at 0515 on Monday and resumed minehunting along QZR 321, north of Heligoland. By Tuesday, we were on QZR 261, off the west Danish coast. At 0800, the wind veered to east-north-east and increased to a lively Force 7, sea state 5, but eased to a more comfortable Force 5, sea state 3 about 12 hours later.

We continued the route survey on Wednesday and into Thursday when, that afternoon, we went alongside *Abdiel* at Heligoland for a well-deserved overnight stand-off. Off we went again on Friday morning, minehunting along another route all day and overnight. Weather deteriorated as the westerly wind increased again to 45kts, sea state 7. Minehunting was abandoned and we maintained station on *Kellington* as conditions very slowly eased overnight and during Sunday morning. At 1440, Exercise Blue Harrier 85 concluded and, with *Kellington* and *Sheraton*, we headed into Wilhelmshaven, getting alongside during the dogs.

The next day was given over to exercise debriefings, involving COs, XOs and the exercise directing staff ashore in the headquarters building. On our final day in Wilhelmshaven we prepped for departure and, in the afternoon, a cold move onto *Sheraton* and a 1–0 victory over *Sheraton* at football.

The *Tons* and *Abdiel* departed Wilhelmshaven on Wednesday 1 May and enjoyed a leisurely passage back to Rosyth, where I left *Brinton*, my fleet time in *Tons* completed.

Overall, I'd had a great time in *Gavinton* and *Brinton*. I'd learned so much, consciously and subconsciously. Stuff embedded in my brain and memory through repetition of serials like OOW manoeuvres and MOBEX. I appreciated the complexity and dangers of minesweeping, taut wires and heavy bits of kit streamed and recovered. My bridge watches were excellent, honing my previous MN experience in the now familiar 'small ships' environment. It was odd to be OOW yet under the control of XO in his cramped ops room a couple of decks below during minehunting, as he monitored the sweep of the hull-mounted sonar to detect MLOs.

Tons' ship's companies were definitely different from their 'big ship' counterparts. It was more intimate, cosy and friendly in a 'small ship' of 30-odd blokes compared to my *Fearless* experience of 500+ souls. Muppets (mine warfare specialists) and bubbleheads (clearance divers) were a rough-and-ready, down-to-earth, but competent and professional crowd in their own world.

4. A Bleak Midwinter in Rosyth

I'd become fond of *Tons*. They were great little ships with decades of illustrious service as MCM and fishery protection workhorses. Their wooden construction, ancient bridge equipment, pungent smell of diesel that perpetually pervaded the accommodation via the aft door were typical features. The novelty of lying in my top bunk, the ship pitching and rolling, cold drips of water seeping through the deckhead and splashing my face, disturbing my slumber. I lived in a bygone era on the bridge, braced against the ship's heavy rolling and pitching, clad in off-white Coastal Forces roll-neck sweater, clutching a steaming mug of kai (cocoa), communicating with the Captain via voice-pipe. Brilliant!

En route from *Brinton* to *Exeter* for the second half of my fleet time, I went on a familiarisation course at Royal Naval Air Station (RNAS) Yeovilton.

On passing out from BRNC, we were issued with a Task Book, a blue, A4, four-ring folder, crammed with a myriad tasks to achieve during fleet time. It wasn't just a multitude of simple tick-off sheets, but a crucial learning tool, supplemented with our own notes and diagrams. It was our prime revision aid in preparing for Fleetboard examinations at year's end.

The tasks were divided into three types – mandatory (pink sheets), good to do (blue), useful extras (yellow) – covering each department on board a warship. Like my Seaman Officer peers, I'd signed off as many as practicable during my time in MCMVs, but it was impossible to make meaningful headway on warfare, S&S, WE, ME and NBCD tasks.

A couple of mandatory tasks were the Junior Officers' Air Acquaint Course (JOAAC) and the submarine equivalent Junior Officers' Submarine Acquaint Course (JOSMAC). I managed to avoid the latter. I was terrified of being confined in a black tube, deep underwater. The mere thought made me quake with fear in my steaming boots. I'd crossed the Atlantic, Indian and Pacific Oceans many times with Blue Star, but I never liked being out of my depth in water. As for being a submariner and the escape tower training … forget it! JOAAC sounded great fun, learning about planes, helos, flying in general and what WAFUs (Wet And F***ing Useless, as FAA personnel were described) actually did.

There were several old chums from Dartmouth on the course. Classroom 'stuff' during the day and evenings in Royal Naval Air Station (RNAS) Yeovilton's wardroom bar. We enjoyed flights in different types of FAA helos, but my best memory was flying in a Hawker Hunter. The afternoon before, we had ejection seat training. A CPO gathered us around an ejection seat, described its component parts and how it worked. He demonstrated how to sit in it and strap yourself in.

Importantly, he went through the ejection sequence. If the pilot deemed it necessary, he'd shout 'Eject, eject, eject' through the headset. Ensuring elbows and knees were tightly tucked in, pull the toggle (from either between your legs or the headrest), and the seat did the rest. Rocket-propelled from the cockpit, the seat launched you into the sky, its parachute opened and you gently floated to earth. Easy!

The next morning, the class gathered and suited up in flying overalls and bone-domes. We met our respective pilot and off we went. At that time, Airwork Services had the contract to operate Fleet Requirements and Air Direction Unit, providing a variety of services to FAA. They operated Hawker Hunter jets and other aircraft. Their employees were retired old-and-bold FAA or RAF pilots who enjoyed nothing more than whizzing around the skies, reliving their good old days in uniform. I'm sure they particularly enjoyed flying Russian missile profiles to 'attack' warships leaving Portland Naval Base during the 'Thursday War'. This was a tense event wherein warships (British and foreign) undergoing operational sea training (OST) departed in formation at action stations, navigated through imaginary narrow channels bounded by minefields whilst being attacked by Soviet missiles and aircraft (Airwork Services' Hunters).

To get an idea of the Hunter, watch *The Black Arrows*, a 1960 episode of the famous *Look at Life* short film documentaries. RAF 111 Squadron flew Hunters and performed aerobatic displays as Black Arrows from 1955 to 1960, a predecessor of today's Red Arrows.

My pilot (I don't recall his name, so I'll call him Jock) was an ex-FAA, 50-odd year-old Scotsman with a gentle, comprehensible accent. As we walked to the Hunter, we chatted about this-and-that. I climbed into the cockpit and strapped myself into the right hand seat. Jock did likewise in the left seat. The Hunter two-seat trainer had twin seats rather than tandem. I could see everything he was doing. Fascinating!

The cockpit canopy closed, Jock taxied to the runway and awaited clearance for take-off. He asked about ejection seat training. I rehashed the procedure. Despite his face-mask and bone-dome, I detected a creased smile on his face. 'All good', he calmly said, 'but if we have to eject, you'll hear "Eject, eject", but you won't hear the third "eject" 'cos I'll be gone.' Hmmm, I thought.

We raced down the runway, soared into the air and climbed quickly to umpteen thousand feet. In the cockpit, there was ambient noise from the jet engines, plus a bit of whistling wind and crackling on the radio/intercom. Outside, we were in the wide blue yonder, among the clouds, the Somerset countryside far below. It was a different experience to a commercial aircraft, squinting through a tiny window. Here, my view was unobstructed. We whizzed around and Jock pointed out a little black dot in the distance. I could barely see it, despite my perfect seaman's eyesight. The dot enlarged and was another Hunter.

4.17 Top Gun ready for his flight

I don't know my flight's duration (an hour?) but it was an exhilarating, unforgettable experience. Jock even let me take the controls for a couple of minutes. We landed, taxied off the runway and parked. After climbing from the Hunter, I thanked Jock for the ride and walked to the office to return my flying overalls and bone-dome. There was a course debrief before we departed Yeovilton.

The following week, I joined *Exeter* in Pompey.

5.

Armilla Patrol – Up the Gulf

5.1 *Exeter* crest
(Nick Barwis, www.jackstaxi.net)

5.2 *Exeter*
(Michael W Pocock, www.MaritimeQuest.com)

After JOAAC, I joined *Exeter* in Pompey, for my 'big ship' fleet time experience. Fortunately, she was deploying to the Persian Gulf for six months. Glorious!

A Batch 2 Type 42 destroyer, *Exeter* was laid down at Swan Hunter, Tyne and Wear, on 22 July 1976, launched on 25 April 1978 and commissioned 19 September 1980. She was 125m long, 14.3m in the beam and displaced 4820 tonnes. Her twin Rolls Royce Tyne and twin Rolls Royce Olympus marinised gas turbines drove twin shafts, each with a five-bladed controllable pitch propeller. Tynes for cruising, Olympuses for sprints of nearly 30kts. Any combination of these four engines was available, depending on the task. *Exeter* was a Falklands War veteran, her Sea Dart missiles had shot down three Argentine aircraft.

The RN's 14 Type 42s were guided missile destroyers to provide fleet area air defence. The main armament was a twin-launcher Sea Dart surface-to-air missile and a 4.5" gun on the fo'c'sle. On each side were a Phalanx close-in weapon system (CIWS) gun and a triple ships torpedo weapon system (STWS) torpedo launcher. Sensors were a Type 1022 long-range radar, Type 996 target identification radar and two Type 909 fire-control radars to control the Sea Dart and 4.5" gun. Type 2016 and Type 192 sonars were used for search and sea bottom profiling, respectively. To detect, deter, spoof and jam the enemy, an electronic warfare suite and decoy system were fitted.

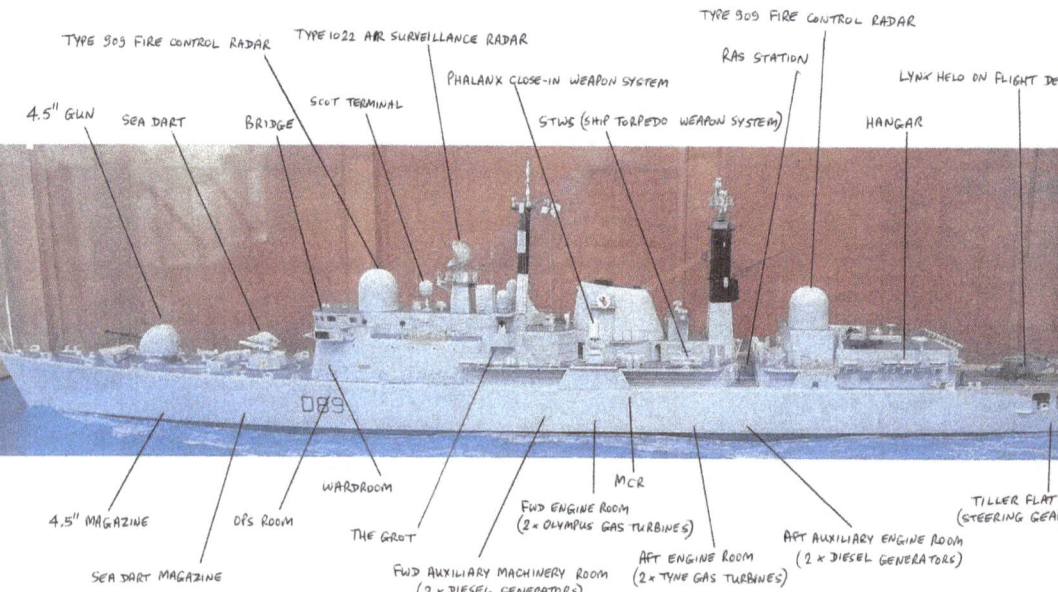

5.3 *Exeter's* main features

5. Armilla Patrol – Up the Gulf

Lastly, a Lynx helo was embarked, capable of using anti-ship missiles and anti-submarine torpedoes. It was housed in the hangar and operated from the flight deck. To handle all this 'stuff' and victual everyone, ship's company was 287 officers and ratings.

Exeter had completed mandatory OST at Portland during March and returned to Pompey in time for Easter leave. Final preps were underway for our deployment.

There were four OUTs: me, Neil Hunter, Kieran Nash and Max Rance. Neil was a fellow graduate entrant, a term behind me. Kieran, an Irishman with a distinctive broken nose, was a fellow SL. We were Seaman Officers. Max was a GL Pusser. The Grot (our cabin) was on 01 Deck, right aft on the port side. Immediately on its right were top and bottom bunks for Kieran and Max, with their built-in off-yellow metal drawers, wardrobe and fold-down desktop opposite. Beyond their partition was my and Neil's space with the same configuration and the added bonus of a tiny scuttle giving us limited natural light. The Grot was equipped with a couple of washbasins but shared heads and showers were down the alleyway.

The Grot was cramped, about half the size of my cabin on each of my merchantmen, where I had en suite facilities. Fortunately, Neil, Kieran, Max and I got on famously. The Grot was permanently filled with fun and laughter. We seemed popular with younger members of the wardroom as we always had a visitor or two. If any of us felt down during the deployment, the ghetto blaster went on full volume and we exploded into dance to lift our spirits before the working day began.

Our Training Officer was Lt Cdr Lloyd Bridgewater, a Principal Warfare Officer (PWO) air defence specialist. He had a rather scruffy beard and thinning hair and seemed a decent bloke. He explained our training regime. We'd split up and rotate through every department on board. Neil, Kieran and I would also spend much time on the bridge as 2nd OOW, while Max was involved in Supply's sub-specialisations (writers (clerks), caterers, stores, chefs, stewards). The onus was on each of us to complete as much of our task book as possible.

Lloyd attached each one of us to a division of sailors so we'd learn how to be divisional officers (DO), viewed by the RN as an officer's most important role, The DO had responsibility for the welfare, development, advancement and discipline of their sailors. I was assigned to the gunners, operations seamen who directed and fired guns and missiles. Their DO was Lt Cdr Chris Durbin, a surface warfare PWO. He was a neat, stocky, likeable fellow, from whom I'd learn much about divisional work.

We had a chat with XO Lt Cdr Jerry Parker. He was lively, silver-haired, with a booming voice when required. He had a grip on the ship and everyone in it. He commanded respect and was popular with the sailors. He dovetailed nicely with our Captain, John Tolhurst, an air warfare specialist who'd previously commanded the frigate *Berwick*. After a succession of posts, he took command of *Exeter* in 1984, one of five Type 42s of the 5th Destroyer Squadron. Captain Tolhurst was a tall, barrel-chested man of good bearing, articulate with an excellent power of command, invariably cool, calm and unruffled. A captain I instantly respected and admired.

On the bridge, Neil, Kieran and I interacted with the OOWs. Lt Neil Farrer was an efficient, effective OOW. S/Lt Jon Cox was in his first OOW job as an SD bubblehead seaman officer and was learning the ropes, under close guidance from Lt Simon Gillespie, our NO. Simon was a hard taskmaster on the bridge. We became closest to S/Lt 'Banjo' West, OOW and Fighter Controller. Banjo took to us easily and always got a warm welcome when visiting the Grot. He was calm, confident and in control on the bridge and in the ops room.

These were the main 'players', but the supporting cast of officers and sailors were equally important and I learned much from them during this deployment. Ashamedly, I don't recall any of the sailors, except PO Meyer, my Divisional Senior Rate who gave me nuggets of advice about sailors.

At last, we sailed from Pompey on Tuesday 28 May 1985 for a few days' shakedown exercises and trials. We wended our way down harbour and passed through the narrows between Fort Blockhouse to starboard and Old Portsmouth to port. In The Solent, we moored at No.3 buoy for a compass swing, after which we headed south-west to pass The Needles and onwards to Portland. I recognised my neat handwriting in the Ship's Log during the first watch (2000 to 0001) as Jon Cox's 2nd OOW.

Wednesday and Thursday were full on, with many serials and exercises. MBDD, MOBEX, steering gear breakdown, flying serials and electronic warfare calibrations filled both days into the evenings. At 0030 on Friday morning, we anchored at Spithead, 8½ cables (1.5km) off Fort Gilkicker – my parents' house was a further kilometre inland. More trials and serials took place before berthing on North Wall at 1430 for weekend leave.

Exeter sailed on Monday 3 June for a week of shakedown exercises off Pompey and Portland, returning to overnight either in Pompey or anchored off Portland. Our Lynx embarked so we frequently went to Flying Stations to allow Andy Greenall (pilot) and Mike Seward (observer) to complete flying serials.

5. Armilla Patrol – Up the Gulf

I had my first experiences of replenishment at sea (RAS) on the bridge as Captain Tolhurst made his approaches to Royal Fleet Auxiliary (RFA) ships *Grey Rover* and *Regent*. RAS allowed a warship to resupply with fuel, ammunition and stores. Sometimes the helo was used for vertical replenishment (VERTREP), flitting between ships to transfer personnel or mail. NATO's standardised RAS fittings meant any member nation's warship can be replenished by any other member's tanker/supply ship. Such specialist ships were capable of RAS'ing three warships simultaneously: port, starboard and astern.

RAS'ing was fraught with potential disaster as *Exeter* closed the RFA tanker until alongside about 30m off. *Exeter's* RAS station sounded three short whistle blasts to warn the RFA's crew before the dildo (a yellow and orange projectile) and attached gunline was fired across to the tanker by SLR. Provided our gunline was successfully captured, our RAS station blew the all-clear whistle signal. The RFA deck crew tied the gunline's end to a heavier line which was hauled back across to *Exeter*, bringing with it the fuel line and its probe. The probe clunked securely into its housing and refuelling began.

During a RAS, the RFA maintained her course and speed, the warship continually adjusted its course and speed to maintain station. A distance line rigged on the fo'c'sle allowed Captain Tolhurst to monitor our distance off. Concentration was required throughout the procedure. With refuelling complete, tanker hauled back the probe. *Exeter* recovered the distance line and executed the breakaway manoeuvre.

I was excited and tense witnessing RAS from the bridge, observing the close teamwork required within the bridge team, particularly between Captain, QM (helmsman) and stoker on the engine controls. Close communication was also necessary between the bridge and our RAS station, about 50m abaft the bridge. So Captain Tolhurst focused ahead but needed eyes in the back of his head to 'see' the action at the RAS station. No matter the conditions, the Captain remained cool and calm throughout. His firm, confident helm and engine orders cut through the general silence on the bridge. What a man – my hero!

By Friday, we were southbound to start our deployment. Exercises continued at a relentless pace. Added to the routine exercises I'd previously experienced, there was a focus on warfare: air defence; surface warfare; gunnery; electronic warfare; communications; and flying. We rendezvoused with *Charybdis* and RFA *Bayleaf*, our companions for Armilla Patrol, the RN's permanent presence in the Persian Gulf during the 1980s and 1990s.

The UK had withdrawn forces from the Persian Gulf in 1971 as part of its retreat from 'East of Suez'. The exotic appointments of Flag Officer Middle East and Senior Naval Officer, Persian Gulf, disappeared forever. Tensions in the Gulf remained high, so RN warships maintained a regular presence. The threat to British shipping and other interests increased when the Iran–Iraq war broke out in 1980. *Coventry* (Type 42 destroyer) was dispatched to the region and Armilla Patrol was born. Of six months duration, it typically comprised two warships (a frigate and a destroyer) with an RFA tanker.

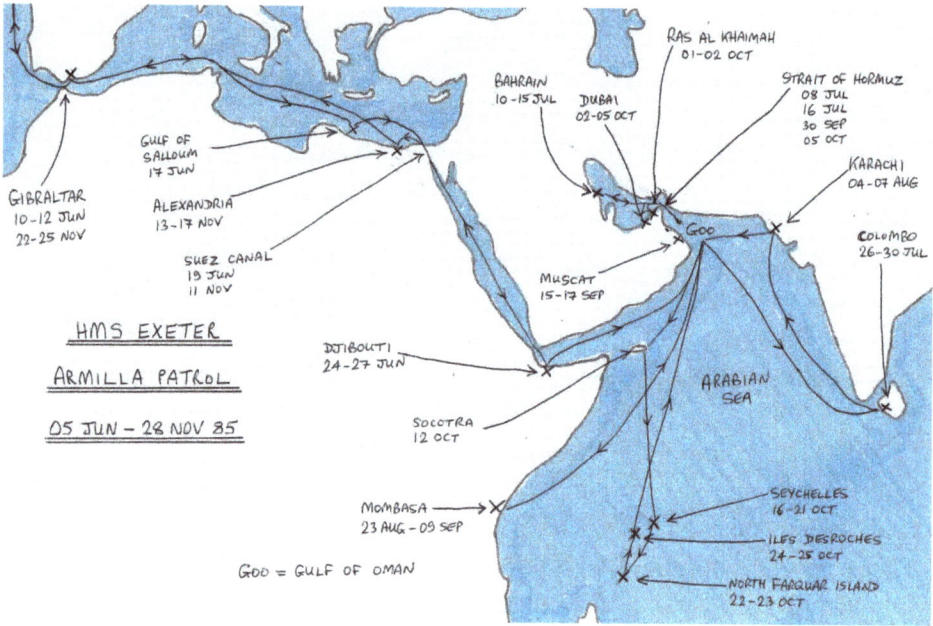

5.4 *Exeter's* Armilla Patrol

Charybdis (affectionately nicknamed *Cherry B*) was one of 26 RN *Leanders*, the RN's most numerous and long-lived class of frigate, built in three batches between 1959 and 1973. They gained a high public profile, due to the popular BBC television series *Warship*, which I'd watched as a teenager. *Phoebe, Danae, Diomede, Hermione, Juno* and *Jupiter* masqueraded as *Hero* (using *Phoebe's* F42 pennant number). The *Leander* design or its derivatives were built for the New Zealand, Chilean, Australian, Indian and Dutch navies. Our workhorses covered various roles within the same hull design and were a little smaller all-round compared to Type 42s. *Charybdis* was armed with Exocet and Sea Wolf missiles, plus a Lynx.

Bayleaf was one of four *Leaf*-class support tankers (*Brambleleaf, Orangeleaf, Appleleaf*). Commissioned in 1982, she was 170.7m long, 25.9m in the beam, 11m draught and displaced 37390 tons. She was a big ship compared to *Exeter* and *Charybdis*, but lumbered along at 15kts.

Our formation headed south-south-west across a benign Bay of Biscay. We rounded Spain's north-west headlands and continued south, the coasts of Spain and Portugal on the port side. Pivoting around Cape St Vincent, we altered course to south-east and steamed across the Gulf of Cadiz, land disappeared from view due to the gulf's curve. Landfall was regained off Cape Trafalgar as we approached and transited the Strait of Gibraltar, which linked the Atlantic to the Mediterranean and separated Europe from Africa. The Strait is narrowest (13km) between Point Marroquí in Spain and Point Cires in Morocco. It was another lovely, bright sunny day with good visibility. High pressure yielded warm temperatures, light winds and a pleasant sea state 2 or 3.

Rear Admiral Thomas (Flag Officer 2nd Flotilla, FOF2) embarked courtesy of our Lynx on the evening of 9 June. 5th Destroyer Squadron (*Exeter, Southampton, Liverpool, Nottingham, Manchester, Gloucester*) with 2nd, 4th and 8th Frigate Squadrons formed 2nd Flotilla, some 36 warships … when we had a Fleet. The following forenoon was packed full of exercises before we went starboard side to at 41 Berth, Gibraltar, for a short visit.

Nothing much happened in Gib. And we didn't have the dreaded Rock race. On both evenings, we went ashore for a few beers. I was back on board earlier than the others. Neil scuppered a few too many beers and tried to get into a night club. 'Security' stopped him. He got a bit punchy. An exchange of blows occurred. Luckily, Neil was rescued by one of *Exeter's* sailors and escorted back, his nose broken and cut. The incident's true nature was never reported, our Medical Officer (MO) banned Neil from contact sport until his injuries healed sufficiently. He was a sight, with facial cuts, a black eye and a plaster across the bridge of his nose.

We sailed from Gibraltar at 0830, Wednesday 12 June. Heading east in the Mediterranean, the weather improved further, with a light easterly wind, sea state 1 or 2. The hectic schedule of exercises and flying resumed. The next afternoon, we completed our first RAS with *Bayleaf*. Passage towards Port Said was unremarkable as we passed between Sicily and Tunisia's Cape Bon on Friday night and across the Ionian Sea at the weekend.

Sunday was more relaxed after the forenoon's flying stations and RAS. A deck hockey tournament was held on the flight deck. It was my first experience of this ruthless, violent sport. Inter-mess rivalry was intense, scores were settled under the guise of 'sport'. Naturally, the wardroom was always the team that everyone wanted to smash. Ship's company cooled off during 'hands to bathe' in the first dog.

Monday morning brought a different experience. *Bayleaf* continued her passage to Port Said while *Exeter* and *Charybdis* headed south towards the Gulf of Salum, just inside Egyptian waters. We went to defence watches at 0530, the intelligence team closed up, Lynx launched. Salum Gulf was a favoured anchorage for Soviet warships. We took a quick whizz around, ensuring we didn't enter Egyptian territorial waters, to spot, photograph and gather intelligence on four or five Soviet warships anchored there. I noticed their hulls were a darker grey than ours and their steel decks were painted a red-lead shade. My neat manuscript in Ship's Log showed we spent a short period at 24kts during this intelligence-gathering task, the familiar whistle and winding up of the engaged Olympus gas turbines in lieu of the cruising Tynes. A rousing sound.

Late afternoon, another couple of Soviet warships were spotted inshore from us. We closed in on *Neulovimy*, a 1958 *Kildin*-class guided missile destroyer. According to the Ship's Log, Captain Tolhurst stationed *Exeter* two cables (400yds) off *Neulovimy's* starboard side for mutual intelligence-gathering and photography. A little later, we observed *Zhdanov*, a vintage 1950s *Sverdlov*-class cruiser. After this early evening excitement, we rejoined *Charybdis* and *Bayleaf* for a pedestrian 9kt overnight steam.

Air temperature gradually rose as we headed along the African coast. Another great naval tradition was introduced. Water coolers filled with Pusser's limers appeared in the wardroom, senior and junior rates dining halls and *Exeter's* main passageways. Limers was a strong soft drink made from Pusser's lime crystals, sugar and water. It was issued when warships operated in hot climates to prevent scurvy due to its vitamin C content.

Mariners had a long history of suffering from scurvy (amongst other ailments and diseases). Sea captains, scientists and doctors conducted much research for hundreds of years to find a means of preventing it. In 1747, Dr James Lind demonstrated that scurvy could be treated by supplementing the diet with citrus fruit, in one of the first controlled clinical experiments reported in the history of medicine. As *Salisbury's* naval surgeon, Lind compared several suggested scurvy cures. In *A Treatise on the Scurvy*, he explained his clinical trial and concluded that citrus fruits were the most effective remedies for scurvy at sea. Hence, limers, which I found very refreshing and have enjoyed lime cordial ever since.

After another busy day of RAS and VERTREP, we moored to buoys at Port Said on the evening of Tuesday 18 June to await our Suez Canal transit.

On Wednesday, *Charybdis'* Lynx transferred some lucky devils ashore. It was the norm to land personnel for 'pyramid leave'. This was a legitimate means of qualifying ship's companies for local overseas allowance, which was designed to ensure service personnel received a more accurate contribution to additional costs incurred when serving overseas. It meant we all got an extra few quid per day in our pocket for serving in Egypt. Excellent!

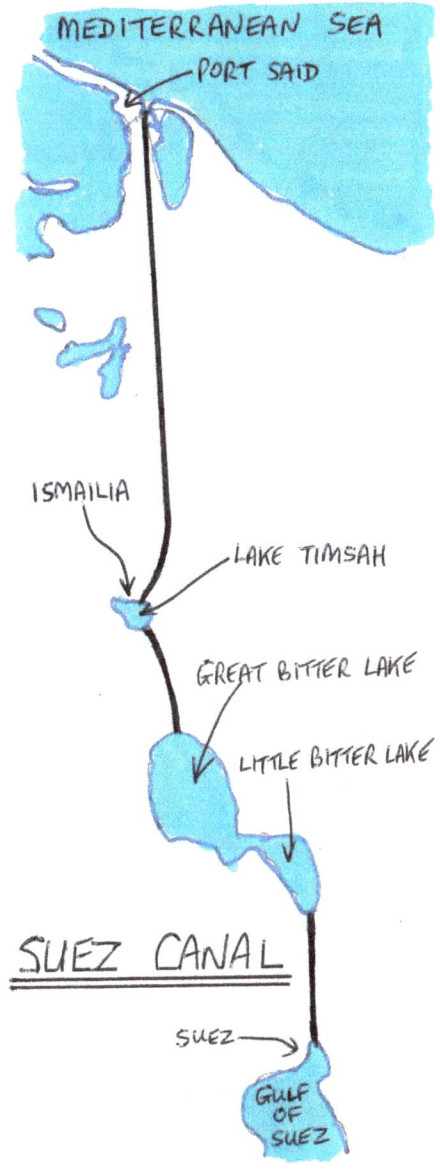

5.5 Suez Canal

At 0117, we slipped from the buoy with the pilot and the Suez Canal Authority for'ard searchlight team embarked. To assist the pilot, the Authority required all ships to have a searchlight fitted in the eyes of the ship to illuminate the canal and its banks ahead.

This was my third southbound transit. My first was 2 November 1980 on *ACT 5* (24212 ton refrigerated modular container-ship of 1334 standard 20ft container capacity, 217m long, 29m beam, 10.5m draught). That was my first trip to sea. I'd signed on at Seaforth Container Terminal, Liverpool, in October 1980, went around the world to Australasia and east coast USA and paid off in Tilbury in March 1981. That voyage had also included a Christmas Day transit of Panama Canal. It certainly whetted my appetite for a seafaring career and travel. My other transit was on *Mandama* (8219 gross ton seven-hatch refrigerated cargo vessel, 161m long, 21.7m beam, 9.1m draught) loaded in Brest with 4500 tons of frozen chickens for Red Sea and Persian Gulf ports. This was during the Falklands War, which we followed via the BBC World Service.

I saw a beautiful, warm, humid dawn as the sun slowly rose above the Sinai Desert. The pink sky became orange until that golden orb dominated as it climbed in altitude. The desert sand shimmered with heat on both sides of the blue Canal. Along the west bank, a narrow band of cultivated green fields and palm trees was interspersed by small hamlets and villages. At intervals, Egyptian military emplacements and posts were identifiable by radio aerials, artillery pieces, small barracks and a large national flag flying. Sinai looked uninhabited and harsh, its sand and rock stretched to the eastern horizon and beyond.

5.6 View from *Exeter's* bridge

5. Armilla Patrol – Up the Gulf 133

5.7 View aft

5.8 Great Bitter Lake anchorage

By 0800, our convoy (including *Charybdis* and *Bayleaf*) anchored in Great Bitter Lake to watch the northbound convoy steaming through. My neat handwriting in the Log shows I was on the bridge for departing Port Said until anchoring. We weighed anchor at 1414 to resume a steady 9kt steam southwards in convoy.

At 1800, we emerged from the Canal, increased speed through the Gulf of Suez and on into the Red Sea. During the evening, we sucked fuel from *Bayleaf*. The weather was typical of my previous experience in the region – dry, hot, a light breeze and sea state 1.

Late afternoon the following day, an accident occurred. CPO Taylour, a weapons maintainer, suffered a severe head injury in the BMARC workshop. BMARC was a 22mm gun fitted in Type 42 destroyers. Our MO recommended landing the patient ashore at the nearest hospital. As this was Jeddah, urgent diplomatic clearance (DIPCLEAR) was sought from Saudi Arabia to permit *Charybdis'* Lynx to transport Taylour to hospital. Meanwhile, *Exeter* flashed up her Olympus turbines and raced at 28kts to close the Saudi coast. Fortunately, red tape bureaucracy was swiftly completed, enabling *Cherry B's* Lynx to head to Jeddah only 75 minutes after the incident was reported. Taylour survived the ordeal and was repatriated to the UK when deemed fit to travel.

After that 'excitement', our task group resumed passage down the Red Sea. At 1738 the next day, we rendezvoused with the homeward-bound Armilla Patrol group (*Manchester, Andromeda* and their RFA). Overnight, the four warships and two RFAs remained in designated stations. In the morning, a busy day began of VERTREPs and boat transfers of heads of department (HODs) between warships for briefings. Olympus turbines were clutched in, the Tynes at two minutes notice, and a mid-afternoon set of OOW manoeuvres took place. The four warships whizzed around the Red Sea, about 150km equidistant between Ethiopia and Saudi Arabia.

It was exciting being part of the bridge team as each manoeuvre was executed, the warships sharply altered course and increased speed to get into the correct station relative to the guide. As OUTs, we operated the Stuarts distance meter, a cunningly simple device to measure the range of an object of known height at between 100yds and 1½ miles. The 'target' vessel's masthead height was set against the left edge of the sliding pointer. The milled knob was turned to bring the top of one image in line with the target's waterline. The range in cables (1 cable = 200yds) was read against the index mark on the sliding pointer and reported to the OOW.

As Neil, Kieran and I got the hang of it and the endless demands for the range of the warship we were taking station on, we found it quite easy. We learned to update, unbidden, an unbroken commentary, to the OOW as range decreased. This made our lives less fraught and the OOW continually aware as he manoeuvred *Exeter* into position and reduced to formation speed. The next signal was transmitted, giving time for all ships to digest and determine how they were to manoeuvre. On 'Execute', off we all went again, whizzing around at umpteen knots in close proximity to each other. There was little/no margin for error. The risk of collision ever-present if one warship made the wrong immediate helm order.

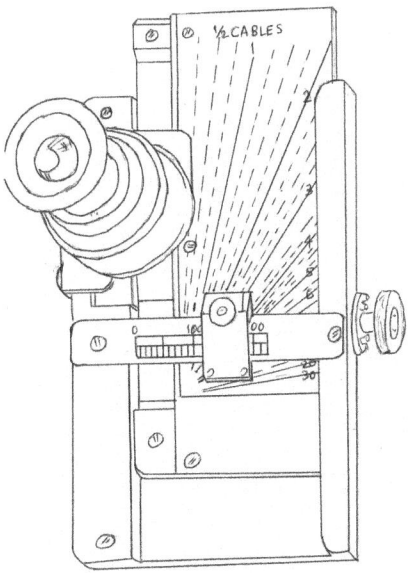

5.9 Stuarts distance meter

I'd enjoyed OOW manoeuvres in *Tons* but that was at a sedate 14kts. Now, we performed at nearly twice that speed. It was exhilarating, despite the evident tension on the bridge. On other occasions during the deployment, Neil, Kieran and I took turns as OOW. According to Simon the Navigator, the key was to 'do something' on 'Execute', don't just stand there. He ensured that we knew and understood the next manoeuvre and the crucial first helm and engine orders to get started. Thereafter, with his guidance, we moved *Exeter* from one position to the next, while monitoring the other warships' movements, all under Captain Tolhurst's watchful eye and cool, calm presence.

The culmination of these OOW manoeuvres was Formation Foxtrot. The four warships were in line astern, *Exeter* rearmost. On 'Execute', *Exeter* increased speed, hauled out to starboard and steamed passed the other three warships. As *Exeter* sped past *Charybdis*, she hauled out and followed *Exeter*. After *Exeter* and *Charybdis* passed *Andromeda*, she followed. As *Exeter* overtook each warship, the 'Still' was piped, salutes exchanged, followed by the 'Carry on'. You can't beat a bit of naval tradition, custom and ceremonial.

At the end, *Exeter* became the guide, leading *Charybdis*, *Andromeda* and *Manchester*.

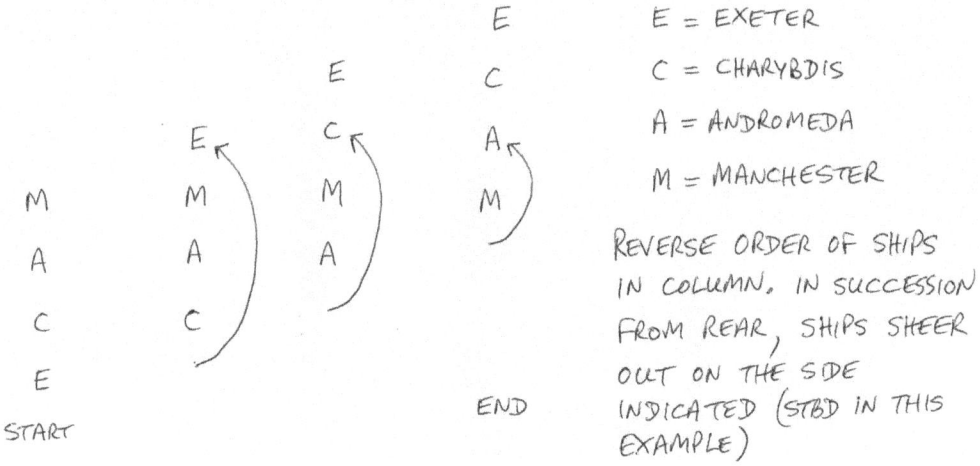

5.10 Formation Foxtrot starboard

At 1435 on Saturday 22 June, Captain Tolhurst assumed command of Task Group 321.1 and Armilla Patrol. Our task group rejoined *Bayleaf* to refuel and continue south. *Manchester, Andromeda* and their RFA set off north, homeward bound, their Armilla duty done.

After the excitement of handover activities, Sunday was a quiet day. The weather remained hot, with light wind, sea state 2, visibility hampered slightly by the constant haze caused by desert sand suspended in the air. In the evening, we transited Bab al Mandeb Strait, the narrow chokepoint at the south end of the Red Sea. We were briefly in the Gulf of Aden before altering course from south to south-west and berthed in Djibouti on Monday morning.

Djibouti (country and capital city) was the pimple on the arsehole of the world. A dreadful place, offering nothing positive. The wharves were lined with large, open warehouses, containing little. Throughout the hot, dusty port, I noticed enormous mounds of grain covered loosely by tarpaulins. I wondered how long they'd been there, untouched. Huge rats were scuttling around, eating well. We fitted extra robust rat guards on our mooring ropes and wires to prevent them boarding *Exeter*.

On the first night in a foreign port was a cocktail party, organised by our BNA, High Commission or Embassy. *Exeter* was usually the host ship, so we were joined by *Charybdis'* wardroom. It was an opportunity to catch up with Monty, as he was one of *Cherry B's* OUTs. Djibouti's 'great and good', plus assorted foreign ambassadors and high commissioners enjoyed our hospitality – as did Neil, Kieran, Max and I. One of us was 2nd OOD and missed out but there were plenty more port visits to come.

Constantly replenished G&T and a variety of tasty 'smallie eats' made for a great evening under the flight deck awning. Navy chefs always produced excellent food for official functions and dinners. It was an opportunity to show off their culinary skills and a change from humdrum daily food production. As we were an integral part of the wardroom, the events were an infinite improvement on the dour ones I'd experienced in *Fearless*. Cocktail parties were a traditional means of 'showing the flag' for the UK and the Navy, enhancing our image abroad, cementing close links with foreign countries.

One evening, the wardroom went ashore. Taxis were expensive. Drinks in the nightclub/disco were extortionate. The atmosphere was pretty awful, particularly as we formed the majority of patrons. Overall, a very disappointing evening. We retreated to *Exeter* earlier than anticipated, our pockets denuded of Djiboutian francs. Our taxis sped through the city, not a single soul on the streets. What a hyper-expensive dump.

A beach trip was organised for the ship's company. The coach was full of 'Jack' in shorts, T-shirts and flip-flops. I don't know what their expectations were but I gathered afterwards that 'Jack' was not expecting to be dumped on a deserted beach – no bar, no facilities, no shade. They returned dehydrated and a worryingly bright, lobster-red.

Everyone was relieved to depart Djibouti on Thursday 27 June. Nobody's future holiday destination. We steamed eastwards across the Gulf of Aden, rendezvoused with *Bayleaf* to refuel and did more flying serials, that now-familiar routine. We became accustomed to benign weather, sea state and gentle swell under a tropical sun, with warm, balmy sunsets and nights.

Neil, Kieran and I had been 1-in-3 watchkeeping as 2nd OOW on the bridge since leaving the UK. Max was learning about the 'nuts-and-bolts of supply' with the Pusser. With three watchkeepers, noise in the Grot was kept down as much as possible. The most difficult pre-watch sleep was before the middle (0001–0400) as everyone else was around for the evening after dinner. Luckily, I can sleep anywhere, anytime, regardless of ambient noise levels.

Table 5.1 OOW routine for three OOWs

| Time | Watch | Day 1 | Day 2 | Day 3 | |

0001–0400	Middle	1	2	3	For OOW 1, 2 and 3 Full cycle completed every 3 days
0400–0800	Morning	2	3	1	
0800–1200	Forenoon	3	1	2	
1200–1600	Afternoon	1	2	3	
1600–1800	First dog	2	3	1	
1800–2000	Last dog	3	1	2	
2000–0001	First	1	2	3	

When working in *Exeter's* other specialisations, Neil, Kieran and I did night watches only. As a future pusser, Max was banged up in S&S but joined us for training in other departments. Specialist sailors and Senior Rates explained the functions and activities of their respective sections. Unlike my *Fearless* experience, in *Exeter* we were welcomed, integrated as far as possible and learned much, sadly long-since forgotten. During this training, we focused on completing pink, blue and yellow tasks in our Task Books. Particularly important tasks required repetitions to reinforce our new knowledge.

Seaman officers were charged not only with bridge watchkeeping and seamanship but also, when qualified as PWOs, war fighting from the ops room. This dimly illuminated, 'gloom room' was filled with circular radar screens, banks of switches and panels of indicator lights. Here, the CO fought the battle assisted by his PWOs, Ops Room Supervisor and a miscellany of specialist operators (radar, sonar, gunners/missilemen and 'gollies' (electronic warfare)). On quiet patrol days, especially overnight, manning was minimal. In times of tension, the 'gloom room' was packed. Every desk/station occupied by an operator in overalls, anti-flash, his once-only suit, lifejacket and respirator around his waist, headset and microphone clamped to his skull. Communication was chiefly by 'command open line', a circuit that connected ops room personnel and all out-stations, especially the bridge.

We learned much about *Exeter's* warfare systems. We drew block diagrams of the Sea Dart and 4.5" gun to understand how missiles and shells were moved from their magazines several decks directly below and connections to the ops room and fire control radar. Such systems involved the weapon engineers (WEs), responsible for maintenance and repair of the mechanics and electronics. I found it interesting to learn how seemingly disparate departments dove-tailed to make our fighting warship.

To drive *Exeter* around, marine engineers (clankies and greenies) were required. They operated and serviced the gas turbines, generators and supporting ancillary systems that powered our warship. My father was a Civilian Instructional Officer at HMS Sultan, the Navy's School of Marine Engineering. When I did my time 'down below', I discovered he had taught many of *Exeter's* stokers, mechanicians and artificers. Thus, I was immediately nicknamed 'Little Ted', after my dad, although I don't know whether this helped me at all. It was fascinating to see how all these pumps, machines, engines, shafts, miles of pipework and cables mysteriously fitted together. I carefully drew block diagrams of these systems, expecting questions on them during my Fleetboard oral examination.

Max enjoyed his ME time. As the days wore on, he developed doubts about whether being a pusser was his true calling and considered changing to the engineering specialisation. Poor Max tortured himself for days and sought our collective advice in the Grot. It boiled down to 'in your heart of hearts, do you really want to be an engineer, Max?' Ultimately, Max remained a pusser. His 'infatuation' with engineering was genuine but temporary. I like to think Neil, Kieran and I were of help with our counselling. No one beyond the Grot was aware of Max's internal trauma.

As well as the Task Book, we had a journal, an A4 hardback book, in which we wrote articles throughout our DTS and fleet time until passing Fleetboard. The ship's OUT training officer ensured his charges wrote an article monthly, inspected and marked by him, XO and CO.

The journal's object was to: practice self-expression; expand powers of observation; write clear, concise and accurate English, using basic Service writing; and develop a neat, logical style of presenting written and diagrammatic information. Sketches, maps and diagrams illustrated the text. Each one drawn on a sheet of paper cut to fit the journal and inserted by cutting out a page and gluing the illustration sheet to the remaining stub. What a rigmarole!

Using a fountain pen, we wrote within our faint, hand-drawn, pencil margins. Any mistake, that page was carefully cut from the journal and started again. Lloyd gave us our monthly topics, a submission date and awarded marks for content, structure, English and legibility. English was out of 40 marks, the others out of 20, yielding a maximum 100 marks.

Kieran wrote in a flowery, non-naval style. Service writing ran counter to his romantic poet nature. Neil, Max and I did our very best to help and cajole him, particularly as the deadline approached. Articles were in black ink. Everyone knew that. For an unaccountable reason, Kieran submitted one article in green ink. We were mortified. Green ink was customarily used exclusively by the captain. Lloyd came to the Grot to discuss this with

Kieran, whose natural charm mollified him, so he allowed him to rewrite it pronto in black ink. We thought the world of Kieran, a real character.

GL seaman officers were required to gain their ocean navigation certificate (ONC). Simon the Nav tried to persuade us to complete it. We were in an ideal environment, bimbling around the Indian Ocean with passages to various ports. Neil decided to do it but regretted it after a couple of days as Simon piled on the work. Neil used a sextant for astro-navigation, calculated our position at morning and evening stars and noon. Unlike a merchantman, *Exeter's* course and speed varied depending on RAS, flying stations and miscellaneous commitments. These delaying serials had to be accounted for. He monitored fuel state and calculated courses and speeds required to achieve ETA at our next port, data he plotted graphically. Simon was a hard taskmaster and applied a navigator's high standards. He was like a dog with a bone. Instead of the standard three days' work, Simon forced Neil to do five or six days. Kieran and I were pleased not to have enrolled. The Grot was delighted when Neil was awarded his ONC. Well earned, Neil.

A couple of days after Djibouti, the guardrails and parts of *Exeter's* superstructure were fitted with radar-absorbent material (RAM). Depending on their composition, thin RAM 'pillows' lashed to the ship absorbed specific radar frequencies. This reduced a warship's radar cross-section and its 'visibility' to the enemy. I have no idea how effective RAM was, but it took our seamen all day to rig.

Saturday evening was film night in the wardroom. After dinner, we moved the armchairs into rows to face the screen. Leading Steward Battersby set up the Bell & Howell projector behind the armchairs. XO and HODs occupied the front row. Sometimes the Captain was invited, so an armchair beside XO was reserved for him. Everyone else sat where they liked. Naturally, we four, the most junior members, gravitated to the rear.

RN and RFA ships were supplied with movies by Services Sound and Vision Corporation (SSVC), a British registered charity set up in 1982. SSVC's purpose was to entertain and inform Britain's armed forces around the world. It included the British Forces Broadcasting Service (radio and television), SSVC Cinemas, the British Defence Film Library and Combined Services Entertainment (for 'live' events). Walport provided a similar service to the MN. Each film was in a large square steel box within which were the (usually) three reels, each in its own circular steel case.

When ready, XO's voice boomed, 'Lights out, Batters. Start the film.' After each reel, drinks were replenished while Batters changed reels. We always had ice cream after the first reel. These enjoyable evenings brought the wardroom closer together socially. At the end, we returned the furniture to its usual positions, Batters stowed the reels and the projector. We put our used glasses and cups on the bar for washing up. Everyone thanked Batters for his sterling service. It wasn't in his terms of reference, but he seemed to enjoy the evening.

Night watches (first at 2000–0001, middle at 0001–0400, morning at 0400–0800) were quiet. Our task group headed east-north-east off the coasts of Yemen and Oman. Overnight, *Bayleaf* was the guide, *Exeter* and *Charybdis* stationed off her port and starboard quarters, usually a box defined by a 40° sector in bearing and a range of 2000–6000yds. These limits gave the warships some freedom of movement. Overnight speed was generally 14–15kts.

Call the hands at 0700 kick-started a new day, leading into the routine daily serials: flying, gunnery, MOB, MBDDs, RAS. Occasionally, we had a maintenance day when *Exeter* stopped in the water for five or six hours to allow the engineers to conduct routine or necessary system and equipment maintenance. This was alien to me, a former merchant seaman, as cargo ships raced between ports to discharge and load cargo, every hour cost money. I was in a different 'game' now.

The patrol area was in the Gulf of Oman (GOO), divided into zones to dictate our task group's posture: outfield, midfield and front line. The last included the Strait of Hormuz and its immediate vicinity, within and outside the Persian Gulf. On 4 July, we entered the front-line zone for the first time and went to action stations at 0630. When everything had been duly checked and the Captain and XO were happy, we relaxed into defence watches.

Action stations and defence watches required us to wear No.8 uniform (action working dress) covered by overalls, white for officers, blue for sailors. We wore a once-only suit, respirator (gas mask) and life jacket around the waist and anti-flash gear. This last comprised a hood and gloves made of Nomex, a flame-resistant, meta-aramid material developed in the early 1960s. Anti-flash provided protection to the head, neck, face and hands from short-duration flame exposure and heat. Wearing all this 'clobber' in the tropics was tiring, even in our air-conditioned environment. I was pleased to hear the main broadcast pipe 'relax anti-flash' so I could take off hood and gloves and tuck them into my waistband.

The day passed quietly as we toured a couple of anchorages with cargo ships waiting for entry to their next port. One was Khor Fakkan, where I'd paid-off from *Mandama* on 9 September 1982. We'd loaded 4500 tons of frozen lamb carcasses in Timaru, New Zealand, bound for Bandar Abbas, Iran. A tug transferred us ashore to a minibus the ship's agent had arranged to take us to Dubai Airport for a Gulf Air flight to Blighty. It was a pitch-black night. We could have been mugged and murdered en route and no one would ever have known our fate. We just had to trust the agent and his hired driver.

Our only excitement was when two DLF decoys fell overboard and inflated (I've no idea what DLF means). This passive, off-board, decoy system provided soft-kill anti-ship missile defence for our warships. They must have been a bit 'secret' at that time because the on-watch PWO ordered everyone not to take photos of these large octahedral floats ('killer red tomatoes') bobbing about in the GOO.

Exeter settled into a daily routine of serials and exercises whilst 'up-threat' in the GOO. It didn't feel tense, but I sensed the command team were wary of our proximity to Iranian waters. We were occasionally overflown by Iranian Hercules aircraft. We came across several US Navy warships on similar duties to us. The ops room notified the bridge if radar detected a warship. This initiated the bridge team to train their eyes and binoculars along the reported bearing. We became competitive about spotting it first and then identifying the vessel's nationality, type and class. It was normal to close the Americans to exchange identities and have a brief chat.

On Monday 7 July, the task group assumed action stations, 'relaxed' to defence watches an hour later to prepare for our transit through the Strait of Hormuz. I was struck by the number of people on the bridge. We were a warship and the Strait was bounded to the north by Iran, the perceived main threat.

My most recent transit of Hormuz had been on *New Zealand Star* (168.9m long, 25.2m beam, 9.4m draught, 17082 gross tons, refrigerated container-ship of 721 container capacity), my last ship before I joined the RN. I'd passed my exams and needed another four months sea time to get my Second Mate's Certificate of Competency. The Master put me on forenoon/first watches for the duration of two round trips, four months, between the Gulf, the Indian sub-continent, Colombo, Singapore and Australia/New Zealand. Going through Hormuz at night at 22kts, alone on the bridge, being overtaken to starboard by a large French container ship, was a fantastic experience.

Our task group made its way north into the Strait, Iran to starboard, Oman's Musandam Peninsula opposite. We pivoted to port around the northern tip of Musandam to a south-westerly course. I detected tension on the bridge but Banjo West remained calm and confident as OOW. I gave him as much support as possible. Our lookouts were briefed to be especially vigilant as there were always a large number of small, ill-lit, fishing-boats bobbing about in this seaway.

The Persian Gulf opened out under a bright moonlit night. On the distant horizon were the familiar gas/oil platforms, revealed as dark shapes on spindly legs as we got closer. Their bright orange flares, burning off waste products, lit up the immediate vicinity. Light airs, warm temperatures, slight seas – marvellous.

On Wednesday 10 July, we got alongside No. 5 Berth in Bahrain's Mina Salman, the prime port located on the north-east tip of Bahrain, in its capital, Manama. Bahrain is a generally flat, arid archipelago of 50 natural islands and 33 artificial islands, centred on Bahrain Island (about 83% of the country's landmass). Bahrain lies between Qatar and the north-east coast of Saudi Arabia. The King Fahd Causeway to Saudi Arabia was still under construction at this time.

The British Ambassador came on board, briefly welcomed Captain Tolhurst and then off they trotted ashore for the customary courtesy calls on civic and military dignitaries. Preparations for the cocktail party were made, first rigging the flight deck awning. This was a full-scale seamanship evolution, POs in charge, sailors grunting and groaning to erect it. An awning's original purpose, when warships didn't have air conditioning, was as a canvas canopy secured over the ship's deck to protect sailors from sun and weather. Old photos of battleships often depicted awnings over the fo'c'sle, quarterdeck and for'ard and aft gun turrets. Awnings gradually became primarily associated with wardroom cocktail parties in foreign outposts.

My main memory of Bahrain was of Neil and me playing hockey for *Exeter* on a concrete pitch against Bahrain Bankers' Club. Neil was the far better player. It was an intense, hot, dry heat, magnified by the pitch's pale concrete slab. The bankers were most hospitable post-match – a good tea and free-flowing beer for all.

We left Bahrain on Monday and headed back to the GOO. Clear of Bahrain, we went to action stations, then relaxed to defence watches for the passage to and through Hormuz the following afternoon. I was getting used to front-line routine but not to the discomfort of two layers of clothing and the associated kit around my waist. I scuppered a fair volume of limers on these occasions, but the inevitable result was a rigmarole to take a pee.

On Wednesday afternoon, *Exeter* RAS'd with *Bayleaf*. Having witnessed several, I settled down on the bridge to observe this fascinating serial. This one was different as, an hour after connecting up, the bridge lost all power, communications and steering. An emergency breakaway was initiated and *Exeter* pulled away swiftly and safely from *Bayleaf*.

An emergency breakaway was an accelerated standard breakaway to disengage quickly without damaging the rigs or endangering/injuring personnel. Emergency breakaway was always part of the RAS briefing and was regularly practised. Various criteria required an emergency breakaway, including this example when *Exeter* suffered an engineering defect. Sound-powered phones and hand signals were the primary communications during a RAS. But the most positive and rapid method was the emergency sound signal of six short blasts on the ship's whistle/siren.

When this occurred, the reactions of all involved on the bridge, at the RAS station and on *Bayleaf* were immediate. *Exeter* sheared away sharply as soon as it was reported that all lines and rigs had been released and were not in danger of fouling our propellers. Phew!

Thursday 18 July was a very busy day in midfield routine. We rendezvoused with USS *Sterett* and French warship *Quartier-Maître Anquetil*. The former, a Vietnam veteran destroyer, was reclassified as a guided missile cruiser in 1975. The latter, a Type-A69 light corvette, was designed for coastal anti-submarine defence and high seas escort missions.

After the rendezvous, *Exeter's* and *Charybdis'* Lynxes flew sorties between all four warships before OOW manoeuvres took place. It was my first time operating with foreign warships but, as they were NATO partners, the sequence of manoeuvres was easily accomplished, despite some complexity. Before lunch, I was one of several *Exeter* personnel to transfer by Tornado rigid inflatable boat (RIB) to the French corvette. It was a short, pleasant ride at speed across the GOO's mirror-like surface.

We clambered up the pilot ladder and were welcomed by the French. I regretted giving up French in 3rd Year as an O-level in the language would have been useful. As it was, I made do with some basic greetings and phrases. Tactfully, I resisted 'Zut alors', 'tout de suite' and 'ooh la la'. Our hosts gave us a ship's tour. It didn't seem much different from our warships.

We had lunch in the wardroom, where red wine was de rigueur at lunch and dinner, and in the Senior and Junior Rates' messes. French warships were traditionally built, with integral wine tanks, just as freshwater, ballast and fuel oil tanks were normal for any ship. I knew American ships were 'dry' – how bloody miserable. In the RN alcohol was available, although sailors were strictly rationed to three cans, per man, per day. In the wardroom, we never considered havng a glass of wine at lunch, leaving such a treat to enjoy with dinner.

After a pleasant, companionable lunch, we returned to *Exeter* by Tornado. A few other folks had visited *Sterett*. I doubt they'd had as good a trip as I had. It was good to interact with other NATO warships on such missions, protecting merchantmen, showing the flag and providing a presence.

The following week or so was unremarkable. Daily routine exercises continued apace for fire, flying, balloon runs, streaming Type 182 Sonar, gunnery shoots and OOW manoeuvres. We patrolled in the GOO outfield area before heading south-east on an uneventful two-day passage to Colombo.

On Friday 26 July, we entered Colombo from the north to berth at Queen Elizabeth Quay, virtually the same berth where I'd joined *New Zealand Star* in September 1983. Blue Star flew me direct from Heathrow. After a night in the Hotel Oberoi, our ship's agent collected and delivered me to the ship. A few hours later, cargo operations completed, we departed for Singapore. I did my first solo watch that night (2000 to midnight) steaming down the coast at 22kts, avoiding innumerable tiny fishing boats with only my lookout for company.

I signed up for a trip to Kandy. A couple of coachloads were driven from Colombo, up into the luxuriant, densely forested hills and mountains of central Sri Lanka. We arrived in Kandy after four hours and checked into twin rooms in a city centre hotel. That evening, we witnessed the annual Perahera procession through the town.

The Esala Perahera (Festival of the Tooth) is held annually in July and August in Kandy, to pay homage to the Sacred Tooth Relic of Buddha. A unique symbol of Sri Lanka, the procession includes traditional fire dances and costumed local performers. The endless procession of dancers intermingled with a large number of flamboyantly decorated elephants. There was a constant rhythmic throb of drums and clashing of cymbals, a joyful noisy crowd and an occasional elephant's roar as the cavalcade paraded through the streets. The festival ends with the Diya-kepeema ritual, a sacred water-cutting ceremony at the Mahaweli River at Getambe.

The next morning, we returned to Colombo, stopping off to visit a tea plantation.

5.11 Costumed elephants at the Perahera, surrounded by festive crowds

On Sunday, Max was duty. Neil, Kieran and I went to the British High Commission compound to play tennis and swim in the pool. With the facilities to ourselves, we had a great time and it was good to escape from *Exeter*.

5.12 Neil and Kieran playing tennis ...

5.13 ... and leaping into the pool

There was a craze to buy Noritake bone chinaware, as it was much cheaper here than in UK. Noritake grew from a trading company established by the Morimura Brothers in New York in 1876, importing chinaware, curios and other gift items. From 1904 in Noritake, near Nagoya, Japan, they created western-style dinnerware for export. Several officers bought full dinner services. I succumbed to an exquisite 'Blue Hill' tea set – a beautifully shaped teapot, milk jug, sugar bowl, cups, saucers and tea plates. Luckily, the box was sufficiently petite to store in my wardrobe and survived the deployment unscathed.

We sailed from Colombo during the last dog on Tuesday 30 July. Twice the next day Indian Navy aircraft overflew, checking us out. Neither time did they respond to our courtesy radio calls.

Halfway across the Arabian Sea, we conducted a high seas firing of our Sea Dart missile. This 1960s-design, surface-to-air guided missile system was fitted to Type 42 destroyers from 1973. Sea Dart was a two-stage, 4.4m long missile weighing 550kg. At launch, its solid-fuel booster accelerated it to supersonic speed to kick-start the Rolls-Royce cruise motor, boosting its speed to over Mach 2.5. Primarily anti-air, it could be used against small surface targets, over a range of 56km. In the Falklands War, Sea Dart shot down seven Argentinian jets.

The upper deck was out of bounds for the firing. The bridge and ops room teams closed up. The bridge wing doors were shut, no spectators allowed. The count down ran smoothly and the Sea Dart launch was successful. Another Sea Dart travelled up from the magazine on to the twin launcher to replace the expended missile. Everyone stood down and that was that. I can't say I heard or detected the missile's launch from my observer's position in the ops room.

On 4 August, we entered Karachi from the south and berthed at 1100 at No. 1 Berth in the commercial port. Opposite was the naval dockyard and Karachi Shipyard and Engineering Works. Apart from the cocktail party and a bit of shopping, Karachi was unremarkable, except for the hurly-burly of heavy road traffic, crush of pedestrians and a heady atmosphere of noise, heat and exhaust fumes. I'd previously been here on *New Zealand Star* in November 1983 but hadn't got ashore. I realised I hadn't missed much.

We left Karachi on 7 August. Almost immediately, the first bouts of tummy trouble occurred and spread among the messes. Our MO managed the situation by insisting on intense hand washing, designating certain heads and bathrooms for the 'sickies' and some segregation. These measures contained the outbreak and, a few days later, it subsided to zero cases. I think about 50% of the ship's company suffered from 'the dog'. Luckily, the Grot was unaffected.

Making our way back to the GOO, we rendezvoused with the aircraft carrier USS *Midway* and her escorts. *Midway* was commissioned into the US Navy in September 1945 and saw service in the Vietnam War. She dwarfed our own *Invincible*-class carriers as her air wing comprised 70 aircraft, including F-4 Phantoms, A-6 Intruders and helos. Our Lynx shuffled Captain Tolhurst to *Midway* for a visit and discussions with his counterpart. We parted from the Americans in the evening to continue our patrol.

Saturday 10 August was a leisurely day as we anchored off Bandar Khayran, an unspoilt, deserted rocky bay and beach with crystal-clear blue water, 50km east of Muscat. A Tornado shuttle service ferried personnel ashore for a banyan, a beach party and barbecue naval tradition during long deployments. Barbecues were made from oil barrels cut in half. Huge quantities of food, especially steaks and burgers, were cooked and scoffed. Sailors drank the day's beer ration, swam in the bay, and played volleyball and football. It was a great opportunity to get off *Exeter* for a few hours and relax in a beautiful environment. All too soon, it was time to return, weigh anchor and resume our patrol.

We remained in midfield for the next week or so. The only interruptions were another quick whizz around the anchorages near Khor Fakkan and a second rendezvous and manoeuvres with the *Midway* group. On 18 August, we headed south-west from the GOO towards Mombasa. We passed close to Socotra, a large island in the Gulf of Aden, off the north-east tip of Somalia – a popular base for pirates.

We crossed the Equator on 22 August. Naturally, King Neptune and his court boarded for the traditional Crossing the Line ceremony. Those souls crossing into the southern hemisphere for the first time were subjected to initiation. This comprised being escorted/carried to and placed on a chair where Neptune's verdict was pronounced. The victim was 'shaved', forced to drink a vile blend of liquids and then tipped backwards into the makeshift pool erected on the flight deck. Organising the ceremony was Senior Rates' perks, which they did with relish.

The entire wardroom was always subjected to this procedure, regardless of anyone's previous experience of crossing the Equator. My first crossing was in October 1980 in the Indian Ocean. My shipmates grappled me and the passage-worker to the poop deck, stripped us to our skiddies and lashed us to the guardrail with cable ties. Barrels of a disgusting cocktail of galley slops, engine-room oil and bilge water were poured over us and then we were 'cleaned' by a high-pressure fire hose. I spent two hours in the shower with a tub of Swarfega to get clean. My skiddies and two towels were write-offs.

Our task group arrived in Mombasa the following day. Approaching from east, the pilot embarked and guided us through the 250m gap between Shelly Beach to the south and Mama Ngina Waterfront to the north. We passed Likoni's Ferry and Floating Bridge, where the seaway widened into Kilindini Harbour. Further on, we berthed at Mbaraki Jetty.

Mombasa, Kenya's oldest city, was the capital of British East Africa until 1907 and known as 'the white and blue city'. Topographically, it's a flat island connected to its growing mainland suburbs by bridges. Founded in about 900AD, Mombasa's strategic location on the Indian Ocean made it a trading centre controlled, in turn, by Portugal, Oman and Britain. Kenya gained independence on 12 December 1963.

This port visit marked the halfway point of the deployment and we had a fortnight's self-maintenance period (SMP). This was an opportunity for personnel to take a few days 'station leave' and for wives/girlfriends to join their husbands/boyfriends.

A rugby tour to Nairobi was organised. I volunteered, despite being a novice, and joined the squad. We had a couple of practice sessions in a nearby park before being transported to Mombasa railway station to take the train to Nairobi. We clambered aboard and settled in for the overnight journey. We must have paired up but I don't remember who my cabin mate was.

5.14 Ready to rumble!
Kieran, me (hidden, second left), Max (foreground)
(Max Rance)

Aptly named Lunatic Express, it was very much a poor man's Orient Express. Ancient coaches with narrow corridors and orange walls. The petite restaurant carriage was ventilated by tiny fans hanging from the ceiling and with limited elbow-room at the dinner table, arms were wedged in tightly by the seats. Cabins were old and battered but comfortable, with flip-down seats that became bunks. Bed linen was fresh, clean and starched. Care was required using the drop toilet as everything went straight onto the track. A quaint relic of the British Empire.

After a good night's sleep, we enjoyed breakfast. Service from immaculately uniformed stewards and crisp, starched, white table linen. Nairobi was a huge, bustling, noisy city surrounded by expanses of slums. A coach took us to our hotel. We had rugby practice in the hotel gardens. Mid-afternoon, we set off for the ground – no idea where. We warmed up. Our initial team was selected, I was a substitute. Our opponents stepped onto the pitch to warm-up.

Team captains tossed a coin, shook hands and kick-off followed. Our opponents were fifteen of the biggest, strongest, fastest, blackest blokes I'd ever seen. It was frightening to watch them score try after try. Nothing stopped them. In the second half, I went on as a winger. My opposite number was enormous! He ran right over me several times. We learned that we'd been thrashed by Kenya's national 2nd XV. We drowned our sorrows in beer. The Kenyans were polite, friendly and fun. Battered and bruised, our bodies ached through the night before the next day's return journey to Mombasa.

Captain Tolhurst decided he didn't need his car for a couple of days and he lent it to Ossie Moseley (Captain's Secretary). Ossie, Mike (our Lynx Observer) and I drove off for a couple of days' safari in Tsavo West National Park, about 160km from Mombasa. In the park, we used a map to find our way along dusty red tracks that extended endlessly into the distance. We saw no other vehicles at all. We'd have been buggered if the car had broken down.

We stayed overnight in a lodge and, from the balcony, watched hippos messing about in a large waterhole. We saw elephants, gazelles and giraffes but no 'big cats'. Luckily, we got back to *Exeter* unscathed.

It wasn't all time-off for us in harbour. Our training continued, one-in-four, as 2nd OOD. We learned the routine and duties of OOD on a big warship, more expansive than those in *Gavinton/Brinton*. The duty watch fire exercise was on a larger scale with a bigger team. Instead of controlling from the gangway, we dived down into HQ1, the nerve centre for NBCD incidents. There were fire-fighting teams, boundary coolers, an incident board operator (who tracked incoming information, plotting it on a ship's deck plan), engineers to provide technical advice, gangway staff controlling access to the ship and the Duty Senior Rate reporting from the scene.

5.15 Ossie and me on the dusty red road to nowhere

5.16 Overnight lodge, Tsavo National Park

5.17 Mike and elephants

We accompanied OOD, one of our Lieutenants, on evening rounds to inspect heads and bathrooms and sailors' messes. The OOD's safe was mustered to check its contents were correct. It held, amongst other stuff, idiot's guides for certain incidents and sealed envelopes of safe combinations. Much of the 24-hour duty period (from morning Colours through to Colours the next morning) was spent in the wardroom or cabin, with forays to the gangway and upper deck. But we were at zero notice to react swiftly to any incident.

I was proud to stand beside OOD on the flight deck for Colours and Sunset. The prep raised, waggled and lowered at the right time. The shrill of the 'Still' and 'Carry on' on the bosun's call, the ship's bell clanged, the hoisting/lowering of the White Ensign (aft) and the Jack (for'ard). Stirring stuff, particularly in tropical white uniform in a foreign port. Marvellous!

OOD was a highly responsible job. With so many components, there was much to learn from our mentors. Great preparation for Fleetboard and beyond, when we entered the Fleet as fully trained Seaman Officers and went solo as OOD.

Throughout our visit, numerous local traders set up stall on the jetty, flogging all sorts of crappy souvenirs. Like many folks, one of the wardroom bought a large wooden giraffe. He mentioned his great bargaining powers to a few of our lads. We asked how much he'd paid for it. '20 Kenyan shillings.' 'You wuz ripped off, Sir. Dusty got 'is for a bar of soap and a pair of Pusser's daps!' The poor chap was ribbed mercilessly.

After respite in Mombasa, the task group headed back to the GOO. It was an uneventful passage to Muscat, arriving late afternoon on Sunday 15 September. This was my fourth visit to, in my opinion, one of the world's most beautiful harbours. Approaching from the north-east, *Exeter* led between Muscat Marine Tower to port and the concrete breakwater to starboard, into Mina Qaboos and went alongside No.6 Berth. The precipices of jagged rocky hills surrounded old Mutrah, now fronted by the extensive Corniche, which wound its way around Mutrah's natural harbour. As the sun slowly sank, the sky changed to orange, the sharp shadows cast across the hills lengthened. Shore lights grew brighter with the onset of twilight and night. The heat eased a little. I felt at home here.

Sadly, after only a couple of days in Muscat we were back in the GOO. Wednesday 18 September was a busy day exercising with Omani Navy and Air Force assets. The splash target was streamed at 0715 and attacked by two Royal Air Force of Oman (RAFO) Jaguars, Anglo-French single-seat, swept-wing, twin-jet supersonic aircraft. Used for ground attack, reconnaissance and tactical nuclear strike, they were armed with missiles, rockets, cluster bombs and a pair of 30mm cannon. RAFO bought 24, based at RAFO Thumrait, southern Oman.

5.18 Muscat's Corniche backed by mountains in afternoon sun. Mutrah Fort in centre

5.19 Banjo, Max and me in the GOO

Their attacks were spot-on. At the end, the pair did a fly-past. The ops room advised everyone to view it from the starboard side. In line astern at full throttle, they flew below deck-edge level, about 50m off. I saw both pilots (Brits on contract to RAFO) glance towards us and wave. They soared away into the cloudless blue sky. Crikey! Stunning! Impressive!

5.20 Neil, Omani fast attack craft, *Charybdis* in background

5.21 Kieran on bridge-wing of *al-Sharqiyah*

Later, we rendezvoused with three Omani fast attack craft (*al-Jabbar, al-Sharqiyah, al-Dhofar*) for OOW manoeuvres and RAS-approach exercises. Kieran was lucky enough to transfer across to one of them and had a great time racing around the rippled surface of the GOO at 38kts.

Our patrol continued for several more days. We anchored off Bandar Khayran for a Sunday afternoon banyan. During this period, we encountered and exchanged identities with a French warship, a pair of Saudi Arabian corvettes and the Sultan of Oman's Royal Yacht *al Said*. Undoubtedly, our most exciting encounter was a day with USS *Kitty Hawk* and her escorts on Wednesday 25 September.

5.22 RAS with *Kitty Hawk*

We rendezvoused during the morning watch and hooked up with *Kitty Hawk* for a RAS. At 81000 tons, 325.8m long, a beam of 86m at the flight deck, tapering to 40m at the waterline and a draft of 12m, she dwarfed little *Exeter*. One of America's supercarriers, she was commissioned in 1961 and carried 85 aircraft: F-14 Tomcat fighters; S-3A Viking all-weather, long-range, multi-mission aircraft; E-2 Hawkeye early-warning aircraft; and Seahawk utility helos. Powerful asset, or what?

After lunch, *Exeter* was designated 'plane guard' for *Kitty Hawk's* flying operations, acting as safety and rescue ship in case an aircraft plummeted into the sea. We sat 400yds (2 cables) on her port bow for the afternoon. We heard and saw her aircraft catapulted off the flight deck and eventually approach and land back on board. Although impressed by the pilot skill required to fly Tomcats, it became rather dull as the afternoon wore on. The climax was a fly past by a pair of Tomcats. Despite being supersonic fighters, they lumbered overhead at about 200ft altitude with undercarriage lowered. Very disappointing after the screeching, close-in fly-past of the RAFO Jaguars. Nevertheless, for me, it was a once-in-a-lifetime experience to be so close to an enormous aircraft carrier conducting flying serials. We remained in company for the evening's flying and parted shortly after midnight.

5.23 *Kitty* and me

After a quiet weekend at sea, our task group headed north to transit Hormuz. As usual, we went to action stations, then reverted to defence watches for a peaceful transit into the Persian Gulf. Shortly afterwards, we berthed at Ras Al Khaimah, capital city of the homonymous Emirate. In 1972, it became one of UAE's seven emirates, sharing the Musandam Peninsula and a common border with Oman's Musandam exclave. Without oil reserves, Ras Al Khaimah developed a diversified economy of manufacturing, high-tech, building materials, financial and banking services, and, increasingly, tourism and real estate.

Exeter and *Charybdis* were the first RN warships to visit this Emirate. Our flag-waving was evidently important. The following afternoon, the ruler, Sheikh Saqr bin Mohammed Al Qasimi, visited *Exeter*. In 1948, he'd overthrown his paternal uncle and father-in-law in a bloodless coup d'état. He watched our departure later as we continued to Dubai, where we berthed at Port Rashid that evening.

I'd been to Dubai a couple of times on *New Zealand Star* but for only about four hours as a container ship's turnaround is so swift. This was my first opportunity to get ashore and see something of the place. It was glitzy but not on the tawdry, tasteless scale it is today. We went shopping at the ubiquitous air-conditioned malls and visited the gold souk and other emporia. Musi-cassettes and fake designer polo shirts were popular purchases. Taxi was the prime mode of transport and booze was freely available in hotels. It seemed a comfortable place to live as an ex-pat on a tax-free salary and attractive package (housing and international schools for the kids). I loved the weather but felt Dubai lacked soul.

We sailed from Dubai on Saturday 5 October and headed back through Hormuz to resume our patrol for the week. We left the GOO on Friday, steaming south-west to Socotra, a popular anchorage for Soviet warships. In defence watches, we swept around and noted *Kirov* (a late-1970s, 28000-ton battle-cruiser, impressively armed with anti-ship, anti-submarine and surface-to-air missiles, plus miscellaneous guns), an *Udaloy*-class guided missile destroyer (slightly larger than *Exeter*) and a *Moma*-class intelligence-gathering ship.

5.24 Banjo, Ray and Neil loafing on the beach

Onward to the Seychelles on an uneventful passage, We crossed into the southern hemisphere to anchor off Port Victoria on Wednesday 16 October. Captain Tolhurst went ashore for his calls and returned to take *Exeter* alongside in late afternoon.

The Seychelles archipelago comprises 115 islands in the Indian Ocean. Victoria, its capital and largest city, is 1500km east of mainland Africa. It was uninhabited prior to its discovery by Europeans in the 16th century, when French and British interests strongly competed for control. It became a British colony in the late 18th century and gained independence in 1976. Seychellois culture and society are an eclectic mix of French, British and African influences.

We enjoyed 'rest and recuperation' for a few days. A car was rented for a gentle drive around the coast of Mahe. Most of our time was spent loafing beside a hotel pool and on the adjacent golden sandy beach. Bliss!

We sailed from Victoria on Monday 21 October. After sucking fuel from *Bayleaf*, our task group split up. *Charybdis* and *Bayleaf* headed north. *Exeter* steamed south-west at 24kts towards Farquar Reef to respond to a distress signal from a merchantman aground. On Tuesday morning our Lynx found *Lion of Piraeus* fast on the reef. A 3000-ton general cargo ship, she was on a voyage from West Africa to India. We continued to close the Farquar Islands. Post-lunch, the Lynx lowered XO and MO on to the stranded ship to assess her situation. *Exeter* established a patrol line nearby but later approached North Farquar to anchor overnight. We checked our swinging circle by lead line to ensure there was sufficient safe water all round.

There's not much to say about the Farquar Group. Part of Seychelles' Outer Islands, they are over 700km south-west of Mahé Island. The group's land area of 5 square miles comprises two atolls and one separate island, but its submerged reefs increase total area to 140 square miles. Not surprisingly, the negligible population is in one settlement on North Farquar.

Throughout Wednesday, a flurry of boat and helo transfers of personnel occurred. *Lion of Piraeus* seemed to refloat but remained fast to the coral. Overnight, her condition deteriorated as the engine-room flooded and generator failed. In the glow of morning twilight, the helo took off to transfer their crew to *Exeter*. By 1030, *Exeter* sped north at 17kts to Isle Desroches. Meanwhile, ship's routine resumed with Captain's messdeck rounds. *Lion of Piraeus* was eventually deemed a 'total loss'.

After disembarking the merchant seamen at Isle Desroches, *Exeter* continued passage northwards at 17kts. On Monday, we rendezvoused with USNS *Ponchatoula*, a 38000-ton *Neosho*-class oiler, for much-needed refuelling. Early Wednesday morning, *Exeter* rejoined *Charybdis* and *Bayleaf* in the GOO, taking a fuel top-up from the latter. We stopped in the water overnight, wallowing gently in the GOO's low swell.

Armilla Patrol was on its final leg as, in the last dog, our task group steered south-west at 20kts, away from the GOO for the last time. The frequency of routine exercises eased as we enjoyed the calm, warm, benign weather conditions of the Indian Ocean. En route, we rendezvoused with *Kitty Hawk's* group again and acted as plane guard. *Exeter* raced off to intercept a Soviet *Udaloy*-class, guided missile destroyer shadowing the US task group. We 'spied' on each other, separated by a few hundred metres before breaking off to resume passage.

We transited Bab-el-Mandeb, leaving the Indian Ocean astern and entered the Red Sea on Monday 4 November. A couple of days later, we rendezvoused with the incoming Armilla Patrol group, *Newcastle, Jupiter* and *Brambleleaf*. It was a busy day of manoeuvres, RAS and inter-ship boat and helo personnel transfers for briefings. We were delighted to see our reliefs.

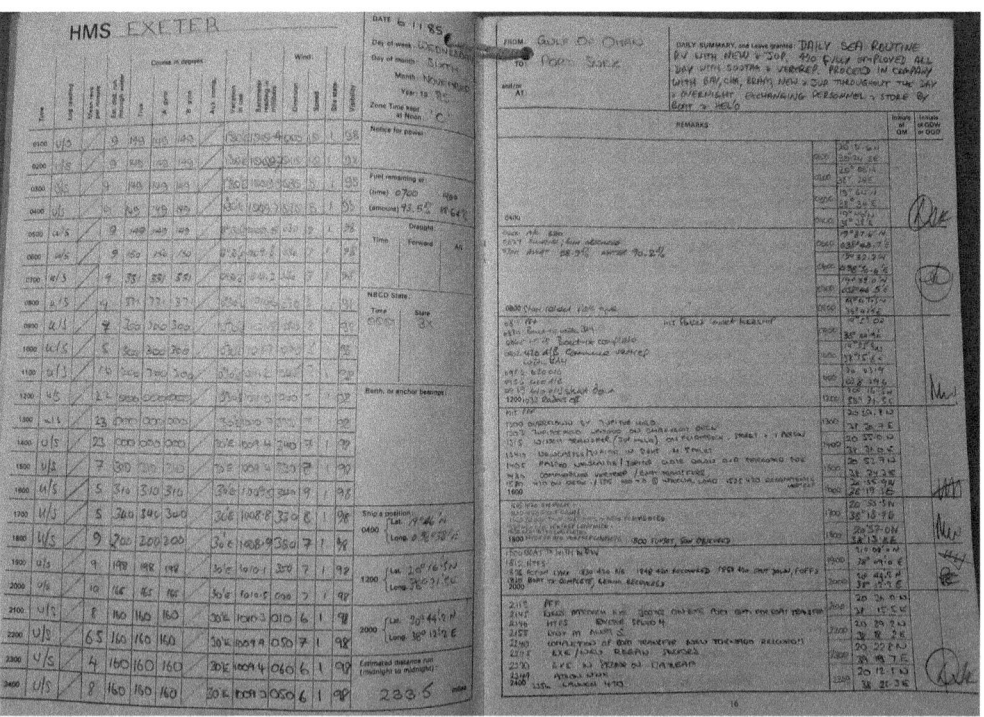

5.25 *Exeter's* Ship's Log, Wed 6 Nov 85. My handwriting for Daily Summary and Last Dog initialled
(National Archives)

Thursday 7 November was official Hand-Over Day, filled with a few more inter-ship personnel transfers, and OOW manoeuvres, which climaxed with a full speed 'Formation Foxtrot' as we bade farewell to *Newcastle*, *Jupiter* and *Brambleleaf*. We were now on 'homeward-bounders'.

5.26 *Newcastle* slides passed …

5.27 … followed by *Jupiter*

5.28 Both Armilla Patrol groups, seen from *Exeter*

We trundled north and anchored off Port Suez at 1740 on Saturday 9 November. The next morning, a Remembrance Service was held on the flight deck, led by our Padre. We monitored the movements of a Soviet icebreaker and a *Kilo*-class submarine in the anchorage.

At 0750 on Monday, we weighed anchor and transited the Suez Canal. Come lunchtime, we passed through the Great Bitter Lake where the southbound convoy was anchored. By 1740, we'd exited the Canal and disembarked the pilot and the signal projector crew. Port Said astern, we steamed towards Alexandria, meeting up with *Fife* (the fifth of eight 1960s *County*-class guided missile destroyers). Our advanced leave party transferred to *Bayleaf* to be landed for their flight home. They'd meet us on our arrival home to become duty watch, allowing everyone else to go on leave immediately.

On Wednesday 13 November we were berthed outboard of *Fife* in Alexandria for a brief visit. Sadly, I recall nothing of Alexandria. We sailed four days later with *Fife* in her role as Dartmouth Training Ship. We embarked 16 OUTs from *Fife* to experience OOW manoeuvres off Alexandria before they transferred back to *Fife* in the afternoon via light jackstay.

This method of transferring personnel and light stores allowed a maximum transfer load of 250kg. The hauling end of the jackstay is manned by at least 25 men, the other end secured by a grommet strop to a slip in the receiving ship. The traveller block is hauled back and forth along the jackstay by the receiving ship's outhaul and delivering ship's inhaul, manned by six men in each ship. The normal working distance between ships was 34m.

I confess, I wouldn't fancy dangling from the traveller block, being man-hauled across 34m of Mediterranean Sea boiling between two warships at a seemingly frightening speed. Both warships subject to differing rolling and pitching, and the chance of getting 'goffered' (soaked) by occasional big waves or even dunked in the sea. No thanks!

We remained with *Fife* for a couple of days. We were fortunate to observe *Exeter* towing *Fife*, a rarely practised but important, complex, often dangerous exercise. There were more OOW manoeuvres and close-range gunnery serials.

5.29 Kieran and me witnessing a gunnery shoot
(Max Rance)

Our task group detached from *Fife* and continued westwards through the Mediterranean to rendezvous with *Ark Royal* for more OOW manoeuvres prior to entering Gibraltar, our final run ashore. We berthed outboard of *Gloucester* and enjoyed a couple of nights ashore in Gib.

The final leg to Pompey was at a sprightly 16kts, rounding Cape St Vincent during the evening of 24 November. In the coastal Atlantic, the weather picked up from the balmy, calm Mediterranean Sea and Indian Ocean to sea state 4 with 25kt easterly winds. The exercise routine tailed off to daily flying stations for the Lynx. Crossing the Bay of Biscay, conditions deteriorated to an uncomfortable sea state 6 and 30kt winds.

On my birthday, we anchored at Portland to clear customs and embark the advanced leave party. Our helo collected FOF2, Rear Admiral Richard Thomas, for a brief visit. His illustrious naval career culminated in promotion to Vice Admiral as Deputy Supreme Allied Commander Atlantic at Norfolk, Virginia, in 1987 and UK Military Representative to NATO from 1989 to retirement in 1992. He then served as Parliament's Gentleman Usher of the Black Rod. *Exeter* weighed anchor that evening and steamed onwards to anchor in Sandown Bay overnight.

Thursday 28 November saw our triumphant entry to Pompey, *Exeter's* home port. Anchor aweigh at 0819, we headed north-east. Rounding Bembridge, the panorama of Southsea seafront opened ahead, bracketed by Hayling Island to the east and Gosport to the west. We saw the four Solent Forts, built by Palmerston to protect maritime access to Spithead and Portsmouth Harbour's entrance, countering the threat of Napoleonic invasion.

The buoyed channel took *Exeter* close inshore, to turn and parallel Southsea seafront and through the narrow gap between Old Portsmouth and Gosport's Fort Blockhouse opposite. In Procedure A, up-harbour we went. My station was at the bullring of *Exeter's* bow. Fortunately, the weather was kind, with light airs, although it was distinctly chilly. My main concern was my cap being blown off my head.

At 0955, we were secure alongside Middle Slip Jetty. Here ended our deployment. And what a brilliant trip it had been. Six months in the sunny, warm Indian Ocean, visiting some old haunts and several new ones. It was novel to rendezvous and interact with foreign navy warships in the GOO, particularly our close proximity to *Kitty Hawk* and red wine with lunch in a French corvette.

Our Armilla Patrol lasted 167 days from Pompey, back to Pompey, of which 52 days were port visits (a ratio of 3.2 sea days to one day in harbour). At sea, we completed 46 RAS, plus numerous VERTREPs, primarily with *Bayleaf*. Flicking through *Exeter's* Ship's Logs, my neat handwritten 'Daily Summary' showed flying serials occurred almost daily, sometimes more, day and night. Add boat transfers, OOW manoeuvres, MOBEX, gunnery serials, NBCDXs, MBDDs, and our Armilla Patrol was very busy, belying the apparent simplicity of bimbling around the GOO.

Neil, Kieran, Max and I considered ourselves extremely fortunate compared to our peers stuck around the UK coast or, worse, on towed array sonar patrols in the grim north Atlantic. We were blessed with a brilliant Captain, a hospitable, sociable, welcoming wardroom, and a bunch of good-humoured, friendly sailors. We four got on famously in the cramped confines of the Grot. No friction, arguments or disagreements … only endless mirth and hilarity. We all recently agreed that we couldn't have wished for a better ship's company and deployment. Time to move on. Fleetboard beckoned!

5.30 *Exeter*, home for six glorious months
(Michael W Pocock, www.MaritimeQuest.com)

6.

Back to Pompey

6.1 Newly striped-up Lieutenant RN

I remained in *Exeter* for another fortnight. It was a busy time. Post-deployment homecoming, final throes of wedding plans but, critically, preparation and revision for Fleetboard. As the culmination of a junior Seaman Officer's training, passing this full day of oral examinations meant we were almost on the Navy's trained strength.

Fleetboard took place at HMS Excellent on Whale Island, just north of Pompey Dockyard. There was a rolling sequence of Fleetboards prior to Christmas leave as those Seaman Officers who'd passed out from BRNC the previous Christmas completed their year's fleet time. I pitched up at Excellent and found my cabin. Unsociably, I got down to some last-minute revision rather than mooch about seeing who else was around. At dinner in the wardroom, I met several of my peers and enjoyed 'swinging the lamp' and spinning dits about our fleet time experiences. I discovered a few contemporaries had chosen to resign. After a post-dinner beer, I scuttled back to my cabin for further revision.

After breakfast, we candidates assembled in the classroom. The first event was a written ROR exam. After four years as a MN deck cadet, I passed an intense oral ROR exam by the Principal Examiner of Masters and Mates in Liverpool to earn my 2nd Mate's 'ticket' so I knew ROR by heart. During fleet time, ship's NOs were obliged to set monthly ROR exams for all Seaman Officers on board. I'd passed them all comfortably and learned 'special manoeuvring rules' applicable to warships conducting various serials and the hierarchy of responsibilities depending on such activities: helos, MCM, RAS, landing-craft ops, flying ops. Like my MN oral exam, the pass mark for Fleetboard's written exam was 100%. Zero margin for error.

My confident start led to a matrix of oral exams with various officers to test our respective knowledge of their specialisation: operations/warfare; marine engineering; weapon engineering; supply; admin; discipline; divisional work; seamanship and so on. About 30–45 minutes was allocated per oral exam. The examiners were all Lt Cdrs or Cdrs and experienced warship HODs.

This is where the hard graft in completing the myriad tasks in the Task Book, plus associated ancillary work/study/drawings/notes, paid dividends. Each oral exam was intense. A clear head was required. Panic kept at bay. It didn't matter to me in which order I was timetabled for each topic. After one, I moved on to the next and waited outside the room until called in.

The Fleetboard President was a Captain. His exam covered anything and everything as he saw fit. He spouted scenarios and sought my solutions. He delved into the decision-making process and asked further amplifying questions. He threw in a few ROR scenarios, too. This was the most fraught of the day's quizzings.

We were all relieved to be told individually by the President that we'd passed. Big sigh of relief as this huge hurdle was successfully surmounted. At day's end, we bomb-burst back to our warships or to Christmas leave. I left *Exeter* a couple of days later, crossing Pompey harbour on the Gosport ferry with my kit. My parents picked me up and took me home.

My well-earned Christmas leave was busy. Sue and I got married, went on honeymoon and moved into furnished married quarters (MQ) in Gosport in the New Year. 1 Nasmith Close was a large three-bedroomed house in a corner plot of a small MQ estate, opposite the Cocked Hat pub and a short walk to Stokes Bay. On a good weekday, it was about 40 minutes each way to attend OOW Course which began at HMS Mercury, RN Signals School, on Monday 6 January 1986.

6.2 OOW 55, drawn by Bob Edwards
(Martin Jones)

Commissioned in 1941, Mercury was established at Leydene House, East Meon, near Petersfield. For many years it was home to the communications and navigation faculties of the RN School of Maritime Operations (SMOPS) and trained generations of naval communicators and navigators. We were the next tranche. There were 18 of us on OOW55, some of whom I'd joined up with: Monty, Martin, Traps, Jamie, Chris Davies, Neil Boughton. Kieran, my erstwhile shipmate from *Exeter* was there. Others were blokes I'd heard of but never really met. Our unelected 'leader' was David Higgs. He was Senior Sub during our final weeks at BRNC before we passed out. We grads were a little wary and unsure of him. Senior Sub had to be a bit of a stickler for rules and regulations. He swiftly allayed our concerns as he was a great bloke and good company, with a terrific sense of humour.

The lads lived-in at Mercury. As the only married man on the course, I was the only one living out. I missed out on whatever high jinks young, single, junior naval officers got up to during empty evenings and weekends. All they had to do on weekday mornings was fall out of bed and stumble down to breakfast. I had a daily 30–45 minutes drive from home, depending on Gosport and Fareham's awful traffic congestion.

The big change for everyone was promotion. Our seniority date was 1 January 1986 and we wore the rank, but not 'effective' until 1 May, on successful completion of OOW Course. We A/SLts were now Lieutenants, the Middies were Subbies.

OOW Course kicked off with navigation and a bit of signals and Morse code reading thrown in. Recalling my poor flashing-light Morse code experience during college phases of my deck cadetship, I dreaded standing outside on cold dark winter mornings staring trance-like at the Yeoman's Aldis lamp. Fortunately, most of us seemed equally as bad and it wasn't taken over-seriously by the Yeoman. After this frosty start, we moved into the classroom for navigation training.

Our class instructors were Lt Charles Barker-Wyatt and Lt Jeff Austin, a US Navy exchange officer. Charles was very well-spoken, tall, slender, topped with a vast mop of black hair which perpetually flopped over his forehead and eyes. He continually flicked it clear with his hand. Jeff was a good chap, professional and competent. We all liked him. Unusually for an American, he also had a sense of humour.

These two shared the teaching. The syllabus consolidated and formalised the noddy introduction we'd had at BRNC with our practical experience gained during fleet time. I rather enjoyed the classroom as it reminded me of my cadetship college phases at Liverpool Poly and covered the same material. Easy! The culmination of the navigation module was a week's practical training at sea. In Pompey, we embarked in *Northella*, the RN navigation training vessel.

Built in 1973 for J Marr & Sons, Hull, *Northella* was a 1238 gross ton stern trawler of 70m length, 12.8m beam and 8.1m draft. She and three sister-ships (*Farnella, Cordella, Junella*) and another trawler (*Pict*) were requisitioned to form 11th MCM (Trawler) Squadron in April 1982. Manned by RN personnel, they gave invaluable service during the Falklands War in minesweeping and mine disposal roles. Post-Falklands, *Northella* was retained and converted into a navigation training ship until being sold off and converted into a research vessel in 1999.

6.3 *Northella* entering Pompey harbour, Isle of Wight ferry astern
(Photoship)

Northella was spacious below deck as her fish-deck was now a large chartroom – where we students prepared our charts and notebooks for the coastal navigation exercises – containing a blind pilotage compartment, in which we acted as Blind Pilotage Officer (BPO) in harmony with the lucky bloke conducting visual pilotage on *Northella's* bridge. We were accommodated in small twin cabins and ate in the large communal saloon. The chefs knocked up excellent food.

The week was spent bimbling around The Solent and Isle of Wight. Each day was a sequence of following the navigation plan between various anchorages. For each 'leg' and anchorage, one of us was 'navigator', one plotted fixes on the chart and informed the navigator of their outcome, another provided a similar service as BPO. The rest of us were in the chartroom preparing the next run or psyching ourselves up to follow those already performing up top.

We rotated and cycled through each job for five busy days. With sunrise about 0745 and sunset around 1640, there were ample opportunities to conduct anchorages during twilight and darkness. It was quite testing. Charles and Jeff were pretty busy too and alternated each serial, which enabled them to immediately debrief the blokes who'd just completed an anchorage. Then get ready for the next trio while the trio between were on.

We were all aware of NO's preparation for entry/departure, anchoring and weighing anchor from our fleet time. It wasn't until we did it ourselves that we realised the time and volume of work it entailed. In the MN, Second Mate (navigator) didn't do anywhere near as much in-depth preparation. We made landfall, arrived at the pilot station, embarked the pilot, who then took the ship into and alongside in the port.

Blind pilotage was also something new for me. It was equivalent to visual navigation on the bridge but relying totally on radar. BPO was important not only for monitoring the radar picture for new contacts and identifying navigational features but, in thick fog, NO moved to BPO's position to continue his warship's safe navigation in confined waters.

Through these exercises and roles, we now fully appreciated how and why this rigmarole was used by navies worldwide.

On our second day at sea, we watched the tragic Challenger Space Shuttle disaster unfold on TV in *Northella's* saloon. We were all saddened and did our best to collectively console Jeff, visibly upset at the news. Everyone was rather subdued that day.

At week's end, we'd all done well enough to be assessed as satisfactory navigators. It was a great relief to disembark and go home for a quiet weekend.

OOW Course continued with various other modules. I don't recollect the exact programme, but we spent several weeks on operations and weapon systems at SMOPS in HMS Dryad.

Dryad had an interesting history during World War II. The estate included Southwick House, a late-Georgian style mansion built in 1800. The three-storey house had a two-storey foyer, lit from a cupola, and a series of elliptical rooms. The front colonnade of paired Ionic columns had a central semi-circular portico. In 1940, the estate owners permitted the Navy to use it for overnight accommodation of naval navigation students. By 1941, it was requisitioned and renamed HMS Dryad.

6.4 D-Day Map Room, Southwick House
(The Gosport Shed)

In 1943, with D-Day planning underway, Southwick House became the forward command post of Supreme Headquarters Allied Expeditionary Force. In the run-up to D-Day, it metamorphosed into the headquarters of the top allied commanders, including Supreme Commander General Eisenhower, Naval Commander-in-Chief Admiral Ramsay and Army Commander-in-Chief General Montgomery.

A huge wooden D-Day map used to plan and monitor Operation Overlord was affixed to a wall in the map room. This was the very place where Eisenhower gave the fateful 'Go' order for D-Day on 6 June 1944.

Post-war, Dryad resumed its functions and Southwick House became the wardroom. I was thrilled to sit in the map room, designated the wardroom ante-room, wallowing in its important role in recent history while drinking tea/coffee and reading the newspaper.

At some point, we moved to HMS Excellent, Whale Island, to complete a fortnight learning how to be a Divisional Officer (DO), considered a naval officer's prime role. Never mind being a PWO, pusser or engineer, being a competent, effective DO and leader was essential.

The divisional system dated back to 1755, when Vice Admiral Thomas Smith ordered his captains to organise their ships' companies into divisions, commanded by junior officers. His aim was to improve discipline, the running of the Fleet and sailors' well-being. The divisional system yielded immediate benefits to the Navy: treatment of sailors became more humane; their efficiency improved; and the level of disease fell. The divisional system has proved itself sufficiently robust to deliver leadership and welfare, and flexible enough to adapt to changes in warship design, warfare and technology.

On board, ship's company is split into divisions, each with an officer appointed as DO. The CO is the XO's and HODs' DO. XO supervises the organisation and administration of the ship's divisional system and is the focal point for disseminating policy, supported by the Master-at-Arms (MAA) or Coxswain.

The DO's primary task is to command, lead and manage their people and to supervise and prioritise the work of their Divisional Senior Rate (DSR).

'Walking the patch' was emphasised. To know and lead our sailors was best done 'face to face'. A DO built trust via eye contact and body language by meeting his sailors on their territory and learning about them, their background and family. The value of a brief chat couldn't be underestimated and improved cohesion, morale and effectiveness. A DO's single biggest failure was when a division perceived that they didn't know or never saw their DO. 'Walking the patch' offered an opportunity to assess sailors' professional standards, attitude, dress, hopes and fears. Engagement was key to making individuals feel valued by the Navy.

We'd been Assistant DOs during fleet time so this course consolidated and formalised our recent experience, which definitely varied widely amongst us. Some had participated more heavily than others. By the end of the DO's Course, we comprehended the importance of being a DO and knew our way around *BR1992 Divisional Officer's Handbook*, an invaluable source of information found in every officer's cabin on every warship.

Also located on Whale Island was HMS Phoenix, the Navy's firefighting and damage control school since 1946. We were instructed in methods to combat fire and flood on board a warship. Practical exercises took place on nearby Horsea Island, opposite the magnificent Roman Portchester Castle.

Horsea had a long naval history. From 1804 to 1849 it was a Royal Powder Works, then a torpedo testing range in 1889, and in 1909 a high-power shore wireless station with a forest of tall masts. In the 1950s, the lake was a testbed for improved Martin-Baker ejection seats to reduce or eradicate serious compression injuries to the spine suffered by naval aircrew in catapult launch accidents on aircraft carriers.

In the 1960s, the telegraphy station closed and Horsea Island became home to HMS Phoenix. Its steel structures simulated three decks inside a warship. Fires were set in these trainers for practical instruction and exercises in firefighting. The kerosene/water mixture burned in the trainers caused significant water and air pollution and a health hazard for staff exposed to the fumes for protracted periods.

Horsea was also home to the Superintendent of Diving, diver training for RN and Royal Engineers, operational RN diving units and the Sea Survival School.

In the early 1970s, the adjacent Paulsgrove Lake tidal mudflats were reclaimed, mostly as a landfill site, the remainder formed up-market Port Solent, comprising a marina, multiplex cinema, housing, retail outlets and business units. When waiting our turn to extinguish fire in the training units, I felt sorry for swanky Port Solent's residents, constantly inhaling Phoenix's noxious fumes and seeing thick, black smoke besmirching their harbour views. At least it was only on weekdays.

We completed the basic firefighting course, a prerequisite before joining a RN warship. At Horsea, we performed practical exercises under stressful, demanding conditions. By week's end we felt confident in the kit, organisation and procedures.

In damage control, we repaired leaks in pipework, hammered home wedges into split pipes, and shored up great gashes in the 'ship's side' with mattresses, lengths of timber, pad-pieces, and agri-props. Everything was made more difficult by cold high-pressure water interminably streaming in to slosh around our feet, legs and then waists, until the team stopped the leaks. Being February, there was much fumbling around as fingers gradually froze and lost all feeling. Tools and kit dropped to the deck necessitated an underwater soaking in order to find and recover them. Incessant noise echoed around the steel compartment, making verbal communications difficult. At ENDEX, we emerged to shiver in Horsea's exposed windswept wastes.

I'd done a two-day and four-day firefighting course at Speke Airport (now Liverpool John Lennon Airport), as part of my deck cadet training, but Phoenix's version was far more intense and its steel training cubes were much larger than Speke's.

Attacking a fierce kerosene fire in four-man teams had to be properly organised and coordinated. Each team member had a specific job: leader, water-wall hose-man, jet hose-man, hose-handler. It was hard work in searing heat, dressed in a thick Fearnought suit, with breathing apparatus strapped on my back, lugging a heavy charged hose through hatches and doorways and up/down ladders. We were knackered, sweaty, filthy and singed after every exercise.

Our instructors were excellent. On one exercise, Monty was first man down the hatch to fight a massive fire in an oil tank in the bottom. He asked, 'How do we find the fire if we can't see in the smoke?' The instructor replied, 'Oh, don't worry sir, you'll feel it!'. Yep, we certainly did.

We completed basic sea survival at Horsea Lake. After classroom instruction, we dressed in standard orange 'once-only suits', inflated our life jackets, and climbed the ladder to the platform overhanging the lake. In sequence, we edged forward and stepped off the 5m platform and hit the freezing water. If arms and hands weren't in the right position, on hitting the water the life jacket smacked the face and a mass of cold water shot up the nostrils. Naturally, Horsea's 'once-only suits' were as well-used and battered as BRNC's. Neck and cuff seals were split, some even had small holes in the body. Everyone got soaked. We clambered into the tethered life-raft and settled down for a few minutes before exiting. We backpaddled to the shore as it's impossible to freestyle or breaststroke with an inflated lifejacket on the chest.

At Royal Arthur, Corsham, Wiltshire, we participated in elements of the Petty Officer's Leadership Course (POLC). We prepared and presented a couple of lectures to the class and other stuff which I don't recall. The staff required us to play dog-watch sport after 'school'. We were a bit boot about that and endeavoured to take it out on them during particularly lethal, aggressive deck hockey. The staff team weren't shrinking violets. They gave as good as they got, including the dodgy deacon, who was particularly violent for a man of the cloth.

Before morphing into Royal Arthur, Kingsmoor Camp was in naval hands from the 1920s. In 1950, at the behest of Lord Mountbatten, it was repurposed as home to the POLC. The six-week syllabus focused on: parade training to improve power of command; written work to enable student POs to express themselves on paper (orders, instructions, directives); public speaking (lectures and presentations to the class and staff officers); and studying important naval BRs (*QRRN, Advancement Regulations, Conditions of Service, Drafting and Rosters*). Personal physical fitness improved through organised sport, gym and evening indoor competitive sport. The culmination of physical activity was Royal Arthur's assault course and a three-day orientation in the Black Mountains.

The camp's estate comprised shabby old Nissen huts for accommodation and classrooms and larger buildings for admin and gym. It all needed a lick of paint at a minimum, if not wholesale refurbishment. No doubt asbestos lurked everywhere.

6. Back to Pompey

The climax of our time at Royal Arthur was spent in the Black Mountains in Brecon Beacons National Park. This wild, desolate area of exposed hills spreads across parts of Powys and Monmouthshire into Herefordshire. It was a favoured locale for SAS training and selection courses. In March, it was bitterly cold but, thankfully, not too much rain. We were billeted in a hut at a small training camp from where we did a couple of orientation exercises before completing a long trek in small teams along different routes. Anyone blessed with map-reading skills was stitched up to be team navigator, who we willingly followed. Uphill, down dale we tramped across varying terrain. Fortunately, there were no freezing streams to traverse. Everyone was exhausted on arrival back at base. Hot shower and a steaming brew defrosted us externally and internally.

At some point, our Appointer visited us. He was responsible for hundreds of junior Seaman Officers, like us about to burst onto the 'trained strength', putting bums on seats in ships, filling up seaman sub-specialisation quotas. Even then, it sounded to me like an incredibly frustrating, difficult job, pandering (or not) to his parishioners' whims but focused on warships' needs. No wonder a high proportion were promoted Commander when they moved on.

After introducing himself and explaining his role, we each gave a brief verbal bio and our desired naval career path. He made some notes. 'Well,' he said, 'I've listened to your hopes and wishes. Some of you are going to be disappointed.' Here we go, I thought. I was confident that Neil Boughton and I were fairly safe as we were designated X(H) before we joined BRNC. But you never knew in this man's Navy! Some wanted to be PWOs, others submariners, a few aspired to becoming aircrew and others MCDOs.

The Appointer stated that there was a 'numbers game', so several would be channelled into submarines. After a few questions from us, he closed the meeting and departed.

A few days later, we were informed of the outcome. As predicted, those wanting to be MCDOs were jobbed for submarines. There were a couple of other 'casualties', notably Monty, who was also now destined for submarines. He was distraught and disappointed. We did our collective best to console him. Monty discussed it directly with the Appointer by phone but his fate was sealed. Regrettably, Monty resigned. We were deeply saddened and angered to see him go. Our last view of him was the back end of his red MG driving through the main gate. It may indeed be a numbers game, but at a time when PWO was also rather problematic for the RN, our (Dis)

Appointer's inflexibility caused the Navy to lose a competent, professional, dedicated young officer with stacks of potential.

At OOW Course's conclusion, we bomb-burst for a spot of leave before our appointment to a warship for our first proper job in the RN.

Neil Boughton and I headed to Guzz to join survey ships and begin our 'makie-learnie' time as Probationary Hydrographic Survey Officers.

7.

Makie-Learnie Droggy

7.1 *Gleaner* crest

7.2 *Gleaner*
(Alchetron)

On Sunday 27 April 1986, I joined *Fawn* as a Probationary Hydrographic Surveyor, abbreviated to Prob H and traditionally called a 'makie-learnie'. *Fawn* was alongside 3 Basin in Guzz for maintenance and defect rectification after running aground on an isolated rock somewhere off Scotland. This incident caused major misalignments between the gearboxes and controllable pitch propeller boxes on both shafts. After trials and assessments, *Fawn* was towed from Troon to Guzz, a voyage of 655km completed in 48 hours.

In these glorious years, the Hydrographic Surveying Squadron included four *Bulldog*-class coastal survey vessels (CSVs) (*Bulldog, Beagle, Fox, Fawn*), a fifth (*Roebuck*) was soon to be commissioned. We had four *Hecla*-class ocean survey ships (*Hecla, Hydra, Hecate, Herald*, known as H-boats), two naval parties embarked in chartered vessels and a large survey team in *Endurance*, UK's ice patrol ship. CSVs focused on bathymetric surveys on the UK continental shelf, out to the 200m contour below which the echo sounder was hopeless. H-boats deployed for deep ocean surveys, primarily in the Atlantic, gathering gravity, magnetometer and bathymetric data. The naval parties surveyed UK inshore and offshore areas while *Endurance's* surveyors conducted detached boat camps on the Falklands and other isolated, inhospitable islands in the South Atlantic. Guzz was our home port, except for the naval parties' survey season until they returned to Guzz for winter demobilisation and Pompey-based *Endurance*.

The first RN survey ship was *Merlin*, an 8-gun yacht built in 1666. From 1681 to 1693, Captain Greenville Collins completed a comprehensive survey of the British coastline in her, the first British warship dedicated to marine survey work. The great age of voyages of discovery (Cook, Flinders, Fitzroy and others) conducted hydrographic surveys everywhere as British influence expanded globally. None of their ships were designed as survey ships. Even after the Hydrographic Service was established in 1795, with Dalrymple as the first Hydrographer of the Navy (1795–1808), we continued to convert older warships into survey ships.

The Victorian era witnessed further effort to survey and chart the oceans and coastal waters in an organised, planned fashion. Beaufort (fourth Hydrographer, 1829–1855) tasked naval surveyors to every quarter of the globe. Constantly urging zeal and commending their achievements, he ensured the Surveying Service maintained its foremost position among the world's chart makers. Seafarers knew they could 'trust in God and the Admiralty chart'.

The famous *Challenger* expedition relied on a *Pearl*-class corvette converted to a survey ship in 1872. Under the auspices of the Royal Society, driven by Richards (sixth Hydrographer, 1863–1874), *Challenger's* 1873–1876 scientific voyage of nearly 128000km of surveying and exploration gathered oceanographic data essential to planning and laying trans-ocean submarine cables.

In the 20th century, converted warships continued to be used up to and throughout World War II. The autobiography of the 19th Hydrographer (1966–1971), Rear Admiral Ritchie, *No Day Too Long: An Hydrographer's Tale*, captured the essence of surveying in pre-War years and during the War itself. His tales of derring-do, surveying newly captured North African, Sicilian, Italian, French and Belgian ports, for which he earned the DSC, make exciting reading. Droggies were involved in pre-D-Day preparations with covert sounding and beach surveys of the Normandy coast, checking that beach gradients and texture were suitable for amphibious landings of tanks and armoured vehicles. *Sounding in the Dark*, a short pamphlet by Lt Cdr Berncastle, who commanded this effort as part of Mountbatten's Combined Operations, described these successful and vital operations using adapted landing-craft.

The large *Halcyon*-class minesweepers, used as survey ships during the War, were replaced post-war by four *Bay*-class anti-aircraft frigates (*Dampier, Owen, Cook, Dalrymple*). They were repurposed as survey ships to find and chart the vast number of uncharted wartime wrecks and mines around Britain's coast. Unarmed, they carried survey boats under davits abreast the funnel and minesweeping gear aft.

In 1954, almost 160 years since the Hydrographic Service's foundation, we finally got a purpose-built survey ship. *Vidal* was the last surface ship built at Chatham Dockyard and the first survey ship designed to carry a helicopter. Named after Alexander Vidal, a 19th century surveyor, her worldwide surveying career most famously included the annexation of the minute islet of Rockall during an Atlantic survey in 1955, landing a three-man party to hoist the Union Jack.

While *Dampier, Owen, Cook* and *Dalrymple* plodded on globally into the mid-1960s, the squadron was enhanced with inshore survey vessels. *Echo, Enterprise* and *Egeria* were based on *Ham*-class minesweepers launched in 1958–1959, 30m long and 150 tons. They replaced wartime motor launches and served for over 25 years as the Chatham-based Inshore Survey Squadron. They were supplemented from 1964 by *Woodlark* (ex-*Yaxham*) and *Waterwitch* (ex-*Powderham*), both *Ham*-class and, briefly, *Mermaid* (ex-

Sullington) and *Myrmidon* (ex-*Edderton*), larger *Ton*-class minesweepers between 1964 and 1968. *Echo, Enterprise, Egeria, Woodlark* and *Waterwitch* shuffled out in 1985–1986, shortly before I joined the branch.

Vidal and *Egeria* feature in a 1962 episode of *Look at Life's Plumbing the Depths* on YouTube. This brilliant ten-minute programme shows many aspects of life in the 'survey navy' on board and surveying ashore. Older droggies will recognise some of the cast.

The Inshore Survey Squadron focused on surveys from the east end of the Dover Strait to the Humber, areas of constantly shifting seabed sands. There were occasional forays further north. The boats laid up in Chatham for the winter. Brian Dyde's book, *This Glorious Profession*, describes life and surveying in the Inshore Survey Squadron as well as his early days in *Vidal, Cook, Scott* and *Dampier*, ending with service in our new CSVs and H-boats. His narrative brilliantly evokes long deployments in the Caribbean and among Pacific Islands, surveying with horizontal sextant angles and station-pointers and, later, new-fangled electronic position-fixing systems and the introduction of sidescan sonar.

At last, in the late-1960s, specifically designed survey ships were introduced. *Hecla*-class ocean survey ships replaced *Cook, Dampier, Owen* and *Dalrymple*. The advent of deep-diving nuclear submarines created a need for more detailed ocean charting and much more oceanographic data. Three H-boats (*Hecla, Hecate* and *Hydra*) entered service in 1965–1966, *Herald* followed in 1974.

Four *Bulldog*-class CSVs entered service in 1968. *Bulldog, Beagle, Fawn* and *Fox* were built by Brooke Marine, Lowestoft. Although planned to operate in pairs overseas, they predominantly operated around the UK coast, with occasional paired forays to the Caribbean. *Roebuck*, a slightly larger sister-ship was commissioned in 1986.

HMSML *Gleaner*, the RN's smallest commissioned ship at 15m long, entered service in 1983 to carry out inshore survey work along England's south coast. She also surveyed elsewhere around the UK coast, with occasional visits to overseas ports.

Two commercial survey ships were chartered to form Naval Parties (NP) 1008 and 1016. A team of surveyors was embarked in each as part of the civil hydrographic programme. NP1008 was the larger vessel and team conducting offshore surveys, NP1016's smaller vessel and survey team focused on inshore surveys, particularly where the newly defunct Inshore Survey Squadron had operated.

Finally, a large survey team was embarked in *Endurance*, UK's ice patrol ship. The surveyors were landed to conduct detached boat camps for several weeks in the Falklands. In 1982, this survey team formed part of the Royal Marines' defence of Port Stanley against the invading Argentinians. Lt Chris Todhunter's monograph, *A Droggie Goes to War*, described his experience of the invasion and participation in retaking the Falklands. *Herald, Hecla* and *Hydra* served as hospital ships during this war.

Continuing the theme of wartime participation, *Herald, Hydra, Fox* and *Fawn* were deployed for surveys off the Iranian coast between Hormuz and the Pakistan border during 1977–1979. As the Iranian revolution evolved, these survey ships evacuated British staff of Chah Bahar Nautical College in January 1979. Ultimately, 260 foreign nationals from Bandar Abbas and another 184 from Chah Bahar in February were evacuated. All evacuees were transferred to waiting US warships and safely landed at Bahrain. The finale saw the survey squadron concentrated off Khor Quwai to steam past HM The Queen in *Britannia*. *Herald* and *Hecla* also participated in the first Gulf War as MCM support ships.

When I joined the droggies in April 1986, the Survey Squadron was in rather rude health with four H-boats, five CSVs, *Gleaner*, two naval parties and *Endurance's* survey team.

The Squadron was managed and directed by Captain, Hydrographic Surveying Squadron (Captain H) in Guzz. His staff included a chief-of-staff, operations officer, marine engineering officer, weapon engineering officer plus ratings for admin support and survey stores. Above Captain H was Hydrographer of the Navy, a droggy Rear Admiral based at the UK Hydrographic Office (UKHO), Taunton.

The survey plan was decreed annually, following on from the previous year's surveys, and allocated to survey ships. The vehicle for this was the *Hydrographic Instruction* (HI), introduced by Rear Admiral Parry (third Hydrographer, 1823–1829), among several other innovations: standard scales for surveys; a requirement for surveyors to render reports on their surveys; sailing directions; light lists; and chart catalogues. As well as these heady achievements, he continued the expansion of survey activity during his short reign, interrupted by his own Arctic expeditions.

The HI was a comprehensive document specifying every aspect of the forthcoming survey, the kit to be employed and the standards to be attained. The Hydrographer issued the HI, Captain H allocated the assets/ships to be used and ship's COs were charged with conducting the survey.

At the end of every survey, the CO was ultimately responsible for collating and checking the accuracy and validity of all records produced, the content of the Report of Survey (RoS) and rendered to UKHO. There, various specialists rigorously dissected their respective aspects of the survey to produce a Survey Appraisal. We dreaded receipt of a Survey Appraisal as they often included tricky points and errors to be explained and resolved. The process could take months, during which some of the droggies involved had moved on to new appointments, leaving their successors to sort out the mess – DSMSMR: 'Don't see me, see my relief'. A thankless task if you hadn't originally participated in the survey.

I stumbled up the gangway to be greeted by the QM who directed me to my cabin. I negotiated the narrow ladders, down two decks to the officers' cabins. I found my cabin and met Neil Spicer, my cabin-mate. I fetched my other baggage from the gangway. Neil and I chatted as I unpacked my kit. He was a rangy, gangly bloke with dark hair and, I must say, a rather scruffy beard. He had enormous shovel-like hands. Still, he was welcoming and friendly. I took the lower of the two bunks. Opposite was a pair of chests of drawers/fold-down desk combos in varnished mahogany. On another bulkhead were matching wardrobes and a sink. I think we had a scuttle, but the dockyard wall blotted out any natural light.

I'd never had a cabin at/below the waterline. In cargo ships, officers' accommodation was three or four decks above the weather-deck, which was itself 10m clear of the waterline. Still, at least we had a scuttle and, at sea, limited natural light would penetrate, interrupted by the whoosh and swirl of waves. Forward of our cabin was another twin berth. Officers' heads and showers were a short distance athwartships, past the ship's office and stationery store. XO's cabin was beyond, on the port side, with the navigator's cabin next door, for'ard.

The next morning, I went up to the wardroom for breakfast, during which XO appeared. Lt Cdr John Partington (aka JP) was a bluff Lancastrian of short stature but, I soon learned, with a great sense of humour. He welcomed me on board. The other officers filtered into the wardroom. Lt Gareth Cann, a Welshman and a similar stature to JP, was Navigator. Lt Tim Dickinson was another droggy. Pusser was Lt Gareth Hughes, a tough, fit, balding Welshman.

At 0900, JP took me up to meet the Captain. Lt Cdr Martin Joseph welcomed me to *Fawn* and explained her situation. It was a mystery to him as to why I'd been appointed when she was banged up in 3 Basin for months ahead. He concluded that I wouldn't learn much about 'droggying' here so he'd investigate alternative opportunities. Meanwhile, to get to know the ship as I'd undoubtedly serve in CSVs when qualified and pick up what I could from JP, Gareth, Neil, Tim and the SRs.

I spent the morning self-touring *Fawn*, up and down ladders, scrutinising the ship's plans framed on the main alleyway's bulkhead and meeting sailors. A CSV was a compact little ship with attractive, graceful lines. I was impressed with the Chartroom. This large space, abaft the comms shack and CO's cabin, was light and airy, dominated by a huge chart table in its centre with an A0 plotter and other chart drawers, bookcases and storage against the bulkheads. The Chartroom was the very hub of survey operations, where surveys were planned, working sheets created and drawn, survey records processed and logged, and inking-in of soundings occurred. More of the Chartroom in a later chapter.

The Chartroom Dodger, a LS(SR), was in charge of the Chartroom, responsible for survey data and records and overall cleanliness and management of the space. Instead of sleeping below in a mess-deck, he was privileged to have his own small cabin at the back of the Chartroom – a perk of the job.

I picked up decent ship knowledge and, after doubling-up with other OODs, joined the OOD roster. Duties were 1-in-8 as OODs included both Gareths, Neil, Tim, me, plus Coxswain (PO(SR)), MEO (a CPO marine engineer) and WEO (another CPO). The Duty Watch was 1-in-4, comprising a Duty Senior Rate (DSR) and a handful of sailors to react to and resolve on-board emergencies (fire, flood, injury, security) under OOD's direction. Weekday duties rotated daily but weekends were 48-hour duties to allow as many of ship's company to escape as possible. Most of our general service sailors lived in Guzz, mainly in the massive St Budeaux married patch overlooking the naval base, so there were few 'travellers' at weekends. If not duty, everyone went home after work.

This was a novel experience for me. In the MN, sea-going personnel lived anywhere they wished. The company arranged travel to join a ship anywhere in the world and home again after paying-off months later. Cargo ships didn't have a home port. Depending on their trading route, some never touched Europe or UK. Dry-dockings occurred wherever convenient or cheapest – I did one on different ships in Bremerhaven, Singapore and Oskarshamn, Sweden.

The days rolled by. I settled in and read important surveying reference books. *General Instructions to Hydrographic Surveyors* (*GIHS*), or *Green Book* due its cover's colour, first issued by Rear Admiral Beaufort (fourth

Hydrographer, 1829–1855). *Notices to Mariners* was another of Beaufort's innovations. *Admiralty Manual of Hydrographic Surveying Volume 1* (*AMHS*, nicknamed *Henry*) was a massive 800-odd page tome, first published in 1938, that described traditional survey principles and methods, superseding eighth Hydrographer (1884–1904) Rear Admiral Wharton's *Hydrographic Surveying*. *AMHS Volume 2* comprised seven booklets on particular topics and represented an updating of *Henry* to modern methods. I found *GIHS* and *AMHS Volume 2* very useful. There was all sorts of interesting droggy 'stuff' on the Chartroom bookshelves.

I learned from *Henry* that hydrography originated in the need for the production of charts specially designed for the mariner and critical to the foundation and expansion of sea-borne trade. No two surveys were exactly the same in character, often presenting the surveyor with new problems to test his skill and ingenuity. Fieldwork was sometimes arduous and trying but, unlike many occupations (certainly in the military), resulted in a tangible and permanent record of a droggy's labours. It was of historical interest and the data furthered scientific knowledge.

Henry also informed me that whether in charge of a sounding boat, a detached boat camp, or command of a survey ship, the surveyor must 'possess, develop and foster a capacity for man management'. He must have knowledge of algebra, trigonometry and mathematics. In the old days, draughtsmanship was an asset as most records were hand-drawn. A droggy needed an unlimited capacity for taking pains and a conscientious devotion to accuracy of detail and a methodical, orderly mind. Sloppy work and a lack of attention to detail wasn't tolerated. Crikey, no wonder the surveyors' motto was 'no day too long, no task too arduous'.

Meanwhile, the CO had resolved my 'makie-learnie' problem. *Fawn* had been programmed to survey off the Isle of Man, taking charge of *Gleaner*, who was doing her bit up there. He'd liaised with her CO to transfer me to *Gleaner* for a while. Sounded good to me, rather than kicking my heels in *Fawn*.

I joined *Gleaner* on 13 May in Liverpool's Princes Dock, a few hundred metres north of Pierhead and the Liver Building. Nearby, at the corner of James Street, was Albion House, Blue Star Ship Management's headquarters. I'd been in there many times to sort out expenses during my college phases at Liverpool Poly (now Liverpool John Moores University).

Gleaner had arrived on 9 May for weekend leave. She looked a neat, compact unit on my first view of her sparkling white hull and superstructure, White Ensign flying at her stern.

Built at Emsworth Shipyard, launched on 18 October 1983, commissioned on 5 December, *Gleaner* was the RN's smallest commissioned 'warship' at 14.8m long, 4.7m beam, 1.6m draught and 22 tons displacement. Powered by two Volvo Penta TAMD 122 diesel engines, her maximum speed was 14kts. Commanded by a Lieutenant, her Ship's Company comprised a PO(SR) and six junior rates (a stoker for propulsion, a weapon engineer to maintain the 'wiggly-amp' kit, and survey recorders (SRs)).

SRs, RN sailors specialising in hydrographic surveying, arose because of the impossibility of employing two survey officers in each boat attached to survey ships and utilise the full boat power of the vessel. In 1904, Hydrographer proposed training intelligent POs or seamen to perform the duties of second officer of the boat. As an inducement to attract suitable personnel, he recommended these sailors be categorised as Recorders and awarded extra pay.

To retain these trained men, the Admiralty Board approved that those POs with an aptitude for surveying become Recorders 1st Class when promoted to CPO and drafted to survey ships as CPO(SR) 1st Class. In 1922, a chronic shortage of SRs occurred due to excessive voluntary discharges. Survey ship COs were required to carefully recruit and train suitable volunteers selected from their younger, promising general service ABs.

Training courses for SRs evolved in the following decades such that the ratings' and officers' courses were held at Royal Naval Hydrographic School (RNHS), HMS Drake. To reflect their professional skills as hydrographic surveyors, droggy officers and SRs were given Special Service Pay (Hydrographic).

I met the CO. Lt Bob Mark was my class's navigation instructor at Dartmouth. It was great to meet him again. He introduced me to his crew, a cheerful bunch of young blokes.

That evening, *Gleaner* slipped the berth and, via a lock, entered the Mersey. Heading north-west, we left the Wirral to port, Liverpool's old docks and Royal Seaforth Container Terminal to starboard. The latter was where I joined my first ship (*ACT 5*) in October 1980 to begin my MN deck cadetship with Blue Star. *Gleaner* was very different from *ACT 5*, a 218m long, 29m beam, 10.5m draught, 24212 gross ton refrigerated container ship. *Gleaner* would easily fit across her fo'c'sle.

At the Mersey's mouth, sea state and wind picked up. *Gleaner* pitched and rolled as she passed Bar Light and into the unforgiving Irish Sea. On the bridge with Bob and the helmsman, one of the SRs, I gripped the chart table, braced against the boat's unpredictable, increasingly violent motion. I'd never been seasick but felt queasy now. Bob suggested I retire to the aft cabin and get horizontal until I felt better. I staggered below, fell into a comatose state, occasionally waking to tumble towards the sink to spew, run the tap and use my fingers to work the foul mess down the plug hole. Disgusting, but I was beyond caring. I never mentioned this to Bob and never knew if he suspected anything. Belated apologies, Bob.

7.3 'Cap'n Bob', me (both centre) and some of his motley crew
(Bob Mark)

Recalling nothing of the passage to Douglas, my senses detected *Gleaner's* movement ease on entering Douglas harbour. I emerged, dishevelled and embarrassed, into a calm, dark night. The lads secured *Gleaner* to the buoy. Lights switched off, engines and generator shut down, last man out locked the door and we trooped ashore to our accommodation at a typical English seafront B&B. A favourable rate had been negotiated wherein the landlady did our dhobying. In my single room, I unpacked my kit and fell into bed, exhausted even after being comatose for the voyage.

Daily after breakfast, Bob briefed us on the day's programme and off we went. Usually, Bob, I and most of the crew flashed up *Gleaner* and headed round to the survey ground. Bob's task was HI243 Ramsey Bay to King William Banks (at standard 1:25000 scale), a vaguely diamond-shaped area radiating from Ramsey, the island's second largest town on its north-east coast.

7. Makie-Learnie Droggy

A recce in February sorted out accommodation, stores and a chartroom facility to retain and work on survey data. *Gleaner* sailed from Pompey on 7 April. After overnight refuelling stops in Portland, Dartmouth, Guzz, Newlyn, Pembroke Dock and Holyhead, *Gleaner* arrived in Douglas and commenced HI243 on 21 April.

During my weeks in *Gleaner*, I learned much about surveying. Every cubic inch of *Gleaner's* compact cabin was filled with her survey systems. Depths were acquired using a Type 780 echo sounder, universally fitted to all our survey assets. A single-beam echo sounder, it recorded depths on a continuous paper-trace. Its stylus 'burnt' the sea-bottom's depth onto paper causing a noxious smell which filled any confined space. It took some acclimatising to as that distinctive pong mixed with *Gleaner's* motion potentially caused nausea.

7.4 HI243, Ramsey Bay to King William Banks
(UKHO Archive)

The Waverley 3000 Dual Channel Sidescan Sonar yielded a 'picture' of the seabed to a range of 150m each side. The towfish body was streamed from the stern and linked to a recorder, which used 'wet paper' to illustrate the seabed. As more of the wet paper rolled through the recorder and dried, an SR carefully 'fan-folded' it. Seabed texture was deduced from this paper record. A seasoned user could interpret the nature of the bottom (sand, mud, rock) and identify wrecks or other man-made debris. Allied to this, seabed samples were taken at grid intervals across the survey ground, using traditional lead line armed with tallow.

Tide rises and falls, so soundings must be 'reduced to chart datum'. UK hydrographic survey chart datums are connected to, and always below, Ordnance Datum (Newlyn) (OD(N)). The prime datum of the UK's land levelling system, OD(N) is defined as the average value of sea level recorded at Newlyn from 1915 to 1921. To connect *Gleaner's* bathymetry, a tide pole and Kent Automatic Tide Gauge were established on Ramsey pier and levelled to nearby Ordnance Survey benchmarks. Our observed tidal readings were applied to the echo sounder paper trace to give true depth at that time.

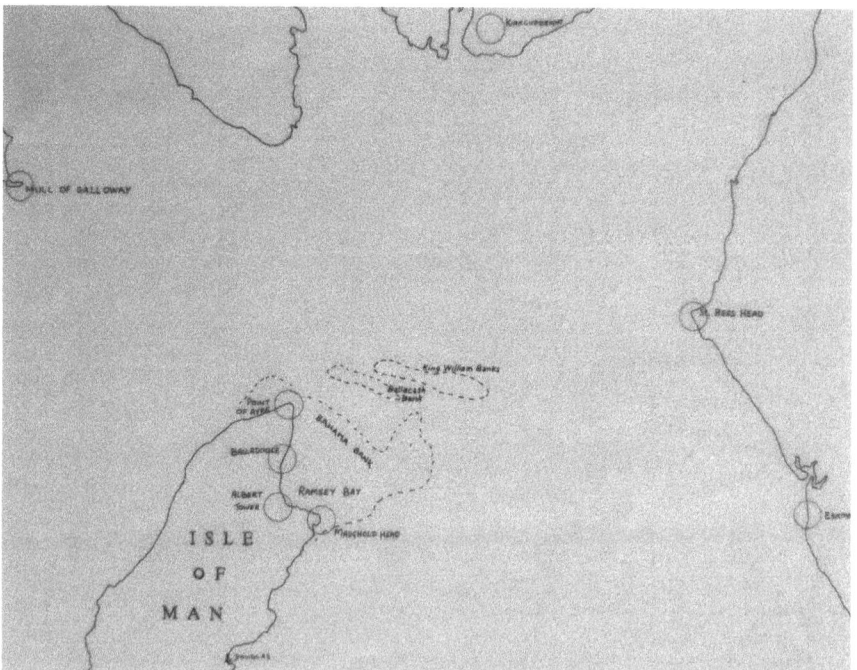

7.5 Trisponder network
(UKHO Archive)

Position was determined using Del Norte Trisponder. Eight transponder units, powered by heavy duty 24V DC batteries, were established ashore at points selected from the Ordnance Survey of Great Britain (1936) Datum to form a comprehensive network. 'Pinged' by the on-board transceiver, the range (80km maximum) of four operator-selected stations were collated within the transceiver to yield a position accurate to +/-3m. The four selected stations yielded the best fix. Sometimes it was necessary to switch out one station for another to retain fix 'strength'.

7.6 Trisponders at: Balladoole; Maughold Head; Point of Ayre lighthouse
(All UKHO Archive)

Time is used to tie-in sounding, sonar and position data. All systems were connected to a computer time source, which initiated a fix mark at two-minute intervals on the paper records. Progress was monitored using an automatic plotter, which also marked a 'fix' at two-minute intervals to create a track plot.

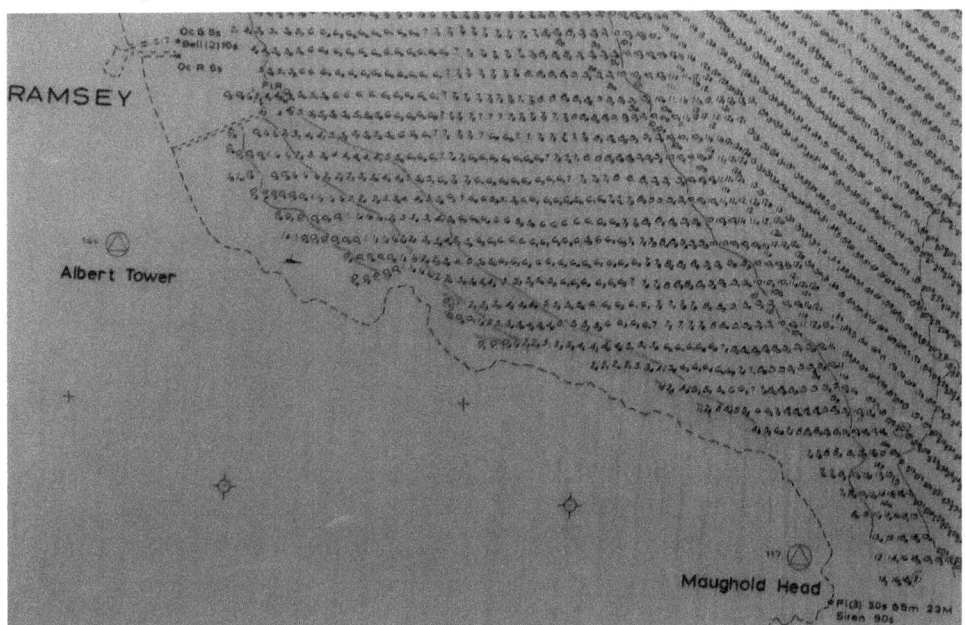

7.7 Extract from sounding collector
(UKHO Archive)

It was rewarding to go out for a day's surveying, run sounding lines across the survey ground collecting data, returning to Douglas in the evening. Meanwhile, the shore party in Douglas replaced Trisponder batteries, checked the tide gauge and worked in the shore office, including applying tidal readings to the echo sounder trace. An SR 'read out' depths on the fix and at three or four points between fixes for the PO(SR) to 'ink in' with a 0.1mm Rotring pen on the sounding collector, an A0 sheet of Ozatex opaque film aligned to the track plot beneath. This collector showed the survey ground filling with soundings, indicating our progress. Unlike any other job in the military, there were tangible, visible results of a day's work in this pre-digital age, ultimately used to update relevant Admiralty charts, available to mariners worldwide. What a great job!

The daily three or four hours commute between Douglas and Ramsey ate into every survey day. This was further reduced when weather and sea state precluded surveying as *Gleaner's* 'rocking-and-rolling' caused poor data gathering. The echo sounder suffered from 'quenching' when the transducer 'pinged' into fresh air and the side-scan towfish wire was subjected to jerky movements. On any odd 'slack' day 'Cap'n Bob' always found tasks for us: changing Trisponder batteries; checking the tide pole and tide gauge; and 'fairing-up' survey records. Bob plodded away at the RoS. I quickly learnt that any fair records to be rendered to UKHO had to be rigorously checked and required the checker's signature. This process ensured that noddy clerical or gross errors were avoided. For every survey, personnel were allocated to fair-up and check survey records.

Evenings were free. The lads went to the pub and, often, the casino. Bob and I enjoyed a couple of pints and dinner somewhere along Douglas' seafront.

A month later, *Gleaner* returned to Liverpool for the 5–7 June weekend at Albert Dock, showing the flag as part of Maritime History Festival Week. I rejoined *Fawn* in Guzz, where nothing much had changed. Same old routine bimbling along as dockyard maties and ship's staff continued to rectify her defects. I got home to Gosport for a couple of weekends.

Luckily, a month later, Bob requested I return to *Gleaner* to assist with the passage back to Pompey. I flew from Southampton to Ronaldsway Airport in a Manx Airlines twin-prop aircraft. It was a novel experience to see the blur of the rotating propeller and hear the engines roar. Cabin soundproofing wasn't top-notch. The stewardess offered passengers a boiled sweet to suck on as we descended to the runway.

Bob picked me up and drove to Douglas in *Gleaner's* Land Rover, an invaluable asset for the shore party to set up, refresh and recover Trisponder stations and tide gauges. *Gleaner's* crew had already recovered the survey kit, packed the shore office and loaded everything on a naval lorry for shipment to Pompey.

On 7 July, *Gleaner's* crew were privileged to attend Tynwald, the opening of the Isle of Man Parliament. Claimed to be over 1000 years old, it's the world's oldest continuous parliament. Prince Edward presided over the open-air ceremony on Tynwald Hill, just off the main road between Douglas and Peel. In the afternoon, the voyage to Pompey began, berthing in Conwy that evening.

The next day we searched for the wreck of *Resurgam*, one of the UK's earliest submarines which sank off Rhyll on 25 February 1880. Sea state and a heavy swell precluded detecting its location. Bob called off our search. *Resurgam* must have been found in later years, because Mick Slater (retired WO(SR) and ex-Operations Director, Bibby HydroMap) sent me images of her. He explained that Bibby HydroMap used *Resurgam* as a calibration site for sidescan sonar and multibeam echo sounder.

 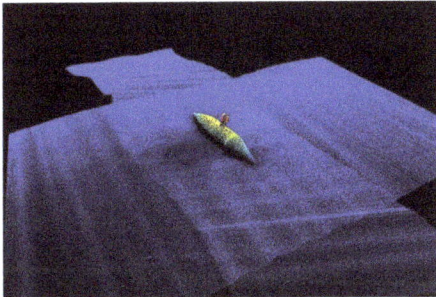

7.8 Sidescan sonar and multibeam echo sounder images of *Resurgam*
(Mick Slater)

Gleaner night-steamed through Menai Strait, an interesting and difficult passage, even in daylight. Differential tides at each end produce very strong currents flowing in both directions at different times, dangerous conditions accentuated by near-surface rocks causing overfalls and local whirlpools.

Unscathed, we berthed at Caernarvon and thereafter at Fishguard, Newlyn, Guzz and Portland before arriving in Pompey on 13 July – days at sea bathed in warm sunshine and benign conditions. Bob and I shared the load as OOW. Off-watch, I sat at the stern and read my book. In each port, we berthed at a marina and used their facilities. Naturally, 'Jack' went ashore nightly for a few 'sherbets', fortunately without incident. In Newlyn, a neighbouring large cabin cruiser befriended them. Their hosts made the mistake of inviting them on board and finally nudged them off in the early hours.

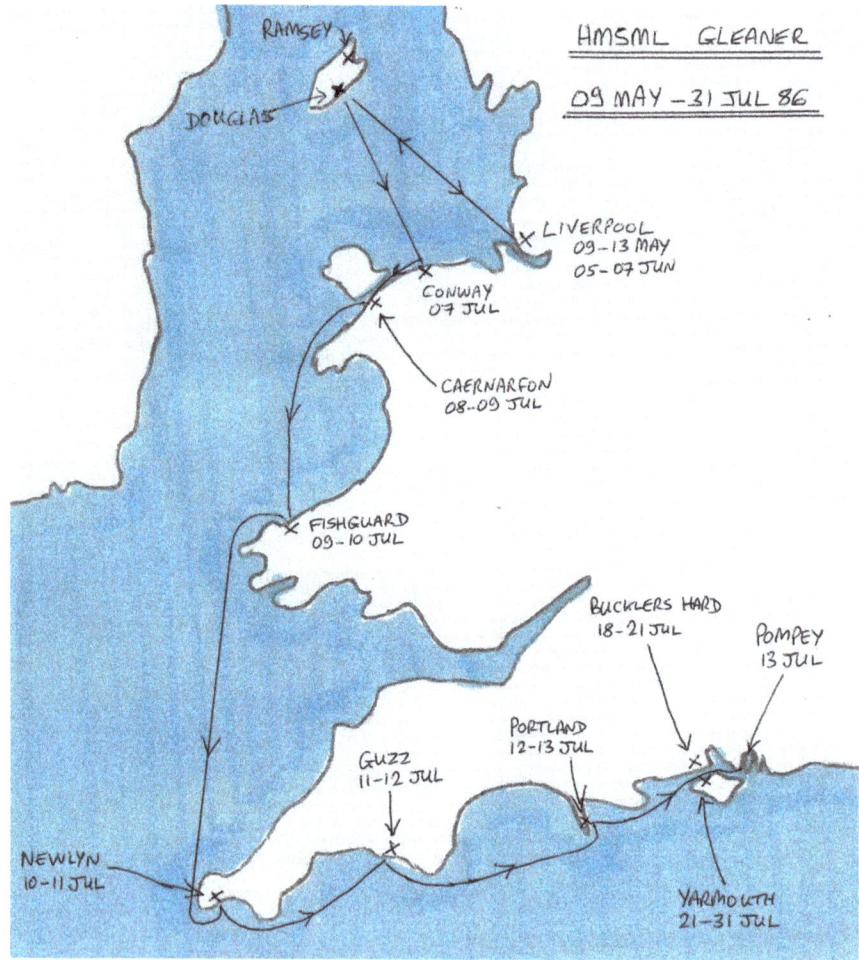

7.9 My travels in *Gleaner*

After a couple of days' leave, we set off to commence HI266 Needles Channel on 17 July, based at Yarmouth. The weekend was spent in Buckler's Hard Marina. Our wives booked rooms in the Master Builder's House Hotel. An intense afternoon of preparations ensued before the cocktail party. The lads in their No.1 uniform, Bob and I in No.5, wives and girlfriends in summer frocks. The guests arrived. Captain H presented a framed reproduction of an early survey of Beaulieu River to Lord Montagu for Buckler's Hard Maritime Museum, marking the formal affiliation of

7. Makie-Learnie Droggy

Gleaner to Beaulieu and Buckler's Hard. Bob arranged the loan of a RM bugler to provide a 'ceremonial sunset', a fitting climax to the function.

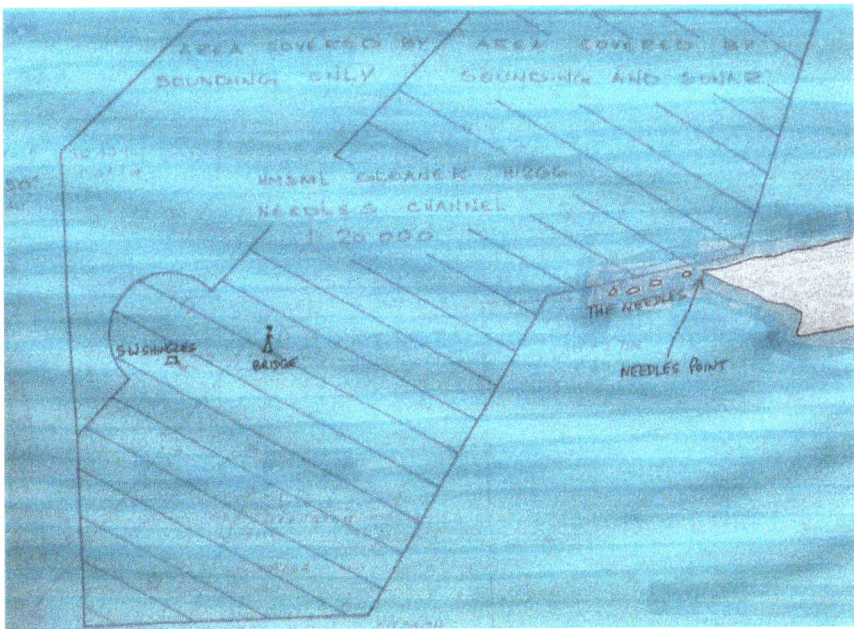

7.10 HI266, Needles Channel
(UKHO Archive)

We sailed on Monday 21 July and got on with HI266. I stayed with *Gleaner* until the end of the month, returning to *Fawn* after summer leave. Post-leave was a busy period as Sue and I arranged to relocate from Gosport to Guzz. I don't recall exact dates, but I think I managed to wangle a couple of days off for the move. The wardroom kindly dined me out and presented me with a beautiful drawing of *Fawn* as a leaving gift. It proudly hangs on the bulkhead, sorry wall, of our study at home.

I thoroughly enjoyed my time as 'makie-learnie'. Despite *Fawn* not going anywhere or doing anything, I got the feel for life in a survey ship. I was bound to be appointed to a CSV at some point. Meanwhile, in *Gleaner*, I learned much from seeing and doing droggying under Bob's tutelage, ably assisted by his SRs. The work covered the spectrum of survey activities performed by our survey ships, giving me a solid foundation for my Basic H Course in September at the Hydro School, HMS Drake. I knew I'd chosen the right sub-specialisation to pursue my naval career.

7.11 Present from *Fawn's* wardroom

8.

Back to School – Basic H Course

8.1 Hydrographic Office crest

Our house move from Gosport to Guzz was seamless. Our MQ in Plymstock was a newer property. Semi-detached, 43 Easterdown Close nestled in a pleasant crescent of about 30 such houses, a stone's throw from Plymstock Broadway shopping area, only a half-hour (traffic permitting) to Devonport and the coast.

My basic hydrographic course started shortly after unpacking, on Monday 8 September. The Royal Naval Hydrographic School (RNHS) moved from Chatham in 1966 and now occupied a stretch of 19th century, thick-walled buildings perched atop a steep slope overlooking Weston Mill Lake at the north end of HMS Drake and Devonport Naval Base. RNHS trained droggies and SRs.

To the left of the main door ran a long corridor, off which were classrooms, chartroom, library and staff offices at the end. Their large windows gave much natural light. In the opposite direction lay store rooms and the crew mess, where the sailors on the staff were based. Several static displays throughout the building illustrated various aspects of droggying to students and visitors. The well-stocked library had a range of technical volumes and general books related to surveying.

As was the naval norm, first morning on course covered admin, introductions and the programme. Cdr Rodney Browne, Officer-in-Charge RNHS, welcomed us to the school. Lean, fair-haired, but stooped with an arched back, an appearance that made him seem much older than he probably was.

Lt Cdr Geoff Rayner was our Course Officer, a well-built, charming chap. He never showed anger or displeasure at his students, no matter how thick or slow we were. Geoff's wingman was a Dutch droggy on exchange, Lt Maarten Gerding, a slightly tubby, dark-haired, bearded bloke with an excellent command of English, as all Cloggies seem to have.

The only other officer on the staff I remember was Lt Cdr Brian Lupton, a schoolie affectionately nicknamed 'Loopy'. He'd been involved with our branch for many years and had been at RNHS for a long time as Computer Officer. Schoolies were the Navy's IT/software/hardware specialists. A soft-spoken, fair-haired, bespectacled chap, he had a ready sense of humour and was always willing to help struggling students.

Other RNHS staff were CPO(SR)s Jones and Roberts, PO(SR)s Steve Hawes and 'Spock' Bidmead, four LS(SR)s, a PO stoker, a couple of stokers and a pinkie. Their main role was to cox and maintain RNHS' 9m survey motor boats (SMBs) berthed below at a pontoon in Weston Mill Lake.

The long hydrographic course, a qualification to look forward to in a few years' time, was in its final weeks. There were probably about eight on that course, some of whom we'd either already served with or had heard of. Droggies were a compact sub-specialisation of some 80 officers and 90-odd SRs. In such a small community, we quickly learned of names, personalities and reputations, many good, others not so. It seemed that once someone had a reputation, he was very much stuck with it.

There may also have been an SR Part 1 or Part 2 Course in residence. We inevitably bumped into all these people, depending on each course's programme, but particularly at stand-easy.

There were seven of us on Basic Course. Geraint West was the only other married bloke, living in Peverell with wife Janet. Sue and I got to know them both well, with frequent dinners and lunches at each other's homes. I knew Neil Boughton fairly well as we'd joined up the same day, were in different Divisions but were classmates at BRNC, had further contact in the confines of DTS and, recently, on our OOW Course. 'Swampy' Marsh and Paul Randall were younger party-boys. Mick Malin had moved upwards from PO(SR) to become an officer. A chubby-cheeked, rotund bloke, he gave the impression he knew it all having completed all SR courses plus his survey ship experience. He wasn't easy to get on with, had an air of unwarranted superiority and looked down on us raw Lieutenants. The last student was Iswinardi (shortened to 'Win'), a short, tubby, young Indonesian survey officer. Earlier in 1986, we'd decommissioned and sold *Hydra* to Indonesia so, post-course, Win would return home as one of their droggies.

For each subject in the syllabus, we were issued with extremely comprehensive handouts. So good, in fact, that we didn't need to take our own notes, except the odd extra scribble. Throughout the course, much calculating and computing was required. RNHS was equipped with electronic Hewlett Packard hand-held 'scientific' calculators, desktop computers and Amstrad 1640 personal computers. The pioneering forefront of information technology!

The course kicked off with a week-long mathematics module. We were shocked by an initial assessment test that covered algebra, linear and quadratic equations, exponents and radicals, logarithms, plane geometry, solid figures, trigonometry, solutions of triangles, radian measure, conic sections, calculus and matrix algebra. None of us had revised, hoping to 'wing it'. When the results were announced we'd failed.

The remainder of that first week covered instruction in differential and integral calculus, partial differentiation, matrix algebra, two-dimensional coordinate geometry and plane trigonometry. Fortunately, we collectively pulled our socks up and passed the module exam. Quite a relief.

Thereafter, we settled into a routine of classroom lectures from Geoff and Maarten across the full spectrum of survey topics. This isn't the place to delve deeply into these subjects, so here's a flavour of the syllabus.

I found it interesting but hard work learning about geometric and physical geodesy, the geoid, determining position on the geoid, deviation of the vertical, properties of the spheroid, and its relationship to the geoid. The prime reference was Bomford's *Geodesy*, a thick, wordy tome which helped make sense of a complex subject. Geophysics was touched upon, another interesting subject. From there, it was a short hop to gravity and geomagnetics and their associated instruments (gravimeters and magnetometers respectively) as fitted in our survey ships. Onwards to the principles and uses of projections used in surveying and computations on projections, particularly Universal Transverse Mercator (UTM).

Surveying control consolidated our practical experience as 'makie-learnies'. Planning and preparation of geodetic control and the framework of a survey were critical. Horizontal and vertical control were explained. Sadly, network analysis was a dark art to me as it involved inputting data to a computer which resolved and produced an assessment of the network's quality. Clark's *Plane and Geodetic Surveying* was helpful in comprehending survey control. Luckily, Geraint was a surveying graduate, so he was a great help.

The importance of field reconnaissance was stressed and thence the marking of control points ashore. This all led to survey computations, including least squares analysis (horror, more of this in a later chapter), 'reduction of observed quantities to the spheroid/projection' and other 'minor control computations'. Crikey!

Geoff and Maarten continued with describing surveying operations in the deep ocean, searches for dangers and shoals, continental shelf surveys, use of sonar, coastlining, tidal observations (tide poles and gauges), large scale and harbour surveys. Vigia, a new word to me of Spanish origin, was a navigational hazard marked on a chart, although its existence and nature hadn't yet been confirmed. Geoff explained how to conduct a vigia search. Something I never did but ocean floor charts were littered with such reported, unverified features. Following on was guidance on the preparation and the critical importance of checking all this data before rendering to UKHO.

Position and measurement science covered the theory of errors, measurement of angles and then the use of theodolites, sounding sextant, level, electronic distance measuring instruments. We frequently spent mornings and afternoons setting up and using these instruments in the field, at various locations in Drake and around Plymouth Sound.

RNHS had Tavistock T2 theodolites, ancient even in 1986 and a cumbersome beast. I wasn't a natural at levelling it on a tripod. There was a certain knack and definite method and sequence to follow when levelling a theodolite, described in *Henry* of course. The little spirit bubbles were bloody difficult to level using the levelling screws at the bottom of the instrument. *Henry* had notes on 'observing horizontal and vertical angles' and 'methods of observing horizontal angles' using the 'direction method'. The observation procedure was long-drawn-out, taking a morning or afternoon, returning to the classroom to calculate the results.

Introduced in 1957, the tellurometer observed linear measurements for ranges 30–50km by comparing the phase of HF radio transmissions to a high resolution and hence accuracy. Its two portable electronic units (master and remote) were of a similar size and weight, comprising the instrument and its carrying case (18kg) in a custom rucksack, a tripod (4.5kg), a power pack (4.5kg), a 12V battery, barometer and whirling hygrometer.

A tellurometer made a basic measurement of time, converted to distance by an assumed radio wave velocity dependent on ambient temperature, atmospheric pressure and water vapour in the air, hence the hygrometer. These factors were measured simultaneously at each unit. A radio-telephone was incorporated in both units. A 'measure/speak' switch converted the carrier waves into a radio channel, enabling operators to communicate. As both had to switch from 'measure' to 'speech', measurements were paused until switching back to 'measure'.

8.2 Tellurometer
(Military Survey)

Siting the tellurometer was important as it operated on line-of-sight, ideally spanning ground of the same quality, rather than a mixture of land and water. After levelling the instruments on their tripods, setting them up was a long, cumbersome procedure with much exchange of information by 'speech' between master and remote, scribbling various readings on the proforma.

I'm sure we used MRA3 tellurometer at RNHS. We were dropped off at various locations around Plymouth Sound to set up either a master or a remote unit. We then went through the process to eventually yield measurements to calculate the distance back in the classroom.

The kit was heavy and cumbersome. Lugging it from the drop-off point to an Ordnance Survey trig point was a slow, painful trek, especially as the rucksack had a metal frame which naturally dug into ribs, kidneys and back. I distinctly recall being marooned and frozen at Staddon Heights, above Jennycliff Bay, on a bitterly cold morning. These exercises lasted almost a school day, so packed lunches were collected from Drake wardroom galley, often including a still-frozen pasty. As the tellurometer was a microwave instrument, we rather pathetically tried to thaw/defrost our pasties by holding them in front of it. A forlorn, futile action.

Today, such observations are so much faster and more accurate using modern instruments with GPS and digital data logging. Young folk have no idea what they've missed compared to the 'good old days', standing around all morning, frozen to the core at an exposed windswept trig pillar, operating a tellurometer or taking observations with a Tavistock theodolite.

Levelling was a method of establishing the vertical distance between two marks, one known (an Ordnance Survey mark) and an unknown (usually a tide pole). The level, another optical instrument, was moved along in short distances between the points, the observer 'shooting' into a tachstaff each time, logging the reading. This was another frustrating experience if, like me, you weren't skilled or swift at levelling the instrument on its tripod. The results were calculated in the classroom. A school favourite was levelling up the steep road gradient from below RNHS to a mark near one of Drake's magnificent stone buildings. The height difference meant that every observation was over a very short distance to get a reading near the bottom of the tachstaff.

The sounding sextant ('hambone' to droggies) was a simplified, more robust version of the marine sextant I'd used in the MN. It had no shades, a wide-angle, low magnification telescope and was graduated in minutes of arc. It was fitted with either a vernier or micrometer reading device. It had similar errors to the marine sextant: perpendicularity of the index glass; collimation; and parallax.

We practised taking horizontal and vertical sextant angles during our boatwork periods in SMBs in The Hamoaze, between the Dockyard and Torpoint. It was quite difficult if the SMB bobbed about in the swell/waves and in a breeze. Legs braced against the bulwarks, flexing to counter boat movement, elbows tucked in to maintain a steady stance whilst observing. When taken, time and angle were immediately noted and the stance resumed. It was cramped in the SMB well deck with two blokes conducting sextant angling to simultaneously make an observation, a third logging the data. Concentration was required. Even short periods of sextant angling were physically and mentally tiring.

A station-pointer was used to plot the position obtained by horizontal sextant angles. The bevelled edges of the three arms (OA, OB, OC) radiated from the circle's centre. OA (the centre leg) was fixed, its bevelled edge married up with the zero of the graduation circle (0°–180°) on each side. OB and OC were movable and clamped in any position. To obtain position, OA's bevelled edge was set against the centre shore mark, OB and OC were set at the observed angle to left and right and set against the left and right shore marks. Hey presto, the centre of the station-pointer's circle (O) yielded the position. Simple but ingenious. This was the prime position-fixing method for coastal surveying for centuries until nullified by the advent of electronic position-fixing systems. Nevertheless, it remained a valid method in some circumstances, so a useful skill to learn.

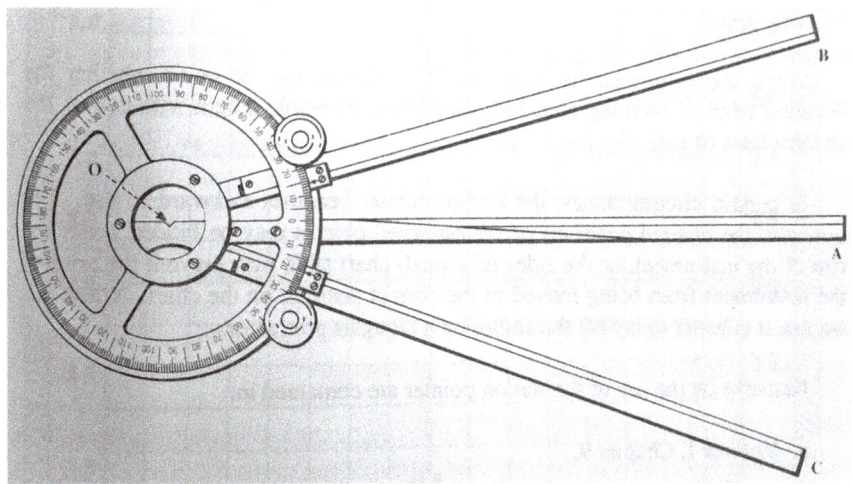

8.3 Station-pointer
(UKHO Archive)

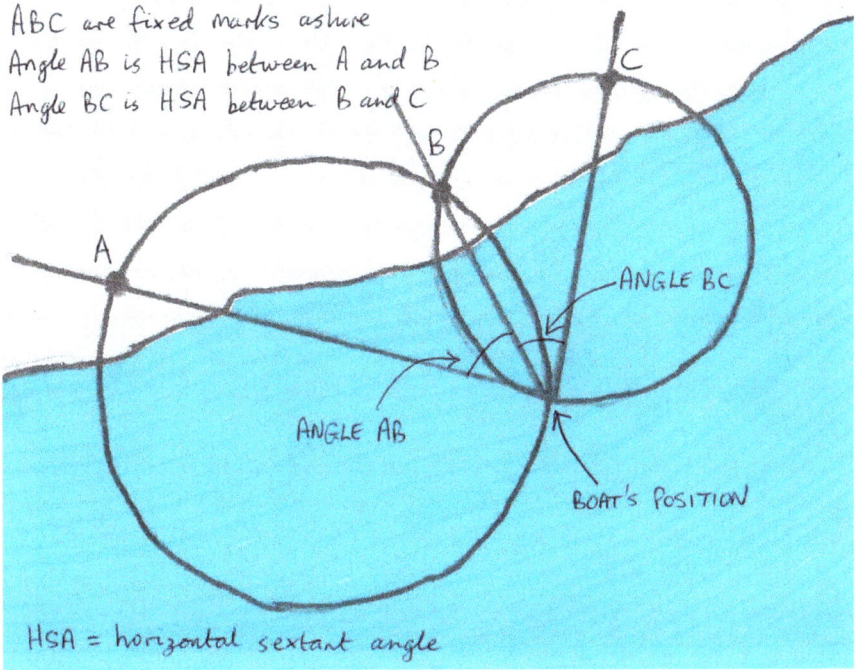

8.4 Station-pointer fix

Coastlining was a method of mapping and delineating the drying line and the coastal topography. The coast within the survey area was walked by the surveyor, logging points of interest to the mariner. A traverse from a known start point to each point, indent or feature, the results plotted and the dots joined up to create a map of the coastline. It was pleasant spending a morning bimbling along the water's edge making observations.

Tides were critical to hydrographic surveys. Geoff and Maarten explained tidal theory, 'real tide', tidal constituents, tidal predictions, co-tidal charts and sounding datums. This led into practical aspects of setting up a tide pole and automatic tide gauge and the importance of tidal observations. Tidal streams were also covered.

Determining position at sea was vital. GPS was in its infancy, so its principles were explained as it was viewed as 'the coming thing' to revolutionise surveying and position fixing. Ultimately, it did, of course. For deep ocean positioning we used the Transit satellite navigation system in harmony with the ship's inertial navigation system (SINS). The latter topic was reserved for long course students. On the continental shelf, traditional methods (sounding sextant and station pointers) were superseded by 'modern' electronic position-fixing (EPF) systems (Trisponder) and hyperbolic systems (Hyperfix). In a CSV, the latter was the prime method of position fixing, the former was secondary.

In addition to *Henry (Volumes 1* and *2)* and *GIHS*, another great reference was Ingham's *Sea Surveying*. Despite being a little dated by 1986, it contained useful information to complement RNHS' wonderful handouts. There was a copy in every ship's chartroom library.

Later in the course, we spent a week at RNAS Culdrose ensconced at the RN School of Meteorology and Oceanography, our first engagement with METOCs. The meteorology and oceanographic sub-specialisation was even smaller than the droggies and provided weather forecasts for the Fleet and FAA. METOCs were found in our aircraft carriers, task groups and naval air stations.

Culdrose (HMS Seahawk) was an exposed, windswept hill-top in deepest Cornwall, near Helston, beyond Falmouth but north of The Lizard. Established in 1944 as HMS Chough (the red-billed, red-legged, black-bodied bird on Cornwall's coat of arms) but changed to Seahawk in 1947 and home to Naval Night Fighter School. Its secondary task was as a base for disembarked front-line squadrons. The skies above Helston filled with the sound of piston-engined aircraft (Firefly, Anson, Sea Fury). In the 1960s naval jet aircraft (Sea Vixen, Sea Venom, Sea Hawk) operated from Culdrose.

Culdrose was designated the RN's main helicopter training base as Hillers, Whirlwinds and Dragonflies arrived in 1958. These were eventually replaced by Wasp, Wessex and eventually Sea King to make Culdrose the largest helo base in Europe. Sea Kings were common to many nations, so foreign aviators joined FAA aircrew for training at Culdrose. In 1960, RN meteorologists moved in and the RN METOC school was established in 1968. I found the METOC stuff interesting, although the job itself looked dull, an endless round of looking at weather info and producing forecasts.

I didn't especially enjoy wardroom life at Culdrose. The building was typical 1960s, inhabited by lots of youngsters at various stages of aircrew training or as qualified squadron pilots and observers. They seemed to think the world of themselves. An aircrew thing? My opinion jaundiced, perhaps, by envy?

The METOC syllabus described physical, synoptic and tropical meteorology, culminating in the analysis of facsimile forecasts which I'd seen and used with Blue Star Line. The most mind-numbing exercise was manually plotting data from meteorological stations to create a weather map. Conversely, physical oceanography was much more interesting. The prime reference was Pickard's *Descriptive Physical Oceanography*, full of good 'stuff' packed into a slim volume. It was a relief to return to Guzz and RNHS after our week's interaction with METOCs and pesky young aircrew.

A memorable afternoon was spent when Cdr Nesbit Glen described and explained his wartime exploits as Second-in-Command of COPP2, an oddity within combined operations pilotage parties as its all-naval team completed particular survey tasks, notably preparations for D-Day. Equipped with a taut-wire measuring machine and echo sounder fitted in 30ft motorboats classified as landing craft personnel (large), Glen and his team conducted surveys into the beaches to be used for D-Day landings and its Mulberry B Harbour.

Their operations began in October 1943. The three boats were towed halfway across the Channel by motor gunboats, then made their own way to the survey ground. The spare boat was anchored as a mark from which Lt Nesbit and his boss Lt Berncastle completed survey lines to as close inshore as practicable around high water springs on moonless nights. To disguise their presence, the boats had underwater exhausts and a light-tight canopy so they could work without showing any light. Around 0400, the spare boat weighed anchor, joined en route by Glen and Berncastle's boats to be towed back to UK.

They carried out five more such operations to the proposed site of Mulberry A and some of the beaches and were never detected. Allied intelligence aerial photographs showed that the Germans didn't start laying beach obstructions until after January 1944.

On D-Day, their role was as navigational leaders for the duplex drive tanks, which had poor forward visibility. These Sherman tanks had a watertight skirt around the top, were watertight below and fitted with propellers and rudders. Glen was allocated to GOLD Beach but when he arrived the tank commanders considered the weather too bad for launching. In the afternoon, Glen went ashore and reported to the beachmaster, who was the captain of the destroyer he'd previously served in. Naturally, they had a small reunion over a bottle of gin in the beachmaster's tent, as the battle was now some miles inland. The following morning, Glen started laying marker buoys for the ships being steamed over from England and sunk to found the breakwater for Mulberry Harbour. What exciting and captivating 'war stories' from a humble droggy. Brilliant!

Talking of small boats, we spent many hours in SMBs, designed in 1971 to conduct visual (sextant angling) and EPFs (primarily Trisponder). They were 9.4m long, 2.9m beam, 1.1m draft and weighed 5.65 tons. A Perkins diesel engine drove a single shaft with reversible gearbox, yielding a maximum speed of 8.2kts and a range of 610km at 8kts.

8.5 SMB, off Newport, South Wales
(Chris Coulter)

With wooden rubbing strakes and an all-round rubber fender, the white GRP hull comprised three sections. A for'ard cabin for domestic facilities and stowages for boat stores. The midships well deck housed the engine and gearbox, batteries, and engineering spares under deck plates, whilst the deck itself was a secondary position for observing horizontal sextant angles.

Survey equipment and plotting took place in the aft cabin with the primary sextant angling position and coxswain at the stern cockpit. There was a cable locker for'ard and, below the aft cabin, were the steering gear and two 35-gallon fuel tanks.

The aft cabin was crammed with survey kit: Type 780 echo sounder, EPF system and sidescan sonar recorder. An SR sat and operated the echo sounder and monitored the other kit. There was also a plotting table upon which sextant angles or Trisponder ranges were plotted along each survey line to yield a track plot. For communications, VHF and HF radios were fitted.

8.6 Example (not on an SMB) of Kitchener gear 'buckets'
(Gerry Quinn)

To provide excellent manoeuvrability, SMBs were fitted with Kitchener gear or Kitchener rudder, better known to us as 'buckets'. The correct name is Kitchen rudder, a combination rudder and directional propulsion system for slow speed boats invented by John Kitchen of Lancashire in the early 20th century. The rudder became a directional thruster. Engine revs remained constant while the buckets were opened, adjusted or closed under the coxswain's control to direct thrust ahead or astern. The cone-shaped buckets were mounted on a pivot either side of the propeller, with the cone's long axis aligned fore and aft when the helm was midships. The buckets pivoted about a vertical axis such that the cone could close off propeller thrust aft of the propeller and directed thrust forwards to create astern movement. Buckets provided excellent manoeuvrability and allowed the SMB to stop almost instantly and turn around on the spot, invaluable when steering survey lines into any coast. Manoeuvring an SMB using buckets was quite a skill, accrued by many experienced AB(SR)s.

With a crew of officer-in-charge, coxswain, two SRs and a stoker, SMBs were designed for day running. Their limited facilities were a small stove and sink, a 25-gallon fresh water tank and food storage, but no heads. It was the stoker's job to keep the surveyors fed and watered. This included knocking up a pot-mess. Typically, a saucepan was filled with tinned spuds, carrots, veg, stewing steak, babies' heads (steak-and-kidney pudding), beans, peas, sausages. Even apricots have been thrown in. Traditionally, the saucepan was never emptied, only added to. Pot-mess was delicious and filling, slices of a white loaf mopped up the dregs, a welcome sustenance during a long day's sounding. This was especially true if sounding occurred daily for a fortnight or more, day running from the ship or a detached boat camp.

Herald was originally fitted with 9m SMBs, as were the four CSVs and, in 1979–1980, they replaced the older 35ft SMBs in *Hecla*, *Hydra* and *Hecate*. Carried in overhead gravity davits, they were hoisted and lowered in up to Force 5, quite a hairy experience. SMBs worked in climate extremes, from harsh Shetland winters to the tropical Caribbean.

Over the years, improvements were introduced. Particularly, a large alternator provided excess capacity to power modern electronic survey kit. With space at a premium, the parent ship fitted the kit suited to its SMB's tasks.

SMBs gave excellent service to the Survey Squadron. Standardisation amongst the boats and the ability to interchange equipment easily and quickly made them potent survey assets. For the development of droggies and SRs, SMBs were great platforms to gain practical experience in seamanship and professional skills whilst gathering survey data. No wonder we spent many hours in SMBs in The Hamoaze and adjacent waters.

I admired the skill of the coxswains in 'steering the (survey) line', manoeuvring the boat at 'end-of-line' in almost negligible water to get onto the next line and head away from danger. The Hamoaze was quite sheltered, so our practical experience was in benign conditions rather than the exposed coasts off which this boatwork frequently occurred. A rolling sea exposed the inherent dangers of lowering and hoisting SMBs. Clear of the ship,

SMBs were susceptible to heavy motion. It was little wonder it was perfectly normal to feel queasy – or worse – when monitoring the echo sounder and operating the sidescan sonar in the cramped, almost airless, aft cabin, with the distinct aroma of the stylus burning the echo sounder paper and the odour of diesel fumes.

Our SMB sessions culminated in a practical assessment of our command and management of the boat by Cdr Browne. He sat in the stern beside the coxswain and got us to each 'take charge' and run some survey lines. It was a relief to know we'd all passed.

As our course neared completion, we were issued an HI to execute a boat survey in the River Lynher. We huddled together to discuss and plan the conduct of the survey. We were responsible for all aspects of it, organising boats, kit, stores, victuals and liaison with SMB crews. In late November, Plymouth's usual wet and windy weather was also cold. We spent the week preparing, conducting and drawing up our survey for Cdr Browne, Geoff and Maarten to appraise. It was quite a management task as time was at a premium and division of labour critical. Still, as on all Basic Courses, we finished the job and were pleased with our end-products. The staff's critique went OK, so all was well.

At some point we had a day trip to UKHO at Taunton. During an escorted tour, we met a few civilian cartographers. A large building housed the chart corrections section and the printworks. The former was a large room filled with rows of draughtsman's desks, each occupied by someone manually correcting charts from the latest *Weekly Notice to Mariners*. So, when charts were ordered and delivered to a customer worldwide, they'd be correct to the most recent *Notice to Mariners*. A dull, tedious, but vital job. The printworks produced the latest editions of charts on huge colour printing presses. We probably had a brief audience with Hydrographer, Rear Admiral Morris, in post since 1985. We certainly met the handful of RN personnel at UKHO, as it was a civil servant-heavy establishment. A good day out.

The final week was exams. We'd survived the progress tests in weeks four and nine. It was now pass or fail time. Failure meant returning to 'general service'. Not something I wished to contemplate. I revised long and hard in my study (our third bedroom in Plymstock), locking myself away for hours every evening.

The five exams were each of three-hour duration: geodesy, projections and computer science; surveying control; hydrographic surveying operations; position and measurement science; and environmental science. The pass mark for each paper was 50% but we had to attain a 60% aggregate overall. Geoff and Maarten informed us of our results at the end of the week. We all passed. I was chuffed and relieved. Cdr Browne presented us with our certificates, we bade farewell to the staff and the lads in the crew mess and shuffled away for weekend leave.

Royal Naval School of
Hydrographic Surveying

H.M.S. DRAKE

This is to certify that
LT. P.J.CARROLL R.N.
has successfully completed the

Hydrographic Officers Basic Course

at the Hydrographic School

this   Twelfth   day of December

Nineteen Hundred and Eighty Six

COMMANDER, ROYAL NAVY
Officer in Charge

8.7 Basic H Course certificate

I was now properly on the RN's trained strength as a newly qualified H2, imbued with the essentials of a survey: POSS+D (position, orientation, scale, shape and detail). I looked forward to joining *Fox* for my first job.

9.

First Job Droggy – Wrecks and Bottom Texture

9.1 *Fox* crest

9.2 *Fox*
(Graham Stevens)

I finished Basic Course on Friday, had Saturday and Sunday at home and joined *Fox* in Guzz on Monday 15 December 1986. As a qualified H2, I now received Special Service Pay (Hydrographic), in addition to LSSB (sea-going allowance) for serving in a sea-going warship. Welcome boosts to my pay packet.

Fox had arrived back in Guzz the previous Thursday after completing HI246 Moray Firth and was getting ready for Christmas leave. On 21 July, she'd begun a crew rotation trial to increase a CSV's time spent on the survey ground. To achieve this, *Fox* didn't return to base port for leave periods but, instead, sent one-third of ship's company ashore for two weeks in every six. Changeovers occurred during a fortnightly 24-hour port visit. Ship's company was divided into three watches (Red, White, Blue) enhanced by several extra bods, so ratings with certain skills were always onboard.

I was delighted to meet Bob Mark again. He'd joined as XO the previous week as a shiny Lt Cdr. I was equally pleased to be assigned to Bob's Red Watch. I went up to meet my new CO, Lt Cdr David Ives, a short, bearded chap with a loud, clear voice, although basically a reserved, quiet man. He was known as a good, solid, professional, competent surveyor. He welcomed me on board and outlined his philosophy on what we were up to and what I should be doing.

As *Fox* was about to start Christmas leave, everyone was on board. I met the rest of the wardroom. Lt Trevor Horne (NO) had been a Long Course student when I started my Basic Course and joined *Fox* about a fortnight before me. Trev was a big, loud, friendly, cheerful bloke, never short of a dit or two. My fellow H2s, Lieutenants Don Ventura and Richard Dobson, had been on board about six months. Don was a soft-spoken Scot and a highly competent, confident surveyor. Richard was a more relaxed chap, well-spoken and smoked like a chimney. The final member of the wardroom was another Scotsman, the Pusser, Lt Steve Shaw, who'd joined in September.

For the crew rotation trial, we were divided between the three watches: Bob and me (Red); Don and Richard (Blue); Trev and Steve (White). The CO was in Blue so when he was off-watch, Lt Cdr Tim Hallpike stood in as CO for a fortnight. Interestingly, when Blue Watch were on leave, Trev retained his NO role, but when Red Watch were off, he acted as XO (in lieu of Bob) while Don assumed NO duties. I learned much later that Trev didn't enjoy crew rotation because, as he pointed out, although nominally NO, he actually only performed as such for two weeks in every six. Meanwhile, neither Bob, Richard, Steve nor I were affected in our roles at all.

Bulldog-class CSVs (*Bulldog, Beagle, Fox, Fawn*) were built at Brooke Marine, Lowestoft – sadly, another now-defunct British shipbuilder. At 1050 tons, they were 58m long, 11m beam and 3.7m draft. Beautiful, graceful compact ships, they resembled palatial beamy motor yachts rather than warships. Their four diesel engines coupled to two shafts with variable pitch propellers gave a range of 6500km and a speed of 12kts. Ship's company numbered seven officers and 38 sailors. They were designed to survey the UK's continental shelf and to deploy in pairs to the Caribbean.

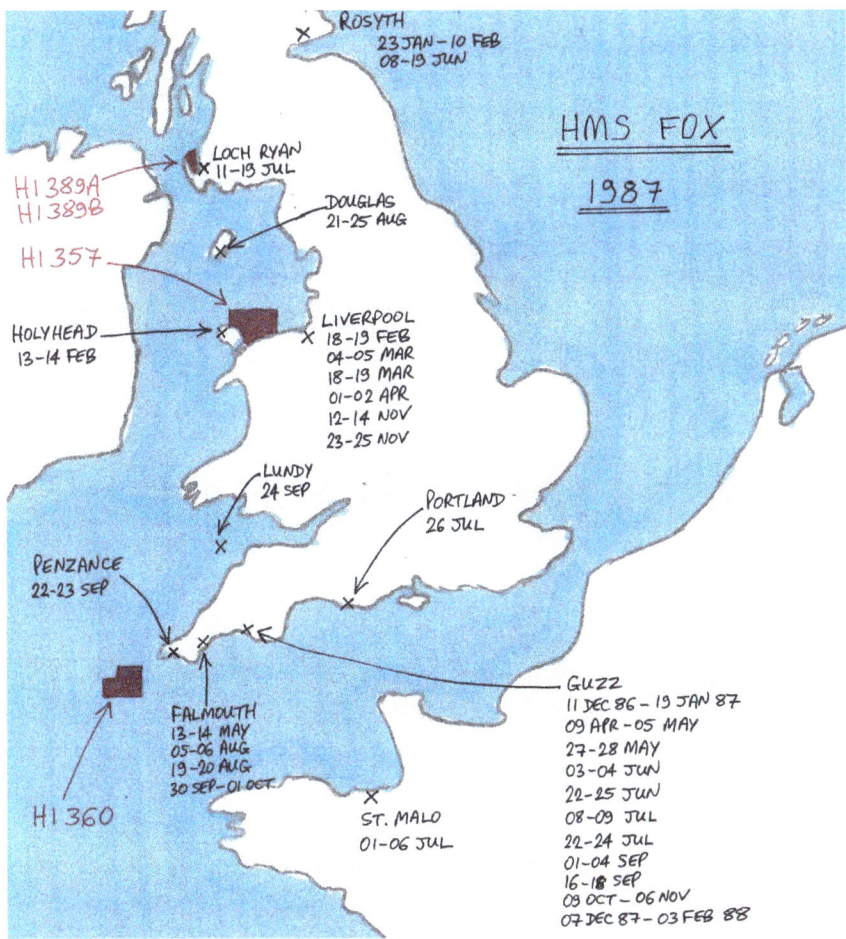

9.3 *Fox* voyages 1987

Fox had a royal connection. In 1973, *Fox* and *Fawn* were surveying off Antigua. *Minerva*, with Prince Charles as Gunnery Officer, also deployed to the West Indies. Charles spent a short period in *Fox*, observing a survey ship at work. Apparently, he enjoyed that time immensely and even had a hand in drawing up the survey fair sheet. More on this royal story later.

Fox's survey suite comprised Hyperfix/Hi-Fix and Trisponder for position-fixing, Type 780 echo sounder, EG&G dual-channel sidescan sonar, magnetometer, expendable bathythermograph (to determine sound velocity in water) and Shipek grab (to acquire seabed samples). SMB

Scorpion was fitted on the starboard gravity davit, on the port side was a Gemini/RIB for boat transfers and MOB. Our main 'armament' was a 2-ton crane on the fo'c'sle which, when trained on any threat, would surely frighten them off! CSVs each had a short-wheel-based Land Rover for setting up, checking and recovering survey kit ashore.

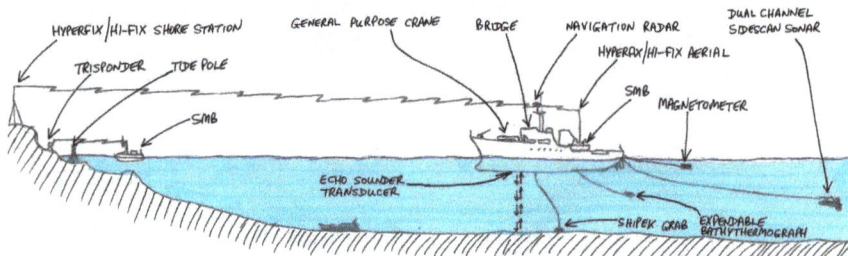

9.4 CSV survey capabilities

Fox moved to 2 Basin, alongside *Fawn*, to enable one duty watch to cover both ships in 'dormant' routine – living in *Fawn* with *Fox* 'dead-ship' outboard. Christmas leave began on Wednesday 17 December, everyone bomb-burst to home, returning on Monday 5 January. After a fortnight's Assisted Maintenance Period (AMP), we sailed for Rosyth with Captain H Staff. They oversaw shakedown training, including damage control and blind pilotage exercises and disembarked at Portland.

The remainder of the passage was in poor visibility, particularly in the Dover Strait. Although I hadn't gone to sea in *Fawn*, my familiarity with her layout was invaluable when *Fox* sailed for Rosyth. I stood my own watches on the bridge and settled into sea routine. We arrived at Rosyth on 23 January, prepared for a hard fortnight of OST alongside and in the Rosyth EXAs. It was pleasant to be back in Rosyth again, a couple of years after my fleet time in *Gavinton/Brinton*. It hadn't changed much in the interim, with a similar daily volume of departures and arrivals of MCMVs and fish-boats, although it was sad to note there were fewer *Tons* as *Hunts* gradually replaced them.

Fox departed Rosyth on 10 February and arrived in Holyhead three days later to start HI357 Irish Sea, Skerries to the River Dee. A couple of days were spent deploying Trisponder stations on the north Wales coast, followed by a few days at sea calibrating Hi-Fix position-fixing system and taking bottom samples. We berthed at the Floating Landing Stage, Pierhead, Liverpool, on 18 February for a 24-hour crew rotation visit.

The subsequent fortnightly periods between rotations focused on surveying, with a couple of afternoons for routine exercises (MOB, MBDD and fire and damage control). There were other interruptions as the Irish Sea's notoriously bad weather caused periodic suspensions of surveying.

I enjoyed the novelty of bridge watchkeeping while surveying. In addition to 'normal' OOW responsibilities, we controlled and monitored the survey operation, continually checked the systems and kit functionality, and general progress of the survey. The bridge had a Glaser plotter upon which the Ozatex A0-size track plot was aligned. The plotter's pen was driven by positional data from Hi-Fix, its ink line showed progress along each survey line and marked a fix at two-minute intervals.

On watch with me were the QM and SR-of-the-Watch. The former was helmsman, whose job was to 'steer the line' when I ordered him to. He did this via a small grey box with a digital read-out of his distance off-line and distance to run to the end-of-line (E-O-L). A decent QM easily steered the line by autopilot, with the odd tweak if *Fox* slightly veered off the line. His role required full concentration as the ship could stray in response to sea, swell and tidal stream conditions.

SR-of-the-Watch monitored the survey kit and alerted QM and OOW as E-O-L approached. He judged when it was necessary to change the paper roll on the echo sounder as it was embarrassing if he saw its end roll through the echo sounder part way along a survey line. The line would have to be aborted, *Fox* turned around to retrace her steps, turned around again back onto the line to resume surveying just before the line was aborted. Not only a waste of survey time but we strove to avoid creating 'holidays' in the data as time would have to be spent later to fill in any gaps.

He also kept an eye on the sidescan sonar trace, a wet-paper record of the seabed topography and features. As the wet-paper (with its whiff of alcohol) rolled through the recorder, it accumulated in a heap on the deck. SR-of-the-Watch carefully fan-folded it when it had dried. At each E-O-L, he snipped off the trace, annotated it correctly and popped it into our home-made sidescan envelopes, old charts cut up and stapled into pockets.

By the mid-1970s, sidescan sonar was essential before any continental shelf area was considered 'surveyed to modern standards'. Our Survey Squadron was equipped with either OAL or EG&G systems, to detect seabed objects of $1m^3$. It was a science to correctly tune the recorder by adjusting its independent controls, but it was an art to interpret the sonograph (the now-dry, wet-paper, fan-folded trace). The prime reference on sidescan sonar was *Professional Paper No.24 Dual Channel Sidescan Sonar Operation & Applications to Hydrographic Surveying*, published in 1977 under the auspices of Hydrographer of the Navy. This excellent little booklet contained everything we droggies needed to know about operating sidescan sonar.

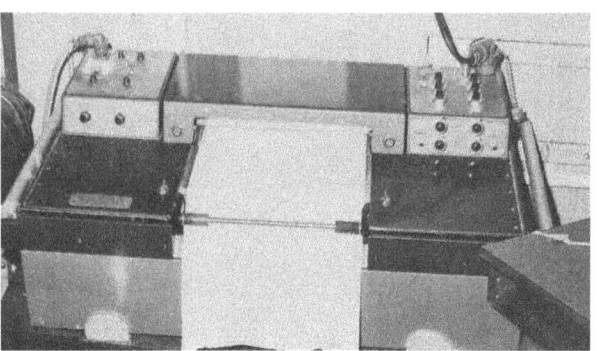 

9.5 Sidescan sonar recorder (left); towfish (right)
(UKHO Archive)

The OAL recorder was a cumbersome beast, 33cm high, 102cm wide, 46cm deep, weighing in at 59kg. It took up the starboard aft corner of the SR's bridge workspace. The 16kg towfish was 137cm long with a diameter of 10cm, its tail-fins spanned 46cm. When not in use, it was secured in a cradle on the quarterdeck.

A well-tuned receiver and towfish at optimum height above the seabed at about 6kts yielded a clear 'picture' of bottom features and texture. Significant wrecks and obstructions weren't always distinctly apparent, although tell-tale signs (solid dark shape and adjoining light shadow) were indicative. Investigations close-in, around and over a wreck, determined its dimensions, orientation and height above sea-floor, reinforced by echo sounder 'least depth' over the wreck.

Before deploying the towfish, a 'rub test' was conducted. The system was flashed up and transmitting. SR-of-the-Watch rubbed the port and starboard transducers in turn. On the recorder, this rubbing caused a dark return on each channel in turn. Hey presto, the system was ready to go.

Streaming and recovering the towfish was a job for on-watch SR and QM, while OOW manned the engine telegraphs and helm. Communication by 'survey broadcast' (tannoy between bridge and quarterdeck) was constant as OOW had to know the exact status of streaming/recovery. It was a relief when the towfish was reported either inboard in its cradle or streamed clear astern. SR and QM then returned to the bridge. Although I'd confidently completed innumerable towfish serials, it was foolhardy to become blasé about the procedures. The sea was an unforgiving environment.

Sidescan had a couple of range settings. For our 1:25000 scale bathymetric surveys we used 150m range scale to each side. This dictated 125m survey line-spacing to ensure total sidescan sonar coverage, with 25m overlap on each line of its adjacent neighbour across the survey ground. It allowed a slight leeway for tiny lapses in the QM's line steering. Survey lines were run along/into the direction of the prevailing tidal stream to minimise uncertainty of the exact position of the towfish. Tidal stream across survey lines could easily push the towfish off the line, causing inaccuracies in plotting seabed texture or, later, finding and investigating a possible wreck.

SR-of-the-Watch monitored the magnetometer (maggy) trace. This bit of kit was sensitive to metal and any other magnetic contacts on the seabed. Normally, its pen trace was a slightly squiggly line, but if we went over or close to a metal shipwreck the trace went bananas, with a brief series high amplitude returns on the trace, before settling back to its steady ambient background squiggles.

OOW managed the whole shooting match, kept the ship navigationally safe and monitored nearby ship traffic. On-line, we streamed the towfish to fly at a height above the seabed of 10% of the range-scale in use. As this was 150m to port and starboard sides, the towfish flew at 15m off the bottom. Survey speed (usually 6kts) and water depth dictated the length of sidescan wire streamed, oftentimes 550–600m. SR-of-the-Watch warned me if the echo sounder depth began to shoal and I'd decide how many metres to haul in to lift the towfish as the depth shoaled whilst maintaining its height at 15m. A little box near the recorder had hoist and veer controls and a read-out of 'wire-out'.

9.6 *Fox* surveying
Ball-diamond-ball shapes (starboard halyard) and red-white-red all-round lights (masthead)
(UKHO Archive)

When surveying we were 'restricted in our ability to manoeuvre'. By day we hoisted three black shapes, ball-diamond-ball, on the starboard halyard, replaced at night by red-white-red all-round lights at the masthead. This privileged state meant virtually every other vessel in our vicinity was obliged to keep clear of *Fox* as she ambled up and down her survey lines.

Each survey line took about 80–90 minutes to run. As E-O-L approached, I keenly watched the distance-to-run reduce and, looking behind me, the Glaser's pen reached the survey area's border. I sent the QM aft, ready to recover the magnetometer. At zero and the Glaser pen on the border, I ordered the maggy be brought inboard as I let *Fox* run on to obtain full sidescan coverage to the border, allowing for the towfish some 550–600m astern. I called 'end of line' and commenced a Williamson turn, normally used when a ship altered to its reciprocal course to retrace her track exactly in order to find and recover a man-overboard. In surveying, we adapted it to turn through 180° to get onto the adjacent survey line, 125m to port or starboard of the line just completed.

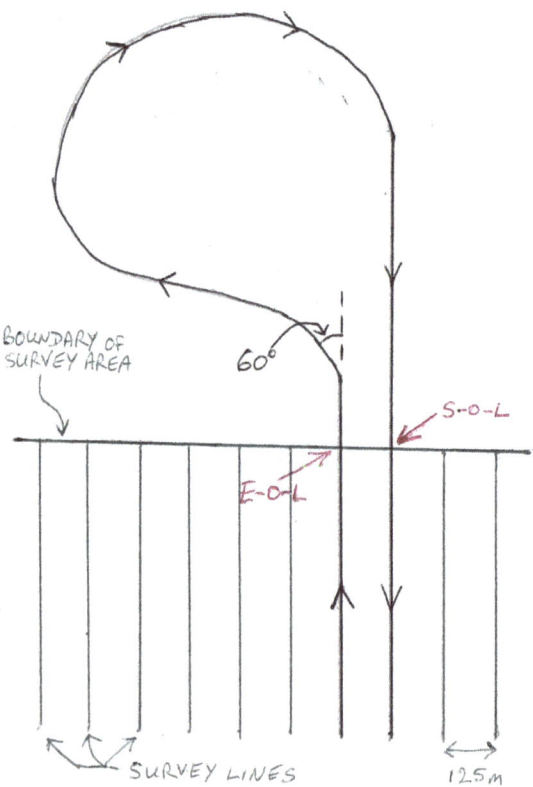

9.7 Williamson turn

9. First Job Droggy – Wrecks and Bottom Texture

At E-O-L, QM remained on the quarterdeck while I increased *Fox's* speed to 12kts, put helm hard over until ship's head was 60° off my original base course, then put hard opposite helm on to bring *Fox* round onto the reciprocal course for the next line and reduced speed to 6kts. Meanwhile, SR-of-the-Watch set the next survey line in the system, did his E-O-L admin, fan-folded the sidescan trace and possibly changed the echo sounder roll. I ordered QM to stream the maggy and return to the bridge, while I manoeuvred *Fox* onto the line for the run-in to Start-of-Line (S-O-L).

It was usually necessary to bring in about 100m of sidescan wire as towfish height dropped during the turn. Bouncing and damaging a towfish on the seabed was expensive in time and costly repairs or replacement. As S-O-L approached, our speed was 6kts, QM was on line, SR-of-the-Watch was ready and sidescan wire veered to the required length so the towfish flew at 15m. At S-O-L on the Glaser and the QM's grey box, I called 'start of line' and off we went.

All OOWs were curious to check time taken from E-O-L to S-O-L, found by looking at the times on the printer's fanfold. As a virgin surveyor, I was initially cautious and ponderous, preferring the QM to be on the wheel for the Williamson turn under my direction, so he went aft before the turn to recover the maggy and again to stream it after the turn. With greater experience, especially as we were operating in a now-familiar area, my confidence and speed increased. It wasn't long until I was on par with my fellow droggies, achieving turnaround times of 80–120 seconds between E-O-L and S-O-L, depending on sea, weather and tidal stream conditions.

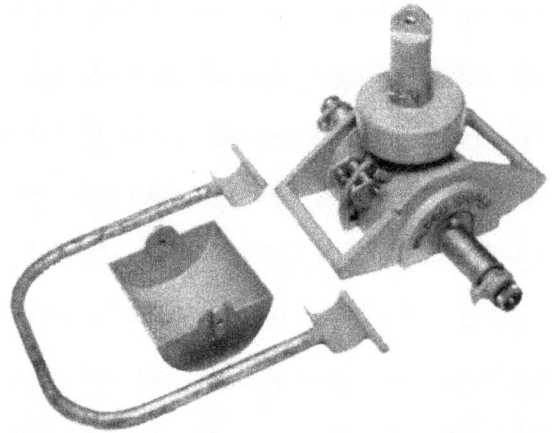

9.8 Main parts of a Shipek grab
(l to r): cocking wrench, bucket, main body

We used a Shipek grab to collect bottom samples. This fiendish, dangerous bit of kit required two SRs to operate. It comprised two concentric half-cylinders: sampler body and sample bucket. The bucket slotted in and the cocking wrench wound the torsion springs to rotate the bucket to fit snugly inside the sampler body. The grab hung from a wire spooled on a winch and remained suspended as OOW drove *Fox* to the sample position. There, OOW reduced speed, went astern to stop *Fox* and veered to give a lee. As soon as possible, from the bridge wing, OOW ordered the grab to be dropped. Released, it plunged by gravity through the water-column. When it struck the seabed, the torsion springs activated the bucket to capture a sample. The SRs winched the grab back inboard and noted the sample's descriptor: fine/medium/coarse sand, shingle, pebbles, stone, mud, broken shells.

The hazardous stages were cocking the grab with the wrench while the grab was suspended at shoulder height and then waiting until ordered to drop it over the side. If the grab accidentally activated when suspended over the deck, it could easily sever a hand or arm. Fortunately, I never witnessed or heard of any such injuries from a Shipek grab.

I enjoyed being on watch. The QMs and SRs were good to be with, general conversation about family, holidays, sport, thoughts on life, career and Navy. There was always humour and wit. They learned when it was necessary to be serious and for events like E-O-L/S-O-L. Due to crew rotation, we all did 1-in-3 watchkeeping, so for each fortnight between 24-hour crew-change, I had the same bridge team.

The QMs were general service ABs. 'Skip' Walters, 'Abes' Abrams, 'Rats' Ratley and 'Bob' Chapman were those I most remember. Skip, a sonar operator, was a blond, tousle-haired, young chap, cheerful and happy with his 'lot'. A dark-haired, bearded, invariably scruffy individual, Abes was a senior AB, good company, although he smoked like a chimney. He famously calculated how our fortnights at sea weren't actually a full two weeks. He didn't count either day of departure or arrival as a sea-day, Wednesday afternoons were 'make-and-mends', 'secure' on Friday was at noon, we didn't work weekends. Subtracting these items from any fortnight, Abes calculated we were only at sea for eight days. 'Jack' never ceased to amaze me with his thoughts and philosophy on life and the universe. Rats was a radar plotter who harboured aspirations to branch change to SR. He thought he was an expert at 'steering-the-line', sadly not borne out by his occasional periods of yo-yoing to-and-fro across the line, necessitating a resurvey of his gaps. I continually monitored poor Rats' steering. Of course, the other QMs good-naturedly but mercilessly ridiculed his performance. Bob Chapman was a boyish-looking, cheekychappy character, seemingly a bright lad who, during my time in *Fox*, applied to transfer to aircrewman. I don't know the outcome.

As a droggy officer, I was DO to the SRs. My Divisional Senior Rate was Coxswain, PO(SR) Rob Lawson, one of *Endurance's* survey team during Argentina's Falklands invasion. Rob was a stickler and rigid disciplinarian. 'Jack' knew not to mess with Rob. 'Kipper' Herring and 'Tony' Hancock were the two LS(SR)s. Kipper was an old-and-bold killick, a glazier before joining the RN in his mid-twenties. Believed to be the only Cockney resident of Scarborough, Kipper was short, pot-bellied, bespectacled and liked his beer. As the prime Chartroom Dodger, he had the little cabin at the aft end of the chartroom. Just as well, as he was a notoriously loud snorer. Tony was Kipper's 'off-sider' as Chartroom Dodger, keeping the space and everything in it well organised and orderly.

The 'new boy' and most junior officer was customarily expected to be Shitty Little Jobs Officer (SLJO) and was allocated the dreadful ancillary tasks (mail officer, public relations officer, affiliations officer). Luckily, I was nominated transport officer and wardroom mess treasurer. The former meant ensuring *Fox's* Land Rover was maintained as regulations required, log sheets properly completed for every journey and Shell fuel card safe. The latter involved collating bar chits, issuing monthly mess bills, keeping the 'books' correctly (for which I had no training whatsoever) and preparing for audits by Steve the Pusser. Overall, I got off quite lightly.

In addition to my OOW role, my survey duties were Wrecks and Bottom Textures Officer. Like all surveyors, I had much to do daily outside my bridge watchkeeping. The previous 24-hours' survey records were moved from bridge to chartroom at 0800. The Glaser track-plot sheet was also changed. In the chartroom, Kipper/Tony checked that echo sounder traces, sidescan fanfolds, printer fanfolds and maggy rolls were correctly annotated and logged. Tide readings were transmitted verbally from ashore by our tide-watcher via HF radio. Chartroom Dodger then applied these readings to the echo sounder roll, marrying up the tide-watcher's times to those etched on the echo sounder roll, using red biro to mark the observed heights of tide, thereby reducing the echo sounder depths to Chart Datum. Later, Kipper/Tony overlaid and aligned the sounding collector atop the track plot, ready for the Captain to 'ink in' the soundings. A joint effort, with Kipper/Tony measuring (with a ruler) and 'reading-out' depth from the echo sounder trace at each fix, the CO scribed the depth with his Rotring pen and called for three or four other depths between fixes. By eye and experience, the Captain judged the number of soundings required to yield complete and even coverage of soundings across the survey ground. 'Inking-in' 24-hours' surveying took a couple of hours hunched over the chart table, taking painstaking care not to smudge any soundings. Chartroom ambient noise was kept to a minimum.

Daily at 0800 (or 0900 after middle or morning watches), I was in the chartroom to inspect and interpret the sidescan sonar trace. I laid the track plot on the chart table, overlaid and aligned my contacts and bottom texture sheet. For each survey line, I looked along the sidescan trace to discern boundaries between different types of seabed. After some practice and familiarity with the survey ground, it was relatively easy to interpret mud, sand or rocky bottom. I used a home-made small scale to take account of the 'layback', the distance from a fix position to where the towfish actually was at that time, 500–600m astern. Gradually, the boundaries between these bottoms joined up as we completed more survey lines. The result was a somewhat primitive map of the seabed showing different textures.

I was also on the lookout for isolated features, as they were likely to be man-made debris or shipwrecks. Included in every HI was a wreck list, extracted from UKHO's extensive wrecks and obstructions database around our coast. Most entries had very little detail, positions were usually dodgy, some derived from fishermen's reports of their nets being snagged somewhere. These were all marked on my textures sheet so it was simple to look for them as I worked my way along each sidescan trace. In my experience, very few were seen on the trace, enabling the CO, using his discretion, to discount many so-called wrecks/obstructions.

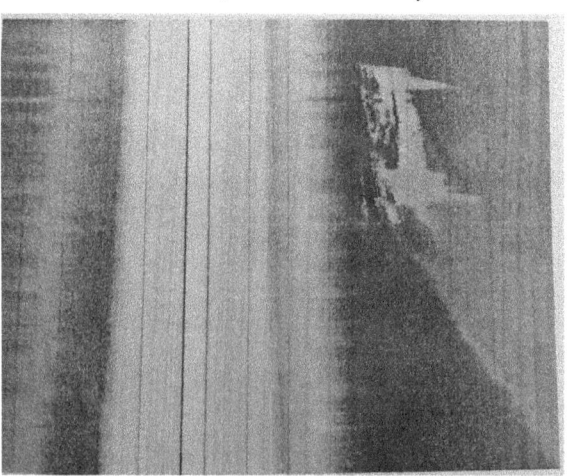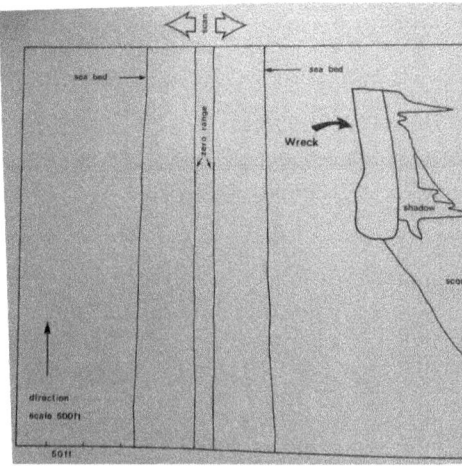

9.9 Wreck on a sonograph (left); interpretation of sonograph (right) (UKHO Archive)

Occasionally we'd detect something unusual. During our survey of the Celtic Deep, sidescan showed a field of about 20 containers that had fallen overboard from a container ship during bad weather. Each was a distinct and separate object of the right dimensions on an otherwise barren sandy seabed.

Sometimes we'd strike lucky, find a proper wreck and conduct a wreck investigation. Its purpose was to position and classify the wreck/obstruction and determine its significance as a danger to navigation. My interpretation of the sidescan trace revealed noteworthy contacts which I logged in my Sonar Contact Book and marked on the Sonar Contact Plot. Daily, I briefed the Captain on new contacts. He decided whether any needed investigating. Those he dismissed, I noted NFA (no further action) in my Contacts Book. Usually, the CO designated a day for investigations to break the daily routine of running survey lines and to catch up on investigations before bad weather, inevitable in the Irish Sea and South West Approaches, precluded surveying.

For each investigation, I prepared A4 sheets for the mini-plotter for each contact and created survey lines around and across it. A wreck investigation began with finding and pinpointing its position, then driving *Fox* to 'box' it with two pairs of parallel sidescan lines at about 3kts. One pair along the wreck's length to give a decent profile of its shape, the second pair across each end of the wreck. The aim was to get good contact in the middle of one sidescan channel's trace. Closely supervised by OOW, accurate steering was required of the QM while SR-of-the-Watch monitored the sidescan trace for the wreck's appearance and thence alerting OOW.

A wreck's position, dimensions and orientation were further refined after these four sonar lines and the towfish was recovered. Now for the tricky bit. A new set of lines at 10m spacing were created perpendicular to the wreck's orientation. *Fox* 'drove' up and down this series of short, narrowly spaced lines to determine the least depth over the wreck. QM really had to be spot-on with his steering. Close sounding lines were re-run as there was absolutely no leeway for being off-the-line. With a 'least depth observed' noted, it was prudent to run another sounding line between adjacent lines (an interline) to check that we'd actually got the least depth.

Much of this work was done 'on the hoof' by OOW: creating sounding lines at correct intervals in the right direction; monitoring QM, sidescan and echo sounder; annotating a mini-plot sheet to show wreck outline and orientation; then its least depth on every close sounding line. It was intense and full concentration was necessary. The bridge team worked in close harmony, focused completely on the task, although OOW was required to maintain a proper lookout for other ships and, particularly, fishing-boats lurking in the vicinity.

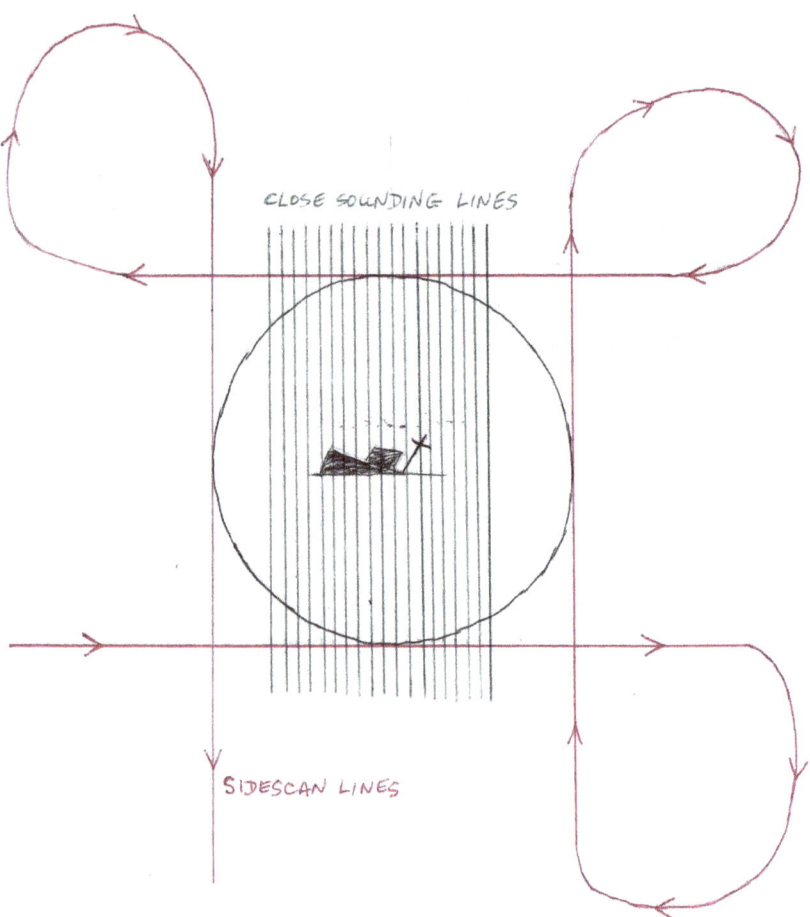

9.10 Wreck investigation

Little wonder that wreck investigations took hours to complete. I enjoyed them as the watch certainly passed quickly. Often, I'd come on watch at night to take over from my predecessor who'd started the investigation. I'd continue with it for my four-hour watch and hand over to my relief to continue and possibly complete it during his watch.

As Wrecks Officer, my work continued in the chartroom where I collated every scrap of data about each investigation: sidescan traces; clippings from the echo sounder trace; mini-plot sheets; maggy trace. A final piece of data was to calculate the wreck's 'height above seabed'. This was crudely achieved using a ruler, simple maths and a calculator. Generally, it broadly agreed with 'least depth by echo sounder'.

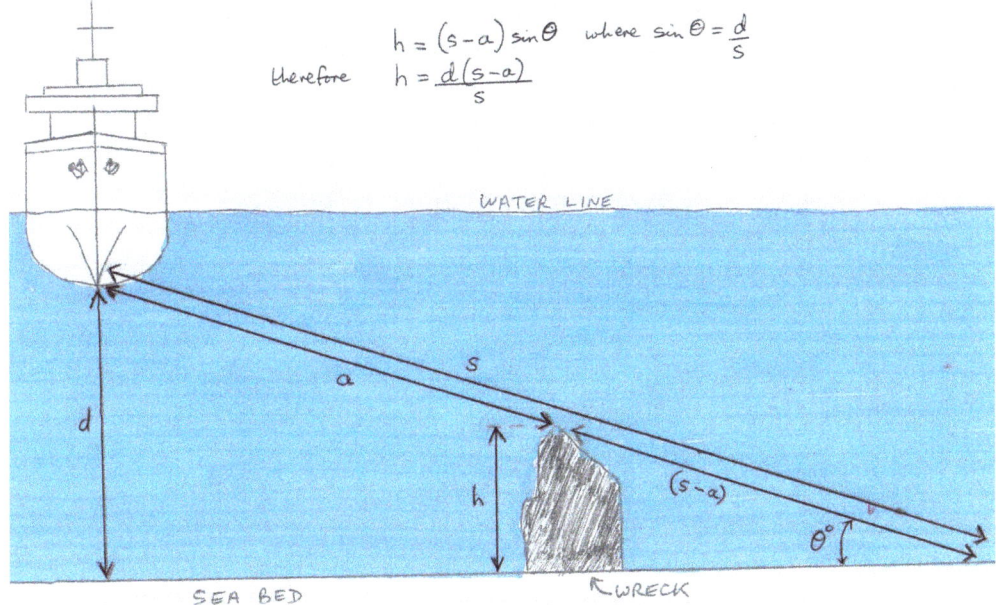

9.11 Calculating wreck's height above seabed
(AMHS Vol 2)

Each investigation had its own annotated A4 manilla envelope in which all this info was placed. Finally, I typed the Wreck Report Form H525. At this time, template forms were used. After inserting one into the typewriter, I carefully aligned by eye each line or box on the form, typing in the relevant information from my notes. Any slight error in typing or alignment of the form meant starting again. It took several attempts to get it right but, like so much in life and work, once I got into a routine and rhythm, I happily plodded along, typing my H525s. It was a laborious, painstaking process requiring the droggy's fabled 'attention to detail'. I'm proud to believe that every one of my H525s and accompanying records were as accurate and precise as possible.

Area 5 of the survey was completed, despite some time lost due to bad weather and fortnightly 24-hour visits to Liverpool for crew rotations. Working close to Liverpool and Holyhead meant visits from Capt H Staff, including Capt 'Jolly Geoff' Hope, who always seemed to enjoy visiting 'his' ships. The Survey Chaplain stayed with us from 31 March until *Fox's* arrival in Guzz on 9 April. Capt H's Staff busied themselves around the ship, checking the engineering departments and chatting to sailors, rarely coming to the bridge. Alas, Chaplains amble everywhere and, unfortunately, gravitated to the bridge if at a loose end. I found such times difficult. As OOW, particularly when surveying, I focused completely on my job so a chatty Chaplain was the last thing I needed. There was no escape, my bridge team were trapped, a captive audience. I know they meant well, but a Chaplain's presence was an unwanted distraction to my happy bridge team.

9.12 Flag Officer Plymouth presented his Commendation to Aussie Austin
(UKHO Archive)

We were alongside in 3 Basin on 9 April for Easter leave and AMP for the remainder of April. Of note, was the award of a Flag Officer's Commendation to AB(SR) Aussie Austin by Vice Admiral Sir John Webster, Flag Officer Plymouth. During our OST, *Fox* had just steamed under the Forth Railway Bridge when MOBEX occurred. Away went the Gemini with Aussie as cox'n and two crew, while *Fox* manoeuvred around, eyes on the bridge, concentrated on monitoring Vlad the MOB dummy. Somehow, Aussie's crew fell overboard so he conducted a real-life rescue of his two sailors under the bridge, in close vicinity of the rocky shoreline. Aussie, his crew and Vlad were hoisted inboard and OST Staff gave *Fox* an excellent report for the exercise.

The other big event was the CO's supersession on 14 April. Although I'd only sailed with David Ives for a few months, I found him a warm, courteous, if quiet man. His successor, Lt Cdr Steve Shipman, a highly competent surveyor, was more outgoing.

9.13 *Fox* conducting a lead-through
(UKHO Archive)

After a couple of days of exercises with *Bulldog* in Plymouth EXAS, *Fox* transited to the Isles of Scilly and began HI360 Isles of Scilly to Land's End, Area 3. This general area, part of the South West Approaches (SWAPPS) was *Fox's* home for most of my time on board. A healthy start was made on the survey, interrupted by a night anchored off St Mary's, Isles of Scilly, sheltering from bad weather and a couple of crew rotations in Falmouth. We berthed at Slip Jetty, Guzz, on 26–27 May for another rotation. We'd completed 80% of Area 3, located and closely investigated three wrecks and, as sidescan and maggy worked well on a flat, featureless sandy seabed, discounted 31 'fisherman's fasteners' on the wreck list.

During the next shortened survey period, three days were lost due to a steering gear defect, repaired in Penzance Bay, before heading north to Rosyth where we berthed on 8 June. *Fox* participated in JMC872. The Joint Maritime Course was a regular exercise from Rosyth, involving warships from several navies. It was a busy fortnight. *Fox* surveyed a couple of exercise areas and conducted two lead-throughs, the first of *Battleaxe* and two Danish frigates, the second of *Ark Royal*. Using Hyper-Fix precise navigation, *Fox* threaded her way through a fictitious minefield and the warships were required to follow exactly in our wake. For the last two days, we were alongside, preparing the survey records for delivery to the Staff of Commodore Minor War Vessels and Mine Warfare on 19 June before sailing that evening.

En route south to the Scillies survey ground, a defect in the starboard gearbox meant the starboard shaft had to be locked. *Fox* limped into Guzz for repairs. Fortunately, we were back in the SWAPPS by Friday 26 June, surveying mostly in heavy mist until breaking off to head for St Malo. This visit was in company with *Bulldog*, *Beagle* and *Gleaner*, plus Capt H Staff. It was primarily a swansong for Capt 'Jolly Geoff' Hope as he was soon to retire. Everyone enjoyed the five days in St Malo. After a cross-Channel ferry trip, Sue and Dobbo's wife joined us. We did a few daytrips near St Malo. The weather was glorious, the beach fabulous, and old St Malo was steeped in history and had plenty of good restaurants.

We departed on Monday 6 July and the ships separated. After a brief survey period, *Fox* headed north to the west coast of Scotland. After an uneventful passage, we anchored at the north end of Loch Ryan on 11 July. We had three short-notice surveys to complete prior to Exercise Purple Warrior. The HI was issued only on 3 July. Our primary task was to establish whether Cairn Ryan jetty could accommodate 7m draught vessels.

Loch Ryan was 13km long on a north-south axis and 4.8km at its widest. A natural harbour, it was an important ferry terminal for traffic to Northern Ireland. Stranraer, the largest town on the loch, was located at its south end. From football scores and leagues, I'd always wondered where such places as Stranraer actually were as Scotland was a geographical mystery to me. Now I knew where Stranraer was.

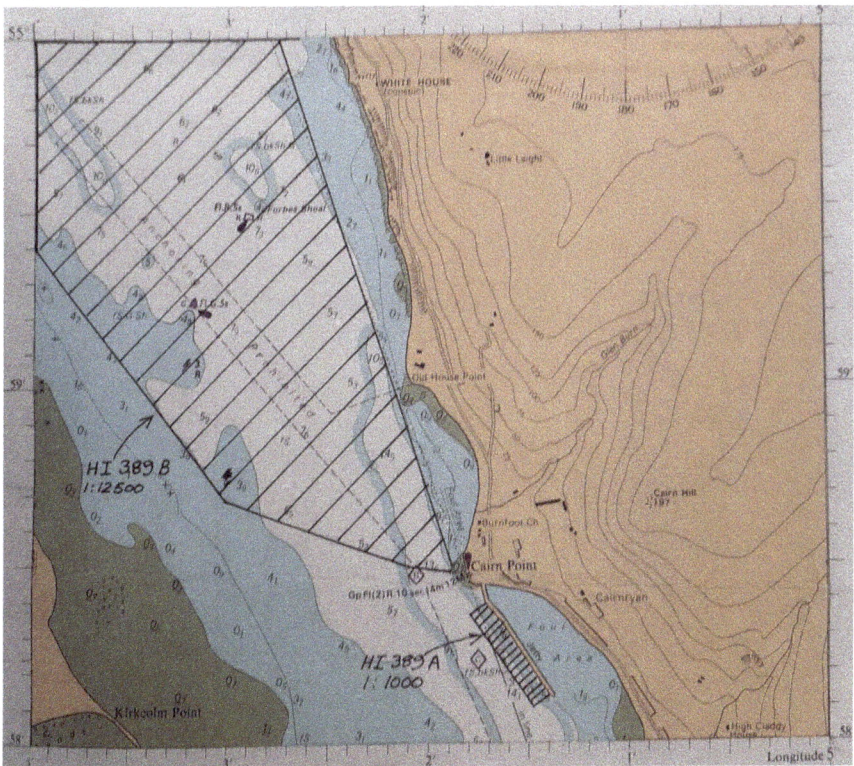

9.14 HI 389 Loch Ryan
(UKHO Archive)

Fox remained at anchor throughout while ship's boats conducted the surveys. I was involved in HI389A, the jetty survey. Our first two days checked survey equipment, levelled the tidepole (set up on the northeast side of the jetty) and established control (a set of transits along the length of the jetty at 5m line-spacing). *Fox's* 18-foot survey boat, armed with echo sounder and sidescan sonar, ran survey lines visually from 50m offshore into the jetty. Often, the boat's bow went under the jetty between its supporting pillars, which required skilled 'driving' by the boat's cox'n to avoid decapitating us.

Cairn Ryan was a popular breaker's yard for many ex-RN warships, most notably the old *Ark Royal*. A sad end to our last true aircraft carrier, star of the BBC TV series *Sailor*, which I avidly watched in 1976. Her slow, lingering death under the scrap man's torch began in 1980, ending three years later. Cairn Ryan was also the final stop for *Eagle* (an older aircraft carrier), the old *Bulwark*, a couple of frigates and several *Ton*-class minesweepers/hunters (*Maryton* (1969), *Crichton, Crofton, Pollington* and *Shavington* (all 1987).

9.15 Pilotage view of Cairn Ryan Jetty
(UKHO Archive)

Our jetty survey revealed a few hefty items 30–50m off the jetty, probably a band of debris corresponding to the outboard sides of *Ark Royal* and *Bulwark*. Sounding and sonar took three days. The weather was dull, misty and cool, but we had long daylight hours in July. Only one day was lost due to adverse weather. We prepared and rushed a tracing of our soundings and areas of seabed debris to Commander-in-Chief Fleet.

Meanwhile, our SMB *Scorpion* did HI389B, surveying Loch Ryan's entrance and the seaway to Cairn Ryan. Three times within the previous six months, Sealink ferries had sustained serious damage when 'taking the bottom'. It was *Scorpion's* job to conduct an exhaustive sonar sweep of the area, locate seabed obstructions and determine limiting depths within the channel. After calibrating, a network of three Trisponder stations was used, a fourth held as a spare. *Scorpion's* crew had an equally busy five days blitzing the entire area by sidescan sonar and echo sounder, investigating all sonar contacts and charted shoals, and conducting cross lines (a series of check lines perpendicular to main survey lines) and bottom samples by lead line armed with tallow. Soundings confirmed the least depth over Forbes Shoal was 4.6m, less than that charted and a 3m isolated rock was discovered just off the bank where it was charted.

A beach survey was also completed of Finnart's Bay on the Loch's eastern shore, near its entrance. *Fox's* Gemini, fitted with a portable echo

9. First Job Droggy – Wrecks and Bottom Texture 231

sounder, surveyed the Bay's approaches, starting on the afternoon of 17 July and finishing on the morning of 19 July. Trevor enjoyed this task as, being a keen ship's diver, it entailed getting into his dry-bag diving-suit.

```
                                                                    H525
                                                                (H.3476/57)
           REPORT ON WRECK EXAMINATION OR SWEEPING

H.M.S.  FOX
H.I No.  389B        of 1987           Wreck Appendix No.   NA
Survey   LOCH RYAN - NORTH CHANNEL
_____

                                    Date located      15 July 1987
   Obstruction (H525/389B/1)        Date examined/swept  18 July 1987
Charted position:   Lat.   NA       Long.
Fixed position:     Lat.   54°59'16".7487N    Long.   005°03'31".7785W
Method of Examination/Sweeping     Close sounding
Fixes

Nav. Decca position (uncorrected)    Not applicable
                                                       Chain
                   Wreck cleared at   NA        metres
                   Wreck fouled at    NA        metres
         Least depth over wreck by E/S   3.8    metres
Estimated height above sea bed (side scan sonar)   1.8   metres
         General depth of sea bed by E/S   5.5   metres
                   Depth of scour by E/S   No scour   metres
Nature of sea bed   Fine sand
Datum to which swept depths and/or soundings are reduced     Chart Datum

Remarks [see GIHS (1982) Article 0945]
This obstruction was first located by sidescan sonar and subsequently examined by close
sounding at 5 metre line spacing. Since both E/S and Sonar returns are similar to those
obtained from a nearby isolated rock there is a strong possibility that this obstruction is
also an isolated rock. Examination by diver is recommended at the earliest opportunity.

(Note: Sections of E/S trace/side scan sonar trace/sweeping diagram to be attached)

                                      Date    19 July 1987
Submitted   T R HALLPIKE                             Officer-in-Charge of Survey
Approved                         Lt Cdr. RN
```

9.16 H525 for an obstruction found during HI389B
(UKHO Archive)

The long days in boats were extended into late hours in the chartroom where data was processed, records 'faired', and preparations and plans for the next day were made. It was pretty full-on for the survey department, relying on unstinting support from engineering and supply departments to keep boats, kit and droggies going. Despite the challenge, tight inflexible deadlines and extremely long working hours, these surveys were a welcome and increasingly rare opportunity to exercise a wide variety of surveying skills, particularly for me as a junior H2.

All kit was recovered on 19 July, *Fox* departed Loch Ryan the next day. During the passage to Guzz, survey records were processed and 'faired up' for rendering after we berthed on 22 July. The next day, *Fox* was fitted out for a trial of the new-fangled global positioning system (GPS, or NAVSTAR). Friday was a Families Day, with 70 guests embarked. From Slip Jetty, we steamed around Plymouth Sound and anchored in Cawsand Bay for lunch. Afterwards, we went up the Hamoaze and Tamar, under the A38 road bridge and Brunel's railway bridge to turn round and return to Slip Jetty. Everyone learned much about the history of this interesting stretch of water from Bob's lively commentary.

Unusually, *Fox* sailed on Saturday morning with five Admiralty Compass Observatory scientists embarked. In Lyme Bay, the GPS kit was fine-tuned before we berthed at Q Pier, Portland, late Sunday afternoon. On Monday, these scientists briefed 20-odd MOD scientists and RN Officers about GPS to prepare for Tuesday's demonstration of the system at sea. Being droggies, we knew of this wonderful, revolutionary system but this was the first time any of us had seen it 'in the flesh', in action. It's difficult to believe that, during *Fox's* trial in July 1986, the general public had no idea of its development and its initial use only by the military. Today, GPS is commonplace and in almost every electronic device.

That Tuesday evening, we off-loaded the kit and visitors and headed back to the Scillies to resume HI360. It was a relief to get back to the humdrum rhythm of our continental shelf survey. But there were a lively couple of days around 8–10 August as *Fox* was inundated by yachts competing in the Fastnet Race.

This classic biennial offshore yacht race covered a 1160km round trip from Cowes through The Needles Channel westward, rounded Land's End, across the Irish Sea to Fastnet Rock and returning around The Scillies to finish in Plymouth. Fastnet Rock is the most southerly point of Ireland, 6.5km south-west of Cape Clear Island and 13km from County Cork on the Irish mainland.

Despite our clearly visible 'restricted in our ability to manoeuvre' shapes, these pesky yachties thought they had right of way because they were racing under sail. Their ignorance of RoR was breathtaking. Several times, OOW used VHF Channel 16 to warn these muppets to keep clear of *Fox* by at least 500m ahead, to port and starboard and 1km astern, as sidescan and maggy were streamed. I'd never had much time for the yellow-welly brigade. I had even less now.

On 18 August, we established a Trisponder station on Bishop Rock Lighthouse. Built by Trinity House in 1858 and further strengthened in 1887, it marked a rock ledge 46m long by 16m wide, four miles west of the Isles of Scilly.

The rocks around the Scillies caused many shipwrecks over the years, including the loss of Sir Cloudesley Shovel's squadron of the British Fleet in 1707, in which 2000 men died. The Elder Brethren of Trinity House decided that the old St Agnes Lighthouse was inadequate and built a replacement on the most westerly danger, Bishop Rock. The first granite structure was completely swept away by a heavy gale in February 1850. Its replacement, 35m tall and 2500 tons of dressed granite, was completed and first lit in 1858. A detailed inspection in 1881 reported extensive damage and structural weaknesses. The solution was to build a new lighthouse encasing the old one and with increased foundations. This increased the light's height by 12m and the building's weight to 5700 tons.

Bishop Rock was still a manned lighthouse. On 18 August, a Sea King helo from Culdrose was used to land *Fox's* WEO on the lighthouse to set up the Trisponder. CPO Hallahan was a trim, soft-spoken chap with a neatly clipped black beard and swept-back hair. In *Fox*, he seemed a kindly grandad-type but could only have been late-40s, having just completed 30 years' service and this was his first helo-winching experience, which I doubt he'd want to repeat.

After a crew rotation in Falmouth on 19 August, *Fox* steamed to Douglas for a four-day visit. Berthed on Victoria Pier's outer wall, there was easy access to the delights of Douglas. But the night of 23–24 August was very uncomfortable due to a Force 6 northerly wind. *Fox* bobbed about, rubbing against the pier all night. Bob, Trevor and I went ashore for a beer or two, leaving Steve the Purser as OOD. Even in the pub, we discerned a deterioration in the weather and curtailed our run ashore. On reaching Victoria Pier, we noticed a yacht in difficulty inside the harbour but off the pier. We tendered our help, the skipper threw us his lines, which we secured to bollards. We asked if he'd just arrived and said it must have been an uncomfortable passage. 'Oh no', he said, 'I was actually trying to sail from Douglas this evening.' We were utterly gob-smacked at that and, reassured he was OK and not going to attempt to sail again, we got on board *Fox*. Yachties! Mad or stupid?

Departing Douglas on 28 August, we returned to the survey ground and completed Area 4 by late afternoon 30 August. Surveying was curtailed due to an easterly gale so we anchored in the shelter of Penzance Bay until it was time to head off to Guzz for crew rotation. There was more adverse weather during the following survey period, with 3½ days at anchor, but otherwise good progress was made. On 23 September, Hydrographer (Rear Admiral Roger Morris) embarked in Penzance for a trip to the survey ground, then onwards to transfer to *Beagle* in the lee of Lundy Island the next day. Surveying continued in beautiful weather until berthing in Falmouth on 30 September for crew rotation. This period was broken on Friday 25 September when *Fox* anchored off Hugh Town in the Scillies for the CO to hold a lunch party to thank local folks who'd assisted us over the past four months.

9.17 Capt Hope presents Hope Operational Efficiency Trophy to Steve Shipman. In background, 'Abes' Abrams
(UKHO Archive)

Meanwhile, technology was moving on. The recently received AMSTRAD 1512 Word Processor made an immediate beneficial impact in completing HI360 Report of Survey. Wow!

The survey was progressed until our return to Guzz on 9 October for AMP into the first week of November. The big news was Capt Hope on board to present to our CO the inaugural Hope Trophy for Operational Effectiveness (1987) to *Fox*. Proof that we'd had a great, productive year. This, surely, was the culmination of Jolly Geoff's long farewell from the RN, starting with the St Malo visit, through his dining-out in October, to the presentation of his eponymous trophy!

We sailed from Guzz on Friday 4 November, heading north to resume HI357 Skerries to the River Dee. The weather was atrocious, forcing *Fox* to anchor for most of the time and even going to Liverpool a day early for one crew rotation. Lt Tim Dickinson (who I knew from my makie-learnie time in *Fawn*) joined on 12 November, taking over from Dobbo who'd left in Guzz during October's maintenance period. Such was the Irish Sea's terrible autumn/winter weather that *Fox* was back in Guzz a day early on 4 December.

The crew rotation trial now ended and it was pleasing that henceforth the whole crew would be on board at all times. Wardroom social life improved as there were more of us around at meal-times. It's difficult to forgot Steward J, never a more unlikely steward. A short, chunky Yorkshireman with a crew-cut above a pock-marked face, Steward J wore the same stained 'white' T-shirt daily. At breakfast, Bob always asked what was on the menu. Steward J listed full English breakfast staples, including 'darkie's walloper' (black pudding), in his broad Yorkshire accent. If soup was on for dinner, I never chose it because Steward J's grubby thumb was always dipped in it as he placed it on the table. Yuk! Nevertheless, he was certainly a character and an integral part of *Fox*.

I enjoyed crew rotation. Its routine of four weeks on, two weeks off suited me. We worked hard when on board but had zero commitments during the off-watch periods. Although it was not quite long enough for 14-night holidays. I never saw the CO's report, but I'm sure the trial didn't sit too comfortably with 'old school' Navy. Crew rotation was never heard of again, until a decade later when *Scott*, followed by *Echo* and *Enterprise*, were commissioned.

Just before Christmas leave, Lt Phil Blackman joined, taking over as Pusser from Steve Shaw. Trev Horne also moved on to take command of *Gleaner*.

For Christmas leave, *Fox* was 'live', with *Beagle* 'dead-ship' outboard in 3 Basin. Martin Jones (*Beagle*) and I volunteered to split OOD duties for the period. Duty for 48-hours on, 48-hours off was an easy routine as nothing was going on in the dockyard with sailors and dockyard maties absent for the festive season. We mutually agreed that Martin did Christmas Day and I did New Year's Eve. On that evening, Sue visited me for dinner and, as midnight approached, we ventured up to the bridge-wing to hear all the ships' sirens sounding off to ring in 1988. Sue repeatedly sounded *Fox's* horn and, shortly after, went home. I followed on 2 January.

Leave ended on 4 January and the remainder of the month was in maintenance. In the survey department, we continued fairing the records from 1987's surveys and prepared for the 1988 season. There was an 'exped' to the Brecon Beacons; *Fox* retained the Survey Flotilla hockey trophy, beating the Naval Parties 5–2 in an exciting match; a couple of major harbour fire exercises, umpired by Capt H Staff; and the entire survey department attended a day's symposium on digital and remotely sensed data in HMS Drake's theatre. Meanwhile, our CO attended a CO's meeting in Guzz, a CO's conference in Taunton, and hosted a lunch and tour of *Fox* for the Mayor and Mayoress of Bideford, our affiliated town.

9.18 Recovered mines on fo'c'sle (left); one of the mines (right) (UKHO Archive)

It was almost a relief to sail, albeit on 3 February, a day late due to hurricane-force winds. We headed north to Rosyth to participate in JMC881, arriving on Saturday 6 February. Briefings on the MCM aspects of JMC881 were given on Monday but sailing was delayed until Wednesday due to that persistent hurricane-force wind. *Fox* spent a week at sea undertaking tasks in support of MCM forces, including recovery of four mines.

We steamed south on 18 February without Rob Lawson as he was to attend the AIB a few days later. We were delighted to learn he'd passed the interview and rejoined *Fox* until he moved onwards and upwards at BRNC.

At first light on Sunday 21 February, *Fox* took in hand HI429 Celtic Deep, an area we grew to love(?), for almost the entire year. For the first few days, we successfully calibrated Hyperfix until we returned to Guzz for the weekend. There, Lt Graham Turnbull (soon to be one of my shipmates in *Hecla*) left for Basic Course, replaced by Lt Jamie McMichael-Phillips (an old shipmate from Dartmouth and OOW Course) as makie-learnie. Don Ventura also moved on, to NP1016. I was sad to see Don go as we'd had such a brilliant, happy year in *Fox*. I missed his soft Scottish burr and sharp wit. I never saw him again. He died suddenly and unexpectedly of a heart attack in March 2023. A tragedy, taken from us far too soon. RIP, Don. Only Bob Mark and I remained from the 'old guard' in the wardroom, plus Steve Shipman as CO since April.

There'd also been changes amongst our SRs. Kipper Herring and Aussie Austin (at least) had gone. Sticky Page was promoted to LS(SR) and did a fine job as Chartroom Dodger. I persuaded AB(SR) Gary Howes to complete the Navigator's Yeoman course. Gary did an outstanding job taking over from Aussie.

Fox spent the first week of March in the Celtic Deep, surveying curtailed by bad weather for only 36 hours, and then headed for Vigo. We crossed the Bay of Biscay under clear blue skies and only occasional ripples ruffled the sea. A school of porpoises frolicked beside *Fox*, ducking and diving around our bow wave. On Friday 11 March, we rendezvoused with *Beagle* off Vigo for a 'formation entry' and berthed alongside Muelle do Laje at 0900. Both COs went ashore for official calls and, on their return, *Beagle's* CO hosted a lunch on board. In the evening, we enjoyed a cocktail party. The Spanish Navy hosted a return reception the following evening and the Port Captain held a lunch for our COs. A combined *Fox/Beagle* football team lost heavily to a local side. Our sailors had a good run ashore in pubs, cafes and to the beach. Warm sunshine prevailed for the entire visit.

Both ships sailed on 15 March. *Fox* had an unpleasant crossing of Biscay in a westerly Force 9 on the beam. It was a relief to berth briefly at Milford Haven to clear customs. Lt Steve Malcolm joined as NO, gapped since Trevor had left. It was another 48 hours of misery until surveying was resumed, before heading to Guzz and 3 Basin for Easter leave from Friday 25 March, followed by an AMP.

We sailed on 26 April, back to the Celtic Deep for a couple of days' surveying until we made a run for Milford Haven to shelter from another Force 9 gale. During May, the survey progressed well between a couple of days of further gales. In fact, the weather was so inclement that we got into Guzz a day earlier than planned, on 19 May.

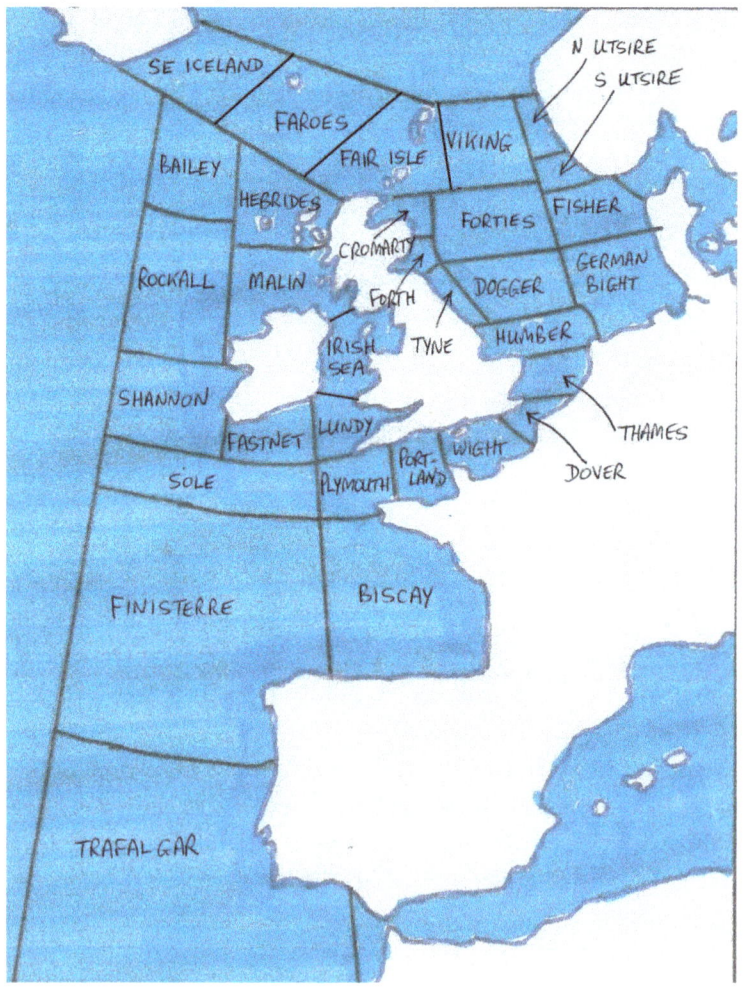

9.19 BBC Shipping Forecast areas, adopted 1949

9. First Job Droggy – Wrecks and Bottom Texture

In this era, we didn't have the luxury of today's accurate and instant weather forecasting. Instead, we relied on the Navy's weather signals, observations through the bridge windows, monitoring falls in barometric pressure on the aneroid barometer (the approach of another depression) and BBC Radio 4 long wave's Shipping Forecasts. These were established by Robert Fitzroy (*Beagle's* Captain during Darwin's voyage and founder of the Meteorological Office). Using telegraphy, Fitzroy issued weather warnings for shipping from 1861. The Met Office introduced gale and storm warnings by areas via radio in 1911.

The BBC first broadcast the Shipping Forecast in 1925. It uses a strict format and text is limited to 350 words, except the 0048 broadcast (380 words to include Trafalgar). Specific words describe the onset of weather events: 'imminent' (within six hours); 'soon' (six to 12 hours) and 'later' (12–24 hours). The forecast's basic order is: gale warnings in force (if any); general synopsis; area forecasts (wind direction/speed, weather, visibility, ship icing). In 2002, Finisterre was renamed FitzRoy, to avoid confusion with the Spanish meteorological service's area of Finisterre. Charlie Connelly's *Attention All Shipping* is an interesting and entertaining history of the Shipping Forecast and each of its sea areas.

Shipping forecasts were a Godsend. The bridge team listened avidly on the HF radio, under the bench abaft the starboard bridge-wing door, to the daily forecasts at 0048, 0520, 1201 and 1754. Famously, the 0048 broadcast was introduced by the distinctive *Sailing By*, a short piece of light music composed by Ronald Binge in 1963. As OOW, I noted the forecasts for Sole, Shannon, Fastnet and Lundy, as these indicated the weather coming at us from across the Atlantic expanse.

During 'silent hours' overnight, we set the HF radio to listen to 208 for Radio Luxembourg, or more commonly Atlantic 252. We were careful with the volume to avoid disturbing the Captain. Calling Steve Shipman at 0630 daily, OOW's report included relevant bits of the 0520 Shipping Forecast as well as survey progress.

We steamed up the Avon for a weekend in Bristol in early June. Past Avonmouth container terminal to port and Royal Portbury Docks to starboard, *Fox* glided upstream and through the Avon Gorge, some 5km upstream from Avonmouth. The gorge, 2.5km long, orientated north-south, cut through a limestone ridge 2.4km west of Bristol city centre. We passed beneath Clifton Suspension Bridge, high above us, based on an original design by Brunel and completed in 1864. It's difficult to believe that *Fox* got into Bristol as the Avon is almost devoid of water at low tide, its width comprised exposed mud flats, except for a very narrow channel.

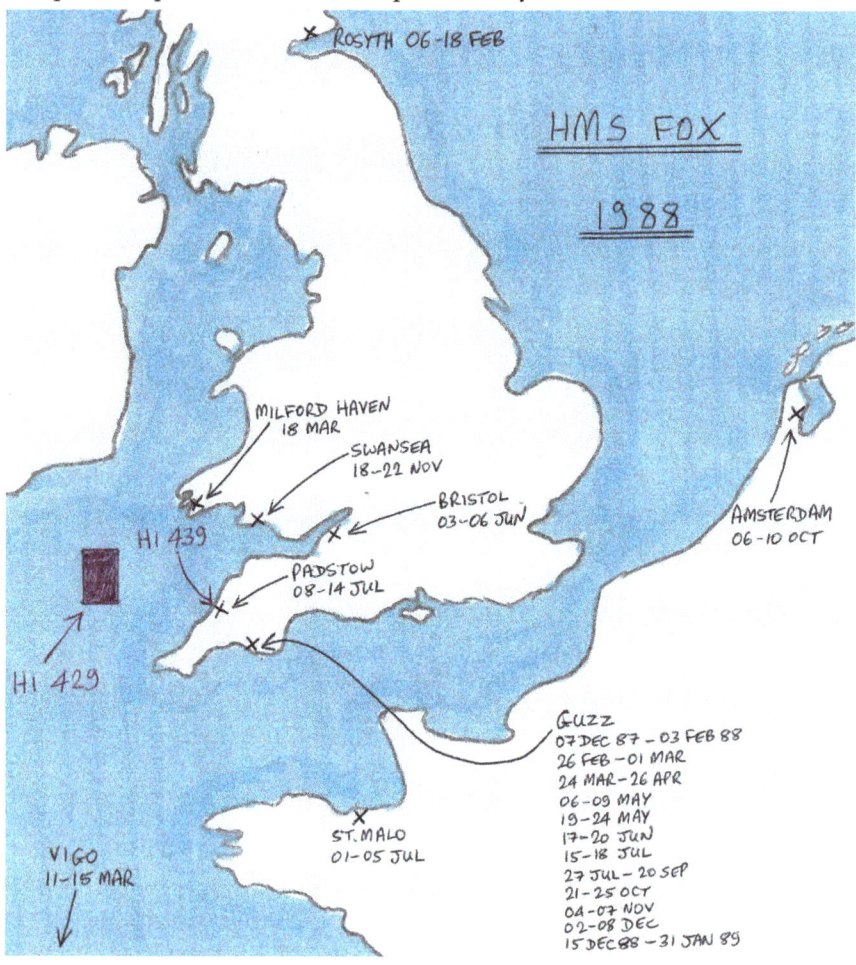

9.20 *Fox* voyages 1988

Departing Bristol, the Survey Chaplain embarked for a full 12 days. It was agonising when, bored out of his skull, the Sin Bosun visited the bridge. As OOW, I was trapped with unwanted conversation distracting me from surveying. SR-of-the-Watch and QM variously requested to fetch tea/coffee, leaving me to entertain the Padre. Luckily, such visits were infrequent and not too prolonged. He certainly busied himself helping the chefs in the galley. It was also pleasant to have someone different at our dinner table. He meant well, like all Sin Bosuns, but I found it quite trying.

Excellent weather in June culminated in a charity barbecue and games night on the quarterdeck on 30 June. Added to the weigh-in for a post-

Easter sponsored slim, over £690 was raised for *Fox's* adopted charity in Bideford. I found 'Jack' was invariably a generous bloke in raising cash for charity.

9.21 *Fox*, St Malo 1–5 July
(UKHO Archive)

Fox spent a long weekend (1–5 July) in St Malo. Despite unseasonal wet and windy weather, it was a rather nautical visit as three French warships and a sail training vessel were also alongside. We cleared customs at Penzance and steamed round to Padstow where the boat camp party were landed. Steve Malcolm was in charge and I was lucky enough to be included. On 8 July, we left *Fox* in SMB *Scorpion* and headed into Padstow, *Fox* returned to the Celtic Deep to resume HI429.

Steve drove *Fox's* Land Rover from Guzz to Padstow and conducted a recce for HI439 Padstow Bay (scale 1:10000) on 6 July. The other seven personnel, including me, met him when we landed in Padstow Harbour, where *Scorpion* berthed overnight throughout. Steve had secured accommodation at Dinham Farm caravan and camping park, near Wadebridge. Fortunately, we were in two on-site caravans. Steve and I shared one with the survey records and kit, the lads in the other. We commuted daily by Land Rover to *Scorpion*.

The first couple of days were spent calibrating Trisponders, establishing Trisponder stations for control and testing *Scorpion's* survey kit. On 10 July, an offshore tidepole was erected and levelled in Hawkers Cove and Trisponders were deployed to Pentire Pillar, Old Stepper Point Light and Brae Hill. The following three days were filled with running sounding lines over the survey area. On 14 July, Trisponders, their associated kit and the tidepole were recovered and we waited in Padstow to rejoin *Fox* when she steamed into Padstow Bay on 19 July.

HI439's primary purpose was to investigate a 9.5m shoal in Padstow Bay reported by Trinity House Vessel *Winston Churchill* in August 1984. We found this very sharp isolated rock pinnacle by sidescan sonar and ran east-west and north-south lines at 10m intervals, towing sidescan sonar to determine the extent and limits of the rock. *Winston Churchill's* reported position was very close to that found by us, the pinnacle's least depth was 7.2m in a general depth of 16m. The results of our investigation were immediately signalled to UKHO, followed by a Hydrographic Note by mail.

9.22 HI439 Padstow Bay
(UKHO Archive)

We then surveyed the River Camel's main channel between Stepper Point (at the river's mouth) and Gun Point, a few hundred metres north of Padstow Harbour. Sounding lines were run east-west across the Camel, plus three check lines north-south down the main channel. *Scorpion* wasn't equipped with a digital surveying system, so Trisponder fixes were manually plotted to yield position, the SMB coxswain driving along range lines from Pentire Point at 50m intervals. It was quite intense work for coxswain and the SRs in the aft cabin. When compared with the most recent previous survey, the drying line on the east side of the channel had migrated west, encroaching into the already narrow navigable channel. Depths in the channel adjacent to Doom Bar were 1m shoaler than charted, possibly due to Doom Bar sediments being moved and deposited in the channel.

We spent five days surveying, lost only a half-day due to bad weather and no time lost due to equipment failure. It was great experience for me. I enjoyed boat sounding and the evening aftermath of processing and logging data and records. Long days but most rewarding to achieve great results. 'Jack' always enjoyed boat camps. When our day's work was done, they got stuck into the 'beer store' in their caravan, led by LS(SR) 'Sid' Ford, an excellent SMB coxswain renowned for his fondness for beer. Luckily, the lads didn't cause mischief or noisily disturb fellow-campers.

After recovering the boat camp crew and *Scorpion*, *Fox* resumed HI429. Of the 15 days available for surveying, 7½ were lost through atrocious weather. We returned to 3 Basin for Summer leave on 27 July, operating a dormant leave routine with *Bulldog* and *Roebuck*. Post-leave was busy, preparing to participate in Navy Days and moving to 4 Wharf. *Fox* logged over 6000 visitors during Navy Days. S/Lt Ian Merchant took over as Pusser from Phil Blackman. Lt Geraint West joined from *Hecate* as H2, relieving Tim Dickinson. PO(SR) Mick Slater joined as Coxswain as Rob Lawson departed for BRNC.

After Navy Days, *Fox* had an SMP during which several events occurred. *Fox* was to be decommissioned at year's end so an enjoyable combined 20th birthday and farewell cocktail party was held on the evening of 2 September. Among the 56 guests were previous *Fox* officers and their wives. Flotilla Week also took place, an opportunity for survey ships' teams to compete in a range of sports. We placed third in swimming and athletics and won tug-of-war. A Defence Sales team visited on 15 September to discuss with Capt H Staff and our CO and XO proposals for *Fox's* forthcoming sale. A sad note for all.

We sailed on 20 September and picked up HI429. Good conditions were short-lived as the Celtic Deep plunged into another violent stormy period. Only 5½ days' surveying were achieved out of an available 10 this month. The remnants of Hurricane Gilbert forced us to run for shelter alongside Pembroke Dock at the head of Milford Haven. We resumed surveying for a few days before making passage to Amsterdam for a four-day visit. Berthed in the city centre, there was easy access to Amsterdam's many bars, cafes and (in)famous red-light district.

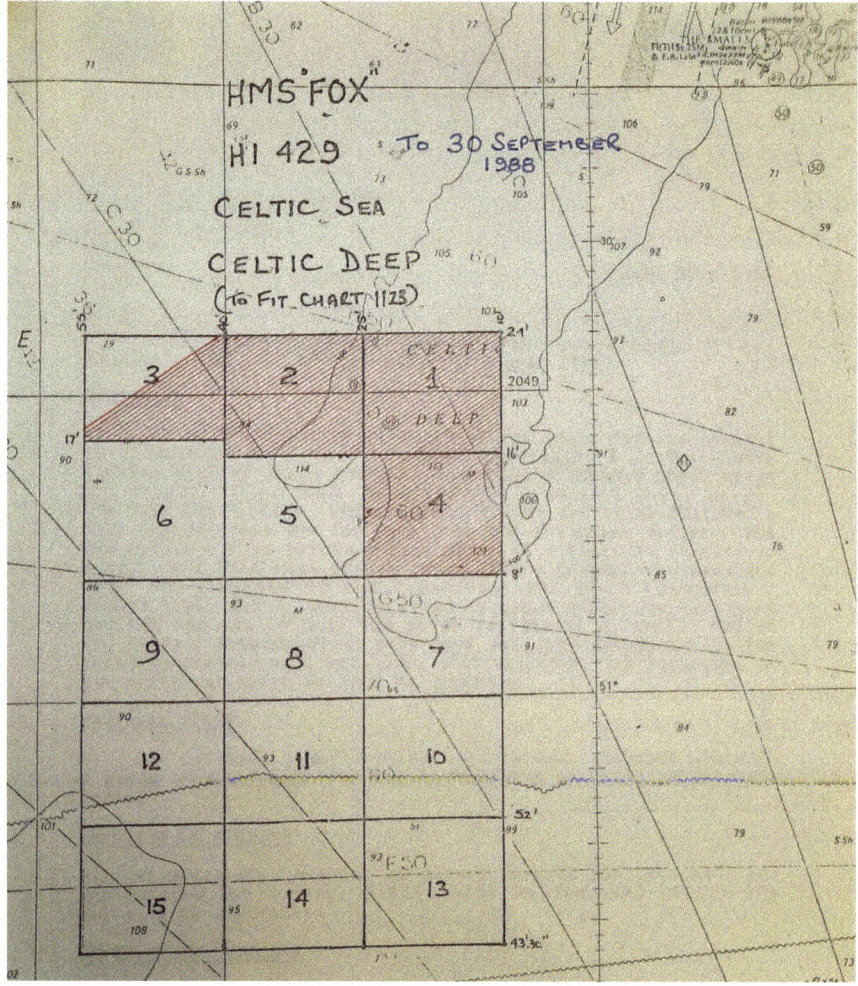

9.23 Progress of HI429 Celtic Deep as at 30 September 88
(UKHO Archive)

By 30 September, we had completed HI429 areas 1, 2 and 4 and part-completed area 3. It was a steady plod, handicapped by time off-task for port visits, leave periods, extraneous taskings and, importantly, bad weather. HI429 comprised 15 areas (each about 13km by 16km) so, if not *Fox*, then other CSVs were doomed to spend another couple of years in the Celtic Deep. But at least they'd enjoy the uplifting sight of Concorde silently flying high above, twice daily, en route from Heathrow to New York. Magnificent!

After Amsterdam, good conditions in the Celtic Deep allowed uninterrupted surveying for the remainder of October, the longest such period since June. We also received regular deliveries of mail and newspapers by a 202 Squadron Sea King helo from RAF Brawdy, Pembrokeshire. A surprising but rarer visitor, a tawny owl landed on 26 October and stayed with us for a couple of days. OOW familiarity with our survey ground meant we played 'chicken' at E-O-L. Knowing the sandy seabed was flat, we challenged ourselves to drag the towfish along the seabed throughout the Williamson turn from E-O-L to S-O-L without damaging or losing it. Fortunately, we never lost a towfish but it was a nervy experience. Thankfully, I don't think Steve Shipman was aware of this practice.

9.24 Tawny owl hitching a ride
(UKHO Archive)

Thank goodness decent weather continued and allowed continuous surveying throughout November, interrupted only by weekend visits to Guzz (4–7 November) and Swansea (18–22 November). A gutsy team of six, led by Ian Merchant, disembarked at Milford Haven to run to Swansea to meet *Fox*, raising £400 for charity. On board, a 'Casino Night' raised a further £200. Jack's 'heart of gold' and generosity continued to amaze me.

After two years in *Fox*, I was very sad to leave on 19 November. I'd learned much as a brand-new H2. I enjoyed my time as OOW, using experience accrued in Blue Star's cargo ships. MN and RN had different philosophies on 'being at sea'. In the former, it was best speed between ports and to reduce time alongside to as short as possible, continuous working was only interrupted with the legal requirement for regular dry-dockings anywhere worldwide. In *Fox*, we conducted our survey role within a programme that included maintenance periods in Guzz, weekend port visits for respite, miscellaneous exercises and leave periods (Christmas, Easter and summer) where all but the duty watch disappeared for a fortnight or so.

As a droggy, I wrought great satisfaction from surveying itself and my roles as Wrecks and Bottom Textures Officer. I was happy working alone in these fields. I knew what I had to do and my deadlines. It was critical to stay abreast of processing data as it accumulated daily, especially as Steve Shipman expected to be briefed on sonar contacts for him to decide if they required investigation or not. I loved collating the records, extracts of sidescan, echo sounder and maggy traces, even typing those blasted H525s on the unforgiving typewriter. A proud sense of achievement. How odd was I?

The greatest difference between MN and RN was that the former comprised 'short' trips of six months or so. The latter was usually trips of two years, often with many of the same folks for the duration. A tighter bond was created, I think. We all learned of people's foibles, characteristics and personalities. I'm lucky to be able to get along with virtually anyone so I found it easy. I certainly grew to respect my superiors, peers and subordinates. Jack's a great bloke with a ready smile and withering wit, but serious and professional in his job.

But, my time was up. I left *Fox*, had a busy few days' leave and joined *Hecla* on 28 November 1988.

10.

To Brazil and West Africa

10.1 *Hecla* crest
(Nick Barwis, www.jackstaxi.net)

10.2 *Hecla*

(Barry Pearce, www.MaritimeQuest.com)

The week between leaving *Fox* and joining *Hecla* was hectic as our first-born was due. Jennifer arrived early morning on Sunday 27 November. Quite a 30th birthday present for me. Fortuitous timing as I joined *Hecla* at 3 Jetty, South Yard, Guzz the following morning.

In November, *Hecla* completed her refit, a week's sea trials and a week-long defect rectification period. There was a turnover of officers. Cdr John Page took over from Cdr Rodney Browne on 1 November, when Lt Martin Clegg also joined as NO. Surgeon Lieutenant (Surg Lt) Russell Keen joined the same day as me. Providing continuity were Lt Cdr Ian Jolly (XO), Lts Graham Turnbull and Paul Randall (both H2s). I knew Graham as he was 'makie-learnie' in *Fox*. Paul and I were on the same Basic Course. Others in the wardroom were Lt Cdr Phil Parsons (Schoolie), Lt Gary Lewis (Pusser), Lt John Fletcher (MEO), Lt Andy Simons (Bosun) and Mid Chris Reeves (undergoing his fleet time).

10.3 Survey Department.
Front (l to r): Dickie Barter, Ryan Ramsey, Martin, me, Cdr Page, 'Higgy', 'Ginge' Woodhouse, 'Kipper' Herring. Back (l to r): Lee Nelson, Micky Peers, Andy Grindall, Steve Coulson, 'Rats' Ratley, Ian Salt, 'Spunky' Seed, 'Jonah' Jones, 'Derby' Allen. Missing (on watch): Graham, 'Scouse' Nicholls. (UKHO Archive)

Among the SRs, I was delighted to see Steve Hawes, one of the PO(SR)s at RNHS during my Basic Course, now CPO(SR). Also aboard were Kipper Herring and Rats Ratley from my time in *Fox*. Due to his extraordinarily loud snoring, Kipper was banned from 1 Mess (the seamen's and SR's mess) and set up a bunk in the depths of the bulk survey store. 'Rats' was now an AB(SR). Pete 'Spunky' Seed had been a very young, wet-behind-the-ears, timid S(SR) in *Fox*, but since then he'd become a keen ship's diver, 'bulked up' a bit and matured into an excellent AB(SR). Chartroom Dodger was LS(SR) Dickie Barter, who managed and organised the chartroom with great elan and was always on top of our data and survey records.

On 29 November, *Hecla* sailed for a few days' shakedown in preparation for OST at Portland. Dinner in the wardroom that evening was unique because Russell pitched up in jacket and tie. This was his first night at sea and he'd assumed that this dress was worn at sea as well as in harbour. We chuckled at his expense, which he took in good heart as XO explained and sent him to change into Red Sea Rig. The weekend of 3–4 December in Portland fully occupied everyone in preps for OST. Not only did each department ready its 'paperwork' but *Hecla* was cleaned and polished internally and externally to present a good impression to the OST staff. There followed an intense week of inspections and exercises at sea and alongside, which we survived satisfactorily. As I was Paul's relief, he escaped this and left to begin his terminal leave. *Hecla* returned to Guzz, berthing at 2 Wharf, North Yard on Friday 9 December, moving into 3 Basin for Christmas leave a week later.

It was a bit of a baptism of fire, joining an unfamiliar ship, thrust straight into sea training and work-up. H-boats (*Hecla, Hecate, Hydra, Herald*) replaced the elderly *Cook, Dampier, Owen* and *Dalrymple*, coinciding with the introduction of our Polaris Submarine Ballistic Nuclear Missile programme. Deep-diving, nuclear-powered submarines with limitless submerged range demanded precise oceanic charts and considerably more oceanographic data. Thus, three OSS H-boats were ordered in 1963. *Hecla* entered service in September 1965, *Hecate* and *Hydra* followed in October 1965 and May 1966 respectively. *Herald* was commissioned in November 1974. In between, *Protea* entered service with the South African Navy in 1972.

H-boats were 79m long, a beam of 15m, 4.9m draught and displaced 2800 tons. Main propulsion of three Paxman Ventura 12-cylinder turbo-charged diesel-electric engines drove a single shaft and propeller to a maximum speed of 14kts and a range of 22000km. A transverse bow-thruster provided manoeuvrability and station-keeping for oceanographic observations.

Above the quarterdeck was the flight deck, from which the ship's Wasp helo operated. It was housed in the hangar abaft the buff funnel. The Wasp was obsolete so none were embarked in H-boats when I joined *Hecla*.

The hull was strengthened for work in ice and air conditioning permitted work in tropical climates. In addition to a spacious survey chartroom, H-boats had wet and dry laboratories, a photographic darkroom, and oceanographic winches for deep seawater analysis and coring. To be able to continue operating alone on long deployments, there was a sick bay with a two-bed ward and an operating theatre with an X-ray machine. A Surg Lt and Leading Medical Assistant (LMA) were integral to ship's company.

SINS was used for mid-ocean positioning, its 'drift' corrected using satellite fixes from Transit Doppler Sat Nav, before the advent of GPS. *Hecla* and *Hecate* were equipped with gravimeters, essential to the data-gathering effort, to record gravity free air anomaly observations.

Data was recorded on the automatic data logging (ADL) system Hydroplot. Installed in 1969, this large computer was housed in its own temperature-controlled compartment. It logged navigational data, gravimeter and magnetometer readings, and drove the Kingmatic flat-bed plotter on the bridge to provide graphic output and to plot the ship's track in real-time.

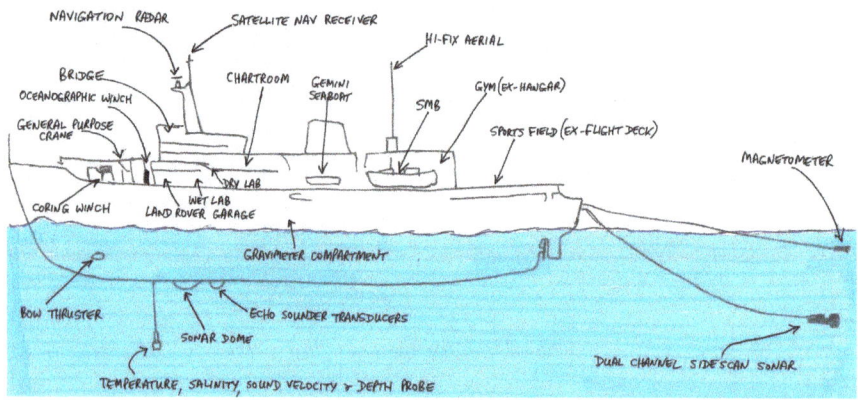

10.4 Features of an H-boat

Post-Christmas leave was a busy time for final preparations for our 6½ month deployment, including the fitting of two Bell Gravimeters (BGM221 and BGM220) by Hydrographic Department technical staff from Taunton. Steve Hawes went on draft, his successor was 'Ginge' Woodhouse, one of the most senior CPO(SR)s in the branch, so the survey department remained in good hands. Ginge was among the party of surveyors captured when the Argies invaded the Falklands. Knowing the value of their recent survey work, Ginge secreted it somewhere and it was safely recovered after hostilities ended. On 9 January, *Hecla* cold-moved to 2 Wharf and Lt Mark 'Higgy' Higgins joined as H2. I knew Higgy as he was a Hawke Senior when I joined BRNC. The survey department spent the next day in Drake Theatre for the annual Hydrographic Department Survey Symposium. The day rounded off with a 15–0 victory over *Roebuck*, to win the Flotilla Football Cup.

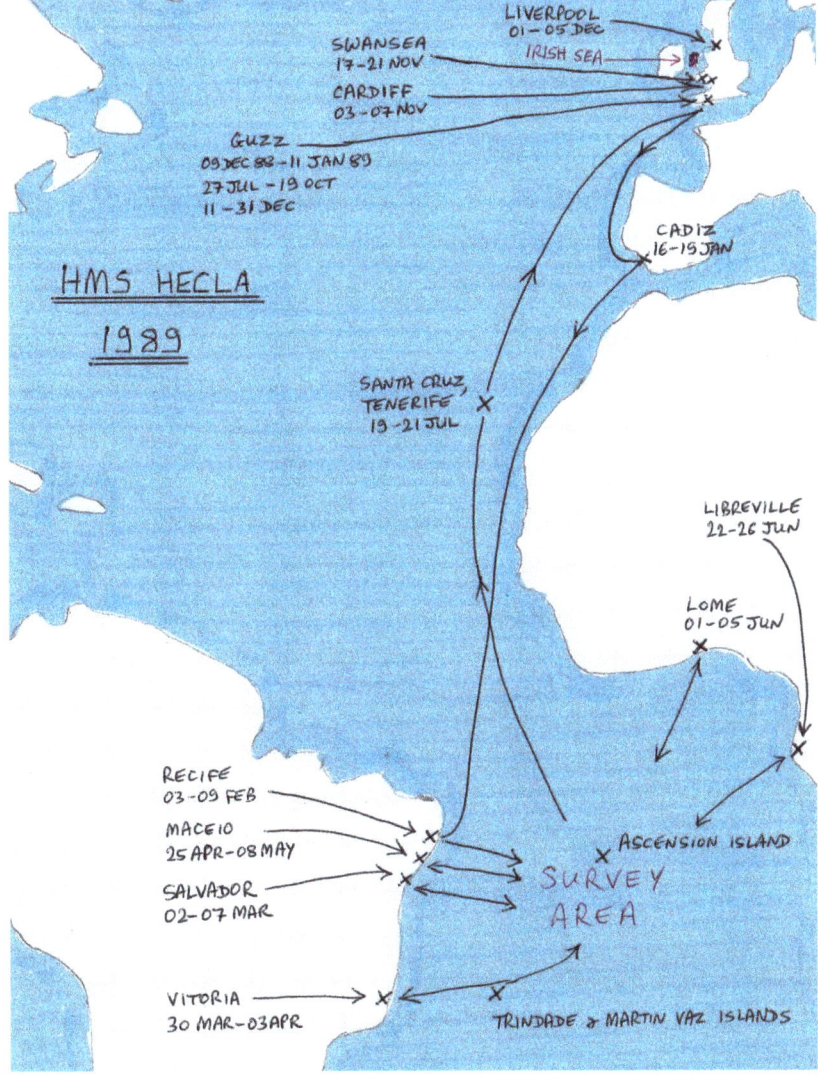

10.5 *Hecla* voyages 1989

We sailed at 1100 on Wednesday 11 January, using the afternoon to check the BGMs at the Eddystone Gravity Range. I recently learned of a FAA Sea King crash near Eddystone Light. Pilot Lt Andy Skinner and a crewman perished at night on 13 October 1988 after taking off from RFA Resource. The other two crew members survived and were rescued. Andy joined BRNC in Hawke the same day as me. An experienced jackaroo, he and Monty often rode BRNC's horses into South Hams. It's poignant and sad that *Hecla* was on the gravity range, not far from the crash site only three months later. Such a tragic loss. RIP, Andy.

We returned to Plymouth Sound to embark Hydrographer, Rear Admiral Roger Morris. Passage across the Channel and Bay of Biscay was rough, causing uncomfortable pitching and rolling. Thereafter, weather and sea state improved, plus warm sunshine as *Hecla* headed south, paralleling the Iberian coast to the east.

At sunrise Monday 16 January, *Hecla* approached Cadiz, firing a 21-gun salute, returned by the battery at Castillo de San Sebastian. With pilot and BNA embarked, we berthed at Alphonso XIII Wharf at 0900. Cdr Page and Hydrographer had a very busy day of official calls ashore, receiving returned calls, hosting a lunch on board and a press conference.

While all that was going on, I had work to do as Gravity Officer. Gravity data was critical to operating nuclear-powered long-range submarines as it impacted the accuracy of their SINS. Gravity data was gathered using gravimeters. *Hecla* and *Hecate* were equipped with two BGM3s. Sensitive to ship motion, they were in the gyro room, located at the waterline, midships along ship's length and on her centreline. On this deployment, they were maintained by a young PO Weapons Artificer with whom I closely liaised regarding the BGM3s 'health'.

When fitted in *Hecla*, our BGM3s were 'connected' or tied into the absolute gravity measurement in Guzz. We'd covered gravity in Basic Course so I had a grasp of the principles but we hadn't used a gravimeter. Higgy (my wingman) and I were coached by the Taunton technical officers in the transfer from a known gravity base station to *Hecla*, using a portable Lacoste & Romberg gravimeter, and how to use its data.

There was a worldwide network of gravity base stations. The HI included station descriptions for each port visit, usually a selection of two or three which were either in the port or at the airport or, occasionally, somewhere in town.

Gravimeters are subject to 'drift' over time. During our 6½ month trip, the BGM3s would 'drift' relatively significantly. The object of the tie-in was to determine the local gravity measurement in port to that recorded by the BGMs and track their 'drift'. A tie-in was conducted over a full tidal cycle of 24.8 hours to account for the variation in height of tide between low and high waters. For a standard four-day port visit, a tie-in on arrival and prior to departure was required.

Provided our tie-in and transfer data were correct, the boffins at UKHO could make any adjustments to the BGM data we collected. Neither I nor the PO gravimeter maintainer were trained to delve into the delicate workings of a gravimeter.

10.6 Feigning interest at Hydrographic Institute.
L to r: me, Graham (hidden), 'Higgy', Martin, BNA, Phil, Spanish officers
(UKHO Archive)

While Cdr Page and Hydrographer engaged in their formalities, ship's company prepared for the cocktail party and our wardroom colleagues busied themselves with paperwork or nothing. Higgy and I stepped ashore to conduct the gravity transfer. The good thing about my job was, as soon as I'd got the tie-in started, I got off the ship to do the transfer. Gravity transfers required a series of measurements to be taken on the wharf as close to *Hecla's* Gyro Room as possible (location A) and at the base station (location B). These measurements were repeated to form the sequence ABABA, three times at *Hecla*, twice at the base station.

The Lacoste & Romberg gravimeter was a 20cm cube carried in a custom box. When set up and levelled, taking a measurement required Higgy and I to kneel and hunch over the gravimeter, dressed in tropical white uniform and cap. This was fine beside *Hecla* on a quiet quay, but looked odd, even suspicious, when at an airport or in town. We always got funny looks from passers-by, staring at two alien officers kneeling, paying homage to a small cube in a foreign country.

By the time we'd finished the ABABA, it was lunchtime. In the afternoon, I faired up the measurements on the relevant proforma. The bonus to being Gravity Officer was that my busy 'first-day alongside' meant I was never OOD and always free to enjoy the customary 'first night in' cocktail party that evening. Brilliant!

The next two days were taken up with official visits. On Tuesday, we attended a presentation on survey systems management by British Marconi representatives to officers of Spain's Hydrographic Institute. In the afternoon, we hosted a tour of *Hecla* by Spanish surveying officers. Luckily, an evening reception at the Hydrographic Institute yielded G&T and tapas. We toured the Hydrographic Institute on Wednesday, sadly not particularly interesting, despite our hosts being so hospitable. Still, part of a warship's purpose was to maintain and further good relations with foreign and allied nations.

Meanwhile, 'Jack' enjoyed Cadiz's bars, organised bus trips to Seville and a visit to a sherry bodega. *Hecla's* football team played well against strong local opposition but conceded three goals in the last 20 minutes to lose 7–4.

Hydrographer disembarked before we sailed on 19 January. Prevailing winds and currents enabled good progress southwards to the survey ground. Off Africa's west coast, the influence of upwelling was startlingly evident. Rich nutrients rose from oceanic depths to invigorate plankton that produced a deep scattering layer so dense our echo sounders had difficulty detecting the seabed. The plankton attracted abundant shoals and, in turn, intense fishing activity by large Spanish and Russian trawler fleets. The rich harvest of fish attracted a wide range of seabirds. Dolphins were also sighted.

At 1456 on Saturday 28 January, *Hecla* crossed the equator. King Neptune was received onboard with traditional ceremony. This was, as usual, organised by the Senior Rates with assistance from some Junior Rates. The 'Policemen' and 'Bears' captured and carried 'first-timers' to Neptune's court. Naturally, all officers were targeted as 'first-timers' regardless. Perched precariously on a chair on the edge of the specially rigged pool, we were each tried, found guilty and punished with a disgusting liquid concoction and dunked into the pool. After holding court on the flight deck, Neptune returned to his watery domain in the Romanche Fracture Zone.

  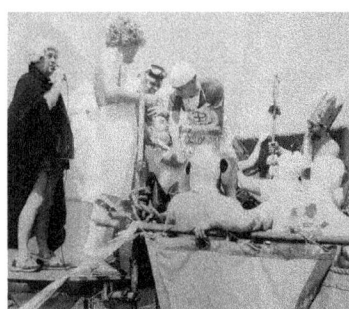

10.7 King Neptune's thugs (left); 'policemen' carry a victim to Neptune's Court; the punishment
(UKHO Archive)

Hecla berthed at No.12 Wharf in Recife on Friday 3 February, for'ard of *Hecate*. Carnival fever swept through Recife, the principal port in northern Brazil. The spectacle and pageant of carnival included incessant street music and non-stop dancing. 'Jack' was soon caught up and carried along by Brazilian ebullience.

We relaxed at the beaches of Boa Viagem and Olinda but the white-knuckle taxi journey there called for an immediate bottle or two of Antarctica or Brahma Chop to calm shattered nerves. One evening, we had a wardroom run ashore, dividing ourselves between a pair of ubiquitous VW Beetle taxis (built under licence in Brazil). Someone urged our taxi driver to overtake the other and a race through Recife's narrow streets ensued. A dice with death as our Nelson Piquet imitators went for it. At any moment an accident could have occurred, wiping out *Hecla's* wardroom.

On another afternoon, several of us went to the beach. Andy Simons was happy to keep an eye on our clothes and valuables while we went for a dip in the Atlantic. On our return, we discovered Andy had nodded off and a thief had stolen some of our stuff, including XO's shirt. 'Securicor' Simons was berated by all. XO had to buy a shirt before we got a drink in the bar of a beachfront hotel.

The immediate waterfront environment was neither attractive nor safe. One evening, in a completely unprovoked incident, three of our sailors were shot at whilst returning to *Hecla*. None were hit, unlike an unfortunate local man shot in a bar not 200m from the ship. Advice to go ashore only in groups was re-emphasised. Fortunately, no one else was robbed or assaulted.

10.8 Recife, post-beach debacle
L to r: Andy, Ian, Phil, Martin, me
(Graham Turnbull)

Whilst all this was going on, S/Lt Mick Rigby joined for fleet time. Mick was an ebullient, gregarious Upper Yardman SR. He livened up the ship as his Geordie accent echoed along the passageways. He was a welcome addition to the wardroom and great fun to be with.

The combination of raw sewage and many corpses, one of them human, floating passed the ship convinced our MO to recommend that the planned dive on the hull be cancelled.

Our football team played in Sporting Recife's 38000 capacity stadium. Despite a spirited performance, *Hecla* lost 5–1 to a strong local team. Nevertheless, it was a great experience for our humble ship's team. A combined *Hecla/Hecate* XI drew 3–3 with the Brazilian Naval Apprentices School team.

For the last couple of days alongside, *Hecate* berthed outboard so we could provide her with power, enabling repair work on her electrical switchboard. After departing together on 9 February, the ships parted company to continue their respective surveys and we didn't see *Hecate* again until four months later in Lome.

Soon after sailing on 9 February, we found that BGM221 was producing invalid data. Despite the PO maintainer's efforts at fault diagnosis, the defect was in the sensor itself, its repair beyond his capability. Hydrographic Department technical staff arranged to meet us in Salvador to resolve the issue. Fortunately, BGM220 and the Lacoste & Romberg gravimeter yielded comparable reliable data to enable our survey to continue.

Hecla settled into an alternating pattern of 24 days at sea and 4–5 days alongside. The survey ground covered the width of the Atlantic, luckily in the tropics rather than the miserable north Atlantic. Survey lines were run either eastwards or westwards, as this was the optimum course to gather gravity data as it impacted gravimeter accelerometers less than other directions. Our survey lines were therefore of long duration at 10kts. As we neared E-O-L, each OOW eagerly tried to predict when that would occur, praying that we'd have the relative excitement of altering course by 90° to head for the next S-O-L. Survey lines were about 4° of latitude apart so the next calculation was when we'd alter course a further 90° onto the next line in the reciprocal direction. I don't know how we contained our excitement!

Graham, Higgy, Andy and I were OOW, a comfortable 1-in-4 rotation, which allowed us to participate in circuit training on the flight deck at 1615 on weekdays and inter-mess sports afternoons on Saturdays. Following the pattern in Table 10.1, we each got 'all night in' every fourth night after the last dog, although it was a long day as the previous watch was the morning. Martin (NO) did the odd watch, which made our routine a little easier.

The SRs were also 1-in-4 watchkeeping but, as there were nine AB(SR)s, they rotated through each survey leg as watchkeepers or day-work in the chartroom or on deck. This provided variety in our watches for each leg. Watchkeeping was an excellent means of interacting with, and learning about the lives, families, thoughts and aspirations of our sailors.

Table 10.1 1-in-4 watch routine

Watch	Day 1	Day 2	Day 3	Day 4	
Middle 0001–0400	1	4	3	2	
Morning 0400–0800	2	1	4	3	
Forenoon 0800–1200	3	2	1	4	
Afternoon 1200–1600	4	3	2	1	
First Dog 1600–1800	1	4	3	2	
Last Dog 1800–2000	2	1	4	3	'Last Dog, all night in'
First 2000–0001	3	2	1	4	

Over the course of every survey leg, a sound working relationship developed, SRs and QMs detected each OOW's particular (or peculiar) foibles as we all had slightly different approaches to running the watch. Regardless, everything went smoothly on the bridge.

Our QMs were general service operations branch ABs. They were under the Chief Bosun's Mate (CBM or 'Buffer'), in charge of the seamen but under Andy Simons' overall responsibility as Bosun. Some ABs liked being QM, others much preferred day-work under the Buffer. For each survey leg, they'd occasionally swap around a little but, generally, we were on watch with the same handful of QMs. They were 'Pusser' Hill (with his broad Leicester accent), 'Oz' Spooner (a Mancunian and skilful footballer), 'Brum' Spooner (a baby-faced Brummie), 'Steady' Eddie McCullough (broad Irish accent and *Hecla's* goalkeeper), and 'George' Purvis (red-headed Geordie). 'George' was a bit of a miserable bloke. My fellow-OOWs preferred not to have him as their QM but I wasn't that bothered. When Martin published our OOW bill for each survey leg, we eagerly wondered who our QM for the period would be. Twenty-four days was a long time to spend watchkeeping with a QM you weren't fond of.

10.9 LStwd 'George' Nicholson and Stwd Warren Strickland
('George' Nicholson)

The 'deck crowd' were managed by the Buffer, PO Pete Edwards, aka 'Peter Huffer, he's the Buffer'. His wingman was LS Al Starkie, strikingly blond and *Hecla's* football team captain. I didn't have much day-to-day interaction with these blokes except observing them at work on the fo'c'sle and on deck. The Buffer took firm charge of his troops from his small 'office' (Buffer's Store) on the upper deck, for'ard of the hangar.

Hecla berthed at No.1 Wharf in Salvador on Thursday 2 March. Cdr Page went ashore for his calls, accompanied by BNA and returned to host a lunch onboard. Meanwhile, Higgy and I conducted the gravity transfer, much the better option. In the evening, we greatly enjoyed the cocktail party. By now, LStwd 'George' Nicholson, an enormous Geordie with short-back-and-sides, ensured our G&Ts remained topped up. As the evening wore on, I detected the proportions of each ingredient were gradually reversed. By the end of every cocktail party George ensured our G&Ts were almost neat gin with a mere splash of tonic.

George had a heart of gold. He looked after us well in the wardroom and kept a tight rein on his stewards. At weekends, he used the library at the aft end of the officers' accommodation as a barber's shop. He only had four styles – No.1, No.2, No.3 or No.4 – and always did an excellent job. His fee raised a goodly sum for charity by the end of the deployment.

10.10 Graham, Martin, me and Mick at Mercado Modelo
(Graham Turnbull)

Salvador was Brazil's capital until 1763 and became the state capital of Bahia. It was the centre of the slave trade until Brazil abolished slavery in 1888. African culture and mystique still abounded in a richly multiracial community. Salvador's architecture was a fascinating blend of old and new, including delightful Portuguese colonial buildings amongst modern high-rise structures.

We frequented the beaches to relax and play American football. Graham was a great fan of the sport and named us the Hecla Green Mambas as we threw the ball around and across the beach. Late afternoons and evenings were spent quietly scuppering 600ml bottles of Antarctica in a bar in the Mercado Modelo. This early-20th-century market occupied the original Customs House and was filled with a couple of hundred stalls selling local crafts and souvenirs. It overlooked the waterfront and was in the shadow of Elevador Lacerda, a lift and walkway from sea-level up to old Salvador's narrow cobbled streets on the surrounding clifftop. Sat at a table on the Mercado Modelo's large balcony at sunset and long into the evening, we ate patatas fritas washed down with Antarctica, illuminated by the lights and hurly-burly of crowds and traffic in the road below.

We sailed on Tuesday 7 March for the survey ground with all sensors operational, the defective BGM having been fixed in Salvador by UKHO technicians. Alas, we suffered a series of survey kit failures. The dual-cartridge recorders for the ADL failed to log data. After repair, one of them failed again five days later. Replacement boards from the spare recorder rectified these problems. Later, the precision depth recorder (PDR) gearbox seized, but we effected a temporary repair. The autopilot repeatedly failed, causing *Hecla* to veer off course, but the bridge teams' quick reactions brought *Hecla* back on track in hand steering without loss of data. The ARPA radar display also suffered a succession of minor defects, which were to be repaired with replacement parts being delivered to Ascension Island. There were also a few engineering defects which were, fortunately, fixed, although the port main engine was out of action for four days.

As this survey leg ended, we headed west towards Vitoria, passing the rugged, barren volcanic islands of Trindade and Martim Vaz, an archipelago about 1,100 km east of the Brazilian province of Espirito Santo of which it forms a part. This archipelago was a waypoint for competitors in *The Sunday Times* Golden Globe Race of 1968–1969, a non-stop, single-handed, round-the-world yacht race, the first of its kind. Peter Nichols' *A Voyage for Madmen* dramatically describes the trials and tribulations of the nine competitors. Nearby was the Davis Bank, a reported shoal of 20m depth. Sidescan sonar was streamed as we cautiously steamed through its centre but found nothing and we hadn't time to conduct a thorough investigation.

10. To Brazil and West Africa

10.11 Off Trindade and Martim Vaz islands

That evening, we enjoyed a wardroom mess dinner to commemorate the Battle of Matapan, which occurred in the Mediterranean, off the southwest coast of the Peloponnese on 27–29 March 1941. British and Australian warships sank three Italian heavy cruisers and two destroyers, for some damage to one of our light cruisers. Although not a decisive engagement, it was Italy's greatest defeat at sea, losing a cruiser division from its order of battle.

The approaches to Vitoria were spectacular. Passing beneath the Terceiro Ponte, spanning the entrance to Baia Vitoria, *Hecla* transited through the narrow scenic Maria da Vitoria river, threading between riverine islands with Forte Sao Joao to starboard, to berth at No.4 Wharf at 0900 on Thursday 30 March. In addition to the usual pattern on arrival, we bade farewell to our OUT, Mid Chris Reeves. He left to join *Ark Royal* to continue his fleet time. We expected he'd find quite a difference between relaxed life in a survey ship and the formal atmosphere aboard one of our largest warships at the time. We'd enjoyed Chris' company and his infectious youthful enthusiasm.

Vitoria was the administrative capital of Espirito Santo state and originally developed through the discovery of gold at the end of the 17th century. Its wealth now derived from exporting iron ore. The nearby port of Tubarao was the largest ore-exporting terminal in the world, shipping some 80 million tons of ore per annum. Vitoria seemed more prosperous than our previous ports, reflected in a less threatening, more friendly, inviting atmosphere. 'Jack' could safely enjoy his run ashore without high risk of violence and danger. The city was blessed with many attractive colonial buildings, superb beaches and magnificent scenery.

Our football team beat the local naval apprentices 4–3, an improvement on their hard-earned draw in Salvador. *Hecla's* golfers were treated to a round at an attractive 9-hole course at Monte Verde, about 160km inland, west of Vitoria. I'd learned that golf was something Senior Rates hooked into because in any port visit there was always an opportunity to get off the ship for a round of golf at a lovely course, generously hosted by hospitable ex-pats.

After an excellent port visit, *Hecla* sailed from Vitoria on Monday 3 April. Beset by a series of machinery and survey kit defects and by heavy seas caused by 25kt headwinds, we lost 42 hours' survey time in the first 10 days of this survey leg. Fortunately, the next westerly survey line over the next seven days allowed us to make up for all that lost time. We anchored for a couple of hours in Clarence Bay, Ascension Island, to collect mail and stores. They were delivered to *Hecla* by Mexeflote and hoisted on board.

10.12 Me and Graham on bridge wing at Ascension; loading stores/parts from Mexeflote (left: Graham Turnbull)

Mexeflote was a diesel-engine powered raft used to move goods and vehicles between ship and shore. Its three components (bow, stern, and centre) were fitted together as required, making it a versatile craft. They were first used in the 1960s by the Royal Logistics Corps in particular, most notably in the Falklands War, but also in humanitarian aid missions.

Ascension is an isolated volcanic island in the South Atlantic Ocean, about 1600km from Africa and 2300km from South America, it holds strategic importance as RAF Ascension Island, a European Space Agency rocket tracking station, a British-American signals intelligence facility, the BBC World Service Atlantic Relay Station and one of four ground antennae for operating GPS.

We used it extensively as a staging post during the Falklands War, most notably for Operation Black Buck, when a Vulcan bomber and accompanying Victor in-flight refuelling tankers conducted the raid on Port Stanley airfield. It provided a refuelling stop for the regular airlink between RAF Brize Norton, Oxfordshire, and RAF Mount Pleasant in the Falklands. RN warships frequently refuelled there southbound or homeward bound – for which the tanker *Maersk Ascension* was chartered to provide bulk fuel storage offshore instead of tanks ashore.

Clarence Bay seemed a pretty place, backed by a sandy beach and, at its south-west end, Georgetown, the island's only meaningful settlement. The island rose inland, surmounted by its dormant volcanic crater. Through binoculars, the landscape looked brown, rugged and barren, although further inland and higher it was verdant with lush forest. Green Mountain National Park had a selection of hiking trails.

On clearing the anchorage, *Hecla* suffered a total power failure and, without propulsion or steering, lurched toward *Maersk Ascension*, her pale blue hull and cream superstructure loomed ever larger. Hand-pump steering in the tiller flat was used to manoeuvre *Hecla* to seaward and safe water. Phew! The end result was departure from Ascension with only one operational auxiliary generator, one steering motor and one main engine almost at the end of its running hours and due to be changed on our return to Guzz, still months away. Regardless, the designated survey lines for this leg were completed and good quality data was recorded.

Taking over the watch was a fairly relaxed but formal event – and unique when relieving Andy the Bosun at night. I got on the bridge to find it in total darkness. Andy dimmed every dimmable light to its minimum. He stuck masking tape over indicator lights that couldn't be dimmed sufficiently. It was annoying and unnecessary, but we all had our foibles. As soon as I'd uttered 'I have the ship' and he'd beetled off below, I removed every scrap of masking tape. There was virtually no danger of not detecting another vessel in the vicinity and very little backscatter from our instrumentation's lights.

The three main engines were illuminated by red (port), amber (centre) and green (starboard) lights when in use. Inevitably, our handovers included the status of the strawberry, orange and lime engines.

Afternoons were my least favourite watches. They prevented my lunchtime sunbathing (bronzing) on the bridge roof after a quick sandwich lunch. Bronzing zones were demarcated. We had the bridge roof, the Senior Rates used the aft end of the bridge deck and the sailors had the fo'c'sle and flight deck.

On watch during lunchtime or weekend afternoons, QM, SR and I saw the fo'c'sle slowly fill with sailors on click-click beds, getting comfortably horizontal, sunglasses in place, 'screaming handbags' and earphones attached. When they'd settled, I sent QM to the bridge roof to twist the windscreen washer nozzles to point away from the bridge windows. On his return, the three of us stood by and, on my command, we pressed the washer buttons. Water jetted out on the fo'c'sle, showering the sunbathers. A short blast was enough to get them splattered. To a man, they removed sunglasses and 'screaming handbags' to look up into a bright blue cloudless sky and wondered where the 'rain' had come from. My bridge team chortled at our childish humour. I don't think anyone realised I'd orchestrated this prank.

Hecla arrived in Maceio on Tuesday 25 April. A straightforward entry to the wide curve of the bay, to swing round nearly 180° to approach and berth in the centre of the main southern wharf. Maceio was a busy commercial port exporting sugar, molasses, wheat and corn. Cargo handling had doubled in the past few years, so berths were at a premium. Within hours, Cdr Page was told we'd have to shift berths tomorrow morning to the seaward extremity of the southern wharf, the only available berth. Having secured alongside on Wednesday morning, the scend caused three springs to part during the day. Cdr Page insisted *Hecla* be moved to a safer berth. This occurred on Thursday and we remained at the western end of the sugar wharf on the port's north side until departure.

Maceio was roughly halfway through our deployment. This fortnight alongside served as a SMP and a great opportunity for ship's company to recharge batteries. Most managed to spend a couple of days 'station leave' in seafront hotels at incredibly cheap rates. Beaches were clean and extensive and the generally welcome atmosphere ashore was devoid of violence or danger. Among the five wives who flew out to join us were Martin's and Graham's. When not duty, most of the wardroom visited their beachside hotel. I have no idea why we didn't leave them in peace. Both couples escaped for a week or so to visit Rio and Iguazu Falls, way down south, straddling the Brazil/Argentina border.

Meanwhile, on-board maintenance and defect rectification continued. Capt H (Capt Myers) visited for a couple of days, accompanied by his Staff MEO and WEO. *Hecla's* footballers suffered a disappointing 3–5 loss to a Portobras team. Interest in golf had soared such that the 'golf club' comprised 27 members. There wasn't a golf course in Maceio so an intrepid dozen travelled 240km by road to Recife for a couple of enjoyable days' golf.

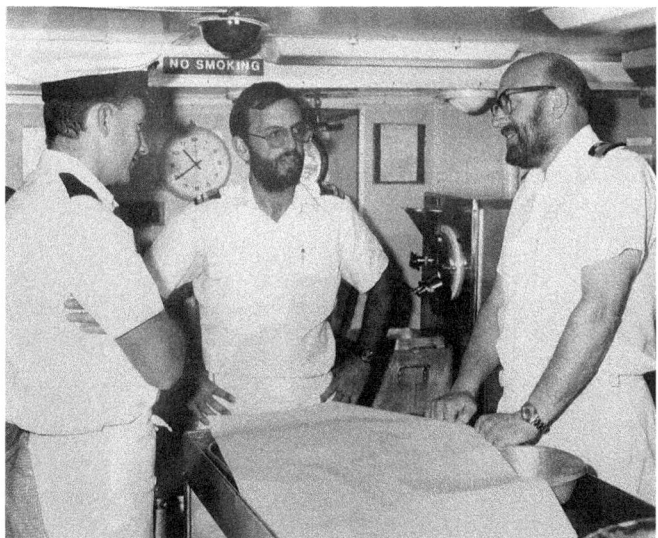

10.13 PO (Cook) McCann and Gary the Pusser chat with Capt H in the galley (UKHO Archive)

The biggest morale booster was receiving mail. On arrival, everyone on board was desperate to see the ship's agent/chandler deliver bags of mail to the MAA. His priority was to empty and sort the bags into batches for each mess. Whilst work continued, there was an undeniable frisson as we waited for the QM to pipe 'mail is now ready for collection'. LHOMs raced to MAA's office to collect their mess' bundle of letters and small parcels, returned to their mess and dished it out to messmates. A wardroom Steward collected ours and placed it in our pigeon-holes in the wardroom. There was a hush at stand easy as we opened and read news from home. Morale instantly sky rocketed.

With no internet or email in those far off days, we waited (impatiently) for each port visit to get mail, our only contact with family and friends, unless an extortionately expensive satellite telephone call was permitted for compassionate reasons. The sole alternative was the 'air mail bluey', a free 'aerogram'. Limited to 30 words, we were entitled to one per week at sea on deployment, I think. We were allowed to 'blob up' two to make 60 words but only after each fortnight at sea. Family could do likewise. I don't think I ever bothered with them as I was used to being away for months in Blue Star without receiving mail, but posted letters and postcards home from whatever exotic port I was in.

SSVC provided a weekly box of video tapes. Each tape labelled by day, containing TV programmes from that day (drama, comedy, sport, soaps). It was a good means of keeping up with TV at home during long deployments. It was important to me to watch them in strict day order. Others weren't so bothered.

On Monday 8 May, *Hecla* left Maceio with only two of three main engines operational and no bow-thruster. Adding to our woes, a pump motor for the reverse osmosis plant burnt out the next day. Our fresh water production was greatly affected, necessitating four days of water rationing later in May to keep consumption under control. The following day, some securing bolts on a generator sheared off, reducing us to one main engine for 14 hours while repairs were effected. As a result, port main engine was stopped every fourth day to check the bolts and prevent a recurrence.

The survey was interrupted by diverting to Ascension to land a sailor for urgent compassionate reasons. We anchored in Clarence Bay, two sailors went ashore for dental treatment and we landed and collected mail and stores. The latter included spares for the ARPA radar so *Hecla* now had two operational radar displays. On leaving Ascension, three main engines functioned so we caught up on the two days lost due to this diversion.

We began surveying in the abyssal plain east of the Mid-Atlantic Ridge. Within days, several new seamounts rising up to 4000m were found. A marked increase in marine life was detected, including shark attacks on the magnetometer. The yellow plastic tubular lure was taken completely, leaving the maggy unprotected and the shark with chronic indigestion. On 23 May, magnetic data suddenly became invalid. When recovered, the maggy had a 1" long shark's tooth embedded in the wooden lure. The strain of the ferocious attack and severe lacerations to the maggy caused several wires to rupture in the cable.

It wasn't all work and no play. Four members of ship's company ran a marathon around the upper deck. Max Jones (NAAFI Canteen Manager or Can-Man) completed the 341 laps in 3hrs 42mins 7secs, raising £464 for the British Heart Foundation. Three other madmen completed half-marathons. A 'village fete' on the flight deck raised £485 for charity, making a total to date of £1700.

A temporary repair using a replacement pump from the hot water circulating system, yielded bow thruster manoeuvrability for arrival at Lome on Thursday 1 June. A testament to our stokers' ingenuity. We berthed outboard of *Hecate* at Quai de Commerce, opposite the naval base.

Lome is the capital and only port in the former French colony of Togo. It exported phosphates and agricultural products and virtually all of Togo's imports arrived here. Togo is a small, tropical country of 57000km², a strip of land only 115km wide at its maximum and a mere 56km of coastline on the Bight of Benin, sandwiched between Ghana and Benin.

As in Maceio, the scend caused both ships to surge continuously. *Hecla* parted two wire spring hawsers. A small portable pump used to boost the fresh water flow rate from the jetty connection was stolen one night.

Apart from Lome market, there was very little to do in this shabby city, coated in red dust, throbbing with heat and thronging with people. We strolled around a bit. Lome seemed safe-ish but we were constantly wary and always ashore in small groups. Thus, the arranged sports fixtures were the main source of escape. Rugby, cricket and volleyball teams were fielded. *Hecla's* footballers were 3–2 up at full-time until the locals equalised in the 17th minute of mysterious injury time. Our Togolese hosts were most hospitable. The golfers experienced putting on 'browns' rather than 'greens'.

10.14 In the throng at Lome market: Martin, Russell and Graham (left); me (right)

For eight days after departing Lome on Monday 5 June, the survey progressed well until the maggy suffered another shark attack. Dorsal fins were regularly sighted, gorging on the abundant prey thriving in the nutrient-rich waters of the Benguela Current. We suffered a couple of steering gear failures in quick succession, caused by defective relays in the autopilot. *Hecla* carried no spares but we discovered that these items cost only £3.75 each. The CO phoned a UK supplier for delivery of several spares at our next port.

Maintaining physical fitness was an integral and important part of life during our survey legs. Wasp helos were withdrawn from H-boats. Its replacement (Lynx) was far too big for the hangar and flight deck. Both spaces were re-purposed as gym and sports field. No excuse not to keep fit on long deployments.

10.15 Circuit training, Buffer in charge (left); gym – tanned, buffed-up 'muscle-bosuns'. Buffer and AB 'Tiny' Little on weights (right)
(UKHO Archive)

On weekdays at 1615, there was circuit training on the flight deck, always well-attended and very enjoyable. H-boats weren't complemented with a PTI so, in our case, the Buffer ran circuit training. His hour-long sessions were intense, hard work and rewarding. He was a big bloke and firmly in charge. After warm-up, we launched into a circuit of some 12 stations, a variety of exercises of 30-second duration for legs, arms or abdoms. Throughout, the Buffer's dulcet tones rang out across the flight deck: 'BIG ARMS, BIG LEGS!'; 'GOOD ABDOMS GOOD F**K!'. He allowed a 30-second respite between each circuit, to walk around the flight deck and regain our breath. 'Fingertips on nipples. In through the nose, out through the mouth', instructed the Buffer. We certainly felt we'd had a great workout after completing three such circuits, breathless and sweat-soaked as *Hecla* continued her survey line in the late afternoon tropical sunshine and calm sea. Other folks did their own thing. Jogging round the upper deck before breakfast or during the dogs. Pumping iron in the hangar. Riding the exercise bike.

In addition, inter-mess sports competitions were organised on Saturday afternoons at sea. Every mess entered a team, keen to show their mettle and skill, as well as settling scores and mess rivalry on the sports field. Junior

Rates always wanted to beat Senior Rates and the wardroom. Everyone wanted to smash the wardroom.

10.16 Flight deck sports
Clockwise from top left: footie, tennis, volleyball *and* cricket
(UKHO Archive)

A wide variety of sports were played: football, deck hockey, volleyball, tennis, cricket. For football and hockey, every mess made balls/pucks from a central core of engineers' cotton-waste or rags, bound tightly with layers of Pusser's black masking-tape. Every ball/puck was slightly different in size, shape and weight. During a game, if the ball/puck went overboard, a replacement from the stockpile was introduced so play continued. The volleyball was somehow secured to a length of cord, the other end of which was tied to the centre of the net strung across the flight deck. A similar arrangement was applied to tennis. In cricket, a tennis ball was secured to a line the length of the flight deck to the aft end and attached to one of the flight deck ring-bolts.

Football and deck hockey were easily the most violent sports. No quarter was given. Deck hockey was played in steaming boots, some folks manufactured thick cardboard shin pads to protect against wild hacking from opponents' hockey sticks. I was astounded there were no serious injuries, just gashes and grazes of varying severity.

These Saturday afternoons were great fun, with much banter and ribbing going on, goading people to get stuck in and have a go at someone. Rough and violent, yes, but never vicious. Scores were settled but we all moved on when the afternoon ended and the kit was packed away.

This survey leg, the deployment's shortest, was our most trouble-free and productive to date. On passage to Libreville, we passed close to the island of Pagalu, surveyed originally by the second *Hecla* (launched 1815) in 1829 after a decade of distinguished service in Arctic exploration.

It was a lengthy passage up the wide expanse of the Gabon river estuary to reach Port Owendo, Gabon's primary port. Gabon, on the Atlantic coast of Central Africa, straddled the equator, bordered by Equatorial Guinea to the northwest, Cameroon to the north, Republic of the Congo on the east and south, and the Gulf of Guinea to the west. Of 270000km^2 in area, it had a population of 2.3 million. It comprised coastal plains, mountains and savanna. The capital and largest city, Libreville, was at the mouth of the Gabon River. The French occupied and colonised Gabon from 1885 until independence in 1960. Over half Gabon's economy is dominated by its oil exports; logging and manganese mining largely provided the remainder. As 85% of Gabon was covered by dense equatorial rainforest, every commodity and virtually all food were imported through Port Owendo. Consequently, the cost of living was extremely high. Libreville was listed as the fourth most expensive city in the world, but with an exceptionally low crime rate it proved a surprisingly safe run ashore.

Berthing on the dolphins at the western end of the single commercial quay, we were welcomed by a 20-piece military band at 0800 Thursday 22 June. As usual, when the CO, accompanied by our Defence Attaché, went ashore for his calls, Higgy and I started the gravity transfer. When we'd finished the first readings beside *Hecla*, transport with driver took us into Libreville, 15km distant. It was unusual that the nearest gravity base station wasn't at the port. Instead, we parked outside Libreville's General Post Office and set up the Lacoste & Romberg gravimeter. We got many strange looks from the locals. Not surprising, as we were two RN officers in tropical white uniform (caps on), kneeling close together hunched over a small metal cube, fiddling with its knurled knobs to get it level and tweaking them to get a reading.

We returned to the Post Office for our second reading a couple of hours later. This time, local curiosity seemed rather threatening, with much chattering and pointing going on. Higgy and I felt quite uncomfortable and were pleased our driver kept the almost baying, inquisitive crowd away. Our sinister presence for a second time made the casual observer wonder if we were white spies gathering goodness knows what state secrets whilst kneeling defenceless outside the Post Office. Luckily, a policeman arrived. We explained (assisted by our driver) that we had Gabonese approval to conduct our measurements. He held off the gathering, vocal crowd. We were relieved to get back in the car and return to *Hecla* unscathed.

Sports fixtures were organised. The Gabonese Naval team snatched a last-minute 3–3 draw, but our rugby team's first outing was a heavy defeat against French Marines. The golfers thoroughly enjoyed their first 18-hole course of the deployment. All post-match social activity was excellent.

10.17 *Hecla's* rugby team
(UKHO Archive)

Back to sea again. We left on Monday 26 June. The following four days were very productive, even though BGM220 yielded erroneous data. The Lacoste & Romberg replaced it and gave good agreement with BGM221. During early July, heavy grey clouds dominated and we endured 3–4m beam seas despite working close to the equator. The resultant ship motion was a bit of a shock. The final ordered survey line was completed on 8 July and *Hecla* headed for Guzz at the end of a highly successful and satisfying survey. Elation spread throughout ship's company.

On 10 July, we rendezvoused with *Hecate* for a boat transfer of some stores and repair kit. Throughout this serial, a pair of sharks cruised between the ships. 'Hands to bathe' was far too risky in these waters. Northbound, a wiring defect was discovered in the ADL, which affected the recording of gravity data. Its repair could only be done alongside so occasional invalid gravity output readings had to be accepted.

Due to a defect, *Hecla* was reduced to a single air conditioning unit for over 24 hours just as the latitude when midday sun was directly overhead was approached. Temperatures below decks rapidly became uncomfortable, illustrating *Hecla's* vulnerability throughout the deployment, with only two of her three air conditioning units fully operational.

Further north, sea and swell calmed sufficiently to enable our upper-deck runners to set a new record of 3hrs 8mins 15secs for the Ringbolt Marathon Relay. In particular, Max the Can-Man ran the fastest mile in 5min 31secs. A fine achievement by all those madmen.

10.18 Gary Lewis sets off on Ringbolt Relay (left); Ringbolt Relay team (UKHO Archive)

Entertainment on board was varied. Throughout the trip, Graham and Phil the Schoolie hosted a radio show on the ship's sound system, broadcasting a wide variety of tunes across musical genres and played requests – if they had that particular song. A ship's magazine was also published during each survey leg and distributed around the messes. In addition to original content, cartoons and strips from Viz were included.

Ship's company functions were held on the flight deck on Saturday evenings at sea. Film nights, barbecues, horse-racing, 'village fete' were all charity fundraisers. Horse race meetings were particularly enjoyable fundraising evenings organised by the Senior Rates, with about ten races with six comically named 'horses'. After auctioning each horse, where bidding strategy was critical, betting occurred. Horse purchases (by individuals or 'syndicates') and betting sums increased as the night wore on, coupled with beer consumption – despite the 'three cans of beer, per man, per day' limit for Junior Rates. The nags galloped towards the finish line at a pace dictated by the roll of enormous dice.

10.19 Horse race meeting on flight deck
(UKHO Archive)

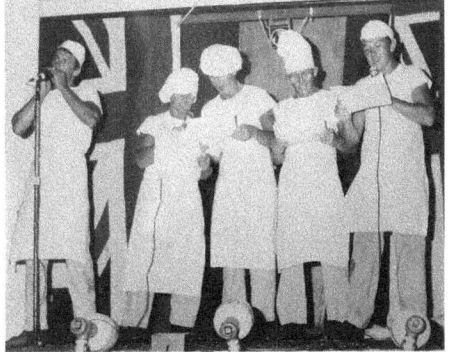

10.20 Scenes from the SODS Opera
(UKHO Archive)

The climax to any RN deployment was the SODS Opera, an opportunity for individuals, duos, trios and groups to perform 'on stage'. Acts took their rehearsals seriously and admirable efforts were made with dress. The evening was hilarious, loud and immensely enjoyable. I was puzzled why stokers always had the best skimpy female underwear for these functions.

As *Hecla* continued along her survey line under starlit skies and tropical temperatures, these social events were greatly enjoyed by all. There was never any 'trouble' as behaviour was excellent.

An important factor in maintaining morale was food. We had superb chefs on board, under the leadership of PO(Cook) 'Scouse' McCann, assisted by PO(Caterer) Mick Harris. They produced excellent daily menus with little repetitiveness, although Saturday night was traditionally 'steak night'. Ship's company's favourite dinner was undoubtedly chicken divine, a simple dish but so popular that extra quantities were made. I always had seconds, it was that tasty.

We supplemented meals with purchases from the NAAFI canteen, managed by Max Jones, a civilian billeted in the Senior Rates mess. All warships had a canteen but only 'big ships' had a Can-Man. In *Fox* (a small ship), WEO acted as such. The canteen offered a variety of confectionery, crisps, fags, soft drinks, toiletries and miscellaneous items. A queue formed at 'stand easy', lunchtime, secure and in the evening as 'Jack' topped up with his luxuries and necessities.

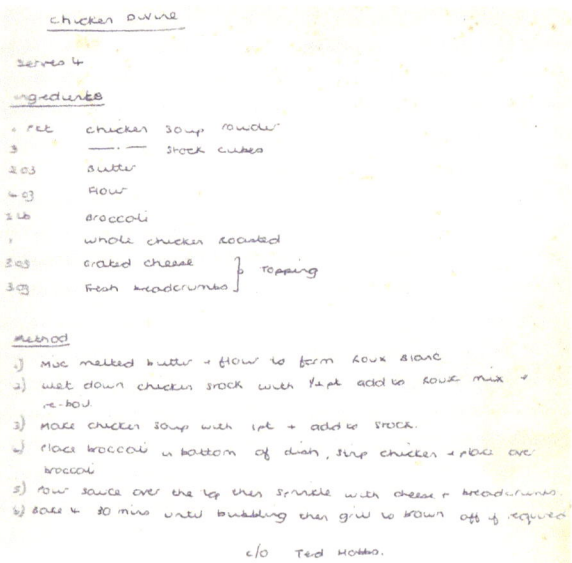

10.21 AB (Cook) Ted Hobbs' chicken divine recipe
(Phil McCann)

10. To Brazil and West Africa

Our final port visit en route to Guzz was Santa Cruz, Tenerife, where we fired a 21-gun salute and the shore battery replied in kind. We got alongside Darsena de Los Llanos at 0915. This was a quiet port visit as we focused on getting home. The only sport played was by our fanatical golfers at an apparently internationally acclaimed course.

10.22 21-gun salute off Tenerife
(UKHO Archive)

10.23 Martin, Higgy and me, Mount Teide in background

Graham, Higgy, Martin and I hired a car and drove up into the mountains to visit Mount Teide, Tenerife's volcano, 64km south-west of Santa Cruz. Its summit (3715m) is the highest point in not only Spain but also in the Atlantic islands. Measured from the ocean floor, its 7500m height makes Teide the third-highest volcano in the world. Its last summit eruption occurred in about 850AD, producing the black lavas that cover much of its flanks. Teide's elevation above sea level makes Tenerife the tenth highest island in the world. Teide Observatory, a major international astronomical observatory, is located on its slopes. We had beautiful weather and the temperature cooled noticeably as the road climbed the foothills through pine forests and opened out on barren lava slopes leading up to the crater. Overall, a great day out.

Santa Cruz was the last time a Defence Courier came out to collect the survey leg's data: the bulky ADL magnetic tape cartridges, Report of Survey and associated forms. On the first day or so of every port visit the chartroom throbbed with activity as we knuckled down to complete our respective annexes, which Martin collated and the CO checked. The Defence Courier Service sent its messengers worldwide to our embassies and high commissions, delivering diplomatic/secret material and returning similar communications to UK. Defence Couriers were elderly ex-servicemen, sometimes rather portly, who sweated profusely after clambering up our steep gangway. We made them welcome with tea/coffee and often lunch as we finished off our submissions. Couriers often stayed in a hotel overnight before collecting our material and returning to UK. It seemed a nice little job and an important role for a retired Warrant Officer or Senior NCO, globe-trotting to interesting and unusual locations, although they didn't have time for tourism.

We steamed at full speed from Santa Cruz for the first three days after departing on Friday 21 July. This allowed us to comfortably maintain the required speed of advance on two main engines in calm seas. We encountered thick fog off Cape Finisterre, a bit of a shock after months of clear visibility. *Hecla* arrived in Plymouth Sound on Wednesday 26 July to clear customs and collect mail before returning to sea to run a series of lines through the Eddystone Gravity range overnight. Hearty cheers echoed through the ship as we tasted our first pint of fresh milk for six months. No more 'low life'!

On Thursday, we anchored in the Sound to embark families by fleet tender for the trip up harbour and into 3 Basin. There were emotional reunions aplenty on board. I held Jennifer at last, grown from newborn into a six-month old babe.

Back on board the next day, we landed the bulk of the survey records and UKHO Technical Staff removed the gravimeters for refurbishment in Taunton. *Herald* berthed outboard of *Hecla* on Monday to double-up for dormant summer leave.

10. To Brazil and West Africa 277

10.24 Ship's company
(UKHO Archive)

August and September were spent in 3 Basin for leave and maintenance. The AMP had several major items of planned work, including structural and electrical repairs in the galley. For a fortnight, we had meals in *Hecate*, now nearby. Whilst maintenance went on, various meetings took place including one at UKHO to discuss the deployment's results and plans for autumn and 1990 surveys. A delegation visited *Hecla's* affiliated town (Salcombe) and played hockey and golf. Cdr Page presented £600 cheques to a Tavistock charity and Hillside School Plymouth, for the latter to improve resources for outdoor education. We were delighted that the Buffer was presented with his well-deserved Long Service and Good Conduct Medal. Amongst those leaving *Hecla* was Graham, off to NP1016. We were sad to see him go after such a fantastic deployment together. But that's 'life in a blue suit'.

The AMP extended into October. We cold-moved to Slip Jetty on 6 October to continue repairs, culminating in a successful basin trial a week later. While defects to survey kit were being solved, Cdr Page and some sailors travelled to the MacIntyre School Wingate, Aylesbury, to present a £1200 cheque towards new playground facilities for its children with intellectual disabilities. I was always impressed by 'Jack's' generosity in donating cash to worthy charities during deployments. Our sailors certainly had hearts of gold.

10.25 Survey department T-shirt
(Martin Clegg)

Store ship, cleaning and preparations for sea continued until we sailed on Thursday 19 October and transited the Eddystone Gravity Range. Not for us the tropical Atlantic, this survey was in the Irish and Celtic Seas. We endured a lively passage across the Celtic Sea in a westerly gale, a shock to all. Good progress was made in the Irish Sea survey for the next three days, when Cdr Page moved us to the Celtic Sea area to take advantage of a favourable trend in the general Atlantic weather pattern.

Unfortunately, by Friday 27 October weather conditions worsened as a small local depression rapidly intensified. Within four hours, winds reached hurricane force and steadied at 60–70kts, gusting over 80kts. Seas mounted to 12–15m. We hove to 70km off Ireland's south coast for the next 24 hours. We used the bow thruster in concert with the main engines and helm to keep ship's head into wind and sea. This required constant concentration and monitoring of the QM's hand-steering. Any lapse caused the ship's head to veer to port or starboard, resulting in heavy rolling. When this occurred, folks phoned the bridge to ask what was going on and fulsomely express their displeasure. With judicious use of bow thruster, main engines and helm, *Hecla* regained her hove to attitude.

10. To Brazil and West Africa

Standing braced on the bridge, I looked through the windows. The wipers worked overtime and the Kent Clearview screens rotated at full-throttle. I saw gigantic green walls of water hurtle towards us, crash over the fo'c'sle and splatter the bridge windows as *Hecla* climbed uphill to the crest and over the top into the inevitable deep trough. Seawater forced its way up the hawse pipes to fountain into the air, adding to the swirling angry green water and white foam flowing overboard. The air filled with sea spray. The wind whistled through the rigging, halyards and gaps between upper deck fixtures, creating an incessant cacophony. The whole of *Hecla* shuddered and vibrated as every green wall struck.

Unlike my *Gavinton* experience in January 1985, *Hecla* suffered minimal structural damage and, thankfully, no one was injured. The hurricane subsided and the sea calmed sufficiently to allow her to be turned safely and return to the Irish Sea for the remainder of the survey leg until our visit to Cardiff. We berthed at King's Wharf, Queen Alexandra Dock on Friday 3 November. Weekend leave was granted to half ship's company, who swiftly organised hire cars and legged it home to Guzz. The rest split their time either on duty or enjoying the delights of Cardiff's nightlife. Fuel, fresh water and fresh provisions were taken on board.

We departed on 7 November with Capt H embarked for a two-day visit. Approaching Fishguard the following morning to land Capt H, light winds rose to gale force in minutes and the sea transitioned from flat calm to 3–4m. The boat transfer was postponed until the next day when conditions were more benign.

Typical of the Irish Sea and the season, a succession of gales hampered survey progress but a marked change in the weather occurred midway through the survey leg as autumnal fog reduced visibility, coinciding with much trawler traffic in the central Irish Sea. To escape, we switched to the Celtic Sea area, although the weather remained unpleasant.

It was a relief to arrive in Swansea for a scheduled visit. Entry into the sea lock was made difficult by strong crosswinds but eventually *Hecla* was alongside on West Wharf, King's Dock. When the pilot embarked, *Hecla* was 'boarded' by a half dozen young ladies, dressed as pirates, from the local Post Office. They held the ship to ransom for the mail in aid of BBC 'Children in Need'. Ever generous, ship's company raised £310 to retrieve the mail and Cdr Page presented the 'pirates' with a ship's crest. This time, Higgy and I weekended to Guzz. It was a terrifying journey as he drove like a man possessed. I was a bag of nerves when I got home. Thankfully, the return journey wasn't at quite such speed.

Our next survey leg was under an anticyclone dominating the northeast Atlantic, bringing stable calm conditions and exceptional visibility, to allow uninhibited survey productivity. By the end of this leg, we'd completed the Irish Sea survey and 80% of the Celtic Sea area. Everyone thoroughly enjoyed the run ashore in Liverpool. We embarked the pilot at Bar Light, entered the Mersey and transited Sandon Dock to berth at Huskisson Dock Branch No.1 on 1 December.

It reminded me of my joining *Benedict* at adjacent Canada Branch Dock as a Deck Cadet in April 1981. *Benedict* and sister-ship *Boniface* were Booth Line 3636-ton general cargo ships, trading between Liverpool/Belfast/Dublin and Belem, in the Amazon delta, via Bridgetown, Barbados, and Port of Spain, Trinidad. Great little ships designed for frequent runs 1300km up the Amazon to Manaus and occasionally to Iquitos, a further 1500km upriver.

It was a busy 'official' weekend as parties of Sea Cadets, CCF cadets and old boys from Chester Royal Naval Association visited and toured *Hecla*. Combined with Liverpool's lively nightlife, we almost welcomed returning to sea on Tuesday 5 December. This survey leg was curtailed by three days as urgent defect rectification work on the 440V motor generator was required. Nevertheless, all but two short lines in the Celtic Sea were surveyed and we made a successful deep-water oceanographic trial to 2000m depth off the edge of the continental shelf to prove the new winch, CTD probe and associated fittings.

Hecla berthed at 2 Wharf in Guzz on Monday 11 December. Work immediately started on the engineering package. The next day, the gravimeters were removed and, the following day, we cold-moved into 3 Basin outboard of *Herald* for Christmas leave.

On the evening of 14 December, a reception for ex-*Hecla* officers and wives celebrated the 25th anniversary of *Hecla's* launch. Among the 45 guests were Hydrographer (Rear Admiral Morris) and two former Hydrographers (Irving and Hall).

Christmas leave commenced on Friday 15 December and marked my leaving *Hecla* after a thoroughly enjoyable and interesting appointment.

11.

Happy Days in the Country Club

11.1 BRNC crest

Towards the end of my appointment in *Fox*, Bob suggested I apply for the droggy's job at BRNC. He was in post when I joined in April 1984 and was my class' navigation instructor. Many of my peers hadn't enjoyed their Dartmouth experience as much as I had.

I gathered that BRNC was the only establishment where the Captain vetted incoming Staff Officers. I wrote a letter to our Appointer, at that time Hydrographer's PA or some similar dog's-body role with responsibility for placing us in droggy jobs. During the latter half of my time in *Hecla*, I learned my application was successful. After a brilliant year in *Hecla* and Christmas leave at home, I joined BRNC on 2 January 1990.

The following snippets of history were extracted from the Britannia Association's little booklet, *BRNC Guidebook*. BRNC's history dated back to 1857 when a formal training scheme for RN officers began in *Illustrious*, a two-deck warship anchored in Haslar Creek, Gosport. She was replaced by *Britannia*, a larger 120-gun, first-rate ship-of-the-line, in 1859. In 1862, *Britannia* moved to Portland, but she was too exposed to the elements and towed to a safe anchorage in Dartmouth in 1863. Cadets were 13-year-old schoolboys whose parents paid for their secondary education. *Hindostan* moored ahead of *Britannia* in 1864 to increase accommodation. A covered gangway connected the two ships.

A slowly decaying *Britannia* was replaced in 1869 by *Prince of Wales*, renamed *Britannia*, in which future officers were educated until the early 20th century. In the mid-1890s, it was decided to build a college ashore. Land immediately adjacent to Sandquay moorings was bought by compulsory purchase in 1898. Aston Webb was appointed to design and oversee construction. A well-respected architect, he'd designed several public buildings, including the Victoria and Albert Museum's main block, Buckingham Palace's façade and Admiralty Arch. Edward VII laid the foundation stone on 2 March 1902 and the first cadets entered BRNC in 1905.

BRNC's impressive frontage made a bold statement about the RN, the training of its officer corps and its standing in Britain at the end of the 19th century. Book-ending the frontage are Captain's House (east end) and wardroom (west end). The whole assemblage overlooks and dominates Dartmouth and its river below. Red brick contrasted with pale Portland stone, capped by a Delabole slate roof. Above the west and east doors corbels depict warship development from 300BC to 1892. Originally, a rose garden was laid in front of the college but this was largely replaced by the parade ground post-World War I, when Osborne Naval College on the Isle of Wight closed, concentrating all cadet training at BRNC.

11.2 *Britannia* and *Hindostan* at Sandquay
(Britannia Association)

On the lawns at either end of the parade ground the figureheads from *Britannia* and Royal Naval College Osborne are permanent reminders of

BRNC's early history. Across the front of the building are words from Britain's first Articles of War, dated about 1653: 'It is under the Navy and the good providence of God that our wealth, prosperity and peace depend'. This encapsulated how the Navy was viewed by Edwardian society and the country at large at that time. I doubt this holds true with today's shrunken, decimated Navy and the UK's low standing and influence globally.

11.3 BRNC façade (centre), wardroom (left), Captain's House (right)
(Britannia Association)

A guided tour of BRNC is well worthwhile. Everywhere in Webb's design and architecture are clever, thoughtful symbols representing the Navy and parts of a warship.

I hadn't been to Dartmouth since passing out in December 1984. Instead of the long flog from Gosport, it was a relatively short hop of 45 minutes from our home in Plympton. I felt very proud to turn left into the main gate at the bottom of Townstal Road's steep hill. I collected my car pass from the MOD Plod sentry box. I drove through the raised barrier, up the steep Prince of Wales Drive, turned left at the junction, glided along Flagstaff Road, parade ground to the right, mainmast on my left, uphill and into the hostel car park. From there, I walked (sorry, marched) up to Hawke Division. Yep, I was appointed as a Hawke DO and I couldn't have been more chuffed to be back at the 'country club'.

I walked through the front door into the familiar expansive hallway. Div Chief Dobson welcomed me and showed me into what was to be my office. There, I met Andy Brook, the droggy I was succeeding. I didn't know him but had met him briefly at our annual Hydrographic Symposium in Drake Theatre and knew of him from other folks in the branch. Pleased to see me, we had a brief chat, interrupted by Lt Simon Carter breezing into the office, which they shared. It was great to see Simon. He was one of those immaculately dressed, fresh-faced, shiny Seniors who'd shepherded us Juniors around when I joined.

Andy showed me to the SDO's office. Divisional posts had been renamed. DO was now SDO (Senior Divisional Officer) and ADOs were DOs (Divisional Officers).

Hawke SDO was Lt Cdr Jon Wakeling, a rufty-tufty Schoolie, swimmer, water polo player and rugger bugger. A little below average height, he was a powerful, muscular bloke with a warm smile, powerful voice and effervescent character. He welcomed me to BRNC, particularly to Hawke, and quizzed me about my background and previous appointments. I instantly liked Jon, a thorough, competent, professional officer and an excellent, supportive boss.

Andy showed me around Hawke and introduced me to my fellow Hawke DOs. The office adjacent to Jon's was occupied by Lt Cdrs Mick Johnson and Rod Williams and Lt Pete Thompson. The former were both MEOs, Mick was an old-and-bold SD, Rod a Manadon graduate GL MEO. Pete was a tall, bearded, pukka GL PWO(U) who described his anti-submarine warfare specialism as 'awfully slow warfare'. They seemed a jolly bunch and I looked forward to working with them.

Andy and I marched down to tour the main college, visiting places and spaces that, as an OUT, I hadn't known existed or had wondered what went on inside them. Andy introduced me to a variety of folks, especially at stand easy in the common room in D Block. This was a great meeting place on weekday mornings, frequented by staff officers and academics mingling and chatting on a range of topics, often about certain OUTs. Here, I first met some of the Hawke-affiliated academic staff, with whom we, as DOs, interacted particularly during the end-of-term report-writing season.

I had a brief appointment with the Captain and Commander Training (Cdr T). Capt Robin Shiffner was the first and only Engineer Officer to command BRNC. A soft-spoken chap, he was a good leader and well-respected by staff and academics alike. His wife was the wardroom wives' stalwart, who organised various events and was involved in arrangements for the end-of-term balls. As Cdr T, Cdr Roger Bishop, a FAA pilot, ran BRNC's training programme. He spoke with a very posh accent and looked down his nose at anyone below his rank. I didn't really take to him.

We had lunch in the wardroom, a hallowed space where OUTs were never permitted. It was another magnificent suite of rooms. The entrance was tucked away to the left of the door to the SGR. To the right was a door to the TV room, ahead was the wardroom anteroom. A high-ceilinged, light and airy space with plush leather chesterfields and chairs arranged around coffee tables. On the rear wall was a long bar, manned by a civilian steward. The anteroom's windows were almost floor to ceiling, those to the left overlooked the parade ground, to the front were the grass tennis courts and the mouth of the River Dart.

11.4 Access to wardroom

From the anteroom, a doorway led into the equally spacious dining room. Our shoes tapped on the highly polished parquet flooring. At the table, the elderly civilian stewards provided excellent silver service. I felt privileged and knew I'd enjoy my appointment here.

We returned to Hawke, via the navigation department in E Block, overlooking the hard tennis courts. Andy showed me round the classrooms, including the bridge trainer and CBT (computer-based training) room. The former was still in its rudimentary layout, but the latter was a recent development, equipped with desktop computers and monitors to enable OUTs to learn and test themselves on ROR. I met the Nav's Yeo (Navigator's Yeoman), a cheerful PO who managed the department's office, equipment, charts and lesson plans. As a Seaman Officer, I was automatically a navigation instructor. Pete and I spent much time to-ing and fro-ing between Hawke and E Block.

We continued the handover in our office. Andy explained our role, what we did and how we did it, myriad commitments and compulsory attendance at certain events. Divisional offices were fitted with Amstrad 464 desktop computers and monitors and used a Lex computer programme for word processing. Wow! This knocked spots off using a typewriter to fill in H-forms in *Fox* and *Hecla*. BRNC even had an email offshoot of Lex. Simon and I shared a printer in the office.

My first day ended and I drove home. The day had gone well, our handover was almost complete. Like any job, much would be 'learned by doing'. I was looking forward to getting stuck in, which began tomorrow when the winter term joined in the afternoon.

We chose to remain in our Plympton home rather than move to MQ in Dartmouth. To reduce my commute and knowing the job was hardly 9-to-5 in an office, I got a cabin in the College and stayed several nights per week depending on commitments. I was allocated a spacious day cabin and bedroom combo tucked above and behind the wardroom. I brought enough kit to tide me over for the week. A perk of living-in was cabin cleaning and, surprisingly, I could leave my shoes and boots out for Sid the Steward to clean and polish. Sid was a great old boy, with striking silver hair and a sense of humour. No return to bulling boots and shoes!

Day 1, Week 0 began with preparations for new entry arrival in the afternoon. Andy bade farewell and shuffled off. Simon talked me through everything for this week. Jon convened a staff meeting to outline his policies and philosophy for OUT training and Hawke Division in general. Meanwhile, the Seniors nominated as new entry guides readied themselves. The morning ended and I enjoyed lunch in the wardroom, a truly magnificent space. Its solid tables and chairs were arranged at an angle within. My shiny shoes clattered on the parquet flooring. I met a few more folks from other Divisions.

After a lazy cup of coffee in the anteroom, I returned to Hawke. We braced ourselves for the onslaught of Juniors. Now our work truly began. Simon and I loitered in and around our office as the first arrivals turned up, parked their cars outside Hawke's front door, as I had six years before. Our shiny Seniors bellowed at them as they stumbled in, clutching their bags and grips before shifting their cars to the far-distant car park. Later, those who'd arrived by train at Totnes and delivered by Tally-Ho coach to the parade ground marched uphill to Hawke. Immaculate Mids pointed them to either the Lower or Upper Dorm.

As a Hawke DO, it was interesting to observe this scene. Juniors' suits and jacket-and-tie varied in standard and quality. For many, it was almost the first time they'd worn shoes as trainers and other casual footwear seemed to be popular with today's youth. Some Juniors appeared nervy and uncertain, a handful seemed outwardly confident.

Later, the Seniors mustered the Juniors outside the front door and marched them down to CJH as the first serial in their 13½ week programme. Back again, they mustered in HGR. Jon gathered his DOs and Div Chief and we trooped upstairs, across the landing, through the double-doors into HGR. Seniors ordered Juniors to 'sit at attention'. We sat along the side, Jon stood at the lectern, introduced himself and welcomed the Juniors to Hawke and the RN. In turn, we stood and each gave a short bio. Then began the Juniors' turn. All too soon, they disappeared downhill for the remainder of the evening's programme.

That was about it for us Div Staff. Jon convened a meeting in his office to debrief the day and seek comments from us about any Juniors who'd instantly impressed or otherwise. Later, I went to dinner in the wardroom and returned briefly to Hawke to see what was going on. A quiet bit of TV in the wardroom before retreating to my cabin.

Thursday dawned. Hawke was alive with Seniors and Juniors, the latter milling around a bit but certainly many seemed aware of what was going on and awaited leadership from our Seniors. Thursday and Friday of Week 0 were filled with the Juniors completing admin, kit issue, familiarising themselves with filling their drawers, wardrobe and shoe-racks correctly.

As DOs, we didn't have much input or involvement. It was interesting to hear conversations and comments as Simon and I sat at our desks. Already, the odd Junior was getting roasted by a Senior, the latter bellowed 'SORT YOUR LIFE OUT!' or 'GET YOUR S**T IN ONE SOCK!' or 'SWITCH ON, FOR F**K SAKE!' at the former. Ah, such memoires of my own first couple of days, although I was never on the receiving end of such diatribes as I'd swiftly gathered what we were supposed to do and when.

I stayed at the College throughout to embed myself just as much as the Juniors, except I really had to know what was going on. Our next commitments were on Sunday. New entry prayers were held in Chapel for CofE folks. The Jocks went to St Giles' Chapel in the main building. As a left-footer, I attended St Philip Howard Chapel, a small room high up in A Block (I think). Staff and Seniors wore No.5, Juniors in their awful battledress uniform.

Our RC sin bosun was Father Tom Burns, a tall, bespectacled character brimming with good humour and great fun. His cabin overlooked the parade ground. Occasionally, during Tuesday or Thursday Divisions, those on the parade ground looked up and saw him standing at his window in his priest's vestments, topped by a bishop's mitre, giving Pope-like waves of the hand. His gregarious personality certainly livened up BRNC, regardless of your religious persuasion.

11.5 BRNC's magnificent Chapel

Sunday afternoon was taken up with new entry sports, a festival of shouting, screaming, raucous mayhem as the four Divisions battled through the various races, relays and competitions. Juniors in divisional T-shirts (Hawke red, Cunningham yellow, St Vincent purple, Blake navy blue), shorts and Pusser's daps. Seniors flitting about, bellowing encouragement, endeavouring to ensure Hawke didn't finish last in anything. Meanwhile, we Staff maintained a dignified stance, wandering around the parade ground, offering encouragement here and there but nothing so unofficer-like as shouting.

So ended Week 0. NGT began in earnest on Day 1 Week 1. I'd settled in comfortably and quickly and had conducted interviews with OUTs in my DO group, about ten Juniors and eight Seniors. The Juniors were a bunch of young blokes from school-leavers to graduates, with a couple of Internationals thrown in. My Seniors included Term 2 Flight (eagerly awaiting their flight grading in Chipmunks at Roborough Airport), Term 3 SLs and GLs (fresh from DTS) and Term 4 GLs. Although undertaking 'academic' studies, they remained under scrutiny from divisional, academic and college staff regarding their C&L (character and leadership). In addition to Div Sub, there were numerous roles assigned to Seniors to test their officer-like abilities: River Rep, Duties Rep, Social Rep, Treasurer, Sports Rep, and responsibilities for organising NEX, general drills and life raft drills.

Assessment of OUTs was ongoing and continued for the duration of their time at BRNC. As DOs, we sought all nuggets of information (good, bad, indifferent) about our OUTs from College-wide sources to create an accurate picture of each man. This data was invaluable in compiling end-of-term reports and, importantly, identifying a weak OUT and providing him with appropriate guidance to rectify his faults. If an OUT fell into this category, he was a marked man whose naval career was blighted at BRNC or could even end abruptly.

Week 1 opened with EMAs, which DOs were required to observe. Naturally, I most detested walking down the interminable steps to Sandquay to witness our Juniors pathetically 'pulling' whalers on the river. Yes, they were just as hopeless as when my entry had done it six years before. After that futile exercise, at least all I had to do was climb the steps up to the College and enjoy a relaxed breakfast in the wardroom. Breakfast was a delight as the 'livers-in' spread themselves around the large dining tables and tucked in while reading a newspaper, no noise, no conversation. It was here that I honed my taste for Frank Cooper's Coarse Cut Marmalade. Bliss!

I most enjoyed squad runs, as the rhythmic beat of boots on tarmac resounded around the College. Ever-present from dawn to dusk was seemingly incessant barking (sorry, 'speaking') of the Britannia Beagles. Our pack was founded in 1878 by Lt Guy Mainwaring, Britannia's First Lieutenant. Hares or badgers were the beagles' prey, a form of pest control which pleased local farmers. The original kennels were by the racquet court (now badminton courts, part-way down Sandquay steps) but, buried in woods, they lacked sunshine. Later, new kennels were built near the corner of the cricket ground. Little wonder their blasted, continual 'speaking' was heard everywhere. Britannia Beagles were originally under the Commander's care. It was oft-quoted that his most important qualification was the ability to ride and hunt with a pack of hounds. Today, the beagles are the remit of the Army Exchange Officer, usually a Cavalryman.

Weeks 1 to 4 were new entry phase, which included standing rounds every evening. DOs conducted these inspections. Juniors were up against time, as I recalled from when I was a Junior. DOs were also up against it when designated to conduct standing rounds. 'Winter routine' meant river activities occurred in the afternoon. After tea, lessons resumed, ending at 1855. If I was teaching navigation until 1855, I had about an hour to return to the wardroom for dinner, change into Mess Undress and march up to Hawke to be punctual for rounds. I became adept at tying my bow tie perfectly first time.

Conducting rounds was illuminating. Early on, some Juniors had great difficulty acclimatising to the routine and the necessary personal organisation. I re-scrubbed the odd bathroom or set of heads as they just weren't good enough. Inspecting Juniors' kit was fun, in a way. They'd largely got it sorted, under their Sea Dads' guidance, but there was always one Junior who couldn't quite hack it. A 'problem child' who might not last the term. Seeing Juniors in their battledress, brilliant white caps with shiny black peaks, bulled shoes and name tallies, reminded me of my own experience. It reinforced my opinion that battledress was a truly awful uniform.

As a Seaman Officer, I automatically became a Navigation Instructor. 'New-joiners' were saddled with teaching international classes (Int1A or Int1B). The latter were generally the worse of the two and, as the most junior nav instructor, I got Int1B. Our Ints were dominated by Middle Eastern nations (Saudi, UAE, Oman, occasionally Qatar) and a sprinkling from Brunei, Singapore, Malaysia, Bahamas and Kenya.

Before every lesson, I popped into the Nav's Yeo's office to collect the folder for my lesson. There were notes and overhead projector slides. No PowerPoint in those far off days. The slides sometimes had little flaps on them, to be revealed as the lesson progressed. Exciting stuff. The syllabus covered the basics of navigation, methods and techniques of navigation, instruments, invaluable reference books (*Admiralty Manual of Navigation, Nautical Almanac, Tide Tables*), chartwork and RoR.

Teaching Int1B (all from the Middle East) was an interesting experience. Their proficiency in English varied. Some really struggled, others (notably Omanis) had an excellent grasp of our language. It was challenging to explain basic principles of navigation in 'noddy' terms. Much repetition was required. Int1B found RoR the most difficult of subjects, especially as the pass mark in tests and exams was 100%. I felt sorry for those in my class who tried very hard to grasp the topic, but no sympathy for those who made little or no effort whatsoever.

There were occasional lessons in the 'Bridge Trainer'. Absolutely nothing like the complex, high-tech, computer-driven, virtual-reality, pitching-and-

11. Happy Days in the Country Club

rolling bridge trainers of today. Ours was a room laid out as a mock-up of an old frigate. 'Equipped' with engine console, helm, pelorus, bridge windows, chart table and Captain's chair, OUTs enacted various bridge procedures following on from our lessons.

Classroom theory was put into practice in BRNC's navigation training ships *Sandpiper* and *Peterel*. These, with *Kingfisher*, *Cygnet* and *Redpole*, were *Bird*-class vessels designed for patrol and fishery protection in coastal and inshore territorial waters. Displacing 194 tons, they were 37.7m long, 7.2m beam, 2m draught and powered by two Paxman diesel engines giving a maximum speed of 21kts. Ship's company comprised 4 officers and 19 sailors. Their main armament was a 40mm Bofors gun mounted aft. Commissioned between 1975 and 1977, they were poor sea-keeping vessels and considered unsuitable for their role. Thus, *Peterel* and *Sandpiper* were employed as training tenders for the RNR and never undertook an operational patrol. After being fitted with an enclosed bridge, they were assigned to BRNC for navigation training duties. Meanwhile, the other three were assigned to Northern Ireland Squadron, replacing *Ton*-class minesweepers.

During new entry term, we accompanied our nav class for a couple of half-days and an overnight trip in these ships. A class was too large for one ship, so it was halved between the two vessels. Every trip required a nav instructor on both *Sandpiper* and *Peterel*. So, nav instructors spent twice as much time in these terrible boats as any nav class.

A large chart table dominated the aft end of the bridge, around which OUTs plotted their fixes and laid off basic chartwork. Clutching their Navigation Notebook and pencil, they gamely ventured outside to take visual bearings of points in Start Bay, perhaps a range off a headland too and then plotted the fix. Both ships certainly had poor sea-keeping qualities. They'd roll on wet grass and were truly dreadful boats. None of us looked forward to these trips. Not for nothing were they nicknamed 'Vomit Comets'.

A bucket was always secured to the foot of the mast for OUTs to spew into … a sad inevitability. On one memorable occasion, I was in *Sandpiper* and noticed an OUT in *Peterel* was permanently kneeling, hunched over the bucket. He was unaware of getting increasingly soaked as *Peterel* rolled and waves splashed up and over him. When we got alongside at Sandquay, medics came aboard, wrapped him in a shiny space blanket and helped him stumble down the gangway and into the waiting ambulance to be carted off to Sick Bay. Poor sod! Apparently a Schoolie, I think he got WFT'ed before the end of term.

11.6 Peterel and Sandpiper
(Flying Fox Association)

When not teaching navigation, DOs were busy in the Division. There was always admin, prep and monitoring the development of our OUTs. Juniors were occupied with classroom instruction across the spectrum of professional subjects (operations & warfare, seamanship, ME, WE, S&S) and leadership.

Leadership was the most significant part of a Junior's syllabus. The basic techniques of 'getting things done' were covered in new entry phase. The leadership package comprised four parts. First NEX then formal classroom introduction to the basic principles of leadership together with some simple evolutions. A series of PLTs around the College and down on the river formed the third phase. The leadership package culminated in the three-day PLX on Dartmoor.

Newly-joined DOs completed a leadership trainers package during Week 1, focused on describing BRNC's leadership programme, taking us through the various elements and showing the various PLT stances in the College grounds and at Sandquay. Guidance was given on conducting and assessing leadership tasks and the 3-minute, 10-minute and 30-minute talks which the Juniors prepared and presented. Like OUTs, we were given a copy of *Getting Things Done*, the excellent booklet describing John Adair's famous three-circle model for action-centred leadership.

Adair's simple and practical model was based on three overlapping circles of task, team and individual. It remains relevant and is still used at BRNC because it describes what leaders have to do, actions they must take in their working environment to be effective: achieve the task; build and maintain the team; and develop the individual. Adair's concept asserts that the needs of task, team and individual are the watchwords of leadership. People expect their leaders to help them achieve the common task, build the synergy of teamwork and respond to individuals' needs.

The task needs work groups or organisations to be effective because one person alone cannot accomplish it. The team requires constant promotion and retention of group cohesiveness to ensure it functions efficiently ('united we stand, divided we fall'). The individual's needs are physical and psychological: recognition; sense of purpose/achievement; status; and the need to give and receive from others in a work environment.

For Adair, task, team and individual need to overlap. Achieving the task builds the team and satisfies the individuals. If team needs are not met or lack cohesiveness, then task performance is impaired and individual satisfaction reduced. If individual needs aren't met, the team will lack cohesiveness and task performance is impaired.

11.7 Getting things done (left); check list of leadership actions (right)
(Monty Birch)

Just as we completed our training, Week 2 introduced the Juniors to leadership. By Divisions, lectures were given on 'What is an Officer?' and 'Qualities of Leadership'. As Week 2 closed, this led to consecutive rolling NEXs to take us into Week 3.

As 'Staff', I was briefed beforehand by my PB cox'n, a Hawke Senior, who assured me that all was in order and everything would run smoothly. It was most pleasant to stroll down to Sandquay at the appointed time, hand my rucksack to an OUT and step aboard. The NEX programme hadn't changed. After slipping from Sandquay and some seamanship evolutions, we went upriver to moor off The Ferry Boat Inn, Dittisham. Pot mess for dinner, then I briefed my OUTs and we were ferried ashore. The OUT teams hiked around South Hams countryside, with a Staff Officer following astern, monitoring their performance, attitude, enthusiasm and map-reading skills.

The evening wore on until the teams trickled back to Dittisham and reported to the Exercise Director outside the Red Lion. They then marched down to the jetty and returned to the PB. Meanwhile, we staff officers scuppered a pint or two. Eventually vacating the pub to get back on board our respective PBs. It was a little more comfortable in the for'ard cabin sharing with my two Seniors and, as usual, I slept well.

After breakfast, we had a church service and lusty singing of the Naval Hymn. Then, downriver we proceeded in convoy, out between Kingswear and Dartmouth Castles and into Start Bay. Here, we greatly enjoyed racing around at top speed, conducting OOW manoeuvres for an hour or so before heading back into the Dart and berthing at Sandquay. I debriefed my OUTs. Overall, I was pleased with their collective performance. An OUT handed me my rucksack and I disembarked, leaving the OUTs and Seniors to scrub out the PB.

The nitty-gritty of classroom instruction about leadership followed. To illustrate bad and good leadership, the presentations revolved around watching selected excerpts from *Twelve O'Clock High*. A classic 1949 war film, it charted the reputation of 918th Bomb Group based at Archbury, a UK airfield. It had become the 'hard luck group', led by its exhausted and demoralised CO whose defeatist attitude permeated his personnel. Ordered to fly another dangerous mission, the CO protests to his friend General Savage (Gregory Peck) at VIII Bomber Command. Savage and his boss visit Archbury and decide to relieve the CO. Savage replaces him and commences the long road back to restoring the group's discipline and morale. Stirring stuff! But valuable lessons in leadership were apparent and discussed back in our Divisions.

Week 4 focused on PLTs, a busy forenoon around the College estate. Small teams marched from stance to stance, everyone given the opportunity to lead the march and run a leadership task. The programme was tight, so teams had to keep track of time, occasionally requiring the DO to give them a kick. I don't recall them all, but a 'pilot' had to be rescued from a tree and there was abseiling from the mainmast down to the grass below. There were a couple at Sandquay. The most memorable was to build and erect a flagpole on one of the pontoons in the river. Almost inevitably, the staves (part of the kit each team carried with them) were not secured sufficiently rigidly. Although a flagpole was erected, in slow motion it slowly curved and arched over such that its top rested on the pontoon. It was enormously deflating for the team, but they just had to soldier on to the next task after an excoriating debrief.

11.8 PLT at the mainmast
(BRNC Archive)

The true test of what Juniors had learned about leadership was encapsulated in PLX on Dartmoor over a three-day/two-night period. Teams of six hiked about 40km, camped overnight and carried all their kit. There were usually five or six PLXs spread across Weeks 5 and 6. As one PLX came off Dartmoor, the next began, making transport coordination simpler.

The programme hadn't changed much since my Summer Term 1984. OUTs mustered in C Block car park where they were inspected and their kit was checked for illicit nutty bars. They stowed their rucksacks in the baggage compartment of the Tally-Ho coach and clambered aboard. Conversation was limited as most OUTs nodded off. As Staff, we sat up front and enjoyed the ride. The start point was either Princetown or Cornwood, depending on where the previous PLX had ended.

After disembarking, Staff briefed their respective team, selected a leader and provided him with the route to Ditsworthy Warren House. He briefed the team and we set off. There was no ETA, just get to Ditsworthy ASAP. Every PLX in which I participated was unique, every team was different, every route too. The standard of map reading varied greatly, particularly as dusk and night fell as it was easy to become disorientated. It was fascinating to observe my team discuss, debate their position and the direction to go.

Staff were issued with their own map so we could monitor progress and whether the team was meandering off-track and in danger of getting hopelessly lost, prolonging the march-on. Time remorselessly ticked along. Dartmoor wasn't a nice place on a cold, moonless night in pouring rain. A contrast from my PLX experience of glorious sunny days and sunset in late evening.

Eventually, we arrived at Ditsworthy Warren. The team were told to select a spot, set up bivouacs and get the hexi-stoves flashed up for dinner and a brew. My day was done. Staff were accommodated in the house. Downstairs was a galley, dining space, heads and bathroom, upstairs was a large bunk space.

Ditsworthy Warren House was built for the keeper of the rabbit warren near the house. Its oldest part dates from the late 18th century or early/mid 19th century, probably on the site of an original 16th century house and is a Grade II listed building. Ditsworthy Warren covered approximately 1km^2, where rabbits were commercially bred and kept for their meat and fur. The rabbits lived in 'pillow mounds', long cigar-shaped structures of stone covered with earth, wherein rabbits burrowed and lived. Dartmoor was suitable for rabbit-keeping as it was poor agricultural land but had sufficient stone to construct 'pillow mounds', walls and vermin traps. There was a 'kennel court' in the adjacent field east of the house, where the warren dogs were kept. Its six-foot-high walls prevented the dogs from escaping. With 53 'pillow mounds', Ditsworthy Warren was the largest rabbit warren in England.

Abandoned in 1947, the house was leased by the Admiralty as part of Dartmoor Training Area. It was used in Steven Spielberg's *War Horse* as the Narracott family's farmhouse. The house was 'dressed' with a thatched roof, window shutters and a lean-to wood store. A cruck-framed building was built close by to serve as the barn. The set was dismantled after filming and the site restored to its pre-existing state.

The Exercise Director (a qualified Exped Leader) and his helpers based themselves at the house. Dinner was laid on and I tucked in greedily.

11.9 Ditsworthy Warren House
(Steve Foster www.treksandtors.co)

Afterwards, I visited my team to check on their location and to ensure there were no injuries or problems. Injuries were usually blisters or shin splints. Blisters occurred early on in term. It was common to see Juniors hobbling around BRNC in Pusser's daps. Anyone still suffering from blisters was forced to delay going on PLX until the 'remedial' PLX for those who'd failed it at their first attempt. I'd never heard of shin splints, which are a pain and tenderness along or just behind the tibia. They develop after hard exercise, sports or repetitive activity. Pain on the front or outside of the shins or on the inside of the lower leg above the ankle was eased by ice on the shin, stretching exercises or taking ibuprofen/aspirin. I firmly believed that blisters and shin splints were the direct result of young people wearing trainers all their lives instead of proper shoes and boots. Harrumph!

An unexpected bonus for Staff was the nightly Land Rover trip to The Royal Oak, Meavy. This 16th century pub nestles beside the village green, the church and the royal oak tree. A handful of us, dressed in exped uniform, occupied a corner booth for a pint or two in this delightful little pub for an hour or so before returning to Ditsworthy for a night's kip in a 'green slug' on a bunk bed. Perks of the job!

11.10 Royal Oak, Meavy
(Steve Foster www.treksandtors.co)

Overnight, it was customary for the Exercise Director and his staff to throw a few thunder flashes near the OUTs' bivouacs and bellow at them to 'lift-and-shift' as they were 'under attack'. After about a half-hour, the Juniors returned to their campsite and settled in for the limited remainder of the night. Call the hands was about 0500. Up they arose, bleary-eyed and tired, to shave, polish their boots and make breakfast. In relative luxury, Staff stirred at 0600 to ablute and enjoy a hearty full English breakfast downstairs.

After the muster and inspection at 0630, the teams set off for a day's hiking and leadership tasks all over Dartmoor. The Juniors carried their kit, plus four staves and a 120ft rope, a hefty jerrican of water was added in the summer term to prevent dehydration. Staff struggled along with a small day pack.

Assessment of performance (collective and individual) was constant throughout. It was interesting to observe the team's interaction and how it evolved during PLX. A reasonable pace had to be maintained between stances to exit a stance before another team's arrival. The programme cleverly ensured that we never met or even spotted another team during the day.

11.11 Leopard crawl across a chasm (left); crossing a chasm on parallel ropes (centre); ascent or descent of a tor (right)
(BRNC Archive)

The ground soon became familiar as the stances hadn't changed since my PLX: the trek around Burrator Reservoir to reach Sheeps Tor; the leopard crawl across Meavy Ford; raft-building to cross the clay pits near Cadover Bridge. There were a good dozen stances, so every OUT led a couple of marches and tasks during PLX.

11.12 Clay pits near Cadover Bridge, scene of many sinking rafts!
(www.dartefacts.co.uk)

At the end of this long day, teams returned to bivouac at Ditsworthy Warren overnight. Previously, teams had camped out on Dartmoor that night, with their Staff Officer in his own little tent nearby and then continued the trek next morning. Now, the second morning repeated the muster and inspection of kit, shiny boots and clean-shaven faces before we set off for a long morning's hiking.

The teams were back at Ditsworthy Warren by about 1300. On arrival, they were told to find a spot within the walled enclosure and have lunch. At 1400, there was a final muster before the Exercise Director issued each team with a route for the march-off to either Cornwood or Princetown. Depending on which of these we'd marched-on from, we marched-off to the other. We bomb-burst from Ditsworthy Warren and set off at a decent pace, knowing this was the final leg and, despite their aches, pains and fatigue, the Juniors knew the end was in sight.

I preferred to march-on at Princetown as, initially, we 'sprinted' along the relatively easy ground of the 'motorway' via South Hessary Tor until rougher ground and tors were encountered for the remainder of the trek to Ditsworthy Warren House. I liked marching-off to Cornwood as once we'd crossed the leat near the house and climbed up to Shell Top, it was virtually downhill all the way to the finish line.

Every PLX ended in what became a 'race-off' as teams could see other teams converging with them towards the final destination. As Staff, we certainly didn't want to be the last team home so we loudly encouraged the team to get a move on and beat any nearby teams to the finish. Potentially brutal but actually quite civilised. It was thrilling to catch up with and overhaul another team so near the finish. Much grit and determination were shown.

At the end, I mustered my team and told them to retire into a snotty heap nearby and await being called individually to me for their debrief and whether they'd passed PLX … or not. I was pleased that the majority passed but saddened if I considered someone had failed. Still, that's 'life in a blue suit'. Some Juniors were simply not cut out for a military life. Those who failed, attended remedial PLX later in the term, when their naval career was most definitely on the line.

When ready, we clambered aboard the Tally-Ho coach and returned to BRNC. Another change was the abandonment of that final test of endurance and willpower, being dropped off to pull a whaler downriver to Sandquay. I was pleased as I didn't relish the possibility of being stranded on a mudflat halfway to await the rising tide.

OUTs survived one PLX. Due to the limited number of DOs and Exercise Directors, we ended up covering two or even three PLXs per term. One term, I returned with my first blisters, don't know how or why this occurred. I saw the nurse in Sick Bay. She gave me some cream and advised me to wear Pusser's daps for a week. I stated I was on PLX in a couple of days. She said, 'But you've already done it.' As I was 'skin-and-essence' in those days, she barely believed I was a DO and nominated for another PLX. I took it easy for a couple of days, my blisters healed nicely and off I went to Dartmoor again, and survived unscathed.

The leadership syllabus included DOs suffering while listening to Juniors' 3-minute, 10-minute and 30-minute talks. The former two were on topics of their own choosing. For the latter, DOs allocated military or naval subjects, which necessitated time and effort in research, writing, preparation, overhead projector slides, and rehearsal to ensure the 30-minutes wasn't exceeded. They also had to be ready to answer questions from the DO group and DO. Rarely were they excellent, mostly satisfactory, and occasionally poor and required a re-scrub.

For everyone, the most enjoyable parts of the leadership programme were the playlets presented by DOs in CJH. There were five, split amongst the four Divisions. *Loyalty* (St Vincent), *Social Behaviour* (Blake), *Discontent* (Cunningham) and Hawke did two (*Plain Clothes* and *Divisional System*). Carefully scripted, they described their topics with some humour to get the message across to the OUTs. Jon allocated roles for our two playlets as he was presenter. Several rehearsals ensured our performances were as slick as possible.

For *Plain Clothes*, we had several changes of clothes and involved a couple of the WRNS officers on the Staff to model the ladies' equivalent to 'dog robbers', 'planters', 'country casuals' and other 'rigs'. I'm not a natural 'actor' and found rehearsals unnerving, but I just had to get on with it in front of the audience and overcame my embarrassment. Sadly, Paddy Watson's memorable pronouncements that 'leather is worn on the foot, not the back', and 'officers do not wear white socks or grey shoes' had mysteriously disappeared from the script. *Divisional System* had several scenes to illustrate how it worked so lines were learnt. Overall, the playlets were good fun and provided light relief for the Juniors whilst putting across important messages.

Sport was an important element of life at BRNC. Saturday and Wednesday afternoons were reserved for team matches against local clubs in various sports, depending on the season. Inter-Divisional sport was keenly followed across a spectrum of sports. In autumn and winter terms, BRNC held a seven-a-side rugby tournament. Each Division was represented by Junior and Senior teams. Of course, Staff had to be seen to participate. In Hawke, Jon was a keen rugger-bugger and press-ganged me into playing for Hawke Staff.

Teams registered with the organisers and then waited until called to play. I don't know who we played first but incredibly I got the ball a few times and made some good runs. I 'skinned' a renowned Cunningham OUT sprinter and scored a memorable try. During the afternoon, I played well, got the hang of it, loafed on the wing, waited for the ball and then ran like fury away from chasing defenders to score. After my overall performance, I was invited to join BRNC's rugby club and regularly played for BRNC 2nd XV as winger. I even had a good match at Manadon against the engineers at the DartMan Games.

There were numerous activities and events throughout each term, depending on the season. For sport, DartMan Games was the lead-in to a weekend of sport against Sandhurst and Cranwell, alternating home and away fixtures. Away All Boats offered opportunities for keen boating and sailing types to show their prowess representing their Division. BRNC sports teams enjoyed fixtures against local teams and clubs, especially away matches as they offered an afternoon out of College.

In addition to 'formal' sport, a gang of DOs played deck hockey in the gym at lunchtimes. These were hard but fair physical games and provided an excellent workout to break up the working day. I also played a bit of squash and badminton in winter and tennis in summer. Happy days.

Training Divisions took place every Tuesday and Thursday morning. Fortunately, there was no Staff involvement so some of us enjoyed watching from the comfort of the wardroom anteroom, sipping a cup of tea as we overlooked the parade ground. Saturday's Ceremonial Divisions required Divisional Staff to attend. Our role, at the appointed moment, was to march down the steps from the bridge, onto the parade ground and split off to inspect a Divisional platoon. Naturally, we felt every OUTs' eye upon us, hoping to spot a DO get out of step or 'tick-tock'. There'd be no end to our embarrassment.

At Divisions, I was immensely proud hearing our RM Band perform. They marched on to their position in front of the mainmast to play stirring tunes. They were faultless. The RM Band Service originated in 1903 when the then RN Band marched into the newly-formed RN School of Music, Eastney in Pompey. Rebranded as RM Bandsmen, they were responsible for providing music to the Navy. In early 1956, the band of *Triumph* (a training ship for RN Officer Cadets) marched into BRNC to become the Band of HM Royal Marines Britannia Royal Naval College. Like every other British military band, ours was much in demand and often absent on tour. It was a shame when they weren't present at Saturday's Divisions. They definitely 'added value' and brilliant 'pomp' to our passing out parades.

Each Division held a termly Mess Dinner and there was always one Combined Mess Dinner per term. These were brilliant functions. Beforehand, OUTs were briefed on mess dinner etiquette and format. It was stressed that care with pre-dinner drinks was necessary to avoid the ignominy of having to leave the table during dinner, taking that long, lonely walk through the SGR and out to the heads, all eyes following the poor sod's embarrassed exit and return. This heinous crime was punished with being fined a round of port, a huge cost considering the number of guests. Seating plans were carefully drawn up so OUTs and Staff sat at alternate places. Mess dinners were training serials in which OUTs practised the art of conversation with folks they'd never met before, just as they probably would at social events when out in the Fleet.

These evenings culminated in retreating to the SGR bar, where more booze was drunk and mess games were initiated. At one Combined Mess Dinner, Chris Patten (the guest of honour) and I were propped against the SGR bar mantelpiece, supping a glass of port while I explained to him the rules and intricacies of mess games. The most popular were tug-of-war, stool-dancing, spinning and mess rugby.

At a wardroom dining-out, one of the 'leavers' attempted to circumnavigate the anteroom without touching the floor. Hanging on by his fingernails and toes, he made good progress around a couple of walls clinging to picture rails, pelmets and dado rail. Alas, he eventually lost his grip and fell in a snotty heap. We all laughed like drains until realising that his arm didn't look right as it was severely bent. Sick Bay was called, followed by BRNC's ambulance and he was carted off to RN Hospital Stonehouse, Plymouth. Luckily, he was so inebriated, he felt no pain whatsoever. We never saw him again.

In Week 12, Divisional Staff meetings were held to discuss OUTs, particularly Juniors. In the forenoon, Jon mustered his DOs and Div Chief in his office. In turn, DOs described and assessed the progress of their Juniors and Seniors. Other DOs input their observations about particular OUTs. The majority were 'grey', 'Mr Average': steady progress, no trouble, but not setting the world afire. There were several excellent Juniors. Sadly, there were also hopeless cases spotted early on in term as 'problem children', subject to DO's close monitoring and mentoring. We gave guidance to these blokes, some hoisted it in and tried hard to rectify and improve their performance. Others were simply unable to adjust and develop into RN Officers. By the end of this meeting, we'd reached an accord on the progress and potential of all Hawke OUTs. Jon submitted our list of 'runners-and-riders' for the categories of formal warning to Cdr T's office.

At 1400 that afternoon, all college staff congregated in the common room for the end of term meeting. Grabbing a cup of tea and biscuits,

Hawke Divisional Staff sat together, similarly the other three Divisions. Affiliated and academic staff found space around the room.

At a table across one end of the common room, Cdr T conducted proceedings, the Captain and the Commander on one side, the Director and Deputy Director of Studies on the other side. Cdr T read out the list of those who'd WFT'ed at 'own request', medically, for disciplinary reasons (very rare), or for further language training (International students). These were cut and dried decisions.

Thereafter, as each OUT's name was read out, his SDO stood and described this chap's lack of progress, remedial actions to date, his attitude, personality, character and potential. The SDO ended with a recommendation: Professional Warning (for sub-standard academic performance); or placed on Captain's Warning or Admiralty Board Warning. The former was usually rectified by these OUTs through knuckling down in class and passing exams. The latter two were far more serious as these poor sods were subject to intense scrutiny and reported on to either the Captain or, worse, the Admiralty Board. Their naval careers were on a knife-edge and depended very much on their reaction and response to this categorisation. The equivalent for Internationals was being placed on National Warning.

Those already on warnings were also discussed. SDOs and Divisional Staff made recommendations for OUTs warranting removal from warning, provided we felt they'd made sufficient remedial progress. Some remained on warning as they still had more work to do.

After SDO had presented an OUT's case history and recommendation, the floor was open for anyone to comment on the individual. There was usually agreement with the Division's recommendation. Occasionally, vociferous discussion occurred amongst the assembly as contrary and supporting views were stated. It was fascinating to observe this process, given the impact of his being placed on warning or, the ultimate sanction, WFT. The top panel listened to every word. The Captain, as the ultimate arbiter, summarised the discussion and announced his decision. The end of term meeting lasted over a couple of hours. I considered it fair and democratic. The DO had monitored, mentored and assessed the OUT. Our Divisional meeting enabled Divisional Staff to discuss and reach a recommendation. Every voice at the meeting was heard, for or against the 'problem child', before his fate was sealed by the Captain.

After the meeting, I needed a cup of tea and biscuits, and many of us stayed in the common room to chat about the outcomes. Meanwhile, Div Chiefs were contacted to notify the affected OUTs, loitering in the

Division. Dressed in No.5, they marched down to the main building and upstairs to the Captain's Flat to await being called in for interview with the Captain. It was a nervous, squitty time for them as they were told their fate.

Weeks 11 and 12 were busy periods for DOs and SDOs. The former were fully engaged with drafting standard report forms (SRFs) for each of our OUTs. As well as being accurate, the report's wording had to marry up with 'scores-on-the-doors'. It was a full-time job. Every term, I spent both weeks in College, unable to escape home to Plympton. Simon and I and the other DOs were at our desks long into the evenings, tapping at the keyboard, reading, re-reading and tweaking our drafts. It was mentally exhausting.

All drafted SRFs were passed to Jon for checking/comments/amendments. There were also frequent trips to the main building clutching draft SRFs for the relevant tutor to read and, inevitably, adjust. Back up to Hawke to insert all the amendments. We were under incredible time pressure as the deadline for submission was inflexible. Report signing was another hurdle. This usually occurred at stand easy in the common room as we moved around the room, hunting down tutors to sign our SRFs. A hurried tea and biscuits was followed by returning to Hawke with final signed SRFs. Phew!

We conducted individual interviews with our OUTs. We read out the SRF, discussed its content and their progress throughout the term. This was the culmination of 13 weeks of Juniors' NGT and Seniors' academic classes, the latter would pass out from BRNC and head to the Fleet for their next stage of training.

Weeks 12 and 13 were busy periods for OUTs as they completed, and hopefully passed, professional and academic exams. Week 13 focused on passing out parade (POP) rehearsals, particularly for those passing out as they practised marching around the ramps, returning to the parade ground to advance in review order. Here they smoothly transitioned from three ranks into two and then marched toward the bridge to halt and salute using their newly-learned sword drill. Next, they slow-marched up the steps and through the main door. The climax of their POP was when the last rank entered the building and the main doors slammed shut. In inclement weather, 'dry' rehearsals on the parade ground were supplemented by 'wet weather' practice on the quarterdeck.

For Staff, a brilliant end-of-term drinks party was held in the wardroom on Wednesday of Week 13. We let our hair down a bit as the term was all but finished, reports written, checked, amended, approved and signed, OUT interviews completed. Our term's work over. All that remained was to get through the last programmed formalities.

11.13 Main doors, through which passers out marched

POP took place the next day. A proud day for those passing out and their families. POP lasted about an hour and a half, after which those who'd passed out met up with their families for a short lunch reception on the quarterdeck. Thereafter, they were free to go ashore but required to return for the Leavers' Service in Chapel at 1730. The Divisional CTP followed at 1830. Hawke's was in HGR – an enjoyable event as it afforded an opportunity for OUTs to introduce us to their families. I made the most of the available G&T and chatted to smiling, proud parents.

Friday was occupied with ball preparations. All OUTs turned-to in the main College to set up the multitude of decorations all over the place. The Captain's wife led a coterie of staff officers' wives to make an outstanding job with floral decorations. When all was deemed ready, OUTs were allowed ashore to meet families, get into Mess Undress and return for the Ball. These fantastic evenings were filled with booze, dancing, eating and conversation, ending with 'carriages' at 0230.

Everyone was 'required on board' for 0800 on Saturday morning for the great clear-up. In the main building, ball decorations were dismantled and either stowed or stuffed into gash bags. Glasses and crockery were collected from various rooms and returned for dishwashing. Meanwhile, cleaning of accommodation and heads and bathrooms was undertaken in the Divisions. The forenoon wore on, everyone itched to escape on leave, which was timetabled to be piped at 1100. That depended on the Commander's inspection in College and SDOs' Divisional rounds.

At last, the main broadcast burst into life, reminding me of my own experience. No sooner had the 'voice' started to say 'Leave …', OUTs raced through Hawke's front door to collect their cars from distant car parks and escape BRNC. Those using the train marched down to the parade ground to clamber aboard Tally-Ho coaches to be taken to Totnes station.

A deathly hush settled over Hawke. Cabins and dorms lay empty and abandoned. Corridors were eerily silent. Jon gathered us in his office for a drink before we bomb-burst home.

So ended my first term as a Hawke DO. I'd settled in comfortably and thoroughly enjoyed being back in BRNC and Hawke in particular. Jon and the other Hawke DOs were excellent company, as were the other SDOs and DOs in Blake, Cunningham and St Vincent. I found OUTs engaging, interesting blokes, different characters in so many ways, yet drawn to becoming naval officers. After my first term as a DO, it was easy to spot 'problem children' amongst incoming Juniors at the start of term.

Not much had changed since my joining in April 1984. The Training Office was well-managed, College organisation and administration seemed to run smoothly, almost effortlessly. But it certainly equated to the swan gliding through the water whilst its feet paddled furiously underwater.

The next five terms of my appointment followed the same general pattern. Staff Officers came and went. In Hawke, Mick Johnson moved on at the end of my first term to be replaced by Neil Moffatt, a submarine nuclear engineer. I took over as Hawke's C&L Coordinator when Simon Carter left at the end of summer term 1990. Clive Walker, another Pusser, was his relief. Clive and I got on well together in our office, although I was always a little wary of sharing our space with his black labrador which occasionally accompanied him. Pete Thompson moved on a year after I'd joined, replaced by Tim Dewing. Charlotte Manley took over from Jon as SDO in winter term 1991. She'd been on DTS previously, so we'd met her when DTS Staff came to debrief us on the OUTs returning to BRNC for term 3. It was the first time I'd had a female boss, but Charlotte was a pleasure to work for and entirely professional and competent as our SDO.

Captain Shiffner was promoted to Rear Admiral and moved on to his last couple of appointments before retirement. His successor was Captain Hastilow, who'd just commanded *Bristol* when she was DTS and had experienced OUTs en masse aboard his warship. He seemed rather aloof compared to Captain Shiffner. Cdr Bishop was relieved by Cdr David Lewis as Cdr T. I thought Hastilow rather pompous and condescending, Cdr Lewis a contrast and a joy to work for. So, in my second year at BRNC two of the top three personalities at the College shifted. The Commander throughout my time was Cdr Chris Morrison, a tall, pukka officer of ramrod military bearing but with a sense of humour. I liked him and Cdr Lewis a lot.

The major change at BRNC was the integration of girls, begun in autumn 1990. 'Women at sea' had been a much-discussed topic for several years but had finally occurred. Talbot Division, located high up in the main building and totally prohibited to males, was disbanded. Female integration into the RN meant the number of girls on this first entry far exceeded Talbot's usual termly complement of 20–25. They were spread evenly across the four Divisions.

An entirely new philosophy was required in BRNC. The 'no touching' rule was introduced. All OUTs were warned that anyone found guilty would be almost immediately WFT'ed. In Hawke, the girls were segregated into a bunch of cabins on the ground floor, as far as practicable from the boys' cabins. Sea Dads were especially wary as they spent more time in close proximity, mentoring the girls and guiding them through the presentation of kit for standing rounds.

Staff were equally aware of the dangers of being close to the girls. As Seaman Officers we'd never had contact with WRNS because a warship was a male-only environment. Everyone swiftly adjusted to this new development.

To further complicate matters, Channel 4 filmed a documentary, *Britannia Waives the Rules,* to follow this initial entry's progress at BRNC (first term) and in DTS (second term). The film crew weren't with us the whole time but turned up for specific stages of training. Many of us DOs, including me, appeared in cameo roles throughout. It's an informative programme and interesting from a historical perspective as this innovation occurred over 30 years ago.

By and large, I found the girls happily integrated within the Divisions and instructional classes, worked hard and tried their best. Several were equal to the best blokes, others on a par with the most useless blokes, the majority were similar to our 'Mr Average'. I can assure readers they were treated exactly the same as the boys. That first term made for an interesting experience but from our second term onwards it became the 'norm' and we didn't consciously notice the gender difference. The girls were 'bollocked' exactly the same as the boys and subject to the same high and inflexible standards.

In May 1991, my second daughter, Alexandra, was born. She was christened by Father Burns in the Catholic Chapel, followed by her christening party on the SGR gallery.

Christmas 1991 marked the onset of the end of my time at BRNC. I'd completed six terms, with a half to go to take me to February. On 26 November, I was one of those 'dined-out' by the wardroom. It was another great dinner, a sociable evening and a late night. As usual, the RM quintet performed brilliantly.

Six-and-a-half terms as a BRNC DO seemed a long time, but I'd very much enjoyed my role. It was incredibly satisfying to play my part in moulding young schoolboys (and later, schoolgirls), bolshie graduates and potential Schoolies into naval officers. I guided their evolution from nervous, under-confident, sometimes immature youngsters, into competent, confident young officers to send to the Fleet for further training and onwards to fulfil their potential in the RN.

A couple of years ago, Lynne, my now-wife, and I were at a Britannia Association dinner at BRNC. As we waited for the port to go round again and Lynne was at the heads, a shadow loomed over me. I looked up to see a giant in Commander's uniform. He thrust an enormous hand down at me and said, 'Phil Carroll?' I stood, dwarfed, as we shook hands, but didn't recognise him. 'Will Peters', he said. I recalled the name and the frame. He'd joined in September 1990, that first term of integration with the girls and was one of my DO group. 'What are you doing here?' I asked. 'I'm the Commander.' Crikey! He'd done well. He continued, 'I'd just like to say, on behalf of your DO group, how grateful we were to you for being our DO and everything you did for us.' Deeply touched, I felt quite emotional. 'This is my last job in the Navy. I've come full circle to end it in the Commander's House, next door to where I started over 30 years ago in Hawke. To cap it all my DO is here, too.' I was incredibly flattered at his words. Anyone in an instructional post or leadership position would secretly hope that they'd had a positive effect and influence on the development of young people in their charge. Brilliant!

In February 1992, I handed over to my relief and left BRNC after a very happy and rewarding appointment. DO at Dartmouth was a great job.

It was an honour and a privilege to have served at BRNC and been a positive influence on so many young people at the very start of their naval careers. I returned to the droggy world.

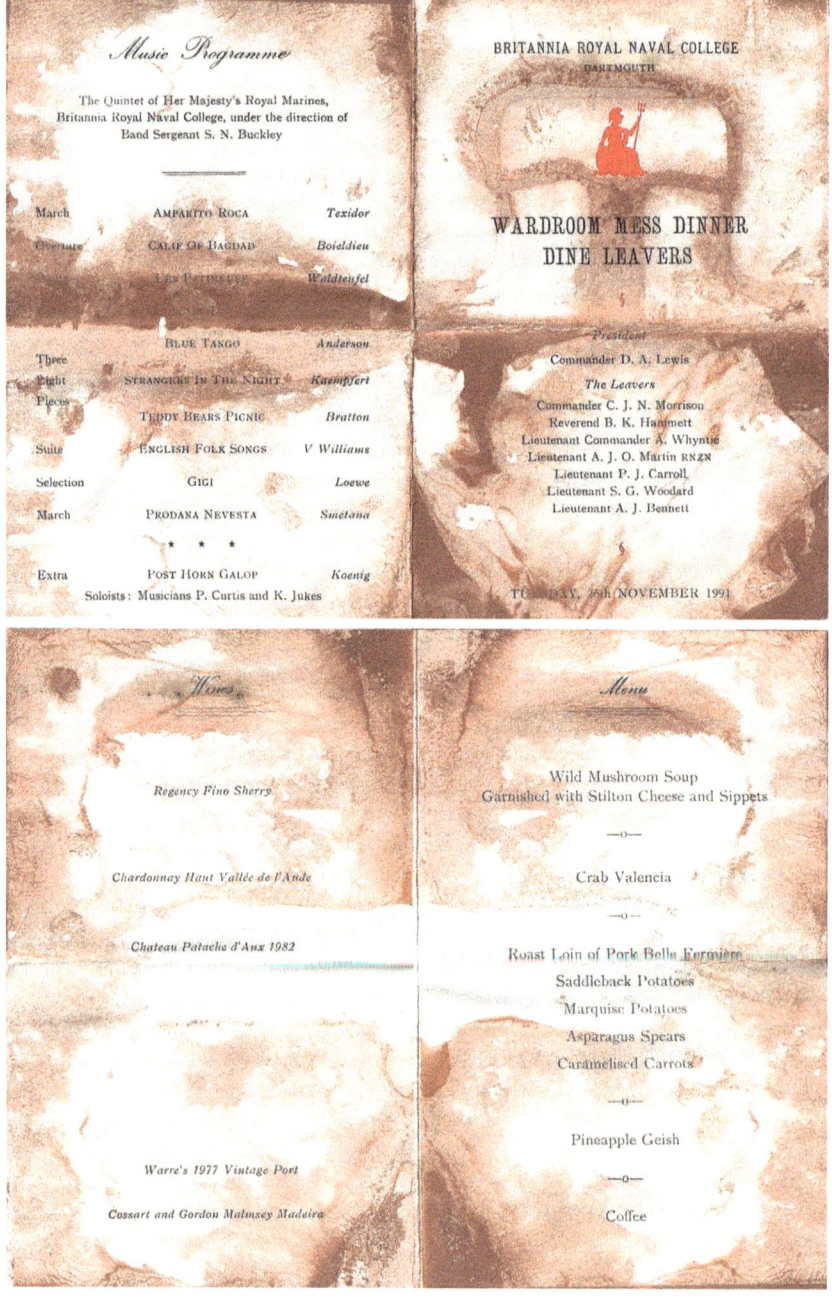

11.14 'Dining-Out': front and back covers (above); menu and wines (below)

12.

A Season in the North Sea

12.1 NP1008 crest

12.2 *Marine Explorer*
(Fotoflite)

In March 1992 I joined NP1008, which along with NP1016, were teams of RN hydrographic surveyors embarked in vessels chartered from civilian shipping companies. NP1016 was, at that time, in *Proud Seahorse* operating in UK inshore survey areas, replacing the Inshore Survey Squadron (*Echo, Enterprise, Egeria* collectively decommissioned in 1985). NP1008 used a larger vessel for UK continental shelf surveys. Previous NP1008 vessels were *Sperus* (ex-lighthouse tender), *Bon Esprit* and *British Enterprise IV* (both deep-sea trawlers) and these contracts weren't automatically renewed.

Annually, NP1008 demobilised for its winter lie-up, typically mid-November to March. This period, based in RNHS, was used to catch up on leave and training courses, to complete outstanding surveys for rendering to UKHO. The latter part of the lie-up focused on planning and preparations for the next survey season.

I joined NP1008 in the offices at RNHS. Lt Cdr Bob Eadie was CO, his XO was Lt Paul Lawrence. Bob had taken command before Christmas and Paul was due to leave a couple of months into the survey season. I relieved Lt Ian Carter as the third of the officers. The rest of the survey team comprised three Senior Rates (WO(SR) Steve Peters, PO(SR)s 'Sid' Ford and Ian 'Horse' Horseman) and six Junior Rates (all SRs).

The complement of 12 was divided into Red, White and Blue Watches for a crew rotation with two watches on, the third on leave. Each watch worked four weeks on, two weeks off for the season. During Bob's absences for watch leave, Paul became CO. As either Bob or Paul were on leave during my four weeks on board, I was effectively XO.

It was the owners' responsibility to ensure his vessel remained operational throughout. Our responsibility was for the survey systems and directing the civilian OOWs when surveying.

This season, we embarked in a newly chartered ship, *Marine Explorer*. Bob, accompanied by Capt H's technical officers and Sid Ford visited our new ship twice to view her progress in refit. This provided an opportunity to design the survey operations room and survey chartroom from scratch. The second visit in early March revealed excellent progress. Joinery in the survey operations room and accommodation was complete, cushion flooring for the decks was being installed. The survey chartroom was fitted with new panelling and concrete laid on the steel deck for its new cushion flooring, desks and chart tables.

Marine Explorer was a 72m long, 2500-ton deep-sea trawler built in Bremen in 1965. She had been *Swanella* until 1984, when she was renamed

Sir Walter Raleigh. Three years later she became *Sir Tristan* before being bought by Eidesvik Offshore in 1990.

Sir Walter Raleigh was the sea-going element of Operation Raleigh. An exciting venture founded in 1984 as a development of Operation Drake, launched by Colonel John Blashford-Snell and the then-Prince Charles, running youth projects from ships circumnavigating the globe to develop self-confidence and leadership in young people through adventure, scientific exploration and community service. During 1984–1988, 4000 young volunteers and 1600 staff steamed in Operation Raleigh's two renovated ships (*Sir Walter Raleigh* and *Zebu*) on expeditions worldwide.

Eidesvik Offshore, headquartered in Bømlo, Norway, was a family-run shipping company founded in 1965. Originally in the fishing industry, it expanded into owning and operating a fleet of purpose-built vessels to service the offshore supply, subsea, offshore wind and seismic industries. Having bought *Sir Walter Raleigh* and renamed her *Marine Explorer*, Eidesvik won the NP1008 contract and retained it until 1995.

We mobilised in *Marine Explorer* at Grimsby on 23 March 1992. Internally, she was clean, functional and comfortable, enabling us to quickly settle in. Some Eidesvik employees were on board to provide technical support and rectified minor defects. Stores were embarked on 24 March, stowed on the ample shelf space of our two new storerooms. The chart and operations rooms were prepared for sea trials.

12.3 *Marine Explorer* alongside Grimsby

Lebus, RACAL, TSS, del Norte and Dowty contractors installed their respective bits of kit. A QUBIT engineer installed SIPS(S) (Survey Information Processing System). During the two years I'd been at BRNC, surveying had moved on a bit, technically and digitally. New kit had been introduced so I had much to catch up on. The Lebus winch powered the hoisting and veering of the Dowty sidescan sonar towfish. The latter was a lightweight successor to the hefty, 'two-man portable' EG&G towfish. Both were improvements on *Fox's* kit. TSS fitted a heave compensator, a marine motion sensor to accurately measure a vessel's roll/pitch/heave movement to provide compensation data to ship's systems, enabling them to yield accurate, reliable data.

The biggest change was SIPS, which moved data gathering, processing and presentation into the incoming digital era. It replaced the old-style echo sounder rolls, marking on the tidal reduction, reading out depths from the echo sounder roll for the CO to ink-in the sounding collector and ultimately draw up the fair sheet, the beautiful end-product of skilled draughtsmanship. There were faults with SIPS and, as no technical sailors were in NP1008, I frequently saw Sid and/or Horse lying beneath the chartroom desks and consoles sorting out problems and faulty wiring.

Marine Explorer was neither a warship nor a RN vessel, but Fleet Seamanship and NBCD teams visited to conduct safety inspections on 27 and 30 March.

The Trisponder outfit was calibrated against EODM (electronic optical distance measuring) at Grimsby on 30 March. Four Trisponder remote units were deployed between Flamborough Head and Whitby the next day.

Mobilisation was completed on 3 April and we sailed at 1800 for sea trials, with RACAL and Sonardyne contractors embarked to trial and demonstrate their systems.

12.4 Stern and A-frame (left); looking aft, sidescan sonar winch and cable's block on A-frame

Clear of the Humber, we headed north. Sea trials are inevitably problematic. We suffered a series of technical and system problems, necessitating a return to Grimsby for defect rectification and the first watch change of the season. All fixed, we sailed on 10 April but were forced to return alongside due to a leak on a main engine cylinder head. Twenty-four hours later, we were off again and HI554 was taken in hand.

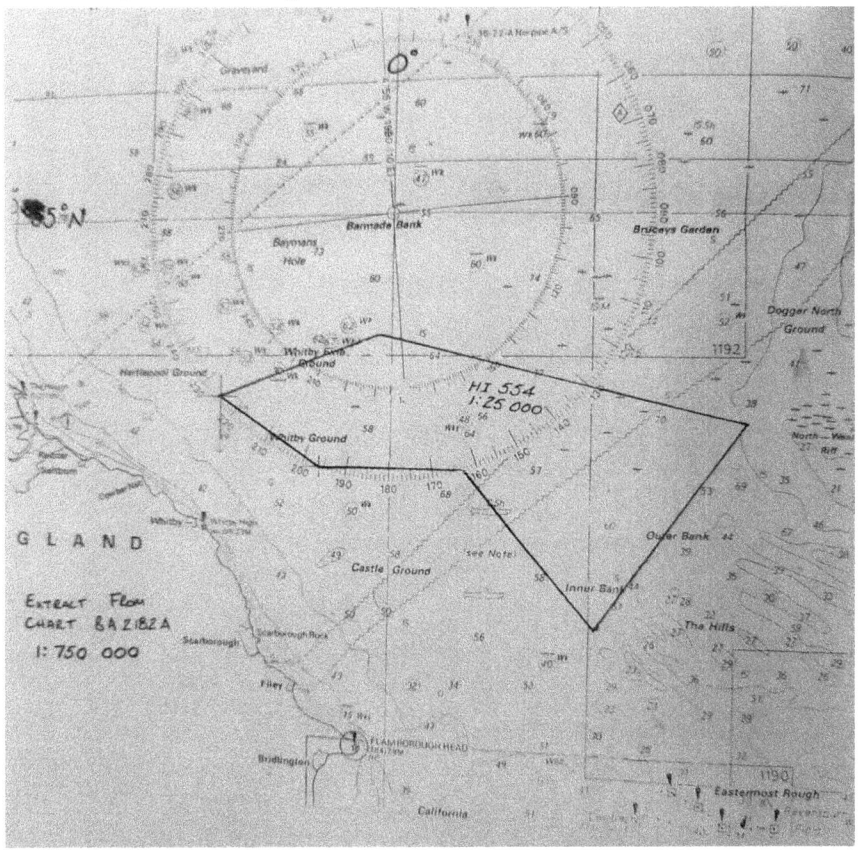

12.5 HI554 (Whitby Fine Ground to Inner Bank)
(UKHO Archive)

The first 48 hours were used to successfully calibrate Hyperfix, carried out against differential GPS (DGPS). Sounding began with cross lines in the early hours of 15 April but, after only one line, a north-easterly gale caused surveying to be suspended. We hove to until the following afternoon and, thereafter, cross lines in Areas 1 and 2 and seabed sampling in Area 1 were completed. After a watch change in Grimsby on 23–24 April, sounding and sonar lines were begun.

Life aboard *Marine Explorer* was comfortable and spacious. Everyone had a single en suite cabin. Mine was a deck below the bridge. It was roomy, completely refitted by Eidesvik, and smelled of newly-applied paint and varnish. We all ate together in the large dining-room, self-service from a wide-ranging buffet of excellent, plentiful food. There was also a large, windowless lounge/TV room located a couple of decks below.

The survey chartroom was a capacious area on the former fish-deck, where the catch was sorted and gutted before storing in refrigerated holds. Our survey operations room was situated on the bridge, abaft, giving us direct contact and communications with the civilian OOW and his helmsman.

The crew, Mate and 2nd Mate were Norwegian but the Masters were British. Graham Hall was a former Trinity House captain, familiar with manoeuvring at close quarters to buoys. He and Jim Clark were good old traditional Master Mariners, highly professional and nearing the end of their seafaring careers. They rotated on a four-week on, four-week off regime, so we interacted with both or just one of them, depending on our own watch cycle. We swiftly established an excellent working rapport, especially after a couple of weeks of survey operations, by which time they knew what to expect from our methodology.

Ashore, in the background, John Grey was the ship manager, another highly experienced Master Mariner. Graham and Jim had regular contact with him and he occasionally visited *Marine Explorer* in Grimsby to check for himself. Only Bob Eadie had 'work' contact with him, our contact was minimal, but he was a friendly chap and was eager to ensure that Eidesvik Shipping and *Marine Explorer* satisfied contractual requirements.

Our survey team worked a 1-in-3 watch system at sea. I was usually paired with AB(SR) 'Chuck' Berry, a tall, gangly young bloke. We worked well together, monitoring survey progress and the E-O-L/S-O-L routine, recovering maggy and hoisting in a few hundred metres of sidescan towfish cable prior to the E-O-L turn and resetting both prior to turning on to the next S-O-L.

When my watch was on board, the other watch pairings were WO(SR) Steve Peters with another AB(SR) and a PO(SR) with an AB(SR). That left Bob as CO plus a LS(SR) running the chartroom and data processing.

Most of our survey season was in the North Sea on HI554 (Whitby Fine Ground to Inner Bank) and HI555 (Southern North Sea Deep Water Route). Our base port was Grimsby. Its glory days as a large, important, vibrant hub for the UK's deep-sea fishing industry were long gone. My forays ashore during crew rotations were depressing as the town was shabby, rundown and grey, with many long-empty shops. A very sad scene.

The docks were devoid of trawlers, long stretches of quayside were empty and underused, long grass and weeds had slowly invaded everywhere. Dockside buildings were increasingly derelict, with broken windows throughout and shards of glass at the foot of the walls with other debris. Tragic. No hope of ever being restored or revitalised.

12.6 *Marine Explorer*
(UKHO Archive)

Every fortnight, *Marine Explorer* berthed in Grimsby for crew rotation and stores replenishment. The off-going watch had packed, eagerly waiting to hand over to the on-coming watch that had driven up from Guzz during the morning. The off-going watch used these hire cars to get home for leave. Meanwhile, the watch halfway through its four-week stint 'enjoyed' 24 hours in Grimsby. Alas, there was bugger-all to do so 'Jack' spent his time in the pub, particularly the Corporation Arms, a scant few hundred metres from our berth in Royal Dock. Sid Ford and his watch-mates holed up in the Corporation from late-forenoon until chucking-out time, when they rolled their way back to *Marine Explorer*. Their collective powers of recovery were impressive as they were never adrift and never visibly hungover at 0800 the next morning.

Access to/from Royal Dock was via a lock into the Humber estuary. Between the two locks, standing tall and proud, visible for miles around, is

Grimsby Dock Tower, a 94m tall hydraulic accumulator tower completed on 27 March 1852. Its 140000-litre reservoir at a height of 61m attained sufficient pressure to provide hydraulic power to Grimsby Docks' lock gates, dry docks and quayside cranes and to supply fresh water to ships alongside and houses on the dock. During World War II, there had been plans to demolish it as it acted as a beacon for Luftwaffe aircraft heading to Liverpool. Post-war, a plaque was laid, paying tribute to minesweeper crews. The tower is now Grade I listed and subject to a preservation order.

Exiting the lock, we were in the Humber Estuary. A turn to starboard took us south-east towards the North Sea leaving, to port, Easington Lighthouse at the end of Spurn, a narrow spit extending from the East Riding coast to form the north bank of the estuary mouth. It had a semi-permanent connection to the mainland until a storm in 2013 made the road to the end of the spit impassable to vehicles at high tide. Spurn is 5km long but only 45m wide in places. Yorkshire Wildlife Trust owned the 181 hectares of foreshore, designated a national nature reserve, heritage coast and part of the Humber Flats, Marshes and Coast Special Protection Area.

12.7 Grimsby Dock Tower on starboard quarter, *Marine Explorer* exiting (UKHO Archive)

Entering the North Sea, we never really knew what sea and wind conditions to expect despite accurate weather forecasts. The North Sea, like the Irish Sea, could be an uncomfortable and unpleasant environment. Still, our survey progressed in generally favourable conditions, dominated by high pressure systems. This was interrupted by a south-westerly Force 8 on 12 May and thick fog on 22–23 May. We discovered the seabed was featureless. Very few sonar contacts deserved further investigation, although two new wrecks were found, investigated and reported.

We had watch rotations in Grimsby on 7–8 May, 21–22 May (when Lt Cdr Bob Maitland superceded Paul Lawrence as XO) and 4–5 June. Area 1 of HI554 was completed on 14 June and half the seabed sampling of Area 2 achieved. In Grimsby on 12–13 June, Trisponder remotes were recovered as we moved to HI555.

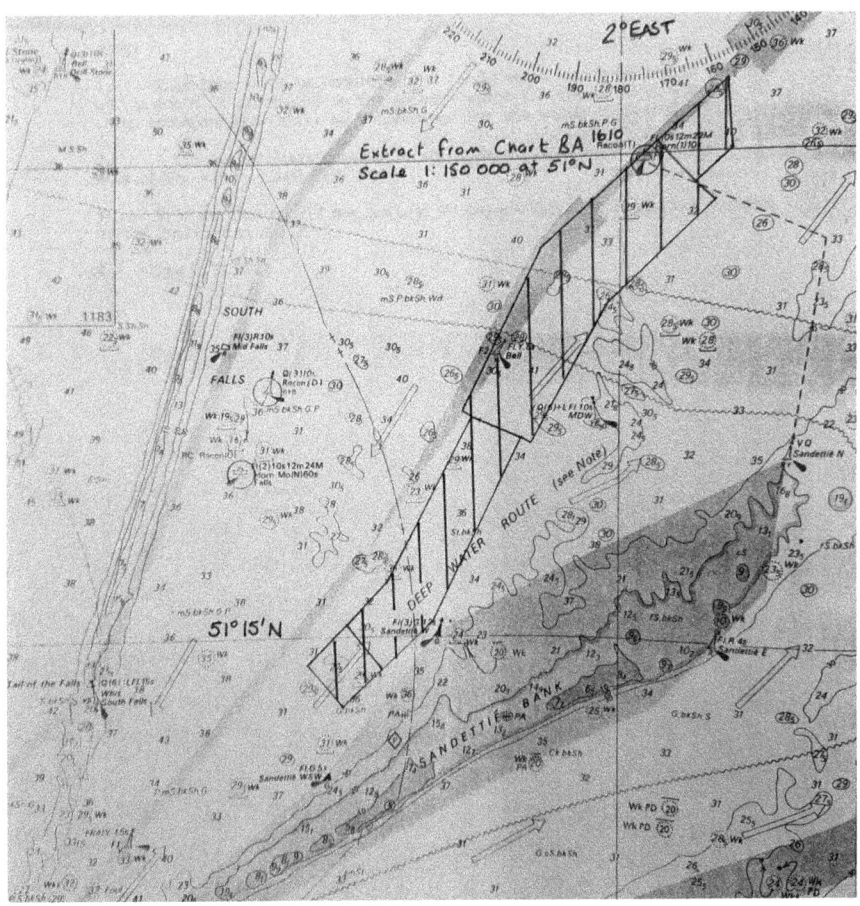

12.8 HI555 (Southern North Sea Deep Water Route)
(UKHO Archive)

Marine Explorer arrived in Dover on 13 June for pre-survey checks, Trisponders were calibrated and deployed on 15–16 June. A 25-hour tide gauge/tide pole comparison was conducted on 16–17 June.

Dover Strait suffered continual northerly and north-easterly winds, frequently gusting to Force 9 during 16 to 21 June, frustrating our efforts to start the survey. At last, the weather broke, permitting Hyperfix calibration on 22 June and sounding started on 23 June. Sidescan sonar revealed changes in seabed texture.

Shipping activity was predictably heavy. Most vessels observed the Dover Strait traffic separation scheme, those that didn't occurred overnight. Dover Coastguard reported these rogues in their half-hourly broadcasts, which also detailed *Marine Explorer's* survey operations and movements of deep draught merchantmen. The manoeuvring required for wreck and contact investigations meant it was safer for all seafarers when conducted during daylight on 28 and 29 June.

A crew rotation in Pompey on 1–3 July enabled NP1008 to brief Staff Officers of Flag Officer Surface Flotilla about our role. The briefing, ship tour and lunch proved a success. For many of the 15 visitors it was their first acquaint with a hydrographic surveying unit. Then, it was back to HI555, which we completed on 7 July. After post-survey equipment checks and recovery of Trisponder remotes, *Marine Explorer* sailed for Grimsby to resume HI554 on 8 July. The usual calibrations were successfully completed, allowing us to start sounding and sonar lines in Area 2 on 12 July.

Thereafter, we continued with HI554 through to the end of the season, interspersed with the regular fortnightly 24-hour visits to Grimsby for watch rotation and logistics support. By and large, the weather was favourable, despite strong north-easterly winds and an uncomfortable swell which forced us to break off and seek shelter in Grimsby from 7 to 13 October. Nevertheless, the survey and its large extension, totalling 1660km^2, were completed on 8 November.

NP1008 demobilised at Grimsby during 9–11 November. We returned to Guzz, *Marine Explorer* sailed for her home port of Bømlo. During the winter lie-up, Area 3 to HI554 was completed and rendered to UKHO, we took Christmas leave and prepared for the 1993 season's surveys: HI581 (Celtic Sea) and HI588 (English Channel – Central Part).

Mobilisation in *Marine Explorer* took place in Falmouth in mid-February. Contractors from Lebus, RACAL, TSS, del Norte, Dowty and Qubit installed and set-to-work their equipment, with some technical support from Capt H Staff.

Marine Explorer sailed from Falmouth at 1800 on 18 February. Embarked contractors ensured that problems or defects were swiftly repaired, yielding successful sea trials. They were landed on the morning of

20 February. The next 48 hours involved: a detour to St Mary's, Scilly Isles, to repair the tide gauge installed by Roebuck and install a second one as a reserve; passage to and from the survey ground; Hyperfix calibration against DGPS; cross-line sounding completed; and a final check of DGPS against Trisponder in Mounts Bay. Phew!

Late on 23 February, HI581 sonar search was begun in the south-east corner of the survey area, adjoining recent modern surveys to the east. Good agreement between our work and recent work was reassuring.

Weather and sea conditions were ideal but interrupted by the passage of a westerly Force 10 frontal system and its residual effects for the following two days. Steady progress was made through the remainder of February and into March, such that data gathering was completed on 12 March. *Marine Explorer* returned to St Mary's to recover the tide-watcher and tide gauge, then headed to Penzance Bay to collect our deployed Trisponders on 15 March. The post-survey calibration on 16 March completed HI581.

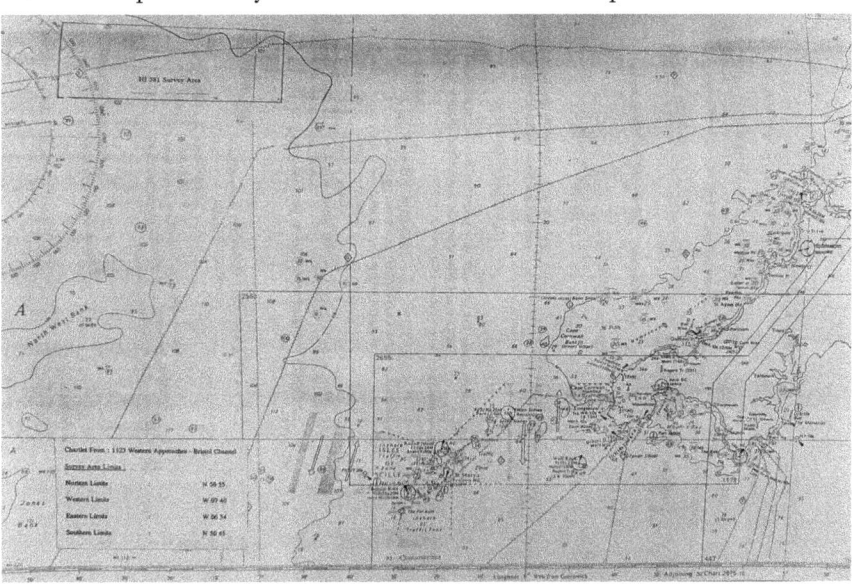

12.9 HI581 (Celtic Sea)
(UKHO Archive)

With my successor, Lt Glyn Thomas, newly embarked in Falmouth, we steamed to Pompey to start HI588. I left NP1008 during the second watch rotation at Pompey on 30 March. I'd enjoyed my year in NP1008, getting back into 'droggying'. Our small team focused entirely on surveying, rather than working in tandem with the myriad activities, exercises and commitments of a warship. *Marine Explorer's* accommodation took me back to my time in Blue Star where, even as a Deck Cadet, I had my own large single en suite cabin. It was pleasing to be amongst MN folks too as I got on well with the Norwegian Mates and British Masters.

Now, boffed up after a year's surveying, I was ready for the challenge of the Long H Course back at RNHS.

13.

A Bajan Interlude

During NP1008's winter lie-up in November 1992 to February 1993, LS(SR) Daz Wake and I were selected, with my oppo Lt Geraint West (then in *Roebuck*), to conduct a boat camp in Barbados.

Apparently, the RN Surveying Service had tendered for this survey in competition with commercial companies. I gather we were the cheapest option, allied to our renowned reputation for high professional standards. Our bid was accepted and correspondence between Hydrographer's staff and Barbados Port Authority ironed out the details. Bridgetown Port Authority wanted to allay their suspicions that the harbour berths were silting up and assess the feasibility of extensions to the harbour.

Daz and I met up with Geraint a week or so before we flew out. Geraint had recently completed Long Course and was our designated leader. We discussed the survey, sorted out and checked the kit required, got it packed and despatched by air freight to Bridgetown. We landed in Barbados on 18 November.

I'd been to Bridgetown a couple of times as a Deck Cadet. On 29 April 1981, I joined *Benedict* (built 1979, 115m long, 17m beam, 6.5m draught, 3636 gross tons, 1967 net tons) in Liverpool. *Benedict* and her sister-ship, *Boniface,* were Booth Line three-hatch general cargo ships. We left Liverpool for Dublin and crossed the Atlantic to Bridgetown. From there, via Port of Spain, to Belém in the Amazon delta. Transiting through narrow Amazonian channels, we called at Santana, a tiny port on the equator in the Amazon delta, to load plywood planks and sheets for the UK. Crossing the Atlantic, I left *Benedict* in Heysham on 22 June. I did a part-trip on her in April 1983 and, after Bridgetown, flew home from Port of Spain. My previous volume, *Under a Big Blue Star*, describes my *Benedict* trips.

Barbados, the most easterly of the Caribbean Islands, was initially claimed by Spain in 1511, Portugal in 1532 and ultimately the British in 1625 to become a wealthy sugar colony. On 30 November 1966, Barbados gained independence.

The economy used to depend on sugarcane cultivation and related industries, but by the late-1970s/early-1980s it had diversified into manufacturing and tourism.

The capital, Bridgetown, was established by English settlers in 1628, and evolved into a major West Indies tourist destination, particularly as a Caribbean cruise ship destination. Bridgetown Port (or deep water harbour) was the prime port of entry for cruise and cargo ships and one of the major shipping and transhipment hubs from international locations for the entire Eastern Caribbean. I had no inkling that a dozen years after *Benedict*, I'd return as part of a RN hydrographic team to survey the harbour.

The Harbour Master met us in arrivals and, after introductions and general conversation, drove us to the Welcome Inn Hotel (today, Barbados Beach Club Hotel), our home for the duration. We unpacked, settled in and enjoyed dinner in the hotel restaurant. An excellent start.

13.1 Home for the duration
(Geraint West)

In the morning, the Harbour Master picked us up and drove to the port, about 11km distant. We became increasingly familiar with this coast road, golden sandy beach, cliffs and the blue Caribbean on one side, clapboard houses (some smart, some shabby) on the other. The road was always busy in both directions.

In his office, the Harbour Master briefed us on the port and its facilities. Most importantly, he confirmed safe receipt of our air freight stores, located in a room reserved for our sole use. This proved invaluable, as we held the key and felt confident that our kit and, importantly, field data were secure. The room had a table large enough to serve as our chart table for drawing up track-plot, sounding collector and fair sheet, as well as fairing up the standard hydrographic proforma. He also offered us the use of any of his small boats for our surveys and provided a coxswain and crew.

13.2 A choice of boats, excluding the big one astern!

The Harbour Master hired a car for our sole use. A good little Isuzu run-around saloon for commuting between hotel and port and to access field locations to set up our survey. He also provided a daily allowance of Bds$50 each per day to cover fuel and expenses. He was courteous, incredibly helpful and keen to ensure we had all the assistance we needed to conduct the survey.

We unpacked and checked our air freight stores, making use of the fitted shelves to stow as much as we could. Chunky, heavy kit and instrument cases were arrayed against the walls. Geraint had already planned the control stations we needed within and beyond the harbour and briefed Daz and me. We stretched our legs with a walk around the port to reconnoitre the 'ground' to end the day.

13.3 (clockwise from top left) Climbing St Ann's Tower; Daz conducting GPS observations; me conducting observations, *Alacrity* in background; conducting trisponder calibration; Geraint at Signal Station
(Geraint West, top right and centre right)

After a busy full first day, we left the port and, a short distance from the dock gate, discovered the Bamboo Beach Bar. We stopped for a cool drink and chose daiquiris. I'd never had one before but found it refreshing. Its basic ingredients were rum, lime juice and sugar. The former was one of the Caribbean's great exports – I recalled loading several tons of pallets of Mount Gay Rum into *Benedict*. Lime is a common Caribbean citrus fruit so there was no shortage of the latter two, either. I've never had a daiquiri since but at the end of every day in Bridgetown, we were refreshed by scuppering two or three in the Bamboo Beach Bar (sadly, no longer in existence) en route back to our hotel.

Over the next couple of days, we checked control stations within the harbour: a pair of existing stations; a secondary station (Signal Station); and a minor station (Breakwater Head). We established two more stations in the vicinity of the shallow draught berths. Ultimately, three were used as Trisponder sites.

Additional control was established at Spring Garden (north of the port) and St Ann's Fort (to the south). The latter, built in 1705, was hexagonal, its walls 50m long, enclosing a 6,000m^2 courtyard. Its Georgian-style construction included vaulted underground magazines and the barracks housed 4000 soldiers. British troops moved out in 1905 and the fort became the headquarters of the Barbados Defence Force in 1979. The tower was one of Barbados' six signal stations, a primary means of communication throughout the island. Daz and I climbed to the top to conduct control observations and place a Trisponder station. The tower's inset stone steps were near vertical. We weren't sure of our safety until we'd reached the top and clambered over the battlements.

During our observations, *Alacrity* (Type-21 frigate) was alongside in her role as West Indies Guard Ship, part of our commitment to secure and protect UK and British Overseas Territories' interests in the North Atlantic and Caribbean. The designated warship primarily conducted counter-narcotics missions and provided humanitarian assistance during hurricane season. We didn't have any interaction or contact with *Alacrity*.

Another two days were used to instal and level the tide gauge and tide pole within the harbour wall at the signal station steps. This location offered protection from most weather conditions. We 'connected' the tide pole to a benchmark on a traffic island just outside the dock gate, about 850m distant. Alas, the two benchmarks listed in the HI were too distant or had been destroyed. We used benchmark data kindly provided by Barbados Land and Surveys Department.

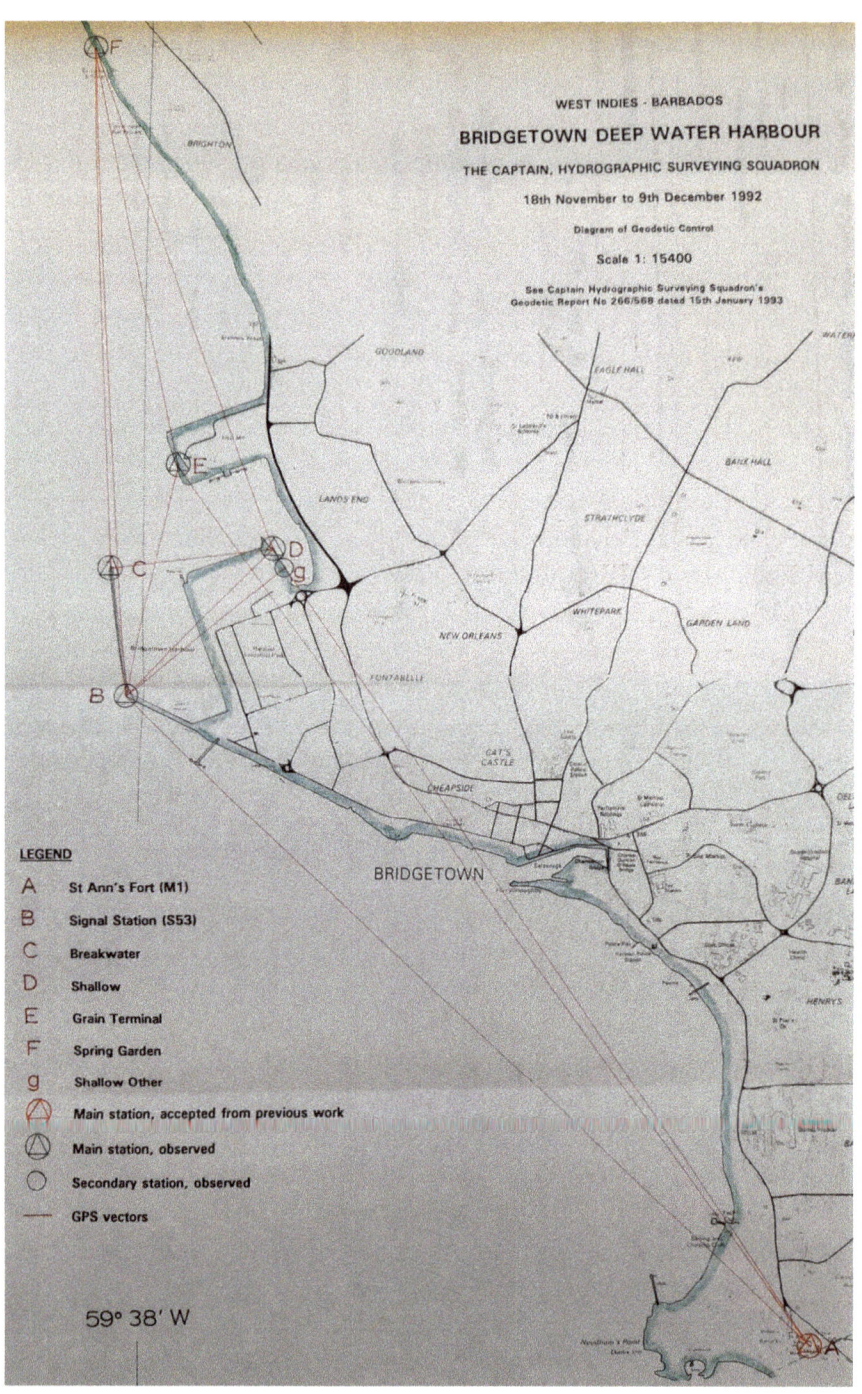

13.4 Control stations
(UKHO Archive)

13. A Bajan Interlude

By then, we'd inspected the boats at our disposal and chose the Barbados Coastguard's Boston Whaler as our sounding boat. This small, flat-bottomed, fibreglass boat proved ideal for boatwork within the harbour. Sounding began on 24 November and a 25-hour tidal comparison conducted.

13.5 HI 568 Bridgetown Deep Water Harbour
(UKHO Archive)

13.6 Daz in Coastguard dory
(Geraint West)

For sounding, we fitted a Raytheon portable echo sounder into each of the boats we used. Pleasingly, this functioned really well throughout the survey. The Coastguard provided a different crew every day, which meant valuable survey time was lost because we had to train each coxswain daily. It didn't help that their working hours were relatively short and quite inflexible, further limiting 'time-on-task'. We switched to the Port Authority's boat and were given a dedicated crew who proved most cooperative and swiftly adapted to our survey requirements. Overall, I think they enjoyed working with us, doing something completely different from their normal work for a few days.

13.7 Our cox'n driving the Port Authority's boat, Trisponder receiver to his right

I'd experienced working with Bajans in the MN. My first ship *ACT 5* (218m long, 29m beam, 10.5m draft, 24212 gross tons, refrigerated modular containership) and *Benedict* had UK officers and Bajan crews. As a Deck Cadet, I spent much time on deck chipping and painting with the Bajans, who I found very laid-back, cheerful and friendly. I was sad to say goodbye to the ABs and Mr Best the Bosun (a squat, powerful silver-haired Bajan, with enormous forearms and thick meaty fingers) when I paid off from *ACT 5* after five months in their company. A truly memorable first trip to sea.

We laid out transits at 12.5m intervals along all berths, using a theodolite and linen tape, checked every 125m by EODM equipment. We ran in on the transits from a maximum of 200m perpendicular to the berth. Distance off the berth during every line was recorded by EODM. With Daz's coaching, our coxswain acclimatised well to steering the transits and he never strayed excessively off the line. If he did, the line was re-run. These transit lines towards the wharves were often suspended for a few hours or even a day as Bridgetown proved very busy, with many movements in and out of the port, so the berths were frequently occupied, blocking our access.

We also used a distance line to maintain correct distance-off for cross lines parallel to the wharf. Daz was in charge of the boat while I grimly held onto the distance line, at great risk of being pulled into the harbour if the cox'n suddenly strayed too far off line, away from the wharf. To get depths along the wharf, Daz walked along it, taking soundings and bottom samples with a lead line 'armed' with tallow. He was able to do so even when a P&O cruise-ship was alongside, although the passengers thought he was a native, dressed in shorts, T-shirt, sandals and splattered in seabed mud and sand from the lead line and tallow.

13.8 Daz in the boat, me holding the distance line to maintain distance-off for lines parallel to wharf
(Geraint West)

Position fixing for the rest of the harbour was by hand-plotting two Trisponder lines of position. We'd prepared lattice overlay sheets to make hand-plotting on line easier. We used the best Trisponder line of position for line guidance perpendicular to the trend of submarine contours. Lines were spaced 25m apart but in areas where the depth was shoaler than 15m (actually, over 50% of the survey ground), line spacing was reduced to 12.5m. A speed of 4kts was used for all sounding. Two cross lines at 250m apart were run at right angles to the main lines, a standard check for gross errors in sounding data.

Seabed samples were obtained using a Dietz La Fond grab at intervals of 250m. The general offshore topography was rugged rock and coral structures, orientated north-west/south-east, interspersed with patches of sand. Inside the harbour basin, depths shoaled to a minimum of 8m at one of the berths but general depths exceeded 10m. The seabed comprised very fine, light-grey material, and not much coarse sand. We found no wrecks or obstructions within the survey ground.

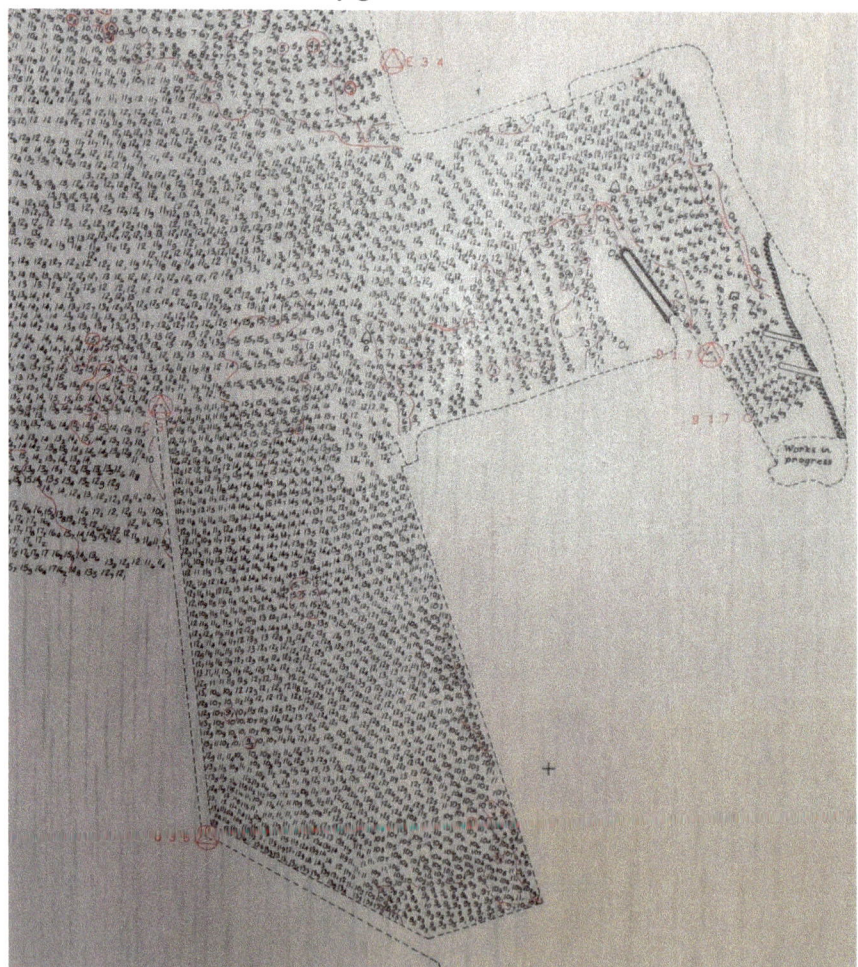

13.9 Extract from HI568 fair sheet, drawn by Daz, checked by me, approved by Geraint (UKHO Archive)

Boatwork was labour-intensive as the three of us were involved all day, every day, from commencement of sounding on 24 November until the final day, 7 December. Daily, we were up at 0530 and on the road to the port by

0600, around sunrise. We worked virtually non-stop until late afternoon, then packed up for the day. We spent 30 November processing our data. No wonder we eagerly anticipated our daiquiris at sunset (about 1730) in the west-facing Bamboo Beach Bar every day.

We were nominally to be in-country for a fortnight. But this had to be extended by a week as Bajan lifestyle meant a slower pace in getting things done than at home. Still, who'd complain about an extra week working in the Caribbean in November/December, enjoying lovely warm sunny days, avoiding a wet and windy winter in Guzz?

13.10 Panoramic view of berths

Our one rest day was 8 December, when we toured Barbados in the Isuzu. I don't remember what we saw or exactly where we went, but it was certainly a relaxing change from the survey. Our last day was spent re-packing kit, dismantling our home-made chartroom and survey store, and a debrief with the Harbour Master. He'd proved an absolute star in his attitude, enthusiasm and support for the survey. We flew home on Wednesday 9 December and set to work in offices in the Hydro School to fair up all our records, Report of Survey, fair sheet and accompanying documents for rendering to UKHO.

Daz drew the fair sheet, I checked it and Geraint's signature approved it. Interestingly, on Daz's retirement as WO(SR), he was presented with a copy of 'his' fair sheet. A brilliant gesture after his long, distinguished naval career. It hangs proudly in his living room.

The Bridgetown boat camp was a great experience. Our trio made a great team, we worked hard and got the job done as efficiently and professionally as practicable. Sometimes circumstances conspired to make life difficult out there, but we just had to roll with the Bajans and adjust our work-day to suit.

Hours were long, but that's normal on a boat camp. It made a difference to work in such a splendid place in excellent weather conditions. Unlike UK weather, we only aborted the survey for part of one day due to incessant heavy rain. But there was always work to do in the chartroom!

14.

Hydro School for Long Course

In April 1993, I pitched up at RNHS to start the 22-week Officers' Long Hydrographic Surveying Course (or Long Course). Mostly based at RNHS, the syllabus included short periods in, and visits to, other learning establishments. The culmination was exams in 'Control and Adjustment', 'Planning, Field and Nearshore Surveying', 'Continental Shelf and Oceanic Surveying' and 'Hydrographic Sciences'. Within each of these core titles lay a large number of topics, some new to us, others familiar from Basic Course but worthy of more detailed study.

14.1 Class photo, for the SMS Newbury module
(RNHS Archive)

Our course was typical in comprising four Brits, two Ozzies and a pair of Cloggies. My fellow-countrymen were Rob Lawson, Andy 'Wadders' Waddington and Derek Turner. I'd last seen Rob as he shuffled off *Fox* and headed to BRNC to become an officer. I knew Wadders from his time in *Fox* as a makie-learnie. I didn't know Derek at all, but he was rumoured to be a very brainy chap. It was great to see Rob and Wadders again. With these two herberts on course, no matter how serious and intense our studies were, we'd always have plenty of laughs. Mike Prince and Mike Beard were experienced Royal Australian Navy (RAN) surveyors, with extensive service in RAN hydrographic ships and *Paluma*-class survey motor launches. Theo Veneboer and Johnny Loog were typical Dutch surveyors, rich in knowledge and expertise in academic and mathematical aspects of hydrography.

The first day comprised the usual admin and welcoming addresses from RNHS' CO, Cdr David Gregan, and his XO, whose name escapes me. Our Course Officer was Lt Cdr Tony Jenks, an old-and-bold droggy. He was assisted by the Dutch Exchange Officer, who shared some of the teaching load. Tony described the course, his expectations and other relevant information. As well as classroom instruction, there'd be lots of practical work in SMBs in The Hamoaze, Lynher River and Plymouth Sound. We'd have to achieve a specified standard in four practical exercises: survey control at RNHS; a large-scale survey; astronomic observations when at the Army's School of Military Survey, Newbury; and a major survey planning exercise.

Around and about RNHS were familiar faces. Brian Lupton was still here as schoolie and computer/IT expert. He hadn't changed a bit. It was great to meet Steve Hawes again, one of the CPO(SR)s on the staff. He was here as a PO during my Basic Course and we had a brief time together when I joined *Hecla* in November 1988. He was CPO(SR) and left *Hecla* in the New Year. I'm sure there were other SRs on the staff with whom I'd sailed or knew since joining the branch, but shamefully I don't recall them.

Despite being forewarned, none of the Brits had done any revision or preparation for the initial maths assessment, which we did after completing the introductory and admin stuff. Not surprisingly, all except Derek failed. I think the two Mikes failed, too. Naturally, Johnny and Theo topped the class. The assessment's purpose was to establish our initial level of maths knowledge. Tony was gravely disappointed in the Brits' performance. Still, things could only get better.

The following paragraphs briefly summarise and indicate the vast content covered by Long Course. My scribblings don't include any detailed explanations. If you're a surveyor, you're likely more knowledgeable than me.

If you're a layman and wish to learn more, there are plenty of text books and references available.

Tony launched into the maths module, beginning with mathematical series, covering simple, binomial, arithmetic and geometric progressions, convergency and divergency of infinite series, exponential series, evaluation of e, differentiation of e^x and logarithmic series. He then moved on to matrix algebra, including least squares which, he said, we'd be studying in some depth at Newbury. I didn't like the sound of that too much.

Onwards into three-dimensional coordinate geometry. This was familiar ground to me as I'd learned much as a Deck Cadet during my college phases at Liverpool Polytechnic, part of syllabus for the 2nd Mate's certificate. This topic led on to vector algebra. A vast body of study involving mechanics, which seemed more relevant to us as surveyors. Tony dealt with Newton's laws of motion and gravity, straight line and circular motion, centrifugal force, satellite motion, effects of Earth's motion on gravity, equipotential surfaces, periodic motion and simple harmonic motion (which was intimately related to tidal theory).

The syllabus had a goodly amount on vector algebra, complex numbers and numerical methods. Fortunately, I managed to dredge up memories of first year maths at university, although that was well over a decade ago and never used or needed since. Still, every little helped in keeping my head above water.

When we'd completed this vast spectrum of mathematics and passed the maths module exam, Tony moved us into the surveying topics. Here, he delved into minute detail on control and adjustment. There was an intense focus on how the Earth's surface is represented by a mathematical figure. Alas, Earth isn't a simple shape. Much time was spent on geodesy, spheroids and radii of curvature.

We conducted computations on the spheroid and how to determine which projection to use for our survey work. All projections have different properties appropriate to certain locations, scale, geographical positions on Earth and the requirements of the survey. Several types of projection used in surveying were described: conical orthomorphic; universal polar stereographic; Mercator (probably the best known of all); transverse Mercator; and Universal Transverse Mercator (UTM), the most commonly used projection today.

Tony revised and elaborated on the types and principles of horizontal and vertical control surveys. He also covered the planning and preparation of triangulation and trilateration networks. This led into methods of adjustment to bowl out errors in observations. Rigorous adjustment of the results of observations involved using 'least squares analysis' and 'variation of coordinates'. I was increasingly squitty about the former as I found it complex to grasp and aware that a goodly portion of our time in Newbury was focused on the subject. The latter involved using a computer programme which crunched the numbers input as a result of our observations to produce a 'network analysis' showing their value and validity. Being computer-illiterate, this subject baffled me but, somehow, I muddled through.

The syllabus included field astronomy. Tony revised the motions of the stars and solar system, and spherical trigonometry. I was very comfortable, as 2nd Mate's college phases included much theory and practice in these topics. They were almost like old friends. I think we even used Clough-Smith's classic *An Introduction to Spherical Trigonometry* text book, too. I still had my own copy at home.

The planning, field and nearshore surveying topic took us back to things with which we were very familiar. Everything to do with planning and preparing to conduct a hydrographic survey was described. As a survey neared completion, we were reminded of the preparation of ship and boat documents and field records. This led to the presentation of data and its rendering to UKHO for their dreaded appraisal and critique of our hard work. Tony explained the measurement of angles and distances in field surveys using the instruments currently in service.

The use of satellite navigation was increasingly prevalent. A multitude of scientific specialisms viewed it as 'the next big thing'. The droggy world was no different. The old Transit satellite navigation system, which I'd used since my first trip to sea as a Deck Cadet on *ACT 5* in late-1980, was being subsumed by America's new-fangled Navstar Global Positioning System (GPS). We learned that the Soviets had developed their own rival system GLONASS, unashamedly copying the Americans' concept and principles. I found how this GPS thing worked fascinating. The mechanics of launching the constellation of 24 satellites into the correct orbits to ensure whole-Earth coverage. The method used to yield an accurate position on a receiver. Monitoring/updating/correcting the system via a global network of ground stations. Brilliant stuff.

We returned to the nitty-gritty of traditional surveying with lectures on large scale and harbour surveys using visual and electronic methods, bobbing about in SMBs. From there, we moved on to continental shelf and oceanic surveying, covering our old friends, EPF systems like Hyperfix and

Trisponder. Tony reiterated the principles and conduct of bathymetric (echo sounder) and sonar surveys (using sidescan sonar).

Lessons on the principles and use of SINS were interesting, given my experience of it in *Hecla* in 1989 and the possibility that my next job may be as Operations Officer in an H-boat, where it was the primary position-fixing system. SINS was also the main navigation system used by nuclear submarines, underwater for months on end during their patrols.

Integral to many H-boat deployments and surveys was the gathering of oceanographic data. This was achieved at planned stations across the survey ground to conduct oceanographic dips (O-dips), where we collected a variety of data through the entire water column, from sea surface to seabed, with specialist bits of kit: bathythermograph (measured temperature against depth and pressure in the upper 300m of the ocean); STDV probe (salinity, temperature, density and sound velocity in water); Secchi disc (a white circular disk 30cm in diameter, attached to a line and slowly lowered into the water such that the depth at which the disc was no longer visible was deemed a measure of water transparency or turbidity); seabed sampling (using Shipek Grab, the life-and-limb threatening spring-loaded grab).

Geophysical surveys were explained. Those who'd served in H-boats had experience of gathering gravity and magnetic data. Although Tony described marine seismic surveys, the RN hadn't done any for many years. They were definitely the province of offshore companies exploring for oil and gas reserves, with ships towing increasingly larger arrays of 'boomers'.

Onwards in the syllabus, we were instructed in 'hydrographic sciences'. This included computer science as applied to hydrographic surveying, describing 'BASIC' language, electronic calculators and desktop computers, and the use of SIPS.

We'd each signed out a swanky Hewlett Packard RPN 32SII scientific calculator for the duration of Long Course. RPN stood for 'reverse polish notation', something I'd never heard of but apparently meant that 'operators (+, -, /, x for example) preceded their operands (numbers)'. The keyboard had loads of functions and 'stores' for calculations that the user 'recalled' when needed for further use. Naturally, there was a compact, dense instruction booklet. Of its time, I supposed it was an impressive calculator.

SIPS had recently been introduced and fitted in our survey ships and I'd used it in NP1008. It highlighted that droggying was evolving from the traditional to the electronic and into the digital age, as new systems were interfaced with each other into full-on, comprehensive, integrated systems.

Other topics were principles of electronics and radio and light wave propagation.

Later, we moved on to the study of tides, revising our knowledge of basic tidal theory, 'real tide' and harmonic analysis. Onwards to tidal predictions, levels and datums, transfer of tidal datum and the use of co-tidal charts. We studied tidal streams, too, and various methods of measuring water flow. All very much our bread and butter.

In the final stages of Long Course, UKHO's Territorial Waters Officer (a long-in-the-tooth Lt Cdr) came down to introduce us to the International Law of the Sea, the 1949 Geneva Convention and the legal liability of Hydrographer and Surveyor for their products.

All the above not only occurred in the classroom at RNHS but also included practical exercises with survey instruments, kit and boatwork in the school's SMBs. These were great as an escape from the classroom, in the fresh air of The Hamoaze, dodging the Torpoint Ferry, and in Plymouth Sound. When in SMBs all day, we lapped up the boat stoker's pot-mess at lunchtime.

Interspersed with time at RNHS, there were several out-of-town trips. The longest and most important was five weeks at Royal School of Military Survey (RSMS), Hermitage, near Newbury, home of the Royal Engineers' survey branch. RSMS originated in 1833 when it was established at the Royal Military Academy, Woolwich. After several moves, it finally settled at Denison Barracks, Hermitage, in 1949, where several Royal Engineers survey, mapping and intelligence units were co-located. In 1979, a major re-build on site provided RSMS with purpose-built facilities.

We pitched up on Sunday 1 June in various cars. I'm sure Wadders and I were together, Rob Lawson came by himself as he lived in Combe Martin on the north Devon coast, and Derek was solo. Not sure what our overseas classmates did, but probably paired up by nationality. The good thing was, we weren't accompanied by RNHS staff. It was assumed that we were big enough and ugly enough to attend school, behave properly and not let the Navy down in this Army environment.

The Officers' Mess was a 1960s-build, neither glamorous nor architecturally interesting. Still, we were allocated first-floor single cabins with a sink, heads and bathrooms along the corridor. The ground floor comprised an entrance hall with lounge (spacious and overlooking an expanse of well-kept lawn), adjacent bar, large dining room and adjoining galley.

On Monday morning, we found the correct block and classroom where we spent our school days for the duration, except for the odd practical exercise within the grounds. Our weekends were free, so the most important question was finding out what time we secured on Fridays. Luckily, I think it was lunchtime, so we'd get home by teatime and travel back on Sunday evenings. It was an easy but long, boring journey (about three hours) as RSMS was just off the A34. We joined the M4 at Junction 13, switched to the M5 at Bristol, which became the A38 at Exeter for the remaining 40 minutes to Guzz.

There were two modules: field survey for four weeks; and a week's air surveying. I confess to not recalling anything of the latter module. The former was focused on least squares analysis and the principles of observing and calculating various measurements, usually astronomic. The basics of least squares had been introduced to us at RNHS but that seemed, almost from the first lesson at Newbury, woefully inadequate. Probably, I hadn't paid sufficient attention to Tony's instruction? Regardless, least squares proved absolutely torturous and, at times, barely comprehensible to me. Realising this very early on, I resolved to fully concentrate at all times and scribble my own copious notes in the handouts. I think Rob and Wadders were in the same boat, but Derek and the foreigners had a far better grasp.

Our lecturer was John Knight, a typical academic, clad in chinos, jacket, shirt and tie, longish unruly dark hair and spectacles. He'd devoted his working life to mathematics, least squares analysis in particular. He was serious about it but gamely tolerated our pathetically slow comprehension of a complex and, to my mind, tediously dull topic. Probably because I found it so hard to follow John as he delved into its depths. It was simply a case of knuckling down and desperately trying to learn enough to pass the module exam.

Ted Price was the other lecturer. He was an 'old school', ex-Warrant Officer, Army surveyor. Invariably immaculately turned out in suit and tie, neat military haircut, with clear diction. He re-hashed some of Tony's lessons on astronomical observations, space geodesy and orbital mechanics. He taught us the calculations involved in resolving astronomical observations by first principles. Then gave us examples to do. These were exceptionally long-winded and prone to easy errors as we worked through them. By having a neat hand, taking care in transcribing figures and constant checking that I'd copied them correctly, I usually got the correct answer, if rather slowly.

Part of the syllabus was using theodolites to take our own observations of celestial bodies and calculate our astronomical position from first principles. These were timetabled for several evenings but, alas, clouds obscured the sky, so we didn't complete these sessions. But that allowed us to scuttle ashore to the nearby pub, The Fox Inn, for a couple of beers before last orders.

We weren't given homework, but it was prudent to at least read through and recap what we'd done in class daily. This took us nicely up to dinner, followed by retirement to the bar for a few 'sherberts'.

It was our first experience of living in an Army environment. Stand easy occurred mid-morning and we made our way to the Mess for tea and biscuits. There were always plenty of the latter, in which I delightedly indulged. I can't help myself with biscuits! We sat down in the ante-room, chatting and reading the newspaper.

What immediately struck us was the presence of numerous dogs in the Mess. Army officers habitually brought their dogs to the office and, at stand easy, brought them into the Mess. Being terrified of dogs, I was very wary of sitting with my face and cup of tea level with a labrador's gaping, tooth-filled mouth and long wet tongue. I got used to it but was perpetually unnerved. One morning, Johnny was drinking his coffee but, unpleasantly and unhygienically, a labrador's arse was almost in his face. Johnny tried to push the dog away but it remained unmoved. At the end of his tether, Johnny ferociously jabbed two fingers into the labrador's backside. It loudly yelped and sprinted away, its owner bewildered at his dog's unusual behaviour. None of us were bothered by labradors in the Mess again.

There weren't many livers-in at RSMS. Our class occupied one dining-room table and there was a scattering of odds-and-sods around the other tables. They were junior Royal Engineers officers on various intense survey courses. After dinner, only a couple of Army surveyors joined us briefly in the bar. The other diners slipped away to resume studying in their cabins.

Throughout our time at Newbury, it was glorious summer weather. The June evenings were light until late. There was only one notable Officers' Mess function when we were there. A 'big noise' in the Mess (Social Secretary?) informed us that it was traditional for the Army to challenge its RN visitors at croquet. The beautiful, well-tended, lawn outside the French windows was the venue as it was clipped and large enough.

The Army were deadly serious. In the week leading up to the match, we observed them practising after work and before dinner. We felt we ought to practise too as none of us had ever played croquet. But, being Navy, we swiftly abandoned the idea and continued our beer-drinking in the bar. On the appointed date, near the end of our course, we wondered if we'd made the right decision. Too late! Royal Navy honour was at stake.

We eight paired off for the four matches. Despite our ignorance of the rules and the hosts' intense practices, we humiliated them 3–1 overall. We miraculously showed some skill at times but generally had the 'rub-of-the-green'. Army faces reddened, jaws dropped, token applause rang across the lawn as the result was announced. We were presented with 'The Shiny Shovel' trophy, highly polished for the occasion. Beer was bought for us during the aftermath but the Army slunk quietly away. We had our most raucous evening in the Mess that night. We suffered for it throughout the next day. It was even more of a struggle to understand least squares. Poor John Knight gamely helped us along.

And so, our five weeks at RSMS ended. We all passed whatever exams were taken, thank goodness. We'd had a good time, but I was relieved it was over and hoped I'd never have anything to do with least squares ever again.

We had a three-day oceanography module at the School of Meteorology and Oceanography at HMS Seahawk, Culdrose in Cornwall. On Basic Course, we'd learned about meteorology but this time focused on oceanography, a subject which interested me more. We stayed in the wardroom, which hadn't changed at all. It was populated with 'wannabe' aircrew, young pups with unbreakable self-belief that they'd earn their wings to become pilots or observers, ignoring the high failure rate. Bless them.

Staying with the RN, we had a day trip to Guzz, to the Royal Navy Engineering College, Manadon. The principles of underwater acoustics were described to us. We learned: the terminology and quantities used in acoustics; acoustic and sonar parameters; propagation of acoustic waves in seawater; generation of acoustic waves; attenuation of acoustic power; effect of reflection, refraction and target strength; and sonar parameters. The parameters included: directivity; factors governing pulse length and bandwidth; factors affecting target detection; and sonar performance. All relevant to droggies in our use of echo sounders and, particularly, sidescan sonar, but equally pertinent to anti-submarine warfare and underwater environmental factors to enable submarines to avoid being detected. It was a full-on day, much to absorb.

I enjoyed the three-day submarine geology module at Bristol University covered plate tectonics, continental drift, the Mid-Atlantic Ridge and Pacific 'Ring of Fire'. I recalled much of these fascinating subjects from my far-off university days. The Department for Continuing Education was housed in a Victorian mansion overlooking Clifton Suspension Bridge. A real treat.

We spent a day at the Institute of Oceanographic Science, Wormley, a small hamlet south-west of London. This research establishment was established in 1949 and moved to Wormley in 1953 to be housed in an ex-Admiralty building, known to the scientists as the Wormley lab. Amongst all the historical kit and scientific gubbins we were shown GLORIA (geological long-range inclined asdic), on her long trailer outside the building. GLORIA was a massive sidescan sonar towed 300m astern of a research ship at 50m below sea surface. It swept widths of up to 22km each side of its body to generate three-dimensional maps of the sea-floor. The first GLORIA was designed and built in 1965 at Wormley, measuring 9.3m long and 3m in circumference. The scientific cruises on which it was deployed mapped ocean-floor features (underwater volcanoes, canyons and tectonic plate boundaries). GLORIA's fourth and last iteration was built in 1993 and retired by the decade's end. Brilliant British innovative science and engineering.

There was a day-trip to Paignton for an EPF module at Racal Marine Services. We crammed into a classroom so tiny that if anyone needed the heads, all those between him and the door had to stand to allow him to squeeze past.

Finally, there was a two-day acquaint visit to UKHO. We were warmly welcomed, had a conducted tour of the offices and several presentations about UKHO's work. One large room was filled with chart tables at which employees spent their days correcting charts by hand. We were impressed with the print room, where swanky new coloured metric charts were produced en masse. A great improvement on the good old days of printing from copper plates in monochrome fathoms. In the evening, we adjourned to a pub and played skittles against UKHO staff. A pleasant beer-filled evening and decent pub food.

We completed the survey planning exercise. It covered everything to do with conducting a survey of Port Sudan in the Red Sea during some sort of crisis wherein the UK had to evacuate its citizens.

We worked together in planning and executing our practical survey exercise, using SMBs and Gemini, plus 'coastlining' along a very muddy bank of the Lynher River. Being autumn in Guzz, the weather was typically wet and windy. Constant rain made the survey a miserable experience. We were perpetually cold, wet and muddy. We finished, faired up our records and rendered the survey to Tony and Cdr Gregan for their critique.

The final week comprised exams and then we awaited the results. We all passed and were equipped for the next stage of our droggy careers. We said cheerio to the foreigners. Mike Prince continued as the RAN Exchange Officer for a couple of years, serving in a CSV. Mike Beard returned to Australia. Johnny and Theo scuttled back to Holland. Wadders went to *Beagle* and Derek took command of *Gleaner*. After Staff Course, Rob joined *Roebuck* and then relieved Derek as CO *Gleaner*. I was returning to *Hecla* as Operations Officer. I was pretty pleased with this appointment and hoped I'd have as great a time as in 1989. As it turned out, I had a fantastic couple of years in the happy *Hecla*.

Royal Naval School of
Hydrographic Surveying

HMS DRAKE

This is to certify that

Lieutenant P J Carroll, Royal Navy

has successfully completed the

Hydrographic Officers' Long Course

at the Hydrographic School

on 8 October 1993

and achieved a second class pass

Commander, Royal Navy

14.2 Long H Course certificate

15.
Happy *Hecla* Again!

15.1 *Hecla* crest
(Nick Barwis, www.jackstaxi.net)

15.2 *Hecla*
(Barry Pearce, www.MaritimeQuest.com)

I joined *Hecla* in Natal, Brazil, on 22 October 1993. She'd sailed from Guzz on 5 October for a geophysical survey in the tropical Atlantic. After Tenerife (11–13 October), *Hecla* trundled south, arriving in Natal the day I joined.

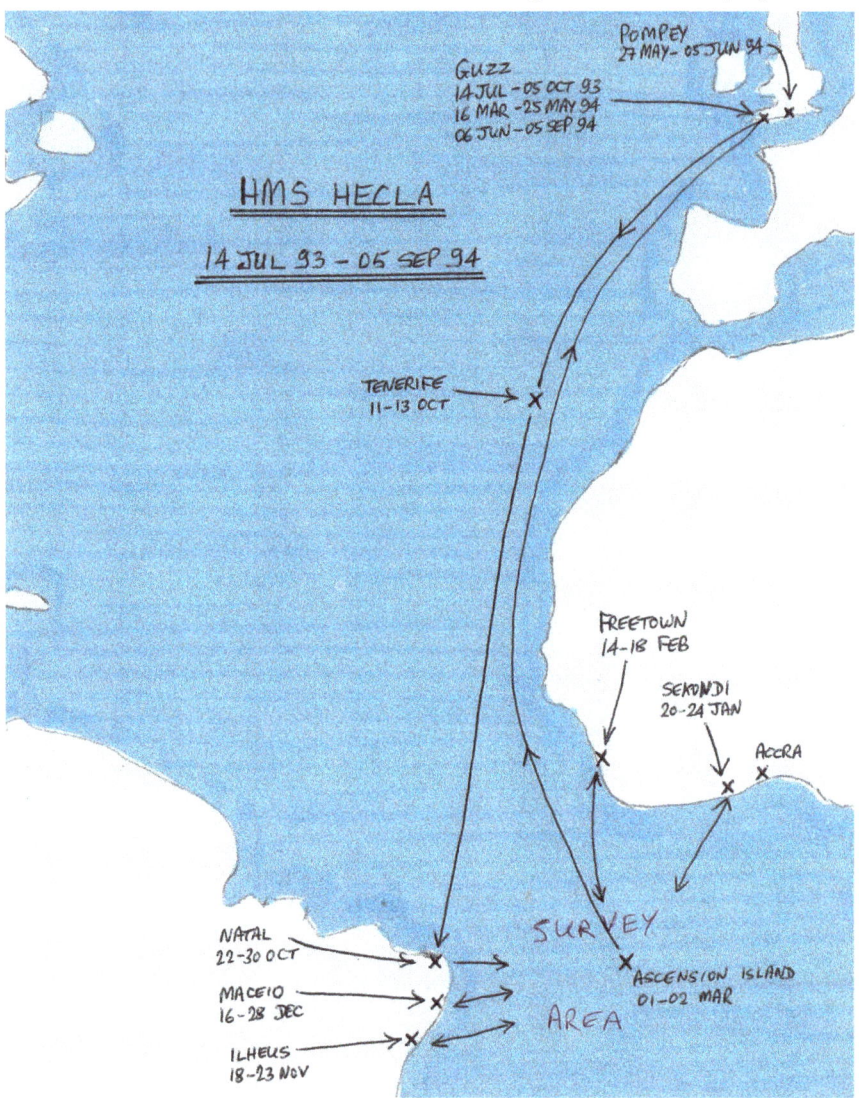

15.3 Atlantic Ocean deployment

I looked forward to a business-class flight from UK to Brazil. Imagine my disappointment when told that because the runway at Ascension Island was closed for upgrading/repair/resurfacing, RAF flights to the Falklands were re-routed via Recife. I drove a hire car from Guzz to Brize Norton to catch a RAF Tristar trooping flight on 21 October. What a let down! No such thing as business-class on 'Crab Air', the food was as poor as expected (bag-meals!) and no in-flight movies or any 'luxuries' of a proper airline.

We landed at Recife at dawn. I was astounded that my luggage was unloaded by RAF blokes based there until Ascension's runway reopened. Other RAF blokes refuelled the Tristar. Luckily, that was the first and last time I flew courtesy of RAF. I mooched about the empty departure area until check-in opened for my Varig flight to Natal, certainly an improvement on RAF Tristar. At Natal, the chandler met me and took me to *Hecla*. It had been a long journey. It was early evening as I clambered up the gangway and was welcomed aboard by the QM. Recalling the ship's layout, I knew my cabin was the second one on the port side, next door to XO.

I dumped my bags and knocked on Martin Clegg's door. It was great to see him again, now Lt Cdr and XO. He welcomed me aboard and after a brief chat, took me to meet the CO. Leaning on the flight deck netting, overlooking the wharf and warehouses, was Cdr Peter Hobson. I introduced myself and we shook hands. He seemed a very dour, grumpy, humourless man. I'd heard he was a jolly good surveyor but my first impression of him remained unchanged throughout the remainder of his time in *Hecla*.

Fortunately, the wardroom more than compensated. Aside from Martin, the other officers were Lieutenants Jon Armstrong (who I was relieving as Ops Officer), Dickie Bird (NO), Simon Hardy (Gravity Officer), Doug Calkin (Magnetics Officer), Andy Morgan (Schoolie), Justin Wilkes (Pusser), Sam Seward (Bosun), Henry Cooper (MEO) and Susie Tanser (MO).

The standard four-day port visit was extended to eight days due to defects on the port main engine. Not a good start but an opportunity to refamiliarize myself with *Hecla* and get to know ship's company. I was delighted to see Mick Slater as my CPO(SR). He'd taken over from Steve Hawes shortly before *Hecla* left Guzz. Chartroom Dodger was LS(SR) 'Willy' Wilcock, who proved an excellent wingman for Mick and me. I'd heard bits and pieces about LS(SR) 'Spike' Hughes, a soft-spoken but highly respected killick. A Welshman of few words but an authoritative presence on the upper deck and during any seamanship serials.

My AB(SR)s during my two-year appointment included 'Dusty' Miller, Gary 'Little Artie' Shaw, Mickey Eastmond, Scott Holden, 'Jacko' Jackson, Mark Hossack, 'Kew' Kewish, Brian Humphries, Pip Cox, Paddy Gibson, plus the original 'Artie' Shaw. An old-and-bold SR, Artie was a legendary hard-drinking Scotsman, yet of an artistic disposition, with a fine hand at drawing. He had a gentle calm about him.

I had much contact with LWEM(R) 'Barney' Barnard. As gravimeter maintainer, he was critical to keeping the survey on track as gathering gravity data was our prime mission. He also maintained the magnetometer, radar and navigation aids so, potentially, the busiest man on board if kit started going wrong.

H-boat geophysical surveys in the Atlantic were classified 'Secret UK/US Eyes Only'. Only those cleared to that level, or higher, 'needed to know' our survey ground's location and extent. Even HI number and title (HI609 South Atlantic) were classified, never mind its contents. I'd undergone the in-depth vetting process before joining *Hecla*. HI609 was held in the chartroom safe, its combination known only to Mick Slater and me. Reading it in the chartroom meant I ensured prying eyes didn't espy a word of it. Only CO, XO (because Martin's security clearance was still valid) and I were cleared to access it. Overall, rather naïve as anyone visiting the bridge could see our position on the navigation chart 'somewhere in the Atlantic' between Brazil and West Africa. Likewise, my SRs could see the survey ground when working on our sheets in the chartroom.

I also took over Jon Armstrong's role as Diving Officer (DivO). I wasn't a ship's diver ('pond life') and had zero interest in diving. In the Mob, you get jobs/responsibilities you don't want. With Jon's guidance, I gained familiarity with the paperwork, buffed up on diving operations and DivO's responsibilities. I shadowed Jon during a dive on the ship's hull. As Dive Supervisor, he had ultimate responsibility for a dive's safe execution.

Hecla's diving team numbered about eight, large for the size of her ship's company. They were keen and willing, attracted by diving itself plus the extra pay concomitant with being a ship's diver. To retain their qualification, ship's divers (like bubble-heads) were required to remain in date by logging a prescribed number of minutes per quarter. When Jon left at our next port, the team would fall foul of this regulation because there was no qualified dive supervisor on board. I was the 'non-diving diving officer'.

One day in Natal, I accompanied the diving team to a beautiful sandy beach along the coast. We'd borrowed a suitable vehicle and loaded it with diving kit. At the beach, Jon organised the dive and, kitted up, pairs of ship's divers strolled into the water to submerge and 'get their minutes in'. At some point, Spike Hughes suggested I have a go. I was scared to death! Reluctantly, I agreed and, under Jon's strict instructions, kitted up and strode off the beach with Spike. At waist-height water, Spike indicated we 'dive'. Down we went, underwater. Visibility was good, I saw the sandy seabed. A few seconds later I became completely disorientated. I had no idea, in about four feet of water, whether I was looking up, down or sideways. It was utterly frightening. I thrashed about in a panic, trying to surface but with no idea which direction to go. Spike saved me and I stumbled onto the beach. This horrendous experience represented my entire diving career and reinforced my dislike and fear of diving.

Back on board, the kit was washed, cleaned, dried and stowed in the diving store on the quarter deck. The team had a good laugh at my expense as we scuppered several 'diver recall signals' (Antarctica beer).

We sailed from Natal on 30 October. *Hecla* slipped from the wharf and headed north in the Potengi River. Shortly, we altered course northeast and passed between Barra do Rio Potengi to port and the exposed rocky pavement of Quebra-Mar da Praia do Forte (Beach of the Strong) to starboard. Leaving Natal astern, we headed into the Atlantic.

Dickie put me in the watchbill. I enjoyed bridge watchkeeping in *Hecla* in the tropical Atlantic. My favourite watch was the morning (0400–0800). After a 'shake' at 0320, I climbed the ladder to the darkened bridge at 0340. Taking over as OOW was smooth. Captain's night orders were simple, the survey systems operational and no shipping contacts within umpteen miles. Our handover completed and, after a brief chat, my predecessor disappeared below. I was enveloped in darkness. The gentle hum of equipment, ping of the PDR echo sounder and heavy clunking of the Kingmatic plotter created a rhythmic, soothing soundtrack.

The increase in temperature and humidity between my cabin and the bridge was noticeable. *Hecla's* accommodation was air-conditioned, but on the bridge we closed the 'punkah-louvres' and opened the bridge doors for easy access to the bridge wings. My tropical uniform (white short-sleeved shirt, white shorts and Pusser's sandals) was comfortable.

I sipped my mug of tea, brought up with me from the pantry as I couldn't start a watch without a 'brew'. I'm a tea man and my mug accumulated a healthy brown staining on its inside. I never washed my mug throughout a deployment so it got a 'draft chit' when we returned to Guzz in mid-March.

Also on watch were QM ('Stan' Baxter) and SR-of-the-Watch ('Dusty' Miller). The only other sailor up and around was the on-watch stoker in the engine room. We didn't ordinarily have contact with him unless something untoward occurred down below. Once per watch, he visited the bridge to sign for 'rounds', confirming all was well in his hot, sweaty, noisy world. At hourly intervals, Stan conducted 'rounds' of the ship to ensure fire hadn't broken out in the accommodation and all was secure throughout.

I continually checked the survey systems on the bridge. PDR happily pinged away, ADL busily marked our progress across the Ozatex trackplot on the Kingmatic plotter. The Transit satellite navigation system was fine, SINS working perfectly. Meanwhile, unseen several decks below, at the waterline and amidships, the gravimeters silently gathered data.

I continuously monitored the radar and kept a good visual lookout for surface contacts. As we were tens, if not hundreds, of miles from merchant shipping routes, I rarely saw any. We were very much off the beaten track as we plodded onwards, gathering invaluable data for use by Britain's MOD and the US Department of Defense.

Although dark when I took over, it was pleasantly warm and comfortably humid in the tropics. I loved standing on the bridge wing, sipping tea, looking up at a clear black sky littered with millions of stars, their magnitude of brightness unaffected by light pollution found ashore. The throbbing rhythm of the engines and generators resonated from the funnel, a lullaby which, perhaps strangely, complemented this tropical maritime environment and the twinkling blanket of stars surrounding our beautiful white ship with its buff funnel gliding through calm, warm ocean.

Stan went below to do rounds and, as it neared 0500, he shook the chef (duty cook), ensuring he got out of his bunk to flash up the galley. Meanwhile, I continued to check the survey and navigation systems were functioning satisfactorily, checked the radar, and took a good 360° look around the horizon for contacts.

Air temperature and humidity slowly increased as the eastern sky began to lighten, the first hint of the pink of dawn as another day opened with the cycle of astronomical twilight, nautical twilight and civil twilight, until sunrise occurred. In these tropical latitudes at this time of year, nautical twilight was about an hour before sunrise, which I calculated using the trusty *Nautical Almanac*. In the west, the sky remained black, untainted by the gradual onset of dawn.

With the rise in air temperature and humidity, *Hecla's* teak decks emitted a distinct, pleasant aroma. Moisture soaked into the wood and released as vapour as air temperature slowly soared. I don't know what chemical and physical reactions caused this, but I loved it. It complemented my keen lookout whilst resting my elbows on the bridge wing dodger, sipping another 'brew'. Combined with the gradual rise in temperature and humidity, I felt enveloped in a blanket of pleasant comfort.

The next hour slowly followed. Stan did his rounds again. Dusty and I chatted about something and nothing. Stan triumphantly returned to the

15. Happy Hecla Again!

bridge with a large plate of bacon sarnies, courtesy of the duty chef. Dusty wetted the tea and we tucked into freshly baked rolls filled with lovely, soft, warm, greasy bacon. Undoubtedly, the most enjoyable few minutes of the best bridge watch.

Out on the bridge wing, I savoured every mouthful of this treat, sipped my tea, and looked out over the tranquil, empty ocean with its long, low, gentle swell. The sun perceptibly emerged from the previously undefined horizon, lightened the sky from pink to orange and ultimately became a bright shiny gold orb. The sea glistened with its brilliance, the warmth and aroma from the teak deck pervaded. Crikey, life was good.

Sadly, these precious luxurious minutes were soon over. We were on the last stretch at the end of the watch and it got a little busier. The odd bloke emerged for a gentle jog around the upper deck, carefully avoiding becoming a casualty through banging his head on the many sharp and solid protrusions of vents and pipework. Others did physical workouts in the hangar or on the flight deck. The occasional curious individual visited the bridge to see where we were – not much different from yesterday as the chart in use covered the entire Atlantic Ocean.

I prepared my script for calling the CO at 0630. Its standard format laid out in Captain's standing orders so I just had to fill in the blanks, but ensure my report was clear, accurate and punctual.

After calling the Captain, Martin usually popped up to the bridge before breakfast in the wardroom. We had a brief chat about the night and survey progress.

Call the hands was at 0700. Although it was Stan's responsibility to perform this ritual, if his piping was poor, OOW (me) copped any grief and ribbing. The wise QM practised with his bosun's call on the bridge wing beforehand. On this occasion, Stan's piping was perfect, so no repercussions.

Finally, our reliefs turned up and we conducted our handovers, which didn't take too long. I went below and headed to the wardroom for a hearty fat-boy breakfast. My job done until my next watch, but I had a day's work to do in the chartroom from 0900.

I disliked afternoon watches. Early, rushed lunch at 1120, an uncivilised hour. Up to the bridge for 1140 for the handover. Then four hours of glorious afternoons continuing the survey, while ship's company enjoyed a lazy hour's lunchtime bronzing before turning to at 1300. Deck space was demarcated: bridge roof (wardroom); Senior Rates (bridge deck); Junior Rates (flight deck and fo'c's'le). Sundays were worse as the bridge team and on-watch stoker were the only folks working.

I couldn't resist repeating my childish prank from my previous incarnation as Gravity Officer in 1989. I sent the QM and SR to the bridge roof to turn the for'ard window washer outwards. We briefly sprayed the bronzing sailors on the fo'c'sle. They reacted the same as in 1989, puzzled at 'rain' despite clear, cloudless, bright blue sky. I should have matured in the interim, as I was a bit more senior as Ops Officer, but couldn't help myself.

The routine at sea hadn't changed since my previous stint in *Hecla* some four years ago. We bimbled along the designated east-west/west-east survey lines across the width of the tropical Atlantic. Line spacing was, I think, 4° of latitude and, after being on one line for several days, every OOW hoped to get the E-O-L and alter course by 90° to head for the next S-O-L.

At the end of this survey leg, shortened due to our extended stay in Natal, we headed for Ilhéus, in the southern coastal region of Bahia, 211km south of Salvador, the state's capital. Ilhéus was formerly one of the biggest exporters of cocoa beans, but its economy was increasingly based mainly on tourism due to its stunning beaches and early Portuguese historical and cultural heritage.

Although Rio Cachoeira flowed through the city, the port was located about 1km north of Ilhéus. It was an easy approach from seaward, steering directly towards the breakwater. After rounding it, *Hecla* berthed, on 18 November, halfway along the inshore side of the breakwater, which actually formed the wharves. It was a short taxi ride to the city centre.

As Ops, I focused on completing this survey leg's RoS, accompanying documents, data cartridges, plus magnetometer data and, crucially, gravimeter data. The trick was to stay on top of the RoS as much as possible at sea to minimise the work required alongside. Mick Slater, Willy Wilcock and I prepared everything in the chartroom, Simon and Doug conducted the gravity transfer, and Barney started the gravimeter tie-in.

The Defence Courier was due on board the next day to collect our large package of data and deliver it to UKHO – an inflexible deadline. CO took a keen interest in our progress when he wasn't engaged in his formal duties. We'd achieved all we could in the chartroom, Simon and Doug completed the gravity transfer and faired-up the forms. We now awaited Barney's tie-in to run its full 24.8hr cycle uninterrupted by power cuts. All went well. It was a relief after the Defence Courier had signed a receipt for our survey data and left *Hecla*.

Simon, Doug and I had time to get ready and attend the cocktail party on the flight deck, covered by the white awning rigged by the Buffer's lads during the day. The chefs' nibbles and smally-eats were of the usual high standard. The stewards, assisted by a few volunteer ABs, kept the hosts and guests topped up with booze. Those G&Ts went down a treat!

Meanwhile, ship's company not on duty went ashore to check out Ilhéus' bars. 'Jack' always found a decent bar and generally Junior Rates gravitated to the same one. Inevitably, when the officers went ashore, we stumbled across 'Jack' who was keen to buy a beer or two. I usually found my SRs and scuppered a couple of Antarctica with them but escaped before getting too involved. If some sort of carnage occurred later, the first question asked was who was the senior bloke there.

It was here that I learned of the prodigious quantities quaffed by the serious drinkers (notably Spike and Artie), often until dawn in Brazil. They slowly scuppered bottle after bottle. The only discernible effect was a bleariness in the eyes, a slight slurring of speech but completely harmless and well-behaved. Amazing!

We departed Ilhéus on 23 November. Out again for the next survey leg in beautiful weather. The tropical Atlantic gave us low sea, slight swell, sunshine, blue sky and warm temperatures. The nights were dark and twinkling stars filled the largely cloudless sky. It was a joy to be at sea.

Circuit training took place every weekday at 1630 and was well attended by 20-odd folks. Barney was in charge and gave us a hard time for an hour with his circuits of arms, abdoms and legs. The last serial was grid sprints. Four random teams lined up behind the hangar threshold. On the whistle, the first four sprinted to the aft net and back four times. When they'd finished, the next four raced. It was highly competitive. Despite my age compared to sprog ABs, grid sprints was my best event.

As a teenager, I was in Hampshire's Under-16 badminton squad, training in the old gym at HMS Sultan. Grid sprints was one of our exercises from one side of the court to each line and back. Good training for badminton as the sport involved short, sharp spurts and sudden changes of direction. Twenty-odd years later, I showed I could still do it. My biggest rival was Spike, a supremely fit bloke, but I beat him more often than not.

To finish the session, we did pull-ups in the hangar. Everyone loudly urged the poor sod hanging off the bar to do 'just one more'. The most I ever managed was eight or nine and I never reached double-figures. Afterwards, I popped to the wardroom to make a pint of tea (two bags, six sugars, touch of milk) and sat against the flight deck nets to recover in early evening tropical warmth before showering and dinner. Bliss!

Other folks did their own thing to maintain physical fitness. Several jogged around the upper deck, a few pre-breakfast, some early evening.

Others devoted themselves to heavy gym work, like Rattler Morgan clad in his familiar shorts, Gold's Gym black vest and red bandana.

15.4 Rattler in the gym
(Dave Olner)

On Saturday at sea, the afternoon was taken up with inter-mess sport on the flight deck. As explained in Chapter 10, five-a-side football, deck hockey, tennis, cricket and volleyball were played. Fierce rivalry prevailed, scores were settled on the 'sports field', particularly through football and deck hockey. Despite evident aggression and violence, there were no serious injuries, just cuts, grazes and bruised egos. And we were all shipmates again at the evening's flight deck barbecue.

We broke off the survey after completing the last line designated for this survey leg and headed to Maceio. Approaching from the north-east, we made landfall at Praia de Ponta Verde early on the morning of 16 December. Sliding south-west and paralleling the coast, we couldn't go too close for fear of scraping *Hecla* on several sets of rugged, low-lying patches of rock, interspersed with the natural pools of Piscinas Naturais de Ponta Verde, an environmental protection area.

Entry to Maceio was simple. We rounded the breakwater that formed the port, a wide turn to starboard to point south-east and go alongside in the sheltered basin on 16 December. Although primarily for SMP, it was an opportunity for wives/girlfriends to spend time with their menfolk for Christmas in Brazil.

15. Happy Hecla Again!   357

15.5 Christmas drinks in Senior rates Mess
(Mick Slater)

I don't recollect if any wardroom wives/girlfriends made the trip, but to save discussion, I volunteered for OOD on Christmas Day. I was used to being away at Christmas after four consecutive festive seasons in Blue Star. My first was Christmas Day 1980, transiting the Panama Canal on *ACT 5* (24212 ton cellular refrigerated container ship) and my last was on *New Zealand Star* (17082 ton refrigerated container ship) in Fremantle in 1983. In 1981 and 1982 I was mid-Atlantic.

We'd had a fortnight's SMP in Maceio in 1989 so Martin and I were familiar with the town and its beaches. It was still a relatively quiet, safe place.

15.6 Dickie, Martin, me in Maceio
(Mick Slater)

The port visit passed uneventfully, particularly my Christmas Day duty. We sailed on 28 December, fully rested and rejuvenated, but 'Jack' poorer in pocket and his liver further damaged by booze.

Leaving Maceio astern, I bade farewell to South America, Brazil in particular. With Blue Star, I first visited Brazil in late-May 1981 on *Benedict* (3636 ton general cargo ship), working cargo in Belém and Santana in the Amazon delta. In November/December 1981, *Rockhampton Star* (10619 ton refrigerated cargo ship) stopped in Rio, Santos, Rio Grande do Sol, Montevideo and Buenos Aires before returning to Rotterdam. More recently, I'd been in *Hecla* to Brazil in 1989. I very much enjoyed Brazil, particularly down the skids in Santos for nights in the Scandinavia Bar and Love Story, good, old-fashioned, whore-filled seamen's bars. Quaffing Antarctica while ogling beautifully tanned Brazilian girls at Copacabana and Ipanema beaches. A great place to live if you're wealthy, terrible if you're poor and live in a favela.

The survey legs continued in the same vein as the preceding ones. I suppose, yes, it was a dull, unexciting, repetitive experience, bimbling along either west or east for several days with nothing to see, surrounded by endless deep blue ocean. I very much enjoyed H-boat life and geophysical surveys. The weather was great throughout, with blue skies and bright sunshine.

Whole ship events were held on the flight deck on Saturday evenings at sea. These included film nights, barbecues, horse-racing night, games nights and, en route home, sods opera. In the tropical Atlantic, good weather and calm seas were virtually guaranteed. Following the inter-mess sports afternoon, a group of Senior and Junior Rates prepared the flight deck and a great evening ensued. Everyone intermingled, regardless of rank, rate or specialisation.

At every event, the 'Phantom Flan Flinger' made a fleeting appearance, clad in black cloak and balaclava, to land a 'flan' in someone's face and disappear into the night. Who was this mysterious figure? In the wardroom, our prime suspect was LMet 'Topsy' Turner, our weatherman. Topsy fitted the bill, being a day-worker, renowned for his keen sense of humour and sharp wit. Was it Topsy? Recently, Dusty revealed that the 'Phantom' wasn't Topsy. Each appearance was highly technical and planned in detail. After each hit, folks started to follow the 'Flan-Flinger' during his escape. To foil their efforts, Dusty was approached to act as a double. Despite everything, the 'Phantom Flan-Flinger' was never caught throughout this deployment or the next. For me, the 'Phantom's' mystique endures to this day.

15. Happy Hecla Again!

As the night wore on and, particularly, when every scrap of barbecued food had been scoffed, all hands joined in the clear-up operation. Folks had gradually started to slip away, especially those on middle and morning watches. By the time the first watchkeepers (2000–2359) came down, the flight deck was empty.

'Jack' was permitted three cans of beer per man per day. Each mess had a beer bosun who fetched the mess' beer ration from the canteen daily when piped. Beer was stowed in the mess beer fridge, padlocked and controlled by the beer bosun or killick of the mess. Not all sailors drank beer, not all sailors drank three tins daily. Cans accumulated in the beer fridge and, post-flight deck function, Saturday night morphed into 'party night' down below. Junior Rates' messes partied noisily for hours, beer fridge gradually emptied, general rough-and-tumble in the mess square, visits from/to other sailors' messes. Stokers in 2 Mess, S&S in 3 Mess, WEs and Comms sailors in 4/5 Mess. I gathered they were pretty raucous nights.

15.7 Saturday night in The Zoo
Dusty Miller horizontal across Artie Shaw, Spike Hughes, Mark Hossack, Emlyn Pearce
(Dusty Miller)

As Junior officers, we were warned never to go down to a Junior Rates mess for a beer. Guess what? Once there, a sprog Subby/Middy was ensnared with endless beers. The first one welcomed and drunk, a second one appeared. Before that was drunk, a third appeared. And so it went on, a pyramid of cans, full then empty, accumulating in front of the hapless Subby/Middy. Dangerous territory.

I went down to 1 Mess (Seamen and SRs) once in 1989 and had a couple of tins before excusing myself. This trip, Spike invited me down to 1 Mess (The Zoo). He handed me a beer. I drank it slowly and accepted a proffered second tin. After that, I bade cheerio to 'my lads' and climbed out of The Zoo despite their protestations. The lads were happy. I was happy to have chatted with them in their own home. They all knew I wasn't the world's biggest drinker and was resolute in getting out of 1 Mess alive.

Between each survey leg, there was a four-day port visit. *Hecla* arrived in Sekondi/Takoradi, Ghana, on 20 January. Embarking with the pilot was a Ghanaian Navy Sub Lt, designated as Liaison Officer for our visit. The pilot guided us onto a berth at the Naval Base, a corner of the commercial port. That evening, we held our cocktail party on board. The next evening the Ghanaian Navy invited us to a reciprocal cocktail party. It was in the wardroom, on the ground floor of Headquarters, Western Naval Command, a short walk from the wharf. They were generous, friendly hosts, welcoming us into their 'home'. A pleasant evening with copious G&T and smallie-eats.

The following morning, *Hecla's* rugby team (including me) boarded a coach and set off to Accra, Ghana's capital, to play a match. No one had any idea how long the journey would take, although we knew we'd be overnighting in a hotel in Accra. I may have been the only officer on this excursion, which put me in a dodgy position if anything went wrong, or we 'lost' someone, or someone got arrested. Despite the lads' background noise and chatter, I cat-napped for most of the 220km journey. From what I saw, whilst eating the packed lunch supplied by our chefs, scenery was mainly jungle on our left side, sea to the right and we passed through a number of small villages of basic brick or timber construction.

We arrived early afternoon at the venue, Accra's polo club. The polo pitch was a huge patch of grass with, nestled within its boundaries, a rugby pitch and posts. After our long journey, we needed a bit of a warm-up. We'd never played together as a team, so training was a bit chaotic. Some of the team were keen rugger-buggers. Barney, our fly-half or centre, had trialled for Gloucester's Cherry-and-Whites. Rattler was a hard, strong, scrum-half from Cumbria. Some had played a bit, others, like me, were rank amateurs.

It was a good, hard game against far better opponents and we were soundly beaten. The only bright spot was our scrummage in the second half near the opposition's try line. Rattler was hard up behind the scrum, urging on our forwards, and I was beside him. The ball squeezed out, Rattler picked it up and immediately passed it to me and I dived through a forest of legs to score our only try. As a winger, I was way out of position, so it was sheer luck to be in the right place at the right time.

We were advised to clean our skin burns from contact with the hard ground as it was impregnated with years of horse poo. This cleansing mitigated the high chance of infection.

After showering, the opposing team hosted us in the clubhouse. Much camaraderie, lots of food scoffed, much beer scuppered. Later, we checked in at the hotel, somewhere in Accra. As in much of Africa, it was exceedingly dangerous to go ashore on your own. We'd been invited to the US Marines' house for more beer. Back on the coach, in darkness, we were driven from the hotel to their compound and had a very beer-laden evening with gung-ho marines. They were part of the US Embassy's security and protection force.

Much later, we poured ourselves onto the coach and eventually retired to our hotel rooms. Departure was at 0800. Needless to say, not everyone was punctual. Barney, Rattler and others kicked those who were adrift out of their rooms. It was a very quiet trip back to Takoradi. Most were heavily asleep, but some stalwarts resumed beer-drinking and noisy banter at the back of the bus. We were back on board by late afternoon.

With hindsight, I'm astounded we survived unscathed. The journeys to/from Accra were the easy bits. In Accra we collectively had no idea where the Polo Club, our hotel or the US Marines' house were in the sprawling capital city. No injuries during the match. No one was lost. No one misbehaved or brought disgrace to *Hecla* or the RN. We returned, somewhat wrecked and dishevelled, but in one piece. Except that Barney's Ray-Ban sunglasses were stolen while we were playing rugby. He's never bought a pair since.

We left Takoradi on 24 January and our next port visit was Freetown, Sierra Leone. We arrived on 14 February, berthing at Queen Elizabeth II Quay, Freetown's port. Like Ghana, Sierra Leone was a former British colony and gained independence in 1961, four years after Ghana. Like many ex-colonies, Sierra Leone had a troubled history of political strife and civil war between factions vying for control and power. During our visit, the country was still in the throes of a nasty civil war. It was too dangerous to go ashore so we were confined on board for the four-day visit. I don't think we missed much at all. Viewed from the flight deck and bridge roof, Freetown looked a pretty crappy place. Fortunately, the gravity transfer and tie-in were successfully completed within the port's boundaries.

No one was sorry to leave west Africa astern when we resumed the survey on 18 February. We managed only another week's surveying until *Hecla's* fragile machinery state caused us to abandon the final survey leg. We slowly steamed towards Ascension, anchoring in Clarence Bay on 1 March. The advance leave party flew home and we weighed anchor on 2 March to head for Guzz.

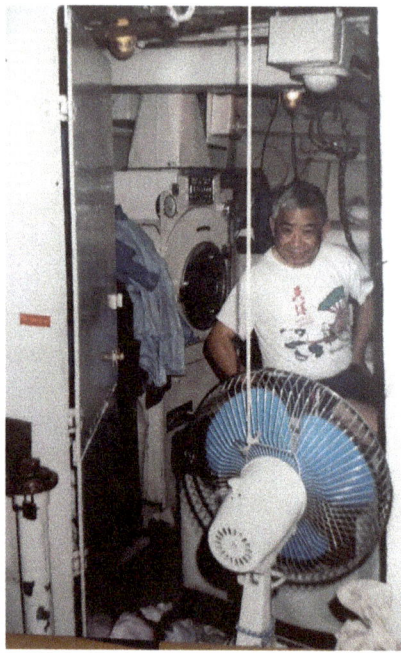

15.8 Jimmy Chan in his laundry

Although most folks on board were new faces to me, there was one very familiar character – Jimmy Chan the laundryman.

The RN had been enlisting Hong Kong Chinese laundrymen to dhobi and press uniforms and white table linen since the 1930s. Around 1950, the Admiralty ordered spaces in warships to be dedicated as permanent laundries. Laundry machinery was designed or procured from well-known manufacturers. Even a laundry school was established in HMS Drake. The whole process of washing, ironing and starching clothes very soon became a science and led to the appointment of a laundry officer, usually MEO. A 20-page *Laundry Manual* was published to ensure dhobying was done correctly.

RN frigates, destroyers, assault ships, cruisers and carriers had at least two Chinese dhobi-men embarked, the largest warships had four or more to cater for the larger ship's company. In *Exeter* we had two, one was 'Sew-sew' (tailor) who did any necessary sewing and also made/adjusted shirts, shorts and trousers. Usually called 'Number 1' and 'Number 2', laundrymen worked under a franchise-type agreement through a mysterious Hong Kong-based businessman known as 'King Dhobi'.

Chinese dhobi-men operated the laundry and charged ship's company for their service. Their laundry was usually squeezed into a tiny cramped unused space and they slept on their ironing boards, surrounded by steam irons and piles of dhobying. Their English was usually poor but they were always quick to complain if there was 'NO FL***ING STEAM!', without which dhobying ground to a halt.

I don't know how long Jimmy Chan had been in *Hecla*, but he was certainly there in late-November 1988 when I'd first joined *Hecla*. Most laundrymen stayed in the same ship for years. As a Deck Cadet in Blue Star, I sailed in two ships (*Rockhampton Star* and *Mandama*) with Chinese crew. All were mid-50s/early-60s and had been on board for years, sending pay home to Singapore or Hong Kong. On *Rockhampton Star*, Bang the Pantry Boy was at least 65. He shouted 'FEEESH, FEEESH!' when serving your fish dish or 'SKAMBO!' when he slapped a plate of scrambled eggs in front of you at breakfast.

Jimmy Chan was a living legend in *Hecla*, an honorary member of the Senior Rates Mess, a popular personality on board and allocated a bunk-space in Barney's 4/5 Mess. He rarely slept there, preferring, like most laundrymen, to kip in his cramped laundry. He provided a great service, but occasionally my white starched and pressed shirts and shorts were marred by the odd crushed button from Jimmy's steam press. I thought his prices were excellent. I couldn't be bothered dhobying socks and skiddies in my sink, so I added them to my dhobi-bag and its list of contents. Our monthly mess bill included payment of Jimmy's dhoby bill. CO, XO, SO and MEO paid Jimmy a lump sum on Chinese New Year. I think sailors paid cash on collection.

After an uneventful passage, *Hecla* transited Eddystone gravity range and anchored in Plymouth Sound on the evening of 16 March. The next morning, met by Capt H (Capt Rodney Browne), *Hecla* berthed at Slip Jetty. On 21 March, we cold-moved into 3 Basin for AMP and main leave was granted on 30 March. Intensive defect rectification and maintenance continued until 23 May, interrupted only by Cdr David Gregan relieving Peter Hobson as CO. I never saw Cdr Hobson again and was saddened to learn of his death in 2024. Another old shipmate gone too soon. RIP, Peter.

A week after my son, Nathaniel, was born, *Hecla* sailed to Pompey on 26 May to participate in Navy Days over the weekend of 28–30 May. At short notice, *Hecla* was tasked as Press Ship for the Spithead Royal Fleet Review as part of D-Day celebrations. Afterwards, we returned to Guzz.

I was sorry to see Martin leave the ship in July. We'd had some great times together in *Hecla*, previously in 1989 and now in 1993/94. His successor as XO was David Pretty. There was a turnover of wardroom personnel after our return from the Atlantic. New MEO (Tony Ford), Bosun (Ross Welburn), Schoolie (Sarah Marston) and Pusser (Andy Young) joined. Among the droggies, Dickie, Simon and Doug left, but Graham Mimpriss joined as NO, with Phil Newell and Mick McCafferty as H2s. Prior to sailing on our next deployment, a new MO (Dan O'Connor) pitched up. MOs were only embarked in H-boats for deployments.

On 5 September, Smudge Smith had a week's handover from Mick Slater as CPO(SR). It was great to see Smudge again as I'd last seen him in *Gleaner* in 1986. I was very sad to see Mick leave a week later, but delighted he was off to Loan Service in Oman, lucky chap.

Hecla sailed from Guzz for a week of shakedown, culminating in arrival at Portland on 11 September for a fortnight's intense OST under FOST's inscrutable eye. All went well, especially in my diving department. A killick bubblehead had been drafted in to run the ship's diving team, although I remained titular DivO. Mac (don't recall his name) went through the department, the team and the diving store like a dose of salts. He knew his stuff and, thanks to him, supported by my ship's divers, we passed FOST inspection in excellent shape. Importantly, my divers could maintain their currency during the deployment. Mac ensured there was a least one dive on the ship's hull at every port visit.

At Portland on 22 September, the living hell of sea training successfully negotiated, UKHO staff boarded *Hecla* to set to work ADL, Bell Gravimeters, GPS receivers and interface units. They remained on board until Gibraltar, providing guidance and continuation training to our largely new survey team.

Navstar GPS became operational in 1993, replacing the relatively primitive Transit satellite navigation system. GPS was the 'new thing'. From the outset, it was designed to provide two levels of performance. The more accurate was intended for use by US and allied military forces. A lower accuracy was available for civil users worldwide. Called selective availability (SA), it introduced deliberate errors into civil GPS signals. For our geophysical survey, we'd still use SINS but enhanced by GPS. But we'd also use P-code GPS instead of the SA version. Due to its high security classification, a US civilian embarked for the trip to babysit and maintain the system. It was all rather hush-hush.

There's plenty of information on the internet if readers wish to learn more about GPS history, development, how the system works and security aspects. Wikipedia is a decent starting point.

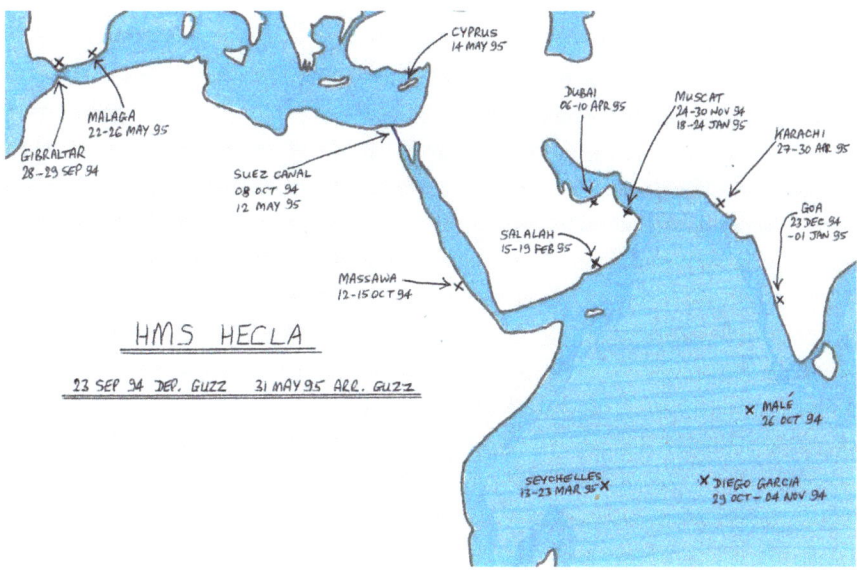

15.9 Indian Ocean deployment

On departure from Portland, *Hecla* transited Eddystone gravity range and steamed south-south-west across Biscay, rounded the north-west tip of Spain and altered course south, the coasts of Spain and then Portugal on our port side. Off Spain's extreme south-west point, we altered to a south-easterly heading and passed through the Strait of Gibraltar.

We paid a brief visit to Gib (28–29 September) where the UKHO staff disembarked. We continued eastwards through the Med to anchor off Port Said on 7 October. The following day, we transited the Suez Canal. I was always captivated by the Canal, its blue strip of calm water carved through the desert, Sinai to the east, Egypt to the west. No adjacent habitation on Sinai but, on the opposite bank, a narrow strip of green trees, crops and mud-brick-type villages, with the desert stretching far into the west.

Our southbound convoy anchored in the Great Bitter Lake to allow the northbound convoy to pass unhindered. During the Six Day War in 1967, the Canal was closed and blocked, reopening in 1975. For eight years, 14 merchantmen were trapped in the Great Bitter Lake, two each of

West German, Swedish and Polish, one French, Bulgarian, Czech and US, and four UK. One of the Brits was a Blue Star reefer, *Scottish Star*. Crews maintained ships' machinery state and cargo gear and helped each other out with spare parts and skills sharing. Nobody knew when the ships would be released so, initially, they were kept at short notice to move. As days, weeks, months, then years passed with no diplomatic progress, it was evident they were there for the long haul. Ship owners gradually reduced crew size to a minimum and rotated personnel. Some returned for another stint and received 'danger money' (about £20 per month) as artillery fire over the top of the ships was exchanged between Israelis on one side and Egyptians on the other.

Despite the uncertainty, crews formed their own 'United Nations', developed a community spirit and founded the Great Bitter Lake Association (GBLA). Sunday's 'church service' was used to place orders for victuals from other ships as the cargoes contained a wide variety of foodstuffs. *Scottish Star* had 6000 tons of Australian apples and pears, dried and canned fruits, casked wine, canned meat and 240 cartons of Swan lager (generously released by the consignee in London). On Monday, 'shopping' was collected. GBLA held a variety of functions and events, including regular sailing regattas using ships' boats. To coincide with the 1968 Mexico Olympics, GBLA held their own Olympics. GBLA's most well-known product was home-made, hand-crafted stamps, which were soon highly prized and sought after by philatelists worldwide.

15.10 Exiting Suez Canal
(UKHO Archive)

From early 1974 to mid-1975, a multinational operation cleared the mines and blockships to reopen the Canal. RN *Ton*-class minesweepers supported by *Abdiel* were among that force. On 5 June 1975, the Canal was reopened and the 14 trapped merchantmen completed their transits, some under their own power, others towed. Like some, *Scottish Star* and her cargo (except for the wool, which had increased in value) were written-off. She was quickly sold to some Greeks and laid up in Piraeus until she was towed to Spain (still in Blue Star livery) for breaking-up in 1979. Chapter 9 of Captain Sandy Kinghorn's *Before the Box Boats* describes his *Scottish Star* experience as Mate in 1968. *Stranded in the Six Day War* by Cath Senker narrates the full GBLA story.

By early evening, *Hecla* was steaming south, enveloped in Red Sea heat, humidity and sandy haze. After an uneventful passage, the ship anchored off Massawa on 12 October. We were the first RN warship to visit Eritrea since its independence from Ethiopia in 1993. Eritrea had a long, troubled history, ruled or occupied in succession by the Kingdom of Aksum, Ethiopia, the Ottomans, Egypt's Khedivate and eventually Italy from 1885. Italian troops spread out from Massawa towards the highlands, to create Italian Eritrea in 1889 until British Military Administration took over in 1942. A decade later, the UN General Assembly made Eritrea self-governing, with a local Eritrean parliament but federal status with Ethiopia for defence and foreign affairs. In 1961, Ethiopia annulled the Eritrean parliament and annexed Eritrea. A bitter, intense, 30-year war of independence yielded de facto independence in 1991, and de jure independence after a 1993 referendum.

15.11 Entrance to Massawa Port

When *Hecla* berthed in Massawa on 13 October, the visual effects of the war were obvious. The port was in a poor state, the majority of the city's buildings were bomb damaged and bullet ridden, many in a state of collapse and dereliction. Massawa was fought over by both sides during the independence war and was captured by the Eritrean People's Liberation

Front in a surprise land and sea attack in February 1990. This cut supply lines to the 2nd Ethiopian Army in Asmara. In retaliation, Massawa was mercilessly bombed from the air, causing considerable damage. Massawa port was inactive throughout the war and the authorities had a long hard slog to make it fully functioning again. Nevertheless, from what I saw, the people seemed cheerful and accepted the vast amount of work required to rebuild Massawa and their new country.

15.12 War-damaged Eritrean Navy vessels

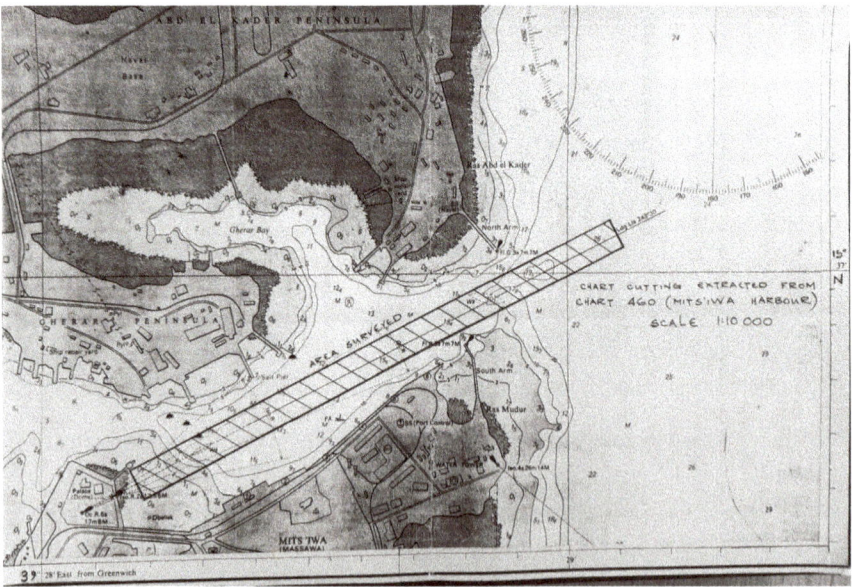

15.13 HI636 Massawa Harbour
(UKHO Archive)

15. Happy Hecla Again!

Luckily, I didn't attend the cocktail party that first evening, hosted by the Eritrean Navy. A couple of the wardroom suffered from 'the dog' for a few days afterwards. Mac McCafferty and I were occupied, with Smudge, Spike and others, in readying our SMB for HI636 Massawa Harbour, a sketch survey of the main channel into port. Preparations stretched into the night and she was ready for a dawn start the next day.

Mac and his crew toiled away for the duration of the port visit. Massawa is noted for mean average temperatures of 30°C (one of the highest in the world) and very high humidity, despite being a desert city. The combination of desert heat and high humidity made apparent temperatures more extreme. Little wonder Mac and his lads were permanently wilted and required constant rehydration. Despite climatic severity, SMB and survey kit worked satisfactorily throughout, including the newly-fitted Del Norte DGPS system. Fairing-up of survey records occupied them after we'd sailed from Massawa.

Shortly after dawn on 14 October, *Hecla's* football team embussed for the short journey to the naval base to play the Eritrean Navy. On site was a small grandstand with changing rooms beneath. Luckily, we were already in our kit and didn't use their primitive facilities. The pitch was sand, like playing on the beach, and very hard work. Even at this early hour, we sweated buckets. Fortunately, we had plenty of reserves so rolling substitutes were frequent. Our opponents were skinny Africans, some quite skilful, all fit and coped well with the weather and pitch. We won a hard-fought match and quickly scuppered the cases of beer brought along as refreshment.

15.14 Footie at dawn

Returning to *Hecla*, most rushed on board for a shower and into civvies as a battlefield tour was scheduled. Back on the coach, the drive through

Massawa was eye-opening. War's devastation was everywhere, roads littered with burnt out, destroyed tanks and armoured vehicles.

15.15 Destroyed tanks (top) and armoured vehicles (bottom) in Massawa's streets

Outside Massawa, we were in an empty desert environment, just the odd building dotted intermittently. The road climbed gradually into the hills and mountains surrounding Massawa's coastal plain. En route, we passed what looked like a war cemetery. I assumed it was Italian war dead, poor devils who fought, died and were buried in this barren, forgotten outpost of Mussolini's Italian Empire.

We reached a long ridge and the battle-scarred remains of an old fort. The coach halted and out we got. There was evidence of trenches plus destroyed tanks. The scene of a long-duration battle in the independence war. Wandering around, we found several skeletons still clad in tattered, weathered uniforms. It seemed so sad, no matter which side they were on, to be killed in battle and left to rot under fierce heat. We didn't have a guide, so we don't know the battle's story, date or duration. We clambered back onto the coach and returned to *Hecla*. An interesting day-trip. Thirty years later, I tried to locate the cemetery and the battlefield using Google maps but without success. I'm rather saddened by that.

15.16 Battlefield remnants (left); standing beside a destroyed tank (right)

On 15 October, we departed Massawa and pressed on southwards to and through Bab-al-Mandeb (Gate of Grief or Gate of Tears), separating Yemen on the Arabian Peninsula and Djibouti and Eritrea in the Horn of Africa. Heading north-north-east through the Gulf of Aden, leaving Socotra over the horizon to starboard and Yemen's coast to port, *Hecla* altered east-south-eastwards to Maldives.

A popular, expensive holiday destination, Maldives lies some 750km southwest of Sri Lanka and India. Its chain of 26 atolls stretches across the Equator from Ihavandhippolhu Atoll in the north to Addu Atoll in the south. Inhabited for over 2500 years, Maldives' history embraced, in turn, Buddhist and Islamist periods before succumbing to protectorate periods under the Portuguese, Dutch and, finally, the British. Independence was gained in 1965.

Hecla trundled through the archipelago from north to south. There was very little to see as the atolls were barely above sea-level. It was overcast throughout our transit, the permanently grey sky did nothing to enhance its appeal to a potential tourist. We anchored briefly off Malé, the capital, on 26 October to foster a spirit of cooperation with the authorities and gauge feasibility and scope for a future boat camp. Weighing anchor in late afternoon, *Hecla* continued further south, leaving Maldives astern, heading 750km to arrive at Diego Garcia on 29 October.

Diego Garcia, a British Indian Ocean Territory (BIOT) atoll, lies just south of the Equator in the central Indian Ocean, 3535km east of Tanzania,

1796km south-south-west of India's southern tip and 4723 km west-north-west of Australia's west coast. It's at the southernmost tip of the Chagos-Laccadive Ridge, a vast underwater mountain range, whose peaks of coral reefs, atolls and islands form Lakshadweep, Maldives and the 60 islands of Chagos Archipelago, of which Diego Garcia is the largest.

This disputed UK overseas territory is also claimed by Mauritius. In the 1970s, the native Chagossians (about 1000 workers contracted to the copra plantation) were expelled, to enable the island's use as a joint UK/US military base. Philippe Sands' *The Last Colony* details this sad tale of legalistic machinations.

Interestingly, Capt Roe DSC and *Vidal* carried out the original survey of Diego Garcia in June/July 1967. Horizontal control was set up from scratch, with geographical position and azimuth established from astronomical observations. *Vidal's* three SMBs (*Stork, Pike, Plumper*) and her other boats deployed daily by dawn and recovered around sunset.

Simultaneously, a nine-man USN Seabees team conducted a thorough engineering study of Diego Garcia to assess its suitability as a base.

Vidal was Roe's last RN sea-going appointment. A highly experienced droggy, including wartime service, he was the most senior RN Captain afloat at that time.

Surveying fully occupied *Vidal* during this 30-month commission, unhindered by general service activities as in today's warships. Ship's routines and surveying practices employed by Roe created an effective, highly efficient, close-knit and happy ship's company. According to a young Ian Austin (long-retired Lt RN and, at that time, *Plumper's* cox'n), our adage 'no day too long, no task too arduous' was never more appropriate.

In 1997, *Herald's* boat camp had a much easier time. Survey technology had improved tremendously. A GPS control station on the atoll was used. But inking-in the contours sheet took days as there were a myriad coral heads to draw around.

Several years earlier, CPO(SR) Mick Slater was based there for four months as sole member of 512 Specialist Team Royal Engineers, part of the US Defence Mapping Department. His role was to download satellite tracking data from the previous 24 hours and check what was tracked against what was predicted using an old Magnavox Transit system. Data was recorded on ticker tape and had to be received in the Florida data centre by 1200Z. Daily, Mick had until 1800 local time to get the data on ticker tape to Diego's Communications Centre for transmission. A cushy job except when, occasionally, the Communications Centre ripped the tape. So, he diligently stayed until transmission was confirmed in case he had to cycle back to his little office to pull off another run of ticker tape.

For the remainder of each day, he was free, mainly at the sailing club maintaining yachts in return for free yacht hire, snorkelling, evenings at the Brit Club and exploring the island. For New Year's Eve 1991, the command booked the Dallas Cowboys cheerleaders to fly in and entertain the troops. Alas, he missed it as he was tasked to remain in his office while the year rolled over in case of any atomic clock issues.

On our arrival, a Fleet Maintenance Group team were on the wharf, ready to get stuck into repairing defects to *Hecla's* main engines. The planned four-day visit was extended to six days, giving us extra days in what looked like paradise. Bummer!

Buffer and his lads erected awnings over the flight deck for the cocktail party. As start time approached the wind increased to gale force, breezing through gaps in the awnings, making it quite unpleasant. CO and XO moved the party down to the wardroom. A great effort by all hands ensured we were ready to receive our first guests on time.

Although it was a UK territory, the tenants (USN and USAF personnel) operated the port and air base. Diego Garcia's value was well-proven. An unsinkable aircraft carrier for B52 bombers during the Iranian revolution, Iraq's invasion of Kuwait and Operations Desert Fox, Enduring Freedom and Iraqi Freedom. It remains a key US presence in the Indian Ocean as a flexible forward military hub facilitating a range of offensive activities.

Naval Support Facility Diego Garcia provided base operating services to lodger units and logistic support to forward-deployed operational forces. USN operated a computer/telecommunications station. USAF units included Space Command and a global HF communications station. The lagoon was an anchorage for US Marine Pre-positioning Squadron Two, cargo ships filled with kit and supplies to support a large Marine force with tanks, armoured vehicles, munitions, fuel, spare parts and mobile field hospital. The runway was designated an emergency landing site for NASA's Space Shuttle, although never used in anger.

Overseeing the US presence was our NP1002. Commanded by a Lt Cdr, it had responsibility for Diego Garcia's civil administration and law enforcement. Its RN and RM personnel were tasked with policing, carrying out customs duties and formed a security detachment. It sounded like an idyllic six-month appointment for an old-and-bold Lt Cdr.

While the clankies sorted out engine defects, the rest of ship's company had a relaxed time on the 'Footprint of Freedom', as the Americans nicknamed the atoll. It was a decent walk from *Hecla* to 'Downtown', on the western limb of Diego. The road was lined with palm trees and scrubby grass. A thin soil covered coral bedrock. When we played NP1002 at football, care was needed as scratches and grazes from the coral subsoil caused infections.

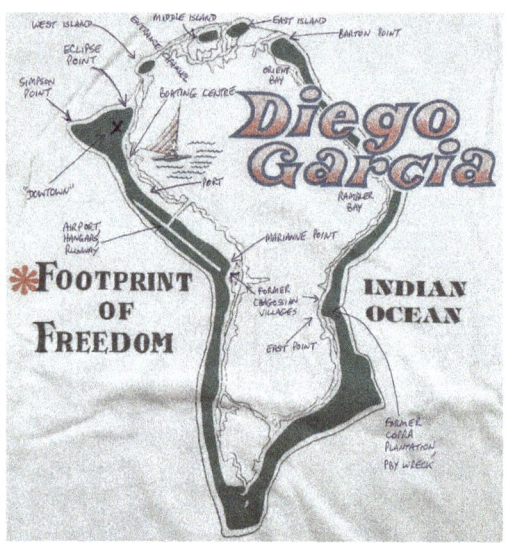

15.17 Diego Garcia

As expected in a US 'main street', there was a fast-food joint, ten-pin bowling alley, commissary, cinema and gift shop, where I bought an eski and a T-shirt (Fig 15.17). Thirty years later, we still use the eski and I wear the T-shirt at the gym, although it's rather tatty today. A well-equipped gym and softball/baseball pitches were nearby. Bikes were the most common mode of transport, tempting as the atoll's average height above sea level was 1.2m and attained a dizzy maximum of 6.7m.

US personnel were accommodated in decent-looking barracks and small villas on side-roads towards the ocean coast. There were also messes for enlisted personnel and non-commissioned officers. But the Officers Club had the enviable prime location at Eclipse Point on the north-west tip of the atoll. A single-storey building which, at the back, opened on a spacious veranda filled with tables and chairs to sit back and enjoy uninterrupted views of golden sandy beach and deep blue Indian Ocean. Even better, was scuppering sundowners watching the sky's ever-changing colours as the sun gradually dipped to, and below, the distant horizon. 'Jack' enjoyed the delights of the Brit Club, run and used by the few ex-patriate contractors.

As Sports Yeoman, Dusty Miller was responsible for confirming sports fixtures in port and was taken ashore to do so by a USN host. En route back to Hecla, they stopped at Brit Club, where they were preparing to host ships company later that evening. A very proud Yank serviceman showed Dusty dustbins full of a cocktail mix for selling to 'Jack' at $5 for all you can drink. Dusty explained it was a bad idea for several reasons: we'd been at sea for 23 days; two bins of cocktail were insufficient; the evening would end in tears. Unfortunately, the Yank didn't believe him. Fast-forward six hours, both bins where empty, it was only 2230 and a hefty number of sailors were present. Apparently, after some raucous behaviour, most of our sailors were escorted back to *Hecla* by the shore patrol. Luckily, no harm was done as the 'trouble' was smoothed over.

One day, we borrowed a small minibus to explore the atoll. Driving south, blacktop petered out to a hard-compacted sand/coral surface. The atoll's southern end was only some 100m wide, bounded by lagoon to our left and ocean to our right. Palm trees dominated on both sides, though not as dense as further north. Driving up the eastern arm, the atoll widened again, scenery unchanged (brown palm-tree trunks, green palm leaves, golden sand and blue water). We stopped occasionally to take photos of this desert island paradise.

We reached East Point and halted at the remnants of a copra plantation. A noticeboard showed the plantation's layout, indicating the use of these derelict buildings, the most impressive of which was the manager's office. Nearby, we came across a seaplane wreck.

15.18 Board showing plan of copra plantation in front of the manager's office

15.19 Flying-boat wreck and explanatory noticeboard
(Tony Jenks)

From February 1942 to April 1946, RAF Diego Garcia and a naval garrison were established. In September 1944, a PBY Catalina flying-boat left its home base of RAF Redhills Lake, Madras, bound for Diego Garcia where it would conduct search missions for a reported Japanese submarine. Unfortunately, the fuel bowser at Kelai, Maldives, sank in a storm, so refuelling wasn't possible. After another 10½ hour flight, the PBY landed at Diego Garcia. Running on fumes from empty fuel tanks, the pilot made it to the mooring buoy. Without beaching gear or undercarriage, it couldn't be pulled ashore. A cyclone blew in overnight. The Catalina, zero fuel and light in the water, bobbed around helplessly like a cork. Washed ashore, it collided with a palm tree which caused it irreparable damage. Fifty years later, we stumbled across her tattered, weather-ravaged remains.

Our extended stay at Diego was a delightful bonus. We left on 4 November and commenced HI636 with the standard east-west survey lines. On leaving Guzz in September, Graham (NO) saw no requirement for me (as Ops Officer) to do watches. Crikey, several months' day-work on a geophysical survey would drive me nuts as I knew I wouldn't be overworked. Insisting I was included, we agreed I wouldn't do afternoons or first dogs (I detested the former and missed circuit training with the latter), but would do weekend forenoons. We had enough OOWs to make this bastardised 1-in-5 routine function. Everyone was happy.

We arrived in Muscat on 24 November. Entry to Mina Qaboos was always a delight, ever since my first visit on *Mandama* in June 1982 to unload tons of frozen chickens. On *New Zealand Star*, we visited twice (6 November 1983 and 8 January 1984) to load/discharge containers – my last trip with Blue Star before joining the Navy. We had a brief three-day visit in September 1985 in *Exeter* on Armilla Patrol. Mina Qaboos was a quaint port with pristine concrete wharves and warehouses and fish souk tucked away in the north-west corner. Right ahead lay the curve of The Corniche, the coast road wound its way from the capital, Muscat, through Mutrah, to old Muscat city. Rising behind and high above the waterfront were precipitous cliffs and mountains.

15.20 Muscat, one of the world's most beautiful natural harbours (top); road winding its way from Mina Qaboos to old Muscat city (bottom)

It was a busy port visit as we landed a boat camp to survey Bandar Khayran, a large inlet 35km south-east down the coast from Mina Qaboos. It was a popular spot for ex-pats and Armilla Patrol warships' banyans.

Mac was in charge of the boat camp, ably assisted by Smudge, Spike and a small team of SRs, a pinkie and a stoker. Detached for a couple of months, there was considerable organisation to ensure Mac's team were fully equipped, stored and victualled to camp on the beach and SMB operational. The survey (Oman HI21b, Bandar Khayran) was undertaken at Oman's behest. Our team worked in cooperation with Royal Navy of Oman (RNO) surveyors.

Mick Slater, now on Loan Service to RNO, did much of the preparations for it before leaving *Hecla*. RNO had promised that its survey launch would actively participate but, sadly, it was in such a poor state it never joined the survey.

Camp was established on 28 November. Mick drove down to welcome them with a couple of cases of beer and to ensure the RNO surveyors were fully involved and *Hecla's* team behaved themselves. The survey was completed on 11 January, with a pause between 23 December and New Year's Day when our team moved into shore accommodation to continue data processing. Hecla's survey team were hosted by Mick and Cdr Steve Bennett (RNO Hydrographer) over the festive season. On Christmas Eve, Mick ferried them to his villa where they were royally 'fed and watered'. The evening went well and they returned to their accommodation late that night. Artie Shaw kipped on Mick's sofa after he'd drawn a fantastic sketch of a horse for Mick's youngest daughter.

15.21 Part of unspoilt Bandar Khayran

15. Happy Hecla Again!

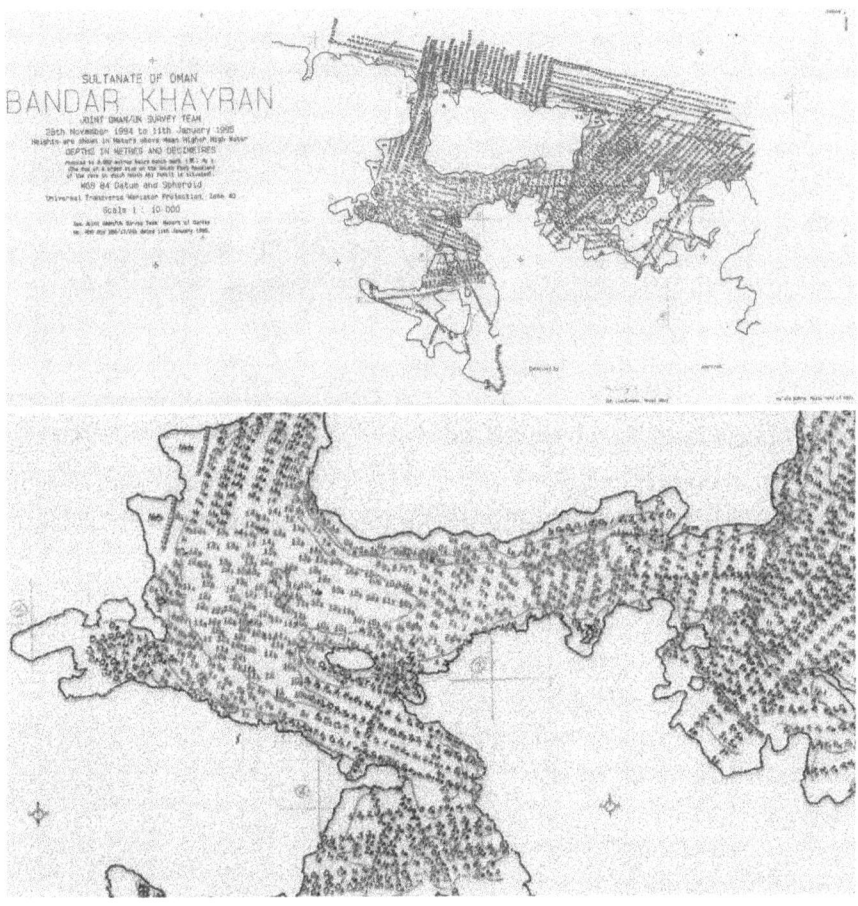

15.22 Extract of HI21b fair sheet (top); detail extract (bottom)
(National Hydrographic Office RNO archive)

In excellent weather, the survey area was sounded and full sidescan sonar coverage achieved. No wrecks or obstructions were found. All charted shoals and dangerous rocks were detected on sonar and one new shoal was found. The seabed away from cliffs and fringing rocks and reefs was flat and featureless mud. Maximum tidal stream was only 0.4kts. So, an unspoilt, beautiful, safe bay and surrounding beaches for ex-pats and warships' banyans to enjoy – mindful of stonefish lurking motionless on the seabed, whose venomous stings can be fatal.

We left them to it and resumed our survey, returning to Muscat on 18 January to recover a well-tanned boat camp team. Joint survey tasks with the Omanis had been a great success. We played rugby on both visits as Muscat's Rugby Club was one of the best in the Gulf, with some talented ex-pat players. Little wonder we lost both fixtures, although AB(SR) Brian Humphries was 'man of the match' in one game.

In the interim, *Hecla* had uneventful, successful survey legs and an SMP in Goa over Christmas. I volunteered as OOD on Christmas Day, pleasing my OOD colleagues. There wasn't much to see or do in Goa, except enjoy the beach, backed by bars for drinks and delicious Goan curry dishes. In Brazil, VW Beetles were built under licence and were ubiquitous taxis. In Goa, the equivalent was Hindustan Motors' Ambassador, fondly called 'King of Indian Roads', introduced in 1957 and based on the Morris Oxford. Another trip down childhood memory lane, recollecting it and its rival, the Austin Cambridge.

Further survey legs alternated with port visits to Salalah (15–19 February), Seychelles (13–23 March), Dubai (6–10 April) and Karachi (27–30 April). Salalah was the prime city in Dhofar province, Oman. It was still rather quaint and smaller than Muscat but gradually growing in size and importance. Mina Raysut, its port, was compact but developing, with new wharfage and warehousing. One of the berths was dedicated solely for the Royal Yacht Squadron. We'd noted the Royal Dhow *Zinat al Bihaar* in Muscat, but here we saw the Royal Yacht *Al Said* and her large support vessel *Fulk al Salamah*.

We'd rented a car in Muscat and toured around modern Muscat, old Muscat and up into the spectacular Hajar Mountains. Similarly, we hired a car to drive around Salalah and its environs, eventually getting up onto the jebel. We stopped for picnic lunch (take-away pizza and coke) beneath the shade of a frankincense tree and continued on to visit Job's Tomb.

15.23 Camels grazing outside Job's tomb

Seychelles was excellent for rest and recreation, much time spent on hotel beaches. As in Muscat, the rugby team played a match against locals and lost again, but post-match socialising was friendly and beer-filled. In Dubai, *Hecla* berthed at Port Rashid. I noted evidence of new building as Dubai surged towards its current state. It retained some charm when we were there, but change was definitely underway. Naturally, we bought fake designer polo shirts. In one shop, I asked the salesman if they were genuine fakes. His face lit up as he confirmed that, yes, they really were genuine fakes. I don't recollect anything about Karachi, but am sure it was still a hot, dusty, crowded, busy city with streets thronged with traffic.

After Karachi, we completed HI636 and started the long trip back to Guzz. 'Days to go' chits started appearing. Soon after we left Guzz on 23 September, somebody proclaimed we had only 251 days to go. I thought, 'Sad bastard. You're in the wrong job, matey!'

Through the Gulf of Aden, squeezing between Yemeni and Djibouti coasts at Bab-al-Mandab and northwards in the Red Sea. The weather was balmy, hot and humid, mostly hazy with sand in suspension. It's likely that the end-of-deployment Sod's Opera occurred – another great night for all.

15.24 Sod's Opera starring: 1 Mess; our own Supremes (4/5 Mess) and Village People (2 Mess Stokers)

At the top end of the Gulf of Suez, we anchored overnight off Suez before an uneventful transit of the Canal on 12 May. I was always captivated by the scenery and my good fortune to have experienced this several times. At Port Said, we dropped the pilot and the useless, lazy Suez Canal Authority lamp party. Emerging into the Med, we headed for Cyprus and anchored off Limassol for 24 hours.

Westwards through the Med, *Hecla* berthed in Málaga on 22 May. Its history spanned nearly 3000 years, one of the oldest continuously inhabited cities in Western Europe. Ruled, in turn, by Phoenicians, Carthaginiana, Romans, Visigoths, Byzantines and Moors, until Castile gained control. Our berth was directly below the old city centre, a short walk up the road to Málaga's many bars and cantinas.

One evening, we took the local metro along the coast to Torremolinos, only 13km and 20 minutes by train. I'd heard of it but never been. Sadly, it was as expected. Lots of beachfront and backstreet bars catering for those awful creatures, 'Brits abroad'. Watneys Red Barrel and fish-and-chips. Brits 'partying', euphemism for getting totally legless and spewing everywhere. We had a beer. The atmosphere was so appalling that, after less than an hour, I banged out and returned to *Hecla's* peaceful civilisation.

We sailed on 26 May, steamed past Gib and into the Atlantic. With good weather, slight sea and low swell, even Biscay was kind to us. It was a quiet few days before arriving off Guzz, espying the breakwater as we rounded Rame Head and then Penlee Point. Passing between the breakwater's western end and Fort Picklecombe, *Hecla* entered Plymouth Sound and anchored to clear customs.

15.25 Stan and Katrina, still together today
(Stan Baxter)

The next morning, families had been given the opportunity to go 'up harbour' on board. Among those reunited were Stan Baxter and his fiancée Katrina. She'd come out to Goa where Stan had proposed. They remain happily married.

We weighed anchor and steamed towards Smeaton Tower, rounded Drake's Island and, with Devil's Point close to starboard and Cremyll Point equally close to port, we continued up The Hamoaze. The Torpoint ferry graciously waited until we'd gone past. *Hecla* used tugs to enter 3 Basin and berthed to complete our successful and highly enjoyable, nine-month Indian Ocean deployment.

15. Happy Hecla Again!

15.26 1 Mess deployment T-shirt
(Willy Wilcock)

15.27 Entering 3 Basin

Easter leave was granted. An extensive AMP began and took us through to the first week of July. Life was relaxed and slow for those not involved in the defect rectification programme. It was a pleasant summer.

On 9 July, *Hecla* sailed for London. We rendezvoused with *Roebuck* and *Bulldog* on 11 July and headed up the Thames. The river snaked through the outskirts of London. On the north side, we passed Tilbury Container Terminal, where I paid off from *ACT 5* after my first trip to sea as a Deck Cadet. What a trip. I'd joined at Seaforth Container Terminal, Liverpool on

17 October 1980, went around the world, transited the Suez and Panama Canals, and arrived in Tilbury five months later, on 23 March 1981. Brilliant!

After passing through the Thames Barrier, the ships entered and berthed at West India Dock, in the shadow of Canary Wharf. The Survey Squadron (*Herald, Hecla, Roebuck, Bulldog, Beagle, Gleaner, Marine Explorer, Proud Seahorse*) was here to celebrate the Hydrographic Office's bicentenary. A full week of official visits, lunch parties, evening receptions and less formal entertainment ensued. Under the collective title of London 200, the week's centrepiece was a royal reception attended by HRH The Princess Royal and 120 VIP guests. The climax was a spectacular fireworks display during which the Band of the Royal Marines played a new march 'The Hydrographic', composed especially for the occasion.

15.28 Bicentenary fireworks at Canary Wharf
(UKHO Archive)

Beagle and *Hecla* opened to the public over the weekend. The Squadron sailed on Monday 17 July. To further mark our Bicentenary, we were all presented with a certificate from Hydrographer, Rear Admiral Essenhigh, the first non-droggy Hydrographer.

The Squadron bomb-burst from the Thames Estuary, to resume their survey taskings. *Hecla* steamed back to Guzz to commence her survey and docking period on 25 July. As this began, much 'emergent work' grew in size and complexity. This coincided with a change in XO as David Pretty shuffled out and Lt Cdr Richard Labone moved in. Richard was far more lively and outgoing, just the man to lead us through an increasingly more challenging docking and repair period. He was on top of everything, particularly badgering Guzz's 'dockyard maties', renowned for their slow and, dare I say, lazy, obstructive attitude. But they had the Navy and its warships by the balls, so it was a continual uphill struggle for ship's company. Sadly, Richard died of a heart attack during a cycling trip in the US in 2024. Another tragic loss and gone too soon. RIP, Richard.

15.29 Departing London, *Roebuck*, *Bulldog*, *Hecla* pass through the Thames Barrier (UKHO Archive)

On 29 August, Cdr David Lye superseded Cdr Gregan as CO and proved as good a bloke to work for as his predecessor. Cdr Lye quickly got to grips with *Hecla's* docking, ably assisted by Richard, with his month's head start on the growing package of work required to sort her out.

I was probably the last of the survivors of *Hecla's* final Atlantic trip and her first Indian Ocean deployment. *Hecla* was still being fixed when I left her on 10 December 1995. I'd had a great time and sailed with an excellent ship's company through the two deployments – my SRs, the QMs (Stan Baxter, Dean Hicks, Nobby Clarkson, 'PC' Constable, Ben Way and others whose names I just can't recollect) plus Barney and Rattler, naturally.

My survey department boys were competent and great fun to be with. It's tragic that Brian Humphries is another young man gone too soon. Most tragic news of all was the loss of Spike Hughes, whose death was a shock to all who knew him. Undoubtedly one of the fittest, most pleasant blokes I've ever met, Spike was highly respected in our droggy world. RIP, Spike.

After just over two years, it was time to move on from 'Happy *Hecla*'.

THE ADMIRALTY - Westminster

Presented to

Lieutenant **P J Carroll** Royal Navy
HMS HECLA

In commemoration of the
HYDROGRAPHIC OFFICE BICENTENARY
12th August 1995

NR ESSENHIGH, Rear Admiral
Hydrographer of the Navy

15.30 Bicentenary certificate

16.

A Dark, Miserable Period

16.1 *Beagle* crest

16.2 *Beagle*
(UKHO Archive)

After Christmas leave at home, I attended the Minor War Vessels CO/XO Designate Course in Pompey. Largely based in HMS Dryad, it comprised short courses in neighbouring 'stone frigates'. It was very civilised as it was mainly classroom instruction, except for getting hot, sweaty, exceedingly grubby, cold and soaked during the sea survival, fire-fighting and damage control courses at Phoenix.

On 13 February 1996, I joined *Beagle* in Guzz as XO. I was looking forward to this job as I felt I'd provide sound, solid support to the CO and run the ship. It was good to return to a CSV, treading familiar territory along passageways and up and down ladders, visiting all her compartments. As XO, I had my own cabin and scuttle and the same deep-brown, varnished mahogany fittings and furniture. *Beagle* was halfway through her refit, begun in November and programmed to end in mid-May.

I confess I didn't much like the CO but was determined to do my very best by him and for ship's company. But my entire appointment in *Beagle* was filled with frustration, disgruntlement, unhappiness and utter misery. I soon learned the CO's top priority in Guzz was to get ashore as soon as possible at the end of the day to commune with his girlfriend in town. Everything else could go hang.

But I had a decent wardroom. Lt Paul Bennion was NO, Lt Glyn Thomas and Sub/Lt Jon Holmes were H2s. I was Glyn's DO in Hawke sometime in 1990 and he'd taken over from me in NP1008. I'd last seen AB(SR) Jon Holmes when I joined *Hecla* in late-1988, shortly before he was drafted elsewhere. I was delighted to see Jon in his first job as H2. Our Pusser was a tall, well-spoken, redhead, Lt John Harris.

I'd witnessed in *Hecla* the general chaos of a refit/docking. *Beagle* proved the same. I attended, with my HODs, innumerable meetings with Devonport Management Ltd ('dockyard maties' in old parlance). These were very frustrating and annoying times as progress was snail-like, with more 'emergent work' suddenly announced. My HODs did their best as the work schedule continually evolved, often at short notice.

Despite our frustrations, collective hard work by ship's company meant various milestones were achieved during the remainder of February. There was pleasing progress in rebuilding main engines and generators. Survey kit (echo sounder 790, Navtex, Navstar GPS and Decca Navigator) was installed. In fact, *Beagle* undocked a day ahead of schedule on 27 February.

Throughout March, compartments were handed back to us to enable the ship's staff move on board to occur on 1 April, as planned. *Beagle* cold-moved to 3 Jetty to prepare for engineering harbour acceptance trials, but a strange noise emanating from the port gearbox, caused by poor meshing on a newly-fitted oil pump, delayed our programme by nearly a fortnight, preventing *Beagle's* participation in Pompey's Navy Days.

Into May, marine engineering harbour acceptance trials were completed, although the steering gear failed shortly after being accepted. Luckily, the fault was isolated and fixed. At last, *Beagle* put to sea on 9 May for sea acceptance trials. Essential milestones were attained: ready for sea date inspection (8 may), contract acceptance date (22 may) and operational date material assessment (28 May). The last meant *Beagle* was 'operational'. These events occurred in this strict order as warships emerged from refit and tiptoed back to the Fleet. I have no recollection of what they entailed for ship's company but they involved long hours for all, particularly cleaning and deep cleaning of every compartment.

The final event was *Beagle's* rededication at Slip Jetty on 31 May. We'd had visits and inspections by various important civilian and uniformed personages, but the rededication had lots of flag rank guests, notably guest of honour Rear Admiral Steve Ritchie CB DSC (former Hydrographer and husband of the ship's sponsor). Nine former COs of *Beagle* attended. The service involved three chaplains (representing CofE, RC and Church of Scotland), capped by music provided by the RM Band, Plymouth. Jon Holmes had moved on in early May, replaced by our RNZN exchange officer. He'd rightly refused to perform a haka at the rededication, despite the CO's persistent pressure. After this intense period, we looked forward to getting to sea and taking in hand survey tasks.

Beagle settled into a short period of surveying flag officer sea training's exercise areas (HI637 Western Approaches to the English Channel) before returning alongside for an AMP from 24 June to 15 July. It never ceased to confound me that after an extensive refit and returning to operational status, warships invariably had to return to base port so soon for defects that emerged after a few days at sea. It certainly wasn't like this in the MN, where I'd done typical three-week dry-dockings on three different ships after which we resumed trading.

During July, Paul Bennion left, Colin Thomson joined as NO. Sub/Lt Pat Mowatt joined as 'makie-learnie'. I liked Pat, he was a strapping, jovial Yorkshireman, enthusiastic to learn about droggying. Alas, occasionally, his big banana fingers were just too large for the keyboards to cope with, resulting in survey system 'crashes', but he was a good lad.

Summer leave filled August and then our focus was on intense preparation for OST. We returned to surveying from 29 August to 6

September, followed by a week's sea/harbour shakedown. Everyone worked their socks off to ensure *Beagle* was ready for OST. I certainly 'put the hours in' as it was to be a predictably very busy period. I'd been through OSTs in *Fox* and *Hecla* and hated every minute. The dreaded Staff in green foulies taking over the ship, running amok, causing mayhem with their sudden exercises. 'Training, not testing' they refrained. That was never our collective impression. Then our clean-up and stowing of kit that followed, readying ourselves for the next serial.

After the initial staff sea check, where all departments' paperwork and admin was thoroughly audited and checked, *Beagle* was day-running for the remainder of the period. OST culminated in the final inspection by Flag Officer Sea Training himself. It was a great relief when it ended on 27 September. *Beagle's* overall performance was assessed just satisfactory. I don't recall the exact 'ins-and-outs' but the upshot was that I was to be replaced. The CO, who I'd increasingly loathed and detested, wrote me a complimentary 'flimsy', praising my proactivity in managing *Beagle*, promoting a safe, corporate and harmonious environment and effective management of personnel, getting the most from a small team. It's a pity this didn't seem evident during OST.

Despite the shocking news, I chose to remain on board until my relief, Gary Brooks, parachuted in. It was neither fair nor honourable to shuffle off immediately, leaving Gary to inherit a pot-mess.

In recent years, I've learned from old droggies at the now-annual Survey Ships' Reunions in Guzz, that there was a quiet, furious reaction to news of my departure. Representations on my behalf were made to Captain H by at least one CO against this harsh decision. Alas, such protestations and sympathetic support (for which I'm extremely grateful since learning of them three decades later) were to no avail. Captain H refused to argue or support my case. So, that was that. Here ended the darkest, unhappiest, most dismal episode of my life and career.

What happens next, I wondered.

17.

A Happy Interlude

17.1 *Scott* crest
(Nick Barwis, www.jackstaxi.net)

17.2 *Scott*
(Michael W Pocock, www.MaritimeQuest.com)

After telephone discussions with the Appointer (fortunately, my old shipmate Martin Clegg), I joined *Scott* on 14 October 1996. The only vessel in her class, she was being built by Appledore Shipbuilders. I believe she was the largest ship the yard had ever built. At 13500 tons, 131m long, 21.5m in the beam and 8.3m draught, *Scott* was the largest ocean survey ship in the western world. Her twin Krupp 9-cylinder diesel engines powered a single shaft with a controllable-pitch propeller yielding a speed of 18kts. In addition to typical navigation and survey systems, she'd be fitted with SASS IV (Sonar Array Sounding System) multibeam depth-sounder. This monstrous bit of kit comprised a longitudinal and a transverse transducer. Separated by several metres, they formed a T-shape on the keel and explained *Scott's* seemingly improbable length.

While *Scott* was under construction on the north Devon coast, she was 'manned' by a small crew led by Cdr Vaughan Nail, assisted primarily by Lt Jim Davies (MEO) based in Captain H's swanky new office building in Morice Yard, between North Yard and South Yard.

Originally No.5 Colour Loft, it was built in 1840–1850 of limestone ashlar with granite designs and a slate roof, capped by a small bell tower on the inland end of the roof ridge. Its three storeys each had seven windows along the long sides and three windows at each end. Internally, the building had been gutted and refurbished, retaining its high ceilings, yielding bright, airy offices. The ground floor was occupied by the survey equipment store, managed initially by a WO(SR), later by CPO(SR), and a couple of civilian storemen. A notable addition to this Grade II listed building was a glass porch, rumoured to be bulletproof, costing some £30000–£50000.

17.3 Capt H's offices and glass porch (left); overlooked by Capt H's residence
(Historic England)

Behind this building and up a couple of long flights of stone steps was a magnificent terraced building. Originally a row of five houses and stables

17. A Happy Interlude   393

for the Dockyard's Officers, dating back to 1720–1724 but reconfigured many years ago as offices and houses, one of which was allocated as Capt H's residence.

Vaughan welcomed me 'on board' and I settled into a support role, grandly self-styling myself XO. Our days were reasonably relaxed and not fraught with problems. Vaughan and Jim dealt directly with the shipbuilders via phone, fax and email. Depending on significant stages in *Scott's* construction, we had day trips to Appledore for meetings. These increased in frequency as *Scott* neared completion.

The shipyard was founded in 1855 on the Torridge Estuary, with Richmond Dry Dock added in 1856. Since then, over 300 ships had been built at Appledore. During World War II, the yard built numerous Fairmile B motor launches and Fairmile D motor torpedo boats. Other vessel types included bulk carriers, LPG carriers, superyachts, ferries and oil-industry support vessels. Our survey ships *Echo* and *Enterprise* were also built there in 2002. More recently, Appledore constructed bow sections of our aircraft carriers and two patrol boats for the Irish Navy.

Scott was built in large sections, under cover, subsequently welded together to form her hull. She gradually took shape and looked increasingly large, dominating the entire shipyard. It was a momentous day when we witnessed the 500-odd ton accommodation block being lifted, manoeuvred and positioned at the aft end of the hull. Now *Scott* looked like a ship.

As she evolved, so a trickle of crew were drafted in, initially mainly Senior Rates. Backfilling of sailors and junior officers occurred a bit later. Our space in Capt H became increasingly crowded. Despite not having a ship as such, there was plenty for the new bods to do. *Scott* was built to a commercial design and standards so most of her kit was off-the-shelf, civilian-sourced, rather than from naval stores. This included life-saving kit, lifeboats, life rafts, cranes and davits. Vaughan tasked me to investigate exactly what civilian courses and 'tickets' our crew required. With my MN experience, I knew where to go and who to contact. The task occupied me fully for the remainder of my time in *Scott*.

In late-1996 or early-1997, *Scott* moved from Appledore to Pompey for fitting-out in dry dock. Meanwhile, we 'lifted-and-shifted' to more expansive office space beside the dry dock in Pompey. 'Manning up' continued. Life was fairly busy as I was continually sorting out courses, but we always made time to attend lunchtime circuit training at the gym. Living in Nelson wardroom made life easy, too. On Fridays, I got a lift home to Plympton with Lt Ben Ripley in his VW Golf, who picked me up on Sunday evenings to return to Pompey.

Not long after settling into our Pompey offices, Bob Mark took command as a shiny new Captain. It was great to see him again. Vaughan shuffled down to become de facto XO, so I assumed the title of Ops/Training Officer.

Scott took shape internally. She was impressive to view from the top of the dry dock as well as looking up at her from the dock's bottom. Crossing the gangway onto the upper deck, I was in familiar territory as she looked exactly like a merchantman. With accommodation aft, surmounting the engine-room and steering-gear compartment, her uncluttered foredeck stretched into the distance to the fo'c'sle and its foremast. What was missing were hatches, MacGregor hydraulic folding hatch covers, mast houses, cranes, derricks and their associated wire-rope rigging with swivels and cargo hooks.

Her accommodation was luxurious for a warship. Junior Rates were paired in en suite cabins, Senior Rates and officers had single en suite cabins. CO and XO each enjoyed a spacious day-cabin, bedroom and en suite facilities. The respective messes were equally capacious. The wardroom had a large anteroom and dining room. The latter's table was impressively long, for which Bob wanted an appropriate silver centrepiece. I think he largely did all the donkey work himself, resulting in delivery of a magnificent silver sculpture of Captain Scott and his four companions hauling their sledge fatefully towards the South Pole, mounted on a huge wooden base. Exquisite.

17.4 *Scott's* silverware table-piece
(Bob Mark)

With the onset of summer, *Scott* gradually became fully manned and, at some point, she would exit the dry dock, get alongside and be commissioned into the Navy. Much planning and administration went into this important ceremony. Naturally, the Ship's Sponsor (Carolyn Portillo) was guest of honour. We joked that husband Michael would accompany her as he was 'unemployed' after Labour's recent landslide General Election victory. He'd be grateful for a free lunch, we opined. Still, he hasn't done too badly since with his excellent railway journey and travel documentaries.

My happy days in *Scott* were almost up as Martin Clegg had ensured my next appointment was secured. I went off to do a trio of instructional and training design courses at HMS Excellent to prepare for the job.

I left *Scott* for summer leave at home. There was much to do as we were going overseas. I was appointed to Loan Service, Royal Navy of Oman, in charge of the Hydrographic Training and Processing Unit. We were all terrifically excited. Oman was the first of three brilliant consecutive overseas jobs, the start of two decades of service in foreign navies.

18.

Postscript

My story has focused on the blokes with whom I joined the RN and sailed with when under training and in the Hydrographic Survey Squadron, as well as on the ships in which I served. What happened to my old shipmates? Since returning from a decade in Australia, I've traced many of them via Facebook or 'word of mouth'.

18.1 Reunited with Monty in his boatshed (left); we haven't changed a bit since summer 1984

I lost track of the majority who joined BRNC in April 1984. On OOW Course, we were deeply saddened to witness Monty, my erstwhile cabin-mate in Hawke, resign and disappear out of the main gate in his red MG. During 2020, I'd made contact with Monty and, in October 2021, we met at his workplace. He'd resumed his former trade as a boatbuilder and director of Avon Boating, Stratford-upon-Avon. He's now Managing Director, has a larger fleet than the RN and has completed the electrification of his boats. He restores heritage boats for a hobby. As with every one of my old shipmates, that first sight and hand shake after so many years was emotional. But then we pick up conversation as if we'd last met a week ago rather than 40 years ago. The bond created decades ago is unbreakable. It was brilliant to meet his lovely wife, Patty, too.

I've met up with Martin Jones, Jamie McMichael-Phillips and Traps Doolan from our BRNC days. Martin and Jamie became droggies. Martin commanded *Quorn* (*Hunt*-class MCMV) and *Echo*, Jamie was CO *Beagle* and *Scott*. Both retired as Captains. Completely unexpectedly, I met Traps in Darwin on a joint naval exercise and, when Lynne and I took a holiday in New Zealand, we met up with Traps and Julie on Auckland waterfront. He'd laterally transferred to the RNZN about the same time as I did likewise to the RAN. Traps commanded HMNZS *Endurance* and retires shortly.

In the last year or so, I re-established contact with my old tennis partner at BRNC, Mark Allibon. After qualifying as a PWO, he commanded *Quorn* and retired to the golf course a few years ago. It took us a year to coordinate our diaries until he and Caroline stayed with us in July 2024, but well worth the wait.

Many Staff Officers at BRNC 40 years ago had distinguished careers, attaining high rank. Andy Wilmett (my DO after DTS) and Richard Clapp (our Tennis Officer) are retired Commodores. Andy went on to command *Edinburgh* and served as Commander British Forces Gibraltar, succeeded by Richard in December 2001, who'd previously commanded *Starling* (in Hong Kong) and *Westminster* and was Commodore Minewarfare and Patrol Vessels Diving and Fishery Protection.

18.2 With Paddy Watson (left); with Bob and Wendy, BRNC in background (right)

18. Postscript

I was always intrigued as to what happened to Paddy Watson, my original DO, an officer of impeccable standards. After BRNC, he commanded *Amazon* and served in NATO's Naval Forces Southern Europe HQ, Naples, completing his career as our BNA in Brunei to retire as a Captain. He'd served as a patrol boat CO in Oman in 1979–1980. I tracked him down as I organised a reunion of Brits who'd served in the Omani Navy and invited him. It was exactly 40 years since I'd first met him. He'd mellowed and was on good form but no mistaking Paddy. He recollected me and we had a great chat about Dartmouth days.

My prime mentor throughout my career was Bob Mark, my class' nav instructor at BRNC and with whom I served in *Gleaner*, *Fox* and, briefly, *Scott*. He, too, had a brilliant career. Without doubt, the best Hydrographer of the Navy we never had. On retirement as Rear Admiral, Bob pursued a successful career in management consultancy, running projects in business strategy, project management, organisation design, logistics and enterprise resource planning IT implementation. In addition, he's devoted several years as a National Council Member of the National Trust and the last seven years on the Board of Trustees of the South West Coast Path Association. Since Lynne and I returned from Australia, we've frequently enjoyed Bob and Wendy's excellent company. Neither have changed a bit over all these years and they're our closest friends.

Post-BRNC, I had a year's fleet time, first in Rosyth in *Gavinton* and *Brinton*. I don't know what happened to anyone in *Brinton*, except Simon Wall's tragically young death. What of *Gavinton's* officers? Sadly, Robin Swaine (XO) died several years ago, but Bernie Bruen (CO) is still going strong. Richard Farrington (GO) and Alistair Halliday (NO) retired as Commodores. Richard's career wasn't overly-blighted by *Nottingham's* grounding on Wolf Rock, off Lord Howe Island in the Great Barrier Reef in July 2002. As CO, Richard reportedly took full responsibility for the incident. Three other officers were also court martialled. Alistair was CO *Bridport* (*Sandown*-class MCMV), *Edinburgh*, *Manchester* and *Campbeltown*.

It's 40 years since my time in *Exeter* and the truly fantastic Armilla Patrol deployment, six months up the Gulf. It took a while, but I finally contacted Neil via the Fleet Air Arm Officers Association. In October 2021, Lynne and I had a week's holiday in Dorset and met Neil and Rachael for dinner at a pub in Piddlehinton. It was brilliant to see him again, just like old times. He'd had irregular contact with Kieran, who had contact with Max.

It wasn't until February 2024 that we finally reunited for lunch at the Naval & Military Club, London. We got on like a house on fire, spinning dits from our wonderful time in *Exeter*. Neil became a helo pilot, serving with distinction, and commanded *Cromer* (*Sandown*-class MCMV). Neil's last RN job was at Defence Procurement involved with unmanned aerial vehicles. This led to a successful second career in this field and he is Director, Business Development of Vienna-based Schiebel, a renowned manufacturer of camcopters, drones and mine detection equipment. Max pursued his Pusser's career with a mix of appointments at sea and ashore (including Cdr S, BRNC), retiring as a Commander. Kieran completed his eight-year commission and was then the RNLI's Inspector of Lifeboats and Operations Manager at Nowcasting Weather. Combined with his naval experience, Kieran had a career in project management, team building and problem solving before establishing twin companies. One guides companies through the internationalisation process, the other provides cutting-edge metocean solutions in oil, gas, offshore wind and coastal ventures. He's lived in Brazil for many years. It was the longest but undoubtedly best lunch I've ever had. Exhausted, I slept deeply on the train back to Exeter.

18.3 Exeter's OUTs reunited – Kieran, me, Max, Neil, Feb 2024

18. Postscript

2025 marks the 40th anniversary of our *Exeter*/Armilla experience, so we're organising a wardroom reunion in Pompey. To date, we've traced and contacted most and they're all onside to attend. Sadly, we've lost Mark Rowledge (PWO(U)) through cancer several years ago. Roger Endersby (Pusser) died more recently. Captain Tolhurst (our hero) had a fine career, commanding *Invincible* and serving as Flag Officer Sea Training and Flag Officer Scotland and Northern Ireland, retiring as Rear Admiral. John became senior military officer at the Defence Export Services Organisation. He was a RNLI trustee for many years and is honoured to be a Vice President, appointed by the Trustee Board as a mark of special recognition of service to the RNLI.

Most of the other officers attained Commander or higher rank. Chris Durbin, my mentor for divisional work, moved on to a new career in the US with his American wife. Since returning to UK, he's written a 16-book series of historical seafaring fiction around our conflicts with the French in the middle years of the 18th century, centred on his protagonists Captain Carlisle and protégé, Holbrooke. And they're jolly good stories, too.

As a droggy, I sailed with so many great characters. I don't know what happened to them all. From *Fox*, Steve Shipman (CO) retired and held an important post at the International Hydrographic Organisation, Monaco for many years. Trevor Horne (NO) commanded *Gleaner* and *Bulldog*. He wangled a trip up the Rhine to Basel in *Gleaner*. Richard Dobson (H2) retired after Loan Service to Oman as RNO Hydrographer. A couple of years after our Long Course, Rob Lawson (Coxswian) commanded *Gleaner* and retired to serve as Ilfracombe Harbour Master for many years.

Of my *Hecla* shipmates, Graham Turnbull commanded *Roebuck* and retired as a Commander to live deep in rural Shropshire. Mark Higgins, like many ex-droggies, pursued a successful career as an offshore surveyor. Martin Clegg (NO in 1989, XO in 1993-94) served until his retirement and enjoyed a successful follow-on career in the RNR.

18.4 With Graham, Oct 2021

Bob Eadie (my CO, NP1008) completed his full career commission, then went offshore and established himself as an expert in rock dumping. In fact, his book on this niche topic is a best seller. Brilliant, Bob.

Pat Mowatt, my 'makie-learnie' in Beagle, enjoyed a successful career. He commanded *Enterprise* and *Scott* and was promoted to Captain. In late 2024, he laterally transferred to the RAN. Well done, Pat. A good move.

But, never mind all these officers, what about my sailors? I have an immense fondness for my old ABs and killicks. Having sailed with them for years and had many interesting conversations and innumerable laughs on long, quiet night watches, I've been intrigued about their subsequent careers, in and out of the RN.

In October 2019, Lynne and I attended a weekend reunion in Chester organised by the Survey Ships Association. It seemed a good means of re-establishing contact with old shipmates. Many attendees were of an older era than mine. I was, however, thrilled to spend Saturday evening with Mick Slater, Steve Hawes and Daz Wake, undoubtedly my favourite trio of retired WO(SR)s. Brilliant!

18.5 Surrounded by Steve, Daz and Mick, Oct 2019

I've found and 'friended' a number of my old SRs on Facebook. From *Fox*, Steve 'Sticky' Page owns a driving school and sponsors his local football club, Watchet Town. From *Fox* and *Hecla* 1989, Pete 'Spunky' Seed matured and left the RN to work at Bristol Docks. He frequently posts beautiful photos of views from his 'office'. Mark Hossack is a successful estate agent in the Home Counties. Others have pursued a variety of careers since the 'Mob'. The majority moved into the offshore industry as surveyors, party chiefs, client reps and achieved much. Dusty Miller is a typical example. He left as CPO(SR) and works as party chief for Fugro. Lynne and I were delighted when Dusty and Sarah visited us for lunch.

18.6 With Dusty, Sep 2021

Sadly, I have no idea how my general service QMs have fared. I know Rats branch-changed to SR, but whatever happened to Skip, Abes, Bob from *Fox*? Or Oz, Brummie, Steady Eddie, George, Pusser and others from *Hecla* 1989? CPO Stan Baxter retires shortly from the RN, but what of the other QMs from *Hecla* 1993–1995? I sincerely hope they're all OK, out there somewhere in the real world.

Rattler Morgan is another of my Facebook friends, retired and returned to his native Whitehaven, Cumbria. Gary Barnard is a fine example of an ex-sailor 'done good', in fact brilliantly. It was clear to me he was a bright boy in *Hecla* 1993–1995. When he left the 'Mob', he gained a BSc Electrical Engineering at Portsmouth University and launched into the offshore world with a series of good posts with Schlumberger. Now, resident in Houston, Texas, he's OneSubsea's regional manager for North and South America. Well done, Barney.

Mick Slater organises annual survey ships reunions in Guzz. His WhatsApp group has increased to 300 or so, the reunions attract 150+ folks. Some are deeply sorry they can't make it due to work commitments. But for those present, it's full-on lamp-swinging and dit-spinning. There's no rank, we're all there together. In this way, our droggy community continues despite the passage of years and the shocking, depressing absence of survey ships in today's RN fleet.

Yep, I'm intensely proud of my service as a droggy and equally proud to be a member of this group of old boys. Mick's WhatsApp group is a thriving community where old shipmates meet and spin dits of the 'good old days'. Long may it continue.

What about my ships? Like any seafarer, I retain affection for every ship I've sailed in, curious as to their lives after I'd moved on. In my previous volume *Under a Big Blue Star*, I described the tragic scrapping of *ACT 5, Benedict, California Star, Rockhampton Star, Mandama, Starman Anglia* and *New Zealand Star*. Heart-breaking.

In 1985, *Fearless* decommissioned for three years prior to a two-year refit in Guzz, recommissioned in 1991. For the following four years, she formed part of the Dartmouth Training Squadron. Finally decommissioned on 18 March 2002, *Fearless* awaited disposal in Fareham Creek, moored and mothballed alongside her sister-ship *Intrepid*. In October 2007, *Fearless* was to be scrapped in Belgium. On 17 December 2007, she was towed to Ghent to be broken up, the first warship successfully exported for recycling by any Western government, complying with international agreements and principles of environmentally sound waste management.

After about six months in the Stand-By Squadron, *Gavinton* paid off on 12 December 1986 and was broken up by Brugse Scheepssloperji, Belgium, on 14 October 1991. *Brinton* had a longer career. In October 1987, she served in the Fishery Protection Squadron but returned to 3rd MCM Squadron a couple of years later. On 14 April 1991, she transferred back to fishery protection. *Brinton* and *Sheraton* were the last *Ton*-class to leave Rosyth on 21 September 1993. A very sad day for all former *Ton*-class personnel, to be replaced by those new-fangled *Hunt*-class 'plastic' MCMVs. *Brinton* paid off on 5 October 1993 after 30 years' service and languished, until eventually sold to Pounds Shipbreakers, Pompey, in January 1998 where she was broken up.

18. Postscript

Exeter continued in service well after I left her in late-1985, participating in the 1991 Gulf War. Commanded by Capt Essenhigh, later the first non-droggy Hydrographer of the Navy, she provided air defence to USN battleships bombarding enemy positions. After an extensive refit, *Exeter* completed another Armilla Patrol from September 1999, spending the Millenium in Dubai, until March 2000. As the last remaining RN warship in commission to have served in the Falklands, *Exeter* starred in the 25th anniversary Falklands War commemorations in Newquay. In May 2008, she visited London to provide the centrepiece for the launch of a new James Bond novel the day before its release. A speedboat brought copies of the book up the Thames for a party in *Exeter* as two Lynx helos circled the ship. On 30 July 2008, *Exeter* was placed on 'extended readiness' at Pompey, until her decommissioning on 27 May 2009. She was put up for sale by auction on 28 March 2011. With *Nottingham* and *Southampton*, she was towed away to be scrapped at Leyal Ship Recycling, 60km north of Izmir, on 23 September 2011. *Glasgow, Newcastle, Cardiff* (2008), *Gloucester* (2014), *Edinburgh* and *York* (2015) met the same sad, ignominious fate.

18.7 *Exeter* at ship-breakers, between *Invincible's* remains and a ferry
(Ships Nostalgia)

Exeter's ship's bell is on display in Exeter Cathedral. Exeter Flotilla, an association of RN and RM veterans living in and around Exeter, holds an annual Trafalgar Day service in the cathedral. *Exeter's* bell is repositioned as the centrepiece for the service commemorating Nelson's famous victory at Trafalgar in 1805.

BRNC's dreadful 'vomit comets' *Sandpiper* and *Peterel* remained in the Dart until they were paid off in the mid-1990s. I don't know what happened to *Peterel*, but *Sandpiper* was bought by a Dutchman.

What became of our Survey Squadron's graceful ships? The Hydrographic Office bicentenary celebrations marked the beginning of the end. It was probably the last time that our eight surviving survey ships gathered together, before decommissioning in the following handful of years.

Gleaner carried on with her outstanding harbour and inshore surveys of our Naval Bases and around UK and Europe. She decommissioned on 16 February 2018, after 35 years' service. Stored ashore at Gosport, she was refloated a year later and her survey suite removed. Defence Equipment Sales Authority invited expressions of interest for her purchase. Despite a price tag of £40000, there was no interest by the closing date of 13 July 2019. I subsequently discovered that she was bought. Her new owner took her out of the water to be surveyed but decided to sell her instead of getting her 'classified' with Lloyds. A sad end for a hard-working survey boat.

I left *Fox* in late November 1988. She decommissioned in February 1989. Mick Slater was on board until the end and relates being introduced to the then-Prince Charles three times in one day. In the 1970s in the West Indies, Charles was an OUT in a frigate but spent a brief time in *Fox*, surveying in the area with *Fawn*. In early 1989, *Fox* visited London and Steve Shipman (CO) invited Charles onboard. As Coxswain, Mick and the QM piped him up the gangway and introduced him to Charles. As HRH proceeded between decks, Mick sprinted round the port side, into the chartroom via the aft door, ready to greet him a second time. During his time onboard as a Middy, Charles drew a fair sheet which famously went through the checking process and made it to UKHO Archives. A mistake on it was detected only when critiqued at Taunton. Steve Shipman tasked Mick to arrange delivery to *Fox* of the original fair sheet to provide HRH with the opportunity to correct his mistake. He duly obliged, hunched over the chart table, Rotring pen and scalpel in hand. Mick met him a third time when Charles popped into the Senior Rates' Mess at lunch time to enjoy a half a pint of CSB, typical beer on tap in CSVs.

The icing on the cake occurred at Mick's investiture in 2008. Charles pinned the MBE to Mick's uniform jacket and, well briefed, knew Mick was a droggy. He described his short time in *Fox* as some of the happiest days of his naval career. They chatted about *Fox*. Mick related how he was introduced to Charles three times in one day during the London visit and Charles' correction of his mistake on the fair sheet. Incredibly, HRH said he recollected Mick and the whole visit. A brilliant, heart-warming anecdote.

Fox was promptly sold to commercial interests, where she continued surveying for a while as *HV Fox*. After a reincarnation as *Plus Ultra*, she underwent an extensive refit in 2014 and steams around as *Motor Yacht Toy Heaven* (a truly appalling name), manned by a crew of 18 plus 14 guests accommodated in seven cabins. She looks nothing like my old *Fox*.

18.8 HV *Fox* (left); as MY *Toy Heaven* (right)
(www.shipspotting.com, left; Super Yacht Times, right)

Fawn paid off in October 1991 and was sold to a then-West German interest to become an offshore support vessel operating off West Africa and China as *Red Fulmar*. In 1998, she was sold on and renamed *Seabulk Fulmar*. No idea if she's still at sea in this guise.

Decommissioned on 26 July 2001, *Bulldog* was sold a month later for conversion to a luxury yacht, renamed *Alyssa M.II*. Unfortunately, she was damaged in an onboard fire in May 2004 in Nelson, New Zealand, and deemed a total loss. Last heard of she was under tow to Brisbane, Australia, to be scrapped. A terrible end for such a graceful ship.

The last CSV to go, *Beagle*, was decommissioned on 7 February 2002 and bought a month later by a yacht company in Poole for £750000. She was converted into the four-deck luxury yacht *Titan*, complemented with a 20-man crew and 22 guests. In 2019, a major refurbishment brought her to world-class cruising specifications and she was renamed *Aqua Blu*. With 15 guest suites finished in a black and ivory theme, a crew of 30 and the highest international safety classifications, she provides top-of-the-range luxury cruising. According to the company's website blurb, *Aqua Blu* is the first ever long-range, ocean explorer yacht permanently based in East Indonesia. She is now additionally equipped with 'Quantum Zero Speed stabilizers' (whatever that means!) and operates in Indonesia and surrounding waters. Showing through are the unmistakeable, graceful lines of a CSV.

18.9 *MY Aqua Blu*
(AdventureSmith Explorations)

Roebuck decommissioned on 15 April 2010 and was swiftly bought by the Bangladesh Navy. Renamed *BNS Anushandhan*, she's still on active service and, since 2020, joined by two new Bangladesh-built survey ships.

Of the H-boats, *Hydra* was the first to go, sold to the Indonesian Navy in 1986 and still in service as *Dewa Kembar*. *Hecate* decommissioned in 1994 and broken up at Pipavav, India.

18.10 *SV Bligh* looking shabby in 2002
(www.shipspotting.com)

Hecla paid off and was quickly sold. Thankfully, my old ship continued surveying as *SV Bligh* in the Irish National Seabed Survey at least until 2002

18. Postscript

but I don't know if she remains active today. I found a short video of her in survey action in RTE's archives (www.rte.ie/archives/2021/0715/1235257-national-seabed-survey/). The bridge hadn't changed too much, with the same engine control panel in the for'ard starboard corner beneath the windows. The chartroom looked pretty much the same, too. Pleasingly, the Irish retained her white hull and buff funnel.

Herald was sold in 2001 to private interests and renamed *SV Somerville* until scrapped at Alang, India, the world's largest ship-breaking yard.

18.11 *Herald's* sad end as *SV Somerville* at Alang
(www.shipspotting.com)

Interestingly, South Africa bought the fifth vessel of the class, *SAS Protea*, commissioned in 1972 and still in service Her replacement is under construction. When I was RN Exchange Officer with the German Navy, I was fortunate to deploy on board FGS *Berlin* to South Africa. Whilst alongside in Simonstown, I gave Lynne a ship's tour. Strolling back through the dockyard, I spotted *Protea* in dry-dock. Lynne had never seen an H-boat, so I pointed out various bit-and-pieces to her, including the scuttle of my cabin as *Hecla's* Ops Officer.

18.12 SAS *Protea*, Simonstown, March 2006

Marine Explorer continued as the platform for NP1008 until its disbandment in December 2003. Eidesvik sold the ship in 2005 and she's listed as an offshore support vessel named *Marine Ex*. I couldn't find any further details. NP1016 was disbanded in November/December 2005.

Gleaner was replaced by *Magpie*, procured under Project Vahana. Up to 38 of these Sea-class vessels will be acquired, replacing various RN vessels under 20m in length. They've already superseded BRNC's PBs. The 18m-long *Magpie* is the largest and only commissioned vessel in the series. The new *Echo* and *Enterprise* replaced the CSVs in 2003 but sadly these were decommissioned only 20 years later. Meanwhile, *Scott*, the replacement for all H-boats, plods along with her worldwide continuous surveying activity. She's completed a quarter of a century of service. *Echo*, *Enterprise* and *Scott* employed a crew rotation system to maximise time-on-task surveying, reminding me of *Fox's* own year-long crew rotation trial of 1987.

Sadly, like the once great RN fleet, the current Survey Squadron is a tragic shadow of its former self. Only *Scott*, at one extreme of size, and *Magpie*, at the opposite end, are in service. Never again will 3 Basin, our home in Guzz, be occupied by white-hulled, buff-funnelled survey ships.

18. Postscript

Regrettably, our survey ships were re-painted grey in about 1997. I find the loss of the Survey Squadron hard to accept or comprehend. It seems that 230 years of hydrographic survey expertise has been ruthlessly and thoughtlessly discarded.

18.13 3 Basin with two H-boats and a CSV, two CSVs berthed outside on 3 Wharf (MOD)

I'm extremely pleased and proud I served during the Survey Squadron's heyday. Our graceful ships manned by dedicated hydrographic surveyors, superbly supported by general service folks, many of whom so enjoyed the 'survey navy' that they remained with us for most of their subsequent careers. For droggies, 'no day too long, no task too arduous' rang true. No longer will the refrain 'Get the drying height!' be heard aboard SMBs close inshore or over rock pinnacles. Nor will we hear 'Fix and sound, fix and sound!' echo around small bays during detached boat survey camps.

Hopefully, today's seafarers still 'trust in God and an Admiralty chart'.

Note on Sources

Firstly, a cautionary note to fellow amateur and budding authors. Don't waste your time contacting the Naval Historical Branch (NHB), Portsmouth. I was given contact details by UKHO Archive. The woman at NHB responded negatively to my couple of emails. Apparently, they're 'too busy' to rummage through the records on our behalf. They haven't got time to allow researchers like me to visit and self-rummage amongst the records. So, unless you're a recognised naval historian or have contacts in the RN's upper echelons, don't bother with NHB. Totally useless and unhelpful.

Far more positively, National Archives, Kew holds vast quantities of documents. Use their website's search engine to find the documents you seek, and you can order them for your appointment. Making an appointment is also simple, just follow the steps. On arrival at Kew, your documents will be on a table, ready for you to commence research. I ordered my maximum 40 documents and then looked through and photographed (on a mobile phone) the Ship's Log pages that had more information than I could note down during my day's session. Take your own victuals or use the café on the ground floor.

For droggies, I contacted UKHO Archive and made an appointment. Ian Killick, lead archivist, met me at the main gate and escorted me to the Archive. I spent two days there, separated by a year, and found almost everything I needed. Reports of Survey, Letters of Proceedings, Hydrographic Instructions, plus numerous reference books and miscellaneous documents were brilliant source material.

Anyone researching their time at BRNC should contact Dr Richard Porter and/or Dr Jane Harrold to arrange an appointment to visit. The archive is a large walk-in cupboard off the rear of Richard's office/study and packed full of documents. You'll need a day to rummage through as, although catalogued by shelf, I found all sorts of other 'stuff' that I thought may be useful in my scribblings. Thankfully, BRNC's dress code retains the old standards, especially no jeans!

Overall, I took several hundred photos of documents during my visits to these three wonderful archives. Appointments are relatively easy to arrange. Allow at least a full day for each. Take your own victuals.

References

Books

Aldridge, Nichola (2017). *Britannia Royal Naval College Guidebook*. Pitkin Publishing.
Berncastle, Lt Cdr FM. (1994). *Sounding in the Dark*. HMSO.
Bomford, Guy (1971). *Geodesy*. Oxford University Press.
Carroll, Phil (2023). *Under a Big Blue Star*. Shakspeare Editorial.
Clark, David (1976). *Plane and Geodetic Surveying*. Constable.
Clough-Smith, JH (1978). *An Introduction to Spherical Trigonometry*. Brown, Son & Ferguson.
Connelly, Charlie (2005). *Attention All Shipping*. Abacus.
Dyde, Brian (2012). *This Glorious Profession – Vanished Times in Naval Hydrography*. Noddfani Publishing.
Hoole, Rob (2012). *Last of the Wooden Walls*. Halsgrove.
Hydrographer of the Navy (1965). *Admiralty Manual of Hydrographic Surveying, Volume I*. HMSO.
Hydrographer of the Navy (1969). *Admiralty Manual of Hydrographic Surveying, Volume II*. HMSO.
Hydrographic Department (1977). *Professional Paper 24: Dual Channel Sidescan Sonar*. MOD(Navy)
Ingham, AE. (1975). *Sea Surveying*. Wiley-Blackwell.
Kinghorn, Captain A W (1983). *Before The Box Boats*. Kenneth Mason.
Morris, RO. (1995). *Charts and Surveys in Peace and War*. HMSO.
Pickard, George L (1990). *Descriptive Physical Oceanography*. Butterworth-Heinemann.
Porter, R and Harrold, J. (2005). *Britannia Royal Naval College 1905–2005 An Illustrated History*. Richard Webb.
Rankin, Nicholas (2019). *Defending the Rock*. Faber & Faber.
Richardson, Nick (2001). *No Escape Zone*. Sphere.
Ritchie, GS. (1992). *No Day Too Long*. Pentland Press Ltd.
Sands, Philippe (2023). *The Last Colony*. Weidenfeld & Nicolson

Senker, Cath (2017). *Stranded in the Six Day War*. Cath Senker.
Todhunter, Chris (2016). *A Droggie Goes to War*. Ton Class Association.
Ton Class Association (2012). *Jacks of All Trades*. Ton Class Association.
Ton Class Association (2017). *Life in the Tons*. Ton Class Association.
Winchester, Simon (2011). *Atlantic*. Harper Press.
Winton, John (2023). *We Joined the Navy*. Sapere Books.
Winton, John (2023). *The Good Ship Venus*. Sapere Books.

Official Records

National Archives, Kew
Ship's Logs
- *Brinton* – Feb 85, Mar 85, Apr 85
- *Exeter* – May 85, Jun 85, Jul 85, Aug 85, Sep 85, Oct 85, Nov 85
- *Fearless* – Sep 84, Oct 84, Nov 84
- *Fox* – Jan 87, Feb 87
- *Gavinton* – Jan 85
- *Hecla* – Nov 88, Dec 88, Nov 93, Dec 93, Jan 94, Feb 94, Mar 94, May 94, Jun 94, Jul 95

UKHO, Taunton
Reports of Proceedings
- *Beagle* – Jan 96, Feb 96, Mar 96, Apr 96, May 96, Jun 96, Jul 96, Aug 96, Sep 96
- *Fox* – Nov 86, Dec 86, Jan 87, Feb 87, Mar 87, Apr 87, May 87, Jun 87, Jul 87, Aug 87, Sep 87, Oct 87, Nov 87, Dec 87, Jan 88, Feb 88, Mar 88, Apr 88, May 88, Jun 88, Jul 88, Aug 88, Sep 88, Oct 88, Nov 88, Dec 88
- *Hecla* – Nov 88, Dec 88, Jan 89, Feb 89, Mar 89, Apr 89, May 89, Jun 89, Jul 89, Aug 89, Sep 89, Oct 89, Nov 89, Dec 89 and Oct 93 to Dec 95
- Naval Party 1008 – Mar 92, Apr 92, May 92, Jun 92, Jul 92, Aug 92, Sep 92, Oct 92, Nov 92, Dec 92, Jan 93, Feb 93, Mar 93

Reports of Survey
- Captain Hydrographic Surveying Squadron – HI568 Bridgetown Deep Water Harbour
- *Fox* – HI429 Celtic Sea, Celtic Deep
- *Fox* – HI357 Irish Sea, Skerries to the River Dee

Fox – HI360 England, South West Approaches, Isles of Scilly to Land's End
Fox – HI362 England, South Coast, Mounts Bay
Fox – HI389a and 389b Scotland, West Coast, Loch Ryan
Fox – HI439 England West Coast, Padstow Bay
Gleaner – HI243 Ramsey Bay to King William Banks
Gleaner – HI266 Approaches to the Needles Channel
National Hydrographic Office RNO Archive – HI21b Bandar Khayran

Annual Report of Hydrographer
- 1986–87
- 1987–88
- 1988–89
- 1989–90
- 1990–91
- 1991–92
- 1992–93

Return of Survey
- 1 Jan–31 Dec 86
- 1 Jan–31 Dec 87
- 1 Jan–31 Dec 88
- 1 Jan–31 Dec 89
- 31 Mar 92–31 Mar 93
- 31 Mar 93–31 Mar 94
- 31 Mar 94–31 Mar 95
- 31 Mar 95–31 Mar 96
- 31 Mar 96–31 Mar 97

BRNC Archive, Dartmouth

Britannia Magazine
College Orders
CTMs (Captain's Temporary Memorandums)
Encyclopaedia Britannia
Term Calendar, Jan-Apr 1984
TOTEMs (Training Office Temporary Memorandums)

Television Series and Programmes

Britannia Waives the Rules (1991). Channel 4
HMS Brilliant (1995). BBC
Look at Life: The Black Arrows (1960). ITV Global Entertainment
Look at Life: Plumbing the Depths (1962). ITV Global Entertainment
Sailor (1976). BBC
Warship (1973–1977). BBC
www.rte.ie/archives/2021/0715/1235257-national-seabed-survey/

Film

We Joined the Navy (1962). Associated British Picture Corporation

www.ingramcontent.com/pod-product-compliance
Lightning Source LLC
Chambersburg PA
CBHW051556010526
44118CB00022B/2726